D1035818

INTERNATIONAL DEBT:
SYSTEMIC RISK AND POLICY RESPONSE

International Debt:

WILLIAM R. CLINE

Systemic Risk and Policy Response

INSTITUTE FOR INTERNATIONAL ECONOMICS
Washington, DC 1984

Distributed by The MIT Press
Cambridge, Massachusetts, and London, England

Dr. William R. Cline is a Senior Fellow at the Institute for International Economics. He was formerly a Senior Fellow at the Brookings Institution; Deputy Director for Development and Trade Research at the US Treasury Department; Ford Foundation Visiting Professor at the Instituto de Planejamento Econômico e Social Aplicado (IPEA) in Brazil; and Assistant Professor at Princeton University, where he is currently Visiting Lecturer. Dr. Cline has published many books and articles on international trade, finance, and development, including three POLICY ANALYSES *released by the Institute:* "Reciprocity": A New Approach to World Trade Policy?; *(with C. Fred Bergsten)* Trade Policy in the 1980s; *and* International Debt and the Stability of the World Economy.

INSTITUTE FOR
INTERNATIONAL ECONOMICS
C. Fred Bergsten, *Director*
Kathleen A. Lynch, *Director of Publications*
Michele McCord, *Business Manager*
Stephen Kraft, *Designer*

The Institute for International Economics was created, and is principally funded, by the German Marshall Fund of the United States.

The views expressed in this publication are those of the author. The publication is part of the research program of the Institute, as endorsed by its Board of Directors, but does not necessarily reflect the views of individual members of the Board or the Advisory Committee.

Copyright © 1984 Institute for International Economics. All rights reserved. No part of this book may be reproduced or utilized in any form or by any means, electronic or mechanical, including photocopying, recording, or by any information storage or retrieval system, without written permission from the Institute.

Library of Congress Cataloging in Publication Data

Cline, William R.
   International debt.

   Longer, more detailed and updated version of: International debt and the stability of the world economy. © 1983.

   Includes bibliographical references.
   1. Loans, Foreign—Developing countries. 2. Debts, External—Developing countries. I. Cline, William R.
International debt and the stability of the world economy
Select Bibliography p. 302
II. Title.
HJ8899.C543
1984   336.3'4'091724   83-26518
ISBN 0-88132-015-3
ISBN 0-262-03100-0 (MIT Press)

Acknowledgments

David D. Johnson provided invaluable research assistance for this study, and Celestine Darby and Diane M. Wheeler typed its manuscript. For helpful comments, I am grateful to C. Fred Bergsten, Richard N. Cooper, Carlos F. Diaz-Alejandro, Chandra Hardy, John R. Petty, Nicholas Sargen, Mario Henrique Simonsen, Ernest Stern, Ralph Tryon, and participants in seminars presented at Chase Manhattan Bank, the Federal Reserve Bank of New York, and the World Bank. W.R.C.

INSTITUTE FOR INTERNATIONAL ECONOMICS
11 Dupont Circle, NW, Washington, DC 20036
(202) 328-0583 Telex: 248329 CEIP

C. Fred Bergsten, *Director*

BOARD OF DIRECTORS

Peter G. Peterson, *Chairman*
Raymond Barre
W. Michael Blumenthal
Douglas A. Fraser
Alan Greenspan
Abdlatif Y. al-Hamad
Reginald H. Jones
Frank E. Loy
Donald F. McHenry
Saburo Okita
I.G. Patel
Karl Otto Pöhl
Donna E. Shalala
Mario Henrique Simonsen
Anthony M. Solomon
Dennis Weatherstone
Andrew Young

Ex officio
C. Fred Bergsten
Richard N. Cooper

ADVISORY COMMITTEE
Richard N. Cooper, *Chairman*
Robert Baldwin
Lester Brown
Rimmer de Vries
Carlos F. Diaz-Alejandro
Rudiger Dornbusch
Robert J. Flanagan
Isaiah Frank
Herbert Giersch
Gottfried Haberler
Mahbub ul Haq
Arnold C. Harberger
Dale E. Hathaway
Nurul Islam
Peter B. Kenen
Lawrence R. Klein
Ryutaro Komiya
Lawrence B. Krause
Assar Lindbeck
Harald B. Malmgren
Richard R. Nelson
Joseph S. Nye, Jr.
Rudolph A. Oswald
Ernest Stern
Philip K. Verleger
Henry Wallich
Marina Whitman
Alan Wm. Wolff

Preface

This publication attempts to present a comprehensive analysis of one of the most important and complex problems facing the world economy: the debt crisis. It provides a complete treatment, with full methodology, data and country cases, of the conclusions summarized in the author's *International Debt and the Stability of the World Economy*, released in September 1983 by the Institute as one of its POLICY ANALYSES IN INTERNATIONAL ECONOMICS.

This book version of the study also updates several elements of the analysis through mid-1984, including projections for the current account and international financial positions of the major debtor countries through 1987 and an analysis of the negotiating strategy which has evolved between the lending and borrowing institutions. The technique of publishing a shorter policy-oriented version and a longer, more detailed version of the same study follows the approach also used in our work on IMF conditionality, trade policy, and economic sanctions.

The Institute for International Economics is a private nonprofit research institution for the study and discussion of international economic policy. Its purpose is to analyze important issues in that area and to develop and communicate practical new approaches for dealing with them.

The Institute was created in November 1981 through a generous commitment of funds from the German Marshall Fund of the United States. Support is being received from other private foundations and corporations, and the Institute now seeks to broaden and diversify its financial base. The Institute is completely nonpartisan.

The Board of Directors bears overall responsibility for the Institute and gives general guidance and approval to its research program—including identification of topics that are likely to become important to international economic policymakers over the medium run (generally, one to three years) and which thus should be addressed by the Institute. The Director of the Institute, working closely with the staff and outside Advisory Committee, is responsible for the development of particular projects and makes the final decision to publish an individual study.

The Institute hopes that its studies and other activities will contribute to building a stronger foundation for international economic policy around the world. Comments as to how it can best do so are invited from readers of these publications.

C. FRED BERGSTEN
Director
July 1984

Contents

Text Tables

Text Figures

Appendix Tables

Appendix Figures

Select Bibliography

Index

Introduction

Analysts have kept a wary eye on the growing external debt of developing countries since at least the early 1970s. External debt has always been an instrument with both positive potential for economic development and associated risk of financial strain. In the normal course of world development, capital should flow from advanced countries, where it is abundant and its return is relatively low, to developing countries, where capital is scarce and its return high. Direct investment is one form of this capital flow, but since the 1970s it has been far overshadowed by financial capital, especially in the form of bank loans to middle-income countries.

While these flows have contributed to development, they have also meant increasing financial dependence of borrowing countries and rising relative debt-servicing obligations. They therefore set the stage for financial strains if, because of international recession, commodity price collapse, or domestic mismanagement, a country cannot meet the original terms of its debt servicing. In the 1960s and early 1970s, episodes of debt-servicing difficulty often were viewed as another variant on the need for development assistance (and in some cases, such as India and Pakistan, intentional debt restructuring was even used as an aid vehicle). Beginning in the mid-1970s, however, the sheer volume of external debt began to reach such magnitudes that potential disruptions in debt servicing posed a threat not only for a country's development but also for the international financial system, and the banks in particular. Yet international lending in the 1970s continued to confound the pessimists, as relatively smooth expansion of lending achieved financial "recycling," the channeling of surpluses from oil-exporting countries to oil-importing countries in deficit, after the oil shock of 1974.

By 1980-81, evidence of strain on the system was increasing, however. World recession, high interest rates, and a second oil shock took their toll. Near default in Poland shook the credit markets. Then, in 1982–83 the debt problem became manifest and widespread. All three of the largest developing-country debtors—Brazil, Mexico, and Argentina—were forced to disrupt normal debt servicing.

Debt-servicing disruption or formal reschedulings of debt reached approximately two-thirds of bank debt owed by the developing and East European countries (chapter 2). By the end of 1982, 34 countries were in arrears on their debt.[1] The amounts of debt formally rescheduled rose from $2.6 billion in 1981 to $5.5 billion in 1982[2] to approximately $90 billion (including amounts being renegotiated) in 1983.[3]

Public policy on international debt now stands at a turning point. The debt issue has played an increasing role in economic policy formation, apparently affecting decisions such as the major shift by the US Federal Reserve toward faster monetary growth and lower nominal interest rates in the summer of 1982, as well as the change in the US administration's position on raising resources available to the International Monetary Fund.[4] Exposure of industrial economies to risk from the debt of developing countries has added a wholly new dimension to the effects of international economic interdependence, a phenomenon already of growing importance in recent decades through the more familiar channels of trade and monetary relationships.

Yet despite the clear attention the debt problem is now receiving from policymakers internationally, it remains unclear whether the financial emergencies that surfaced in 1982–83 will be resolved by the various rescue packages already in place. Some analysts and statesmen argue that the debt problem has become so severe that it cannot be managed using past approaches, and that broad new schemes of debt relief are required. In contrast, official statements of international organizations tend to downplay the risk of debt to the international financial system.[5] Despite such assurances, doubt remains about the extent of this risk. Even the most straightforward policy remedies stir heated controversy that the public is bailing out the banks.

While much of public attention is focused on the risks of a debt crisis for the banking system, a quiet crisis already exists in the severe economic recession being confronted by many developing countries, in large part because of their adverse balance of payments positions and debt burden.

Largely because of austerity measures, lower external demand associated

---

1. According to a 15 February 1983 communication with the International Monetary Fund.

2. World Bank, *World Debt Tables*, 1982–83 ed., p. 2.

3. M.S. Mendelsohn, *Commercial Banks and the Restructuring of Cross-Border Debt* (New York: Group of Thirty, 1983), p. 4.

4. As recommended in John Williamson, *The Lending Policies of the International Monetary Fund*, POLICY ANALYSES IN INTERNATIONAL ECONOMICS 1 (Washington: Institute for International Economics, August 1982).

5. Thus, the World Bank took "an unfashionably positive view of the external indebtedness of developing countries" and maintained that "There is no generalized debt crisis . . . ," World Bank, *World Debt Tables*, 1982–83 ed., pp. vii, xvi.

with world recession, and reductions in international lending, average growth rates of nonoil developing countries have fallen from 5 percent in 1973–80 to 2.4 percent in 1981 and only 0.9 percent in 1982.[6] In Latin America a depression of 1930s magnitude has brought average growth to 1.5 percent in 1981, −1 percent in 1982, and −3.3 percent in 1983, with real declines of GDP by 4.7 percent in Mexico and 3.3 percent in Brazil in 1983.[7] The influence of the cutback in bank lending in this depression is examined in a study by Morgan Guaranty bank, which calculates that the decline by approximately $25 billion in bank lending in 1982 translated into a loss of 1½ percentage points in developing-country growth; in turn, slower growth of industrial country exports to developing countries cut one-half of a percentage point off of industrial country growth.[8]

The debt problem not only constrains growth in developing countries and poses potential risk for the international financial system; in addition, it has already contributed to reduced exports and jobs in industrial countries as developing countries have retrenched on their imports. Including members of the Organization of Petroleum Exporting Countries (OPEC), developing countries account for 40 percent of US exports and 42 percent of European Community (EC) exports to non-EC markets. From 1981 to 1982 exports of Organization for Economic Cooperation and Development (OECD) countries to non-OPEC developing-country nonmembers declined by $14 billion in real terms, an amount corresponding to approximately 350,000 jobs.[9] By 1983 the trade and employment effects of the debt crisis were even larger. US exports to Latin America fell by $24 billion from 1981 to 1983, costing approximately 400,000 jobs.[10] Resolution of the debt problem can contribute directly to recovery in industrial countries in addition to reducing the risk of a much larger economic dislocation from international financial collapse.

This study examines the major areas of public policy on external debt. Chapter 1 analyses the origins of the debt problem. Chapter 2 examines the potential risk to industrial country economies and financial systems (primarily through their banks) posed by the debt of developing and East European countries, and reviews the important series of debt packages orchestrated by the International

---

6. IMF, *World Economic Outlook*, 1983, p. 171.

7. Naciones Unidas, Comisión Económica para América Latina (CEPAL), *Balance Preliminar de la Economía Latinoamericana durante 1983*, cuadro 2 (Santiago, December 16, 1983).

8. *World Financial Markets* (October 1982).

9. The decline was from $220 billion to $196 billion, of which a part was attributable to a 4 percent reduction in dollar prices of exports. OECD, *Monthly Statistics of Foreign Trade*, June 1983, pp. 37, 42, 49; and IMF, *International Financial Statistics*, June 1983, p. 56.

10. Sanjay Dhar, "U.S. Trade with Latin America: Consequences of Financing Constraints," *Federal Reserve Bank of New York Quarterly Review*, vol. 8, no. 3 (Autumn 1983) p. 18.

Monetary Fund, the US government, and other official actors in 1982–83 responding to financial crisis in Mexico, Brazil, Argentina, and certain other countries.

Chapter 3 presents a model for projecting the debt and balance of payments of the large debtor countries. This analysis focuses on the fundamental question: is the debt problem a manageable one of short-term illiquidity, or is it so entrenched that it represents country insolvency that must be dealt with by radical measures? In answering this question the level of world economic growth plays the largest role. Chapter 4 analyzes the dynamics of "involuntary lending" under current circumstances, the technical aspects of debt rescheduling, and the calculus of default decisions. Chapter 5 examines the medium-term viability of major financial rescue packages in terms of future maturity bunching, reconversion to voluntary lending, and political sustainability.

Today's debt problem is intimately linked to banking institutions, and chapter 6 examines the adequacy of these institutions (including bank regulation). The final policy implications drawn in chapter 7 match the projections of this study against prospective levels of international financing to examine the feasibility of global debt management of the medium term. The chapter examines some of the plans that have been proposed for more radical debt relief as a solution to the debt problem, as well as a general contingency strategy. It then summarizes the policy conclusions and concrete recommendations of this study. The final text chapter is an epilogue (chapter 8) that reviews developments through mid-1984 and presents updated projections in the light of actual experience through 1983. The appendices present a statistical model for predicting debt rescheduling (appendix A), the technical statement of the projection model used in chapter 3 (appendix B), country detail on the cases of Mexico, Brazil, Argentina, Poland, and Yugoslavia (appendix C), and supplementary statistical materials.

Since the initial development of the central projections of this study in April 1983, the publication of its monographic version in September 1983, international economic developments have tended to confirm this study's basic conclusion that the debt problem is manageable. Most importantly, world economic recovery has begun in earnest, led by robust US recovery. Moreover, the major debtors have met or exceeded their external adjustment commitments, as Mexico and Venezuela achieved extraordinary external surpluses in 1983 while Brazil and other major debtors achieved their planned external targets.

By early 1984, many analysts still maintained that the crisis of international debt stood in the eye of the hurricane rather than the calm after the storm. By mid-year a rise in US interest rates had triggered escalation in political calls for debt relief, and the prospects for agreement between Argentina, the International Monetary Fund, and private banks remained unclear. More broadly, for policymakers in industrial countries the challenge was to consolidate the gains achieved in managing the problem of international debt, most importantly by sustaining for a long period the recent global economic recovery, but also by keeping their markets open to imports from developing countries. For the leaders of major debtor countries, the challenge was to continue adjustment but through increased exports rather than through the reliance on import cutbacks and GNP recessions as in 1983; to achieve, or at least set the stage for, domestic economic recovery; and to avoid the adoption of extreme (and probably self-defeating) measures on debt despite the political pressure from publics under severe duress from the initial burdens of economic adjustment.

Origins of the Problem

The global debt problem stems from forces dating to the mid-1970s, and the first oil price shock (1973–74) in particular. The intensification of the problem in 1982 derived primarily from the effects of global recession from 1980 to 1982, combined with adverse psychological shocks to credit markets caused by events in individual major countries. In a broad sense the problem is a consequence of the transition from inflation to disinflation in the world economy. Funds that were borrowed when inflation was high and real interest rates were low or negative are no longer cheap in an environment of lower inflation and high real interest rates.

Debt Trends

The large magnitude and rapid growth of international debt is shown in table 1.1. For the "nonoil" developing countries (including such new oil exporters as Mexico and Egypt) total debt (including short-term) multiplied nearly fivefold from 1973 to 1982, reaching approximately $612 billion. The estimated debt of five OPEC countries that are not in capital surplus—Algeria, Ecuador, Indonesia, Nigeria, and Venezuela—adds another $80 billion, and net East European debt (in hard currency) accounts for another $53 billion (excluding the Soviet Union).[1] The total debt of these three groups of countries thus stood at approximately $745 billion at the end of 1982.

The bulk of this external debt is sovereign debt: amounts owed abroad by national governments, by their decentralized agencies, or by private firms but with public guarantees. However, a considerable portion of the debt is owed by the private sector without public guarantee. The World Bank estimates that 80 percent of long-term developing-country debt was public or publicly

---

1. The estimates of debt used in this study are described in appendix D. East European debt: *Wall Street Journal,* 4 April 1983 and Wharton Econometric Forecasting Associates.

**Table 1.1 Indicators of external debt, nonoil developing countries,
1973–82** (billion dollars and percentages)

	1973	1974	1975	1976	1977
External debt					
Total	130.1	160.8	190.8	228.0	278.5
Long-term	118.8	138.1	163.5	194.9	235.9
Total, 1975 prices[a]	169.0	175.7	190.8	218.0	250.9
Exports[b]	112.7	153.7	155.9	181.7	220.3
Debt/exports (percentage)	115.4	104.6	122.4	125.5	126.4
Debt service[c]/exports (percentage)					
Reported	15.9	14.4	16.1	15.3	15.4
Adjusted[d]	n.a.	− 1.6	6.5	10.5	9.4
Debt/GDP (percentage)	22.4	21.8	23.8	25.7	27.4
Oil as percentage of imports[e]	5.9	12.6	13.3	15.6	15.1

n.a. Not available.
Source: IMF, *World Economic Outlook,* 1982 and 1983.
a. Deflating by US wholesale prices.
b. Goods and services.
c. Includes interest (but not amortization) on short-term debt.
d. Deducting inflationary erosion of debt.
e. Net oil importers only.

guaranteed in 1981, and 20 percent was private.[2] In some countries, such as
Chile, private debt is a much larger fraction of the total, raising special problems
in cases of debt rescheduling (chapter 4).

The nearly fivefold rise in debt from 1973 to 1982 (table 1.1) represented
average annual growth of 19 percent. However, after deducting for inflation,
the real debt of nonoil developing countries has risen only by a multiple of 2.1
over the last decade, indicating real growth of 8.7 percent annually—still a
rapid rate but one of less startling dimensions. Considering that real growth of
GDP has averaged 4.5 percent in 1973–82 for nonoil developing countries,[3]
the weight of external debt relative to domestic production has risen in the last
decade (from 22 percent of GDP in 1973 to 35 percent in 1982, table 1.1).
Nonetheless, because developing countries have achieved export growth that
is more rapid than GDP growth, the ratio of external debt to exports of goods
and services has risen by considerably less, from 115 percent in 1973 to 143
percent in 1982 (table 1.1).

2. World Bank, *World Debt Tables,* 1982–83 ed. p. viii.

3. IMF, *World Economic Outlook,* 1982, p. 144, and 1983, p. 171.

1978	1979	1980	1981	1982
336.3	396.9	474.0	550.0	612.4
286.6	338.1	388.5	452.8	499.6
281.0	294.7	308.6	331.3	357.8
258.3	333.0	419.8	444.4	427.4
130.2	119.2	121.9	124.9	143.3
19.0	19.0	17.6	20.4	23.9
11.0	6.9	4.9	11.7	22.3
28.5	27.5	27.6	31.0	34.7
13.9	16.2	20.4	21.0	19.9

The reassurance provided by growing exports is less convincing when the debt-service burden, as opposed to debt itself, is taken into account. Primarily because of rising interest rates, debt service (interest on short- and long-term debt plus amortization on long-term debt) has risen from an average of 15.4 percent of exports of goods and services in 1973–77 to 18.5 percent in 1978–80 and 22.2 percent in 1981–82.

To be sure, some of this increase in the debt-service ratio, at least until 1980, was attributable to a higher inflationary component of interest rates. Higher inflation tends to cause higher interest rates. When this occurs, higher current debt service must be paid—because approximately two-thirds of developing-country debt is at floating interest rates tied to the London Interbank Offer Rate (LIBOR).[4] But higher inflation also erodes the real value of the debt that eventually is to be repaid. Accordingly, high interest rates caused primarily by high inflation have the effect of causing a greater present cash flow burden in return for eroding the real value of outstanding debt. In effect, they cause accelerated amortization of the debt in real terms.

This process of inflationary acceleration of debt repayment through higher nominal interest rates was important through most of the 1970s. As shown in table 1.1, the adjusted "real debt-service ratio" deducting the inflationary erosion of principal was considerably lower than the nominal debt-service ratio through much of the period.[5] By 1981–82, however, nominal interest rates

---

4. See chapter 3.

5. For calculation of the adjusted real debt-service ratio, total debt-service payments are reduced by the amount of US wholesale price inflation in the year in question as applied to outstanding debt at the end of the previous year.

were high while inflation was declining. As a result, the adjusted "real" debt-service ratio rose in 1981 to a higher level (11.7 percent) than in any previous year for a decade, and it then proceeded nearly to double (to 22.3 percent) in 1982 as inflation fell sharply while interest rates fell more slowly.

Another disconcerting trend in the external debt is the rising share of short-term debt (original maturity less than one year) in the total. Short-term debt rose from 8.7 percent of the total in 1973 to 14.6 percent in 1974–79 and 18.1 percent in 1980–82 (table 1.1), showing a rise to a new plateau after each oil shock. The susceptibility of short-term debt to sudden disruption in normal renewal, once creditor confidence erodes, makes its rising share a source of instability. And short-term borrowing is an especially unreliable form of financing long-term development. Ideally, loan maturities should match those of investment projects.

Figure 1.1   Total external debt, nonoil developing countries

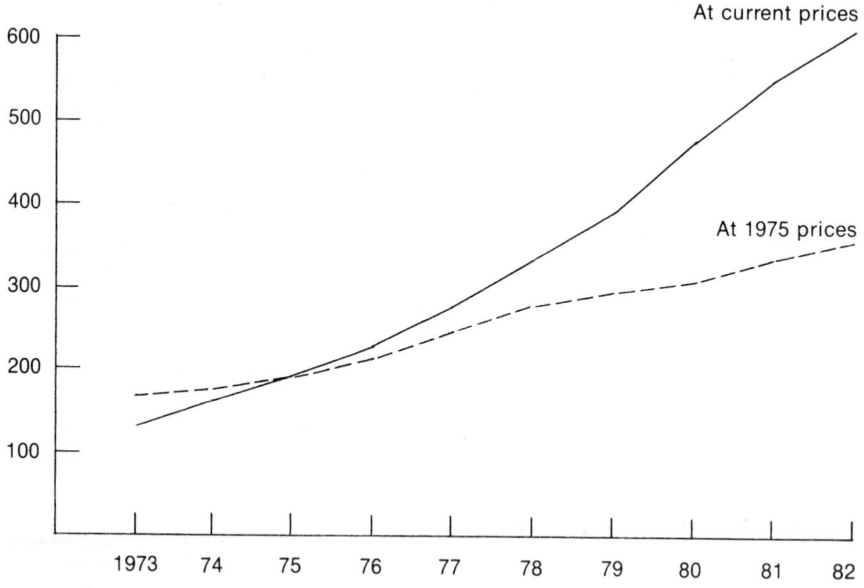

Source: Table 1.1

The broad pattern shown in table 1.1 and in figures 1.1 and 1.2 is that although developing-country debt grew rapidly in the 1970s this growth was much more moderate when judged in real terms and relative to the export base. However, by 1981 the burden of debt rose significantly on all three principal measures—ratio of debt to exports, real (adjusted) debt-service ratio,

Figure 1.2   Indicators of debt burden, nonoil developing countries

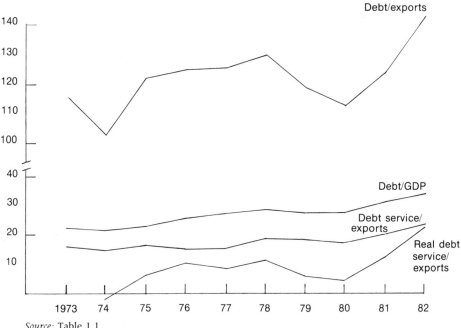

Source: Table 1.1

and ratio of debt to GDP. And in 1982 these measures of debt burden rose still further, to levels (in each case) not previously experienced. As can be seen in table 1.1, an important cause of the sharp deterioration in 1982 was an actual decline in the nominal value of exports (by 3.8 percent) even as total debt continued to rise (by 10.3 percent). Export stagnation was driven both by global recession (which caused export volume growth to decline) and by dollar appreciation and commodity price erosion (lowering the dollar value of export earnings). As discussed below, domestic policies in debtor countries also played a role in increasing debt in important cases. In sum, the underlying data on developing-country debt confirm that significant economic erosion in 1982 lay behind the emergence of acute debt-servicing difficulties in several countries, including the most important debtor nations.

The pattern shown in table 1.1 provides useful aggregate background, but debt difficulties occur at the level of individual countries. Accordingly, tables E-1 to E-4 of the statistical appendix present data on debt trends individually for 33 developing and East European countries. As those tables show, for certain key debtor countries debt trends have shown a greater increase in debt burden than is apparent in the aggregate data just examined. Thus, for the three largest debtors, debt growth has been far greater than the fivefold (nominal)

Table 1.2   Export growth[a] compared with interest rates, 1973–82
(percentage)

	1973	1974	1975	1976	1977
LIBOR + 1 percent	10.2	12.0	8.0	6.6	7.0
Export growth, nominal					
Nonoil LDCs	n.a.	36.4	1.4	16.5	21.2
Net oil importers	n.a.	33.1	1.6	16.3	21.9
Net oil exporters	n.a.	57.3	−0.1	18.9	18.8
Brazil	56.1	33.2	6.1	13.5	19.7
Mexico	26.8	31.6	−0.2	13.3	14.0
Argentina	61.6	25.8	−23.9	30.8	43.6
Korea	85.6	29.4	9.7	60.8	38.2
Venezuela	54.4	126.8	−15.7	2.8	5.5
Chile	49.0	60.1	−21.7	31.7	8.1

n.a. Not available.
Source: IMF, *International Financial Statistics,* selected issues; IMF, *World Economic Outlook,* 1983, and Institute for International Economics debt data base.
a. Goods and services.

multiple for all developing countries (1973–82). For Brazil the rise has been a multiple of 6.4, to $88 billion; for Mexico, a multiple of 9.5, to $82 billion; and for Argentina, a multiple of 5.9, to $38 billion. The debt-service ratio has risen far more dramatically for these leading debtors than for developing countries on average. Compared with a rise from 16 percent in 1973–74 to approximately 24 percent by 1982 for all developing countries, Brazil's debt-service ratio rose from 36 percent to 87 percent, Mexico's from 25 percent to 58 percent, and Argentina's from 21 percent to 103 percent (appendix table E-2). Moreover, although these countries' relative debt burdens gradually increased through the 1970s, there was an especially sharp rise in 1982. Thus, the ratio of net debt (debt *minus* foreign reserves) to exports of goods and services rose from 257 percent in 1981 to 365 percent in 1982 in Brazil, from 209 percent to 249 percent in Mexico, and from 275 percent to 354 percent in Argentina.

The data for individual countries also reveal important cases where the debt burden has been kept at a relatively low level. Thus, Korea had a ratio of net debt to exports of only 104 percent in 1982; Indonesia, 86 percent; and Venezuela (because large reserves offset much of its debt), 104 percent—all well below the average for developing countries. In short, the debt trends for individual developing countries tend to confirm erosion in 1982 in particular but, in addition, a more serious extent of the underlying problem in certain

1978	1979	1980	1981	1982
9.7	13.0	15.4	17.5	14.1
17.2	28.9	26.1	5.8	− 3.8
16.9	26.8	24.2	5.4	− 3.8
18.0	40.4	35.4	7.8	− 3.6
7.2	24.2	29.3	15.7	− 13.4
39.1	40.2	54.3	21.9	7.3
16.3	26.6	13.0	5.1	− 15.7
31.3	13.8	15.6	21.7	2.3
− 0.8	50.2	36.4	10.1	− 22.0
13.8	59.0	32.2	− 2.6	− 3.8

countries (especially in Latin America) where temporary debt-servicing break-downs have in fact occurred within the last 18 months.

Mario Henrique Simonsen, former planning minister of Brazil, has proposed a useful summary criterion to determine whether a country's debt-servicing burden is improving or getting worse.[6] Simonsen's criterion is that export earnings must be growing at a higher rate than the interest rate. Otherwise, the country's debt burden tends to worsen. The logic of this rule of thumb is that there is an automatic "inherited" increase in debt by the amount of past debt *multiplied by* the interest rate, because this amount is the interest due on past debt. If the country is achieving a balanced foreign account (current account) excluding interest, then its debt will grow by this amount. That is, its debt will grow by the interest rate. If the ratio of debt to exports is to avoid increasing (maintaining a constant relative debt burden), exports must also grow by at least this rate. As a consequence, exports should grow at a rate no less than the interest rate.[7]

The sea change in debt-servicing viability in 1981–82 may be seen by examining this summary criterion. In table 1.2 and figure 1.3, a typical interest

---

6. Mario Henrique Simonsen, "The Financial Crisis in Latin America" (Rio de Janeiro: Getúlio Vargas Foundation, 1983; processed).

7. This rule no longer applies when the country is running a trade surplus and transferring net resources abroad rather than receiving them. In that case the debt does not automatically grow at the interest rate, and export growth may be more modest. However, under normal conditions developing countries receive net resource inflows rather than transferring net resources abroad.

rate on developing-country loans—LIBOR plus a spread of 1 percent—is compared to the nominal export growth rate for 1973–82. Until 1980 the interest rate averaged 10.2 percent, while the growth rate of exports for nonoil developing countries averaged 21.1 percent. The interest rate test was clearly being met and overfulfilled. But in 1981–82, the interest rate averaged 15.8 percent, while export growth in these countries averaged only 1.0 percent. The actual decline of exports in 1982 was especially damaging. A sharp change had occurred, with higher interest rates conflicting with slower export growth, and the condition for avoiding deterioration in the relative debt burden was no longer being met. The table also shows export growth for individual major debtors. The declines in average export growth were severe for most of the countries listed that did experience debt-servicing difficulty in 1982–83 (Argentina, Brazil, Chile, Mexico, Venezuela).

The table also shows that once before in the past decade, in 1975, the condition comparing export growth to the interest rate was also violated. In that year the global recession caused slow export growth. However, unlike the 1981–82 period, there was no widespread incidence of debt-servicing disruption in 1975. The difference between the interest and export-growth rates was smaller (6.6 percent in 1975 compared with an average of 14.8 percent in 1981–82), reflecting the fact that the 1975 recession was shorter and less severe. Moreover, the relative severity of the debt burden was milder going into the 1975 recession (as measured by debt relative to exports and GDP, and the debt-service ratio, table 1.1).

In sum, various measures of relative debt burden show a sharp erosion in 1981–82 as well as (by at least some criteria) milder earlier erosion in the 1970s, both in the aggregate and for key individual debtor countries. The principal causes of the eroding debt situation include both global influences and domestic policies of the debtor country. The global, or external causes of the debt problem include higher oil prices in 1973–74 and 1979–80, high international interest rates—especially in 1981–82, and global recession in 1980–82—which not only reduced the growth of export volume for developing countries but also caused a sharp deterioration in their terms of trade. Domestic policies included crucial decisions on exchange rates, domestic budgetary policy, and growth strategy generally. In addition, there is the question of the role of possibly overly accommodative foreign private banks, an issue considered in chapter 6.

Oil Prices

The single most important exogenous cause of the debt burden of nonoil developing countries is the sharp rise in the price of oil in 1973–74 and again

Figure 1.3 Export growth compared with international interest rates

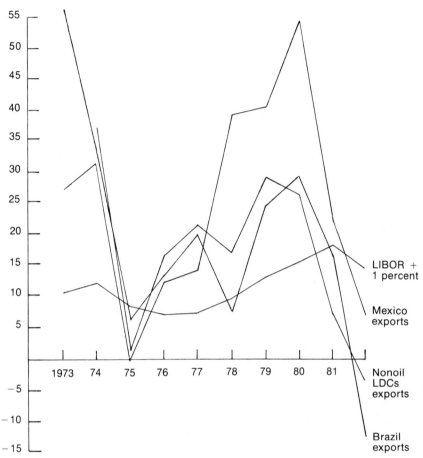

Source: Table 1.2

in 1979–80. As shown in table 1.1, the value of oil imports rose from 6 percent of total merchandise imports in 1973 to 20 percent in 1980–82. Table 1.3 presents a simple calculation of the cumulative additional costs of oil imports imposed on the net oil-importing developing countries by these price rises. The first column shows actual net oil imports by these countries since 1973. The second column shows the amount that would have been paid for these imports if the price of oil had risen no more than the US wholesale price index after 1973.[8] (Note that by 1973 oil prices had already risen by 42 percent from their

---

8. This value *equals* column A *times* the ratio of the US wholesale price index to the index of oil prices (Saudi Arabia), with both indexes set at 100 for 1973.

Table 1.3 Impact of higher oil prices on debt of nonoil developing countries[a] (billion dollars)

| | Oil imports | | Additional cost |
Year	Actual (A)	Hypothetical (B)[b]	(C = A − B)
1973	4.8	4.8	0.0
1974	16.1	5.3	10.8
1975	17.3	5.7	11.6
1976	21.3	6.8	14.5
1977	23.8	7.5	16.3
1978	26.0	8.6	17.4
1979	39.0	10.9	28.1
1980	63.2	11.9	51.3
1981	66.7	12.1	54.6
1982	66.7	11.9	54.8
Total, 1974–82	344.9	85.5	259.5

Source: IMF, *World Economic Outlook*, 1982, p. 163, and *International Financial Statistics*, selected issues.
a. Net oil importers only.
b. If oil prices had risen no more than US wholesale price index from 1973.

1972 level.) As the table shows, the cumulative total of the additional expense on oil imports amounts to $260 billion over the decade. This amount includes no allowance for cumulative interest charges on each year's additional oil bill, which would make the additional debt even larger. On the other hand, the estimates do not refer to actual increases in debt but potential increases before taking account of offsetting factors, especially adjustment measures adopted to reduce nonoil imports and increase exports, and increased exports to OPEC countries.

It is reasonable to ask whether oil-exporting developing countries achieved corresponding export gains that made their debt lower than it would have been. Among the countries grouped as "nonoil developing countries" by international practice,[9] only Mexico is now a major exporter of oil. Yet Mexico's large build-up of debt was almost certainly accelerated rather than deterred by higher oil prices. Mexico first borrowed heavily to develop oil production, and subsequently the promise of oil exports was the main basis for its ability to borrow large amounts more generally in pursuit of a high-growth strategy.

---

9. See, for example, IMF, *World Economic Outlook*, 1983.

Among the other oil-exporting developing countries, it is difficult to argue that the debts of Venezuela, Nigeria, Indonesia, and Ecuador are substantially lower than they would have been in the absence of higher oil prices (with the possible exception of Venezuela if debt net of reserves is considered); indeed, the ratio of their 1982 debt to the 1973 level is higher than for the nonoil developing countries. Accordingly, the net impact of higher oil prices was an unambiguous increase in developing-country debt of extremely large dimensions.

It does not follow from this analysis that the problem of world financial vulnerability to external debt would be relieved by a collapse in the price of oil. On the contrary, by now the oil-exporting developing countries (including Mexico) have built up large debt, and the adverse impact of a sharp drop in the price of oil would be highly concentrated for them while the corresponding benefits for oil-importing developing countries would be more modest (because oil is a much smaller fraction of their imports than it is of oil exporters' earnings from exports). As is often the case in economic (or physical and political) phenomena, the sharp increase of oil prices carried with it certain irreversibilities, including financial strains for the system as a whole that could not now be eliminated by the sudden return of oil prices to their 1973 levels. The issue of the impact on debt of lower oil prices is examined in chapter 3. The main thrust of the preceding analysis is that a legacy of the 1970s is a high level of debt attributable to an international force exogenous to the debtor countries: the sharp rise in the price of oil.

Interest Rates and Recession

If higher oil prices set the stage for a heavy debt burden for many countries in the last decade, the global recession and high interest rates of 1980–82 added sufficiently to the burden to precipitate several major debt crises by 1982.

Borrowers became accustomed to low real interest rates in the 1970s. For 1961–70, LIBOR on US dollar deposits *minus* the US wholesale price increase produced an average real interest rate of 4.1 percent. But for 1971–80, this average was − 0.8 percent: real interest rates were negative on average for the decade.[10] By 1979 and 1980 nominal interest rates were high (LIBOR averaged 13.2 percent) and although (US) inflation was virtually equal to LIBOR, high nominal rates caused a cash-flow squeeze for borrowers as discussed above. By 1981–82 declining inflation without a corresponding decline in interest rates meant high real interest rates (7.5 percent in 1981 and 11.0 percent in 1982), making matters worse.

Because of higher interest rates, caused largely by the unusual mix of

---

10. IMF, *International Financial Statistics Yearbook*, 1982.

monetary and fiscal policy adopted in the United States in 1981–82, the average interest rate on outstanding long-term debt of developing countries rose from 4.5 percent in 1973–77 to 8.5 percent in 1981–82;[11] deducting (US) inflation the real interest rate on this debt rose from −6 percent to +3 percent over the same period.

To obtain a notional magnitude of the increase in debt attributable to higher interest rates, it is possible to estimate the "excess interest rate" in 1981–82 as the amount by which real interest rates exceeded their average level for 1961–80. For the 1960s and 1970s real interest rates (LIBOR *minus* US wholesale price inflation) averaged 1.66 percent. In 1981 this real rate was 7.46 percent, and in 1982 it reached 10.95 percent.[12] Thus, the excess of interest rates above the real level that might have been expected based on the past two decades was 5.8 percentage points in 1981 and 9.29 percentage points in 1982.

Approximately two-thirds of developing-country debt is indexed to LIBOR (chapter 3). Deducting nongold reserves (most of which earn interest), the nonoil developing countries had net floating debt of $240 billion at the end of 1980 and $293 billion at the end of 1981 (rising to $329 billion at the end of 1982). Applying the estimated excess interest costs in 1981 and 1982 to the year-end debts of 1980 and 1981, respectively, total excess interest payments on developing-country debt amounted to $41 billion in 1981–82, beyond amounts developing-country borrowers could have anticipated on the basis of past real interest rates. The basic cause of this excessive interest rate was the mismatch between loose fiscal policy and tight monetary policy in the United States, which drove up domestic (and therefore international) interest rates in textbook fashion.

Coinciding with and in considerable degree because of, high real interest rates, the international economy experienced severe recession in 1980–82. From 1973 to 1979 real growth in industrial countries averaged 3.2 percent annually. It then fell to 1.2 percent in 1980–81 and −0.3 percent in 1982.[13] Commodity export prices for developing countries are sensitive to the business cycle, and by 1981–82 they showed substantial declines. With 1980 = 100, export unit values fell to an index of 94 in 1981 and 90 for 1982 in nonoil developing countries. Import unit values rose to 103 in 1981 and returned to 100 by 1982.[14] Applying these changes to the trade bases (goods and services) of the previous year (table 1.1) the resulting effects were a loss of $25 billion

---

11. IMF, *World Economic Outlook*, 1982, p. 173. For funds borrowed commercially at a typical rate of LIBOR plus 1 percent spread, the corresponding rise was from 8.8 percent to 16.8 percent, in nominal terms, and from −1.6 percent to 11.3 percent in real terms.

12. IMF, *International Financial Statistics*, various issues.

13. IMF, *World Economic Outlook*, 1983.

14. IMF, *International Financial Statistics*, May 1983, pp. 56–57.

Table 1.4   Impact of exogenous shocks on external debt of nonoil developing countries (billion dollars)

Effect	Amount
Oil price increase in excess of US inflation, 1974–82 cumulative[a]	260
Real interest rate in excess of 1961–80 average: 1981 and 1982	41
Terms-of-trade loss, 1981–82	79
Export volume loss caused by world recession, 1981–82	21
Total	401
Memorandum items	
Total debt: 1973	130
1982	612
Increase: 1973–82	482

Source: Author's calculations; see text.
a. Net oil importers only.

in export value and an import cost increase of $9.6 billion in 1981, and a loss of export value in 1982 by $44 billion but no increment in import costs (compared with 1980 prices). Thus, the total loss to nonoil developing countries from deteriorating terms of trade in 1981–82 was an estimated $79 billion.

Real export volume also stagnated as the result of a 1980–82 world recession. Real export growth for nonoil developing countries averaged 8.1 percent in 1971–80.[15] Real export growth was 9.9 percent in 1981 and only 1.8 percent in 1982, giving an average shortfall for the two years that, when applied to the base of exports of goods and services, implies a net loss of $21 billion from trend in real exports.

In sum, high interest rates and the global recession imposed large cumulative losses on the nonoil developing countries in 1981–82. In all, these countries lost approximately $141 billion in higher interest payments, lower export receipts, and higher import costs as the consequence of adverse international macroeconomic conditions.

The (ex ante) impact of all of these exogenous shocks on external debt of the nonoil developing countries is summarized in table 1.4. As the table shows, their combined impact (on an ex ante, or potential, basis) was to increase the debt of nonoil developing countries by $401 billion. The table also shows the total increase in external debt of these countries since 1973, amounting to $482 billion.

---

15. Calculated from IMF, *International Financial Statistics Yearbook,* 1982, using export values as deflated by unit values of exports.

By their nature these estimates are not strictly comparable to actual debt increases after the fact, because countries did pursue adjustment measures to reduce external deficits (and debt) from levels they otherwise would have reached. Thus, in Korea higher oil prices in 1979–81 raised the cost of oil imports from $2.2 billion in 1978 to $6.1 billion in 1982. But because of strong measures to adjust by raising exports, Korea's trade balance actually improved, from a deficit of $1.3 billion in 1978 to one of $0.8 billion in 1982.[16] Accordingly, it would not be proper to conclude from table 1.4 that 83 percent of increased debt ($401 billion/$482 billion) was caused by these exogenous shocks—other influences not measured here could well have contributed considerably more (ex ante) than the remainder of $81 billion, and the final debt build-up was substantially smaller than the sum of all such ex ante influences (because of adjustment). Nonetheless, these figures strongly suggest that a very large part of the increase in developing-country debt in the last decade may be attributed to the impact of global causes that were exogenous to the developing countries themselves: higher oil prices beginning in 1973 and, in 1981–82, abnormally high interest rates and declines in terms of trade and export volume associated with global recession.

Domestic Policies

In addition to serious outside shocks from the world economy, domestic policy errors contributed to the deterioration of the debt situation.[17] In Mexico, the government allowed the peso to become seriously overvalued, and allowed budget deficits to surge to 16.5 percent of GNP in 1982 when the upcoming presidential election made authorities reluctant to carry out effective budget-cutting measures. The government adhered to a strategy of high growth (8.2 percent annual growth in 1978–81) that probably exceeded capacity growth and failed to take adequate account of the substantial weakening of the oil market in 1981.[18]

In Brazil, domestic adjustment policies were stronger and indeed contributed to a severe recession that began in 1981 and continued into 1983. Even so, Brazil's domestic policies bear substantial responsibility for the eventual crisis in 1982. Throughout the 1970s after the first oil shock, Brazil consciously followed a high-risk strategy of pursuing high growth based on rapid accumulation of external debt. The resulting legacy of large debt proved to be an oppressive burden when the international economy weakened and exports

---

16. IMF, *International Financial Statistics*, various issues.

17. For a more extended discussion of domestic policies in Argentina, Brazil, Mexico, Poland, and Yugoslavia, see appendix C.

18. William R. Cline, "Mexico's Crisis, The World's Peril," *Foreign Policy*, no. 49 (Winter 1982–83), pp. 107–18.

declined instead of continuing their earlier rapid growth.[19] Matters were made worse by overvaluation of the cruzeiro after an ill-fated attempt to bring down domestic inflation by placing a 40 percent ceiling on devaluation in 1980. Nonetheless, by 1981 the government was taking adjustment measures and was typically considered by the international financial community to be managing the economy well.

In Argentina a policy of preannouncing an exchange rate devaluation by less than the rate of domestic inflation, in an attempt to bring down inflation, led to a vastly overvalued peso, high imports, poor export performance, and rapidly rising debt by 1981. Ineffective stabilization policy, collapse of the peso, and extremely high inflation in 1981 were followed by the adverse shock to credit markets from the Falklands war and the associated mutual freeze of assets between the United Kingdom and Argentina. In Chile, much more stringent monetary and fiscal policy led to success in bringing down inflation in the 1970s (in contrast to Argentina's failure to do so). Nonetheless, a similar conceptual approach to reducing inflation by preannouncing the exchange rate led to a similar problem of overvaluation of the peso, which, together with a decline in the price of copper, led to rapid increase in debt. In Venezuela, lax management of state agencies permitted build-up of short-term debt after 1976 despite the presence of surpluses in the external accounts and large external assets in the petroleum agency. In Poland, foreign borrowing to avoid domestic economic restraint, and the domestic political clash between the Solidarity trade union and the government, led to increased debt, a severe decline in economic activity, lower exports, and exhaustion of reserves.

In Venezuela and Mexico especially, but also in other cases to some extent, policies led to large capital flight abroad. The basic flaw was maintenance of an overvalued exchange rate on a fully convertible basis, combined with domestic interest rate policy that failed to provide sufficient attraction to retain capital domestically. As a consequence, in 1982 the decline in Venezuela's official external assets reached over $8 billion, although on current account its deficit was only $2.2 billion.[20] Similarly, in Mexico errors and omissions showed outflows of $8.4 billion in 1981 and $6.6 billion in 1982 and short-term capital outflows added $2.1 billion in 1982, for total capital flight of $17 billion.[21] In Argentina, in 1980 and 1981 errors and omissions and short-term capital outflows registered total capital flight of $11.2 billion.[22] Thus, recent capital

19. William R. Cline, "Brazil's Aggressive Response to External Shock," in William R. Cline and Associates, *World Inflation and the Developing Countries* (Washington: Brookings Institution, 1981), pp. 102–35.

20. UN Economic Commission for Latin America, *Preliminary Balance of the Latin American Economy in 1982* (Santiago, January 1983), p. 13.

21. Banco de Mexico, *Informe Anual* (Mexico City, 1982), p. 230.

22. IMF, *International Financial Statistics*, May 1983, p. 68.

flight has contributed nearly one-third of total debt in both Venezuela and Argentina, and approximately one-fifth in Mexico. This fact not only raises the issue of the quality of the economic growth and capital formation purchased by higher debt in these particular countries, but it also raises questions about the advisability of international official financing of such capital flight through the mounting of support packages to put new public and private money into the country from abroad even when national citizens are removing their own assets from the country. At the least it implies the need for strong domestic measures (realistic exchange and interest rate policies) to prevent future substantial capital flight.

In addition to short-term policy errors such as those just enumerated, there have been long-run development strategies that have been less than ideal. Excessive protection in programs of industrialization based on import substitution, inadequate pricing of capital, over-pricing of labor, overly ambitious and inefficient government enterprise activities, and other distortions have hindered efficient development in many developing countries.[23] The cyclical pressures from the global economy have made it more essential that distortions in basic development strategies be corrected.

This review of policy mishaps does not mean that the bulk of developing-country borrowing has been unproductively used. Aside from the notable amounts of capital flight in the three Latin American countries cited above, the use of most borrowing appears to have been productive. Thus, domestic savings did not decline in the 1970s when external financing was heavy. For middle-income oil-importing countries, gross domestic savings were 21 percent of GDP in 1980 compared with 19 percent in 1960, and gross domestic investment was 27 percent compared with 21 percent,[24] suggesting that not only did foreign financing help increase domestic investment, but also that it was not used for the purpose of raising domestic consumption and reducing domestic savings.[25] Similarly, for 10 major borrowing developing countries, the average savings rate rose from 20.6 percent of GNP in 1965–73 to 21.9 percent in 1974–79, and the investment rate rose from 20.4 percent to 22.6 percent.[26]

It must also be recognized that by the late 1970s, a large part of new net borrowing was going merely to pay the interest on past debt (chapter 4, table

---

23. See World Bank, *World Development Report 1983*, Part II (Washington, 1983).

24. World Bank, *World Development Report 1982* (Washington, 1982), p. 118.

25. Note that this judgment is not contradictory to the analysis that higher oil expenditure contributed to the debt. The bulk of oil use in developing countries tends to be as an intermediate input into production (for example, in truck transportation) rather than for consumption (in pleasure driving, for example). Accordingly, it is not appropriate to view oil imports primarily as consumption, and as inelastic response of these imports to higher price as a failure to carry out necessary reductions in consumption.

26. Jeffrey D. Sachs, "The Current Account and Macroeconomic Adjustment in the 1970s," *Brookings Papers on Economic Activity*, no. 1 (1981), pp. 201–68.

4.2). In evaluating the productive or unproductive use of borrowing, it is first necessary to deduct this portion, as a given cost of the borrowing process. The central question is whether the remainder of net borrowing went primarily to capital formation or into consumption, capital flight, and other less productive uses such as military purchases. The available econometric analysis of developing-country borrowing has tended to find that it was associated with acceleration of productive investment rather than used primarily for consumption purposes.[27]

In sum, there have been significant domestic as well as foreign causes of the debt problem. This conclusion has also been found in various detailed studies of the causes of debt-servicing difficulties.[28] Nonetheless, it would be inaccurate to conclude that the bulk of the debt contracted has failed to go into productive investments; the evidence tends to indicate that most borrowing was productively used. But it remains true that because the magnitudes of the external economic pressures on developing countries became so great (especially by 1981–82), as examined above, there was little margin left for domestic policy error. In evaluating domestic policy, it must also be kept in mind that the sharp decline in the global economy, rise in interest rates, and oil price shock of 1980–82 were generally not predicted, and few would have advocated the extremely cautious borrowing policy that would have been consistent with foreknowledge of these global shocks.

Psychology

International debt problems have been aggravated by psychological shifts in the credit markets. In both Eastern Europe and Latin America, a debt-servicing breakdown by a major country has led relatively rapidly to a process of regional contamination that has severely restricted capital flows to most of the rest of the region. Poland's quasi-default in 1981 demonstrated that the "umbrella" theory of Soviet backing for East European debt was invalid, and credit quickly became scarce for the region, pushing Romania into rescheduling and placing pressure on other governments in the region. Thus, the net exposure of Western banks in Eastern Europe declined from $46 billion in 1980 to $42 billion by mid-1982.[29]

The Mexican debt crisis of August 1982, added to the Argentine disruption

---

27. *Ibid.*

28. See in particular Stanley W. Black, "The Impact of Changes in the World Economy on Stabilization Policies in the 1970s," in *Economic Stabilization in Developing Countries,* William R. Cline and Sidney Weintraub eds., (Washington: Brookings Institution, 1981), pp. 43–77.

29. BIS, *The Maturity Distribution of International Bank Lending* (Basle), selected issues.

of debt servicing associated with the Falklands war, caused a similar adverse shock to credit supply for Latin America as a region. In September of 1982 lending to Brazil fell to half its monthly average for earlier in the year.[30] By mid-1983 problems of credit availability and resulting debt rescheduling in Latin America had spread to Brazil, Chile, Peru, and Venezuela, and previous debt-servicing difficulties (and reschedulings) persisted in Costa Rica, Nicaragua, Bolivia, and Ecuador. The only significant exception to regionwide debt-servicing disruption was Colombia, a country that had carefully avoided incurring heavy debt (at the recognized cost of less buoyant growth) and had placed the receipts of the late-1970s' coffee bonanza into reserves instead of using them as leverage for further borrowing. The abrupt curtailment of credit to Latin America was evident in the data for US bank loans outstanding, which rose from $68.1 billion in June 1982 to $69.3 billion in December, an increase of only $1.2 billion compared with $7.3 billion in the same period during 1981.[31]

To be sure, there was also underlying deterioration in the debt-servicing capacity of many of the Latin American countries in 1982, largely because of the depressed level of their exports (which fell from $97 billion in 1981 to $87 billion in 1982 for the region as a whole).[32] Nonetheless, the sharp psychological shift aggravated debt problems and at least in some cases (especially Peru) probably precipitated debt-servicing disruptions that otherwise could have been avoided.[33]

In the autumn of 1983, debt disruption entered the Asian region as the assassination of a prominent political opponent in the Philippines, Benigno Aquino, triggered nervousness among creditors. The Philippines moved to a package of debt rescheduling and adjustment under IMF auspices. However, because the Philippines is a sharp exception to the general pattern of moderate debt burdens in Asia (tables 3.9, E-3), it appears unlikely that a credit freeze will spread to other Asian nations.

Summary

The external debt crisis that emerged in many developing countries in 1982 can be traced to higher oil prices in 1973–74 and 1979–80, high interest rates in 1980–82, declining export prices and volumes associated with global recession

---

30. William R. Cline, "Mexico's Crisis."

31. Federal Financial Institutions Examination Council, *Country Exposure Lending Survey* (Washington), various issues. The figures cited exclude countries in the region that are members of OPEC.

32. UN Economic Commission for Latin America, "Preliminary Balance," p. 13.

33. See the analysis in "A Logit Model of Debt Rescheduling, 1967–82," appendix A.

1981–82, problems of domestic economic management, and an adverse psychological shift in the credit markets. External debt of developing countries has grown to large dimensions, and in 1981–82 that growth outpaced the growth of exports that sustain the debt. Because of the magnitude of this debt and the widespread, if not generalized, evidence of debt-servicing difficulties, the debt problem currently poses a considerable risk to the security of the international financial system.

2

Systemic Vulnerability and Emergency Response

The international financial system is vulnerable to the potential impact of default or serious disruption in the servicing of the debt of developing and East European countries. This vulnerability stems largely from the fact that much of the debt is owed to private banks in industrial countries, and the amounts owed are large relative to bank capital. Because banks play a pivotal role in national economies, and because their loans are highly leveraged on a relatively small capital base, loss of a significant part of their capital from developing-country defaults could place severe strains on the Western economies.

The events of September 1982 through mid-1983 demonstrated graphically that Western policymakers acknowledge the vital importance of the viability of the external debt of several large debtor nations to the international financial system. As temporary debt-servicing breakdowns emerged in or threatened major debtors, the international financial community reacted promptly with financial rescue packages. This chapter first examines the extent of the system's vulnerability to external debt, and then reviews the emergency measures taken and their prospects for success.

Bank Exposure

Significant default on sovereign debt last occurred in the 1930s. But most of the debt was in the form of bonds. While its loss hurt individual bondholders, the damage did not extend beyond them. Today the bulk of sovereign debt to private sources is in the form of bank lending. Because banks are highly leveraged financial intermediaries, the economic damage from default could be multiplied severalfold.

The risk to banks from foreign lending may be gauged by examining the size of their exposure to the class of foreign borrowers most likely to encounter debt-servicing difficulties: developing and East European countries. The exposure in these countries may be compared to the banks' capital base. For US

21

banks, table 2.1 shows the ratio of exposure to capital since 1977 when the country exposure reporting system began. It is evident from this table that the exposure of US banks in nonoil developing and East European countries is high. For all banks this exposure has risen from 131.6 percent of capital in 1977 to 155 percent in 1982. If five OPEC countries not in capital surplus are included (Algeria, Ecuador, Indonesia, Nigeria, Venezuela) the 1982 total exposure stands at 182.8 percent of capital. For the nine largest banks relative exposure is even higher: 235.2 percent of capital for East European and nonoil developing countries and 282.8 percent including the five OPEC countries just cited.

Table 2.1 Exposure of US banks in Eastern Europe and nonoil developing countries, relative to capital (percentages, end year)

	1977	1978	1979	1980	1981	1982	Value, 1982 (million dollars)
All banks							
Eastern Europe	16.7	15.8	16.1	13.9	12.9	8.9	6,278
Nonoil LDCs	114.9	114.4	124.2	132.3	148.3	146.1	103,181
Sum	131.6	130.2	140.3	146.2	163.5	155.0	109,459
Mexico	27.4	23.4	23.0	27.6	34.3	34.5	24,377
Brazil	29.4	28.6	27.3	25.4	26.9	28.9	20,438
Nine largest banks							
Eastern Europe	25.0	23.5	23.9	21.8	19.5	13.9	4,045
Nonoil LDCs	163.2	166.8	182.1	199.3	220.6	221.2	64,149
Sum	188.2	190.3	206.0	221.1	240.1	235.2	68,194
Mexico	32.9	30.4	29.6	37.8	44.4	44.4	12,262
Brazil	41.9	42.4	40.3	39.3	40.8	45.8	13,296

Source: Federal Reserve Board of Governors, *Country Exposure Lending Survey,* various issues.

The trends in table 2.1 highlight the pullback from Eastern Europe since the Polish debt disruption of 1981. By 1982 exposure in Eastern Europe had fallen to slightly over half its size relative to capital in the late 1970s. The table also documents the sharp rise in loans to Mexico: for the nine largest banks, an increase from 30 percent of capital in 1978–79 to 44 percent by 1982, with a similar rise for all banks. The paramount role of Mexico and Brazil is shown in the table: each accounts for about one-third of the capital of all banks and about 45 percent of the capital of the nine largest banks. Together Mexico and

Brazil represent 35 percent of total US bank loans to Eastern Europe, nonoil developing countries, and five OPEC countries.

It should be kept in mind that although exposure to these countries is high relative to bank capital, it is a more modest share of total bank loans. Thus, for the nine largest banks, loans to the set of countries considered here (including five OPEC countries) account for 282.8 percent of capital but only 13.9 percent of total bank assets (primarily, loans). The difference between the two concepts stems from the high leverage of banks, whose loans are as much as twenty times as large as their capital.

The exposures of individual large banks to individual countries potentially in debt-servicing difficulty provide a more direct reflection of vulnerability. Table 2.2 shows the exposure of 18 large individual banks to five Latin American countries that have all experienced debt-servicing difficulties (of varying degrees) in the last year. The exposure is expressed as a percentage of primary capital (the same capital measure as that used in table 2.1). From the table it is evident that certain key banks have considerably greater exposure relative to capital than might be expected based on more aggregate data. Exposure in Brazil is approximately three-fourths of the capital of Citicorp and Manufacturers Hanover; exposure in Mexico equals or exceeds 60 percent of capital for Manufacturers Hanover, Chemical Bank, and First Interstate. Exposure in these five Latin American countries alone exceeds 150 percent of capital for Citicorp, BankAmerica, Chase Manhattan, Manufacturers Hanover, Chemical, and Crocker National.

In short, for the US banking system as a whole and for some of the largest US banks in particular, exposure to developing countries poses a substantial potential vulnerability. Nonetheless, it is necessary to have a general idea of the extent to which this broad class of external debt stands at risk. One simple basis for examining this question is to examine the debt totals for the class of countries that have indeed experienced significant debt-servicing interruptions within the last year. In several cases these include new or former debt reschedulings. In most of the cases (perhaps with the notable exception of Poland), the reschedulings should provide the basis for adequate future meeting of debt commitments, albeit with subsequent reschedulings in certain cases. Recognizing, then, that such a listing tends to overstate the pool of potentially risky loans, the data in table 2.3 present total bank lending (US and other industrial countries) to the 20 countries with the largest debt owed to banks, and the table indicates whether the country experienced debt-servicing interruption in 1982–83 (and reports the ratio of its debt service to exports of goods and services). Perhaps the most severe case of disruption is that of Poland; the least severe (primarily management difficulties in shifting short-term to long-term debt), Venezuela. Using this definition, however, and considering that smaller countries not singled out in the table are having comparable difficulties,

Table 2.2 Exposure as percentage of capital, major banks, end-1982

	Argentina	Brazil	Mexico	Venezuela	Chile	Total	Capital[a] (million dollars)
Citibank	18.2	73.5	54.6	18.2	10.0	174.5	5,989
Bank of America	10.2	47.9	52.1	41.7	6.3	158.2	4,799
Chase Manhattan	21.3	56.9	40.0	24.0	11.8	154.0	4,221
Morgan Guaranty	24.4	54.3	34.8	17.5	9.7	140.7	3,107
Manufacturers Hanover	47.5	77.7	66.7	42.4	28.4	262.8	2,592
Chemical	14.9	52.0	60.0	28.0	14.8	169.7	2,499
Continental Illinois	17.8	22.9	32.4	21.6	12.8	107.5	2,143
Bankers Trust	13.2	46.2	46.2	25.1	10.6	141.2	1,895
First National Chicago	14.5	40.6	50.1	17.4	11.6	134.2	1,725
Security Pacific	10.4	29.1	31.2	4.5	7.4	82.5	1,684
Wells Fargo	8.3	40.7	51.0	20.4	6.2	126.6	1,201
Crocker National	38.1	57.3	51.2	22.8	26.5	196.0	1,151
First Interstate	6.9	43.9	63.0	18.5	3.7	136.0	1,080
Marine Midland	n.a.	47.8	28.3	29.2	n.a.	n.a.	1,074
Mellon	n.a.	35.3	41.1	17.6	n.a.	n.a.	1,024
Irving Trust	21.6	38.7	34.1	50.2	n.a.	n.a.	996
First National Boston	n.a.	23.1	28.1	n.a.	n.a.	n.a.	800
Interfirst Dallas	5.1	10.2	30.1	1.3	2.5	49.2	787

n.a. Not available.
Source: Annual reports for individual banks; *American Banker,* 17 March 1983 and 6 April 1983; Prudential-Bache Securities, "Banking Industry Outlook," May 6, 1983; *Veja* (Brazil), 1 June 1983. Capital figures are from reports of condition (Federal Reserve).
a. Bank capital includes shareholders equity, subordinated notes, and reserves against possible loan losses.

Table 2.3 Debt owed to industrial country[a] banks by developing and East European countries, June 1982

	Debt (billion dollars)	Debt service[b] as percentage of exports of goods and services (1982)	Debt servicing disruption in 1982–83
Mexico	64.4	58.5	yes
Brazil	55.3	87.1	yes
Venezuela	27.2	20.7	yes
Argentina	25.3	102.9	yes
South Korea	20.0	21.1	no
Poland	13.8	n.a.	yes
Chile	11.8	60.4	yes
Philippines	11.4	36.1	yes
Yugoslavia	10.0	30.3	yes
East Germany	9.4	29.0	no
Algeria	7.7	41.0	no
Hungary	6.4	33.0	no
Indonesia	8.2	11.3	no
Nigeria	6.7	5.4[e]	no
Taiwan	6.4	n.a.	no
Israel	6.1	23.7	no
Colombia	5.5	23.9[e]	no
Egypt	5.4	39.0	no
Malaysia	5.3	5.0[e]	no
Peru	5.2	53.4	yes
Subtotal	311.5		
Of which			
Debt disruption	224.4		
Total, LDCs[c] and			
Eastern Europe[d]	374.9		

Source: BIS, *The Maturity Structure of International Bank Lending*, Basle, December 1982; Institute for International Economics debt data bank; and Wharton Econometric Forecasting Associates (GDR, Hungary).
a. Group of Ten plus Switzerland, Austria, Denmark, and Ireland.
b. Excluding short-term principal, including short-term interest.
c. Including Yugoslavia; excluding Middle Eastern capital-surplus oil-exporting countries.
d. Excluding USSR.
e. 1981.

fully two-thirds of the bank debt owed by East European and developing countries was under a cloud of interruption in normal debt servicing in
1982–83.

The thrust of the preceding analysis is that not only does bank exposure to
Eastern Europe, nonoil developing countries, and noncapital-surplus OPEC
countries reach nearly 300 percent of capital for the nine largest US banks and
nearly 200 percent for all US banks, but approximately two-thirds of this debt
is in some sense at risk as revealed by interruption in debt servicing in 1982–
83. Accordingly, potential vulnerability of the financial system must be taken
seriously.

Even under the worst of circumstances, however, this body of debt would
be unlikely to become worthless overnight. Indeed, in the vast majority of
rescheduling cases the debt is carried at book value and, at least until further
evidence of protracted failure to meet rescheduled payments legitimately, can
continue to be carried at full value on the banks' books.

Moratorium Consequences

The stages of debt-servicing difficulty beyond rescheduling include "extended
moratorium" whereby no principal or interest is paid for a period of, perhaps,
more than six months, and outright "repudiation." In the last quarter century
only Cuba and North Korea have repudiated external debt. As discussed in
chapter 4, the costs of repudiation for a country are likely to be so high that
this alternative is rarely chosen. A country in severe straits is more likely to
announce that it can make no payments for a considerable period of time.

For Western banks, repudiation of a substantial portion of loans to developing
countries and Eastern Europe would be crippling. Even widespread moratoria
could have a severe impact on the banks. To gauge the potential risk, it is
useful to consider how far international debt would have to deteriorate to cause
banks to pass beyond certain thresholds of deterioration themselves.

A first threshold is the level of bank profits. Foreign loan losses would in the
first instance be set against profits before affecting capital. In 1982 gross profits
(before tax) of the nine largest US banks amounted to $5.5 billion.[1] Their total
loans to nonoil developing countries, Eastern Europe, and five noncapital-
surplus OPEC countries stood at $82 billion at the end of 1982, or 15 times as
large as gross profits.

Regulatory practice on provisioning (setting aside of reserves) on doubtful
loans has been to require that up to 50 percent be provisioned over a five-year
period. On average, approximately 10 percent of the principal would be set

---

1. Paine, Webber, Mitchell, Hutchins, Inc., "Earnings Models for Large US Banks," *Status
Report,* June 14, 1983.

aside the first, and 15 percent yearly thereafter (although these patterns are not rigid and depend on individual bank decisions). With annual gross profits of $5.5 billion, the nine largest banks could afford to provision only 30 percent of their loans to developing and East European countries out of annual profits.[2]

Nor would there appear to be much relief from the standpoint of offsetting tax effects. Although financial institutions can carry back losses for 10 years and thereby obtain tax refunds, US banks in practice have paid little tax in the past—only 2.7 percent on domestic income for the 20 largest banks in 1981.[3] Accordingly, there would be little in past tax payments to use as a recoverable offset against new losses from external lending.

As a similar, but perhaps even more hypothetical, illustration, consider what would happen if Argentina, Mexico, and Brazil were to miss one year's payment on principal and interest, and were to do so in a sufficiently aggressive way that it seemed appropriate to write off fully the payments missed. The complete loss of one year's payments due from these three countries would cause losses equal to 28 percent of the capital of the nine largest US banks even after taking account of offsetting profits on other loans.[4]

Based on these two illustrations, situations could arise (though with a low degree of probability) in which losses from Third World debt could cut heavily into the capital of Western banks. To pursue the illustration of a write-off of one year's payments from Argentina, Brazil, and Mexico, although the resulting cut in capital would not cause insolvency, it would mean that the banks would have to begin to reduce their total loans sharply in order to reestablish the 5

---

2. Let x be the amount of developing-country loans that must be provisioned and y the amount of gross bank income. Assuming interest of 12 percent on these loans, $.12x$ would be forgone income as the payments are missed, reducing gross income to $y - .12x$. Maximum provisioning out of profits is then $.10x = y - .12x$, or $x = 4.5y$. Considering that total developing-country and East European debt is 15 *times* gross bank profits, only 30 percent of these loans $(4.5/15)$ could be provisioned out of profits. This calculation assumes that missed interest payments would not be counted in profits (i.e., using accrual accounting). Otherwise, there would be little if any "real" provisioning (because such phantom payments would probably exceed the 10 percent yearly provisioning rate), and the bank would find itself having made no effective allowance at all for principal loss.

3. *Internal Revenue Code*, section 172 (New York: The Research Institute of America, Inc., 1980), pp. 160–61; *Washington Post*, 10 March 1983.

4. These three countries owe $31.3 billion to the nine largest banks, whose capital broadly defined is only $29 billion. Together the three countries owe the nine largest banks approximately $3.4 billion in interest, $6.9 billion in short-term debt payments, and $3.4 billion in long-term debt payments for 1983, before recent restructurings. The total owed is $13.7 billion for 1983. By contrast, 1982 profits of these banks were $5.5 billion before taxes. Thus a loss of $13.7 billion would cause total losses of $8.2 billion or 28 percent of capital and, without offsetting items generating taxes, these losses would have to be fully absorbed out of capital.

percent ratio of capital to loans required by regulators.[5] There would thus be a multiple reduction in loans. Potentially the nine largest banks would have to cut their loans outstanding by approximately $160 billion as the result of a loss of $8 billion of their capital from one year's loss of principal and interest from Argentina, Brazil, and Mexico under conditions where these losses had to be written off. Both because of loan cutbacks and because of a sharp increase in the risk premium, the interest rate could be expected to rise, causing recessionary pressure. Even if the Federal Reserve loosened the capital backing of loans temporarily, the potential would exist for economic shock waves through reduced credit availability to American business and consumers and, as a result, increased unemployment.

To a considerable extent, the sequence of events that would follow major bank losses because of country losses remains uncharted waters. The process just described of loan reduction by affected banks seeking to reestablish their capital-to-loan ratios would be clearly contractionary. However, to the extent that central banks made loans to the affected private banks in an attempt to replace at least partially the repayments that otherwise would have been received from countries failing to make payments, there could be inflationary consequences. When a country makes loan payments to bank A, it tends to do so using funds newly borrowed from bank B or else funds drawn from its account of export earnings held at bank B. The withdrawal at one bank tends to offset the repayment to the other, leaving little net monetary effect on the banking system as a whole. But if, in place of the country's payment, the central bank (Federal Reserve, in the case of the United States) makes a loan of comparable size to the private bank, there can be a net expansion of the monetary base, permitting an expansion of the money supply by a multiplied amount for the banking system as a whole. Essentially, a payment from the home country's central bank is an injection of high-powered money that serves as the basis for multiplied monetary expansion. However, the Fed could use other measures (open market sales of Treasury bills, for example) to offset the inflationary injection of these loans, unless it decided that crisis circumstances warranted faster monetary expansion.

In practice some combination of these measures would probably occur in a debt crisis. In addition, the regulatory agencies could permit reduced capital-to-loan ratios; Congress might provide mechanisms to inject public capital if capital ratios fell below a minimal level (as in the case of recent legislation for a safety net for thrift institutions); and write-offs could be spread over a number of years. And the central banks could perhaps gauge the amount of their lending so that the inflationary effect of injection of high-powered money just offset

---

5. Although the capital requirement for large banks has not been rigid, it is becoming more so as regulators respond to increasing congressional pressure. A new formal requirement of 5 percent capital backing for large banks was adopted in mid-1983. *Wall Street Journal*, 10 and 20 June 1983.

the contractionary effect of bank-loan cutbacks designed to restore capital-to-loan ratios.

Despite the fact that the Federal Reserve could respond in a crisis, there would be enormous economic risks from a large-scale banking crisis. If a wider front of country defaults were to occur, many major banks could become insolvent. For the nine largest banks this result would occur if just Brazil, Mexico, and Argentina repudiated their debt, or if all developing and East European countries experienced sufficient difficulty that one-third of their debt had to be written off. Normally bank insolvencies are dealt with by merger, with a larger, sound bank absorbing the bankrupt concern. But in the situations just described, merger would be highly unlikely. There would be no banks larger than the failing banks to absorb them. In the past merger has tended to guarantee the deposits of all depositors. In a bankruptcy of the major banks, however, it is likely that only deposits covered by the Federal Deposit Insurance Corporation (FDIC) would be guaranteed (in the United States), a maximum of $100,000 per account. For the US banking system, deposit insurance covers only 73 percent of total deposit value.[6] For the largest banks, the value of deposits covered by insurance is probably no more than 50 percent of the total.

By central banking principle, the central bank supports illiquid banks but not insolvent ones. Accordingly, a truly massive failure of external debt could bring down many major banks. Regardless of the emergency public measures that might be mounted in response, the potential economic consequences could be devastating. Accordingly, those (including some in Congress and the financial press) who advocate policies that would ignore this risk (for example, opposition to adequate resources for the International Monetary Fund) should be recognized as high-stake gamblers.

In sum, because developing and East European country exposure is so large relative to bank capital, any large-scale write-down of this debt would have dramatic effects on the banks, cutting deeply into their capital and exerting pressure for them to reduce the level and growth of their lending. Potentially serious domestic economic disruptions could result, with possible contractionary as well as inflationary consequences, and with large possible losses for the considerable portion of deposits not covered by insurance. For these reasons most policymakers take the problem of Third World debt very seriously indeed.

Rescue Operations, 1982–83

In view of the potential damage to the international financial system from a collapse of the debt of developing countries, especially that of the largest

---

6. According to information supplied by the FDIC.

debtors, the decisive response of US and other Western officials to the major debt crises of 1982 was reassuring. There were four major rescue operations: for Mexico, Brazil, Argentina, and Yugoslavia. The International Monetary Fund played a major role in all four. US authorities took the lead in the packages for Mexico and Brazil, while the Swiss did so in the case of Yugoslavia. The basic model of the rescue packages included country adjustment, an IMF program, bank lending, and official bridging loans.

Argentina's debt problem lingered over several months as arrears built up after the Falklands crisis. But when Mexico suspended principal payments in mid-August 1982, the stakes were clearly so large that foreign official response was immediate. The United States quickly mobilized $1 billion in commodity credits and $1 billion in prepayment for oil purchases for the strategic oil reserve, and it led a lending package from Western central banks through the Bank for International Settlements (BIS). The loans from central banks were short-term, designed to provide a bridge to expected IMF lending. Private banks agreed to an initial delay in principal payments and subsequently to major rescheduling and provision of new loans. By November Mexico had signed an agreement with the IMF.

In the case of Brazil rapid erosion in capital market confidence led to a large emergency loan from the United States in November 1982 and to recourse to IMF borrowing—a step the government had sought to avoid. An IMF agreement was reached rapidly, and by year's end a rescue operation similar to Mexico's was broadly in place. Argentina's package progressed much more slowly but an IMF agreement was finally signed early in 1983. For its part, Yugoslavia developed payments problems at the end of 1982 as it found itself unable to borrow the required amounts from banks. By early 1983 Western governments, banks, and international lending institutions had put together a $6 billion credit package for Yugoslavia, in a form that avoided outright debt rescheduling.[7]

In managing these rescue packages, the International Monetary Fund adopted a new approach of historical significance. Contrary to previous practice, whereby the IMF merely hoped that an adoption of a stand-by lending program would act as a seal of approval to encourage the return of foreign private lending, the IMF now explicitly told the private banks that if they did not provide new lending themselves there would be no new IMF funds whatsoever. In a situation in which many banks sought to withdraw, this strategy gave them no alternative but to bear their fair share in extending new loans. This approach was an effective answer to the "free-rider" problem (chapter 4), whereby especially the smaller banks seek to enjoy the benefits of increased quality of their exposure from provision of new international lending by large banks without providing any new lending themselves.

The elements of the international rescue packages for Argentina, Brazil,

---

7. *Washington Post*, 21 January 1983.

Table 2.4 Financial rescue packages[a] for Argentina, Brazil, Mexico, and Yugoslavia (billion dollars)

	Argentina	Brazil	Mexico	Yugoslavia
Financial support				
IMF				
Stand-by	1.7	—	—	0.6
Extended Fund facility	—	4.6	3.7	—
Compensatory finance and other	0.5	1.3	0.22	—
World Bank	—	—	—	0.5
Bank for International Settlements	0.5	1.2	0.925	0.5
United States				
Oil payments	—	—	1.0	—
Commodity Credit	—	—	1.0	0.2
Federal Reserve	—	0.4	0.925	—
Treasury	—	1.53	—	—
Private banks, new loans	1.5	4.4	5.0	3.0[b]
Government trade credits	—	—	2.0	1.1
Total	4.25	13.4	14.7	5.9
Debt rescheduling				
Amount[c]	5.5	4.9	19.5[d]	n.a.
Originally due	1982–83	long-term 1983	8/1982 to 12/1984	n.a.

— Zero or negligible.

n.a. Not applicable.

Source: House of Commons, Treasury and Civil Service Committee, *International Monetary Arrangements International Lending by Banks* (London, 15 March 1983), pp. *xxviii–xxix*; *Wall Street Journal,* 9 May 1983, and communication with Manufacturers Hanover.

a. Principal financial support measures through mid-1983.

b. New loans, $600 million; $1.2 billion to repay matured debt; $1.2 billion stretch-out of short-term loans.

c. Public debt.

d. In addition, special arrangements effectively rescheduled $15 billion in private debt.

Mexico, and Yugoslavia are shown in table 2.4. Some key elements of the packages were more limited than they appeared because of their very short-term nature: loans from the BIS, the US Treasury, and the Federal Reserve. These loans had to be repaid typically within 90 days, meaning that they added nothing to the cash flow for 1983 as a whole and served solely as bridging loans until the IMF and bank packages could be assembled. Similarly, the amounts from the IMF and from the banks are not comparable, because the IMF amounts (except for Argentina) were the full amount that could be expected over the next three years (at least in the absence of an extraordinary decision to exceed 450 percent of quota, or new quota increases without reduced percentage-of-quota access), while new bank lending was just for 1983 and additional new bank lending could be expected again in 1984 and 1985, ideally on a voluntary basis but perhaps again on an involuntary basis. Given these nuances, the table shows massive international support in these rescue operations.

Debt rescheduling was a central part of these packages (except in Yugoslavia, where loan rollovers were used to avoid the stigma of rescheduling). Once again, just as the IMF informed banks that it expected new money, it also informed them that the IMF funding would be forthcoming only if the banks committed themselves to reschedule certain portions of debt coming due. Typically rescheduling was on a five-to-eight year basis, involved rescheduling fees (from ½ percent for Mexico to 1½ percent for Brazil), and carried relatively high interest rate spreads (typically about 2 points over LIBOR or US prime). In Mexico, all public debt due in 1982 after August and through 1984 was rescheduled. This amount reached approximately $20 billion, much of which was short term. In Argentina, arrears on short- and long-term private debt had reached $2.8 billion by early 1983, and all public debt in arrears as well as that due in 1983 was rescheduled. In Brazil, only the public long-term debt due in 1983 was rescheduled, because Brazil made an extreme effort to distance itself from being classed as a standard rescheduling case—for fear of injury to its credit standing in the longer run. Instead, Brazil secured commitments of banks to maintain the levels of their short-term exposures, obviating outright rescheduling of short-term debt but setting the stage for subsequent problems as these bank commitments were not fully met (in the component for interbank deposits in foreign branches of Brazilian banks).

Performance to Date

By mid-1983 the principal rescue packages appeared to be functioning relatively well.[8] Argentina and Mexico were meeting their policy commitments under

8. See John Williamson, ed., *Prospects for Adjustment in Argentina, Brazil, and Mexico: Responding to the Debt Crisis* (Washington: Institute for International Economics, June 1983).

the IMF agreements, and both had relatively good prospects of achieving their external current account goals for the year—although primarily at the cost of severe domestic recession as the mechanism for reducing imports in the case of Mexico.

In Brazil, however, the program was proceeding less smoothly. Failure to meet internal targets (such as that for reducing the budget deficit) meant that the IMF suspended its support until additional measures and new targets could be agreed upon. A central problem was that a large devaluation in February 1983 had boosted inflation, thereby making targets established in specific monetary amounts much tighter than originally planned, in real terms. Moreover, of the four-part bank package established for Brazil, the part concerning interbank deposits was failing to meet the target level (only $6 billion was being maintained compared with $7.5 billion planned). As a result, Brazil had built up nearly $900 million in arrears by mid-year.[9]

By the third quarter of 1983, adjustment prospects temporarily dimmed, as continued suspension of the IMF program and bank lending in Brazil led to mounting arrears and Argentina experienced nonfulfillment on some of its IMF program targets. In October the Brazilian congress rejected a crucial law limiting wage indexation. But by November a significant improvement in the near-term prospects had occurred, as Brazil's congress approved a compromise limitation of wage indexing, IMF and bank lending to Brazil resumed, and the election results in Argentina held promise for a new government likely to be able to honor debt commitments (chapter 5).

Despite difficulties in meeting domestic stabilization targets in Argentina and Brazil, the external sector performance of the three major debtors since their financial rescue packages began has shown sharp adjustment, though primarily through cutbacks in imports rather than increased exports. The level of imports in Mexico declined from $24 billion in 1981 to $14.4 billion in 1982 and only $7.7 billion in 1983. As a result, the current account balance shifted from a deficit of $12 billion in 1981 and $4.9 billion in 1982 to a surplus of $5.5 billion in 1983, even though total exports remained practically unchanged (at approximately $21 billion) in 1983 as oil exports weakened slightly.[10]

Imports in Brazil declined from $19.4 billion in 1982 to $15.4 billion in 1983, a reduction of 20.6 percent in value. Exports rose from $20.2 billion in 1982 to $21.9 billion in 1983, an increase of 8.4 percent. Importantly, the rate of increase was considerably faster after the maxidevaluation of February (16 percent in the second quarter over the year earlier and 11.5 percent in the third quarter, after a 4 percent decline in the first quarter).[11] Argentina's adjustment

9. *Financial Times,* 31 May 1983.

10. Banco de Mexico, *Indicadores Económicos,* various issues.

11. *Gazeta Mercantil,* 5 March 1984; Fundaçao Centro de Estudos do Comercio Exterior, *Balança Comercial e Outros Indicadores Conjunturais,* September 1983; and *O Globo,* 6 October 1983, p. 21.

also concentrated heavily on imports, which declined by 42 percent in 1982 and another 20 percent in 1983, while 1983 exports stood at 14.7 percent below the 1981 level.[12]

The aggregate trade balance of Argentina, Brazil, and Mexico together shifted from a deficit of $2 billion in 1981 to a surplus of $24 billion in 1983. Essentially, the three countries cut imports by half (two-thirds in Mexico, half in Argentina, and one-third in Brazil) while restoring 1983 exports approximately to their 1981 level. Accordingly, for the three largest debtor countries the bulk of external adjustment had already occurred by 1983 (and indeed the size of the adjustment for these countries alone was equal to practically the entire cutback in international bank lending). For the future the need is not further increases in their combined trade surpluses, but instead matched increases in their exports and imports to permit reactivation of their economies. As noted in appendix C, domestic adjustment (primarily in correcting inflationary imbalances) was much less successful. The broader question of future growth implications of the sharp external adjustment in these countries is considered in chapter 8.

Tactical Lessons

The most important question about the international management of debt crises to date is whether its underlying assumption is sound: that the problem is temporary illiquidity, not insolvency, and that temporary financing combined with country adjustment is accordingly the proper remedy. An alternative diagnosis would be that the debt problem is so severe that it will never be possible for the key debtor countries to service the full burden of their debt, and that instead radical measures should be taken to relieve these countries of a substantial portion of the real burden of their debt on a permanent basis. In other words, the alternative diagnosis would imply bankruptcy proceedings.

As set forth below, the judgment of this study is that the debt problem so far remains one of illiquidity and that accordingly the basic strategy of dealing with the problem through international measures to provide special liquidity is the right approach. Even within this strategy, however, there are questions about the proper tactics.

One issue is whether there is a special need for bridging loans of the type that have been provided by central banks and the BIS. These loans typically have been at short-term maturities, such as three months (although in some cases the loans have been renewed because of delays in the IMF disbursements that were supposed to be at the other end of the bridge). They have been

---

12. Naciones Unidas, Comisión Económica para América Latina (CEPAL), *Balance Preliminar de la Economía Latinoamericana durante 1983*, cuadro 6 (Santiago, December 16, 1983).

arranged in haste, and made available without policy conditions. The bridge loans may well have been essential in the important early cases of Mexico in mid-1982 and Brazil at the end of 1982, to provide reassurance to international financial markets in the face of debt disruptions of unprecedented size. Subsequently, however, the cases of Argentina and Brazil demonstrated that even the largest debtor countries can go into arrears without precipitating international financial collapse. Net new lending usually is smaller than interest payments under a financial package once it is in place. Accordingly, temporary interest arrears provide an alternative vehicle for financing prior to completion of the arrangements, because they equal or exceed the formal financing that is to be mobilized. Arrears also place pressure on the country to come to terms with the IMF and the banks.

In early 1984 Argentina was precisely in the situation of using interest arrears for temporary financing (instead of official bridge loans) in the period before an IMF agreement. Moreover, when four other Latin American countries did come to Argentina's assistance with a bridge loan (chapter 8), the US Treasury backed up the arrangement with a bridge loan of its own that would only come into effect after Argentina submitted its letter of intent to the IMF. This condition indicated that US officials were moving in the direction of making any bridging conditional on near-agreement with the IMF, in contrast to the unconditional bridge loans for Mexico and Brazil in 1982.

The past public image of the critical role of central bank lending probably has been exaggerated, in view of the short-term nature and limited contribution of this lending. The more important form for official support is through longer term lending by multilateral banks, the IMF, and national agencies. At the national level, the export credit agencies are promising vehicles for this purpose (if legislative inhibitions about their use for balance of payments support can be overcome), considering that bilateral concessional assistance is irrelevant for middle-income countries and in view of the political popularity of export credit. The US Commodity Credit Corporation is another useful instrument. The basic judgment here is that there is relatively less need for the ultra short-term bridge loans than their seeming prominence in past rescue packages would suggest, but greater need in the future for longer term official finance. This judgment also implies that there is no need for a new international agency or arrangement to provide bridging loans; and that instead it would be better to concentrate international efforts on the assurance of adequate funding for multilateral institutions that provide longer term lending.

A second tactical issue concerns the pattern of delays in actual disbursement of loans committed by the banks. Here a problem has been that bank disbursements have been tied to IMF disbursements. If the IMF reviews country performance and finds noncompliance with the policy conditions of its lending program, the agency suspends disbursements of its funds. The agreements between banks and debtor countries typically have tied disbursements of new bank lending to those of the IMF, so that bank flows also come to a halt. However, it may require many weeks or even months formally to reestablish the IMF program. During this period bank funding is absent even though the country may be close to, or actually in, agreement with the IMF once again. A delay of this type can cause difficulties for the banks themselves, by bringing arrears on their interest close to or beyond the 90-day period that causes reclassification as nonperforming. That is, without receiving new bank lending, the country is unable to remain current on its interest payments.

It might be better for all parties if the link of bank lending to IMF disbursements were less mechanical. For example, bank lending to the country could continue according to schedule regardless of the status of the IMF agreement, with the safeguard that bank flows would be suspended upon the specific recommendation of the managing director of the IMF (perhaps with the agreement of the lead banks). If suspended, bank lending could then be reinstated upon a positive recommendation by the managing director of the IMF, even before formal IMF board approval of a new program.

The structure of rescheduling is another tactical issue (although if the option of below-market interest rates, or even the milder alternative of interest capitalization, were considered, rescheduling would become a strategic rather than a tactical issue). The four major rescue operations suggest some patterns on rescheduling technique. Rescheduling over at least two years, as in Mexico, would appear preferable to a single-year rescheduling. Reliance on voluntary maintenance of short-term credits is especially vulnerable for interbank deposits, as shown by the Brazilian case, and is less effective in a country with a more severe underlying debt burden, as shown by the problems of Brazil compared with the relative success of Yugoslavia. However, it remains an open question whether rescheduling of all short-term debt is desirable. Doing so tends to create a later bulge in long-term amortization (Mexico, Argentina) and it could be preferable to identify a level of hard-core trade finance—perhaps half of one year's imports—and maintain at least this much short-term debt without rescheduling. (For further discussion of rescheduling, see chapter 4.)

The nature of the IMF-sponsored adjustment program is another tactical issue. The major rescue packages have shown a common pattern of IMF conditionality. They involve the government's commitment to reduce budget deficits, often by ten percentage points or so of GDP. The packages limit expansion of domestic credit. They also involve commitment to a realistic exchange rate, although by the time the program is in place the country often has already carried out a large devaluation.

The central question about this pattern is whether the IMF is needlessly causing economic recession by recommending contractionary policies. An aspect of this question is the issue of whether the IMF has any right to insist on certain measures aimed at domestic performance, particularly on fiscal balance and inflation, as long as the country is meeting its targets in the external sector.

An in-depth examination of the stabilization approach advocated by the IMF is beyond the scope of this study. However, certain observations are appropriate. First, the macroeconomic consequences of these programs are not necessarily recessionary, especially over a horizon of two to three years (as opposed to the first year). The stimulus to production of exports and import substitutes tends to offset at least partially the contractionary effect of cuts in the budget deficit. Similarly, in at least Argentina and Brazil the large government deficits place such strain on credit markets that reduction in the deficits facilitates expansion of private sector activity by reducing "crowding out" in the credit market.

With respect to domestic versus external targets, it must be said that with both Brazil and Argentina on the verge of hyperinflation—with Brazil's inflation at nearly 300 percent per year in the third quarter of 1983 and Argentina's escalating to nearly 900 percent immediately before the October election—medium-term sustainability of favorable trade performance has limited credibility unless inflation is reduced. These unacceptable rates of inflation also tend to reinforce the need for budgetary and monetary austerity, even taking into account the presence of excess capacity.

Whatever the specific tactical lessons drawn from the experience of international financial rescue through 1983, broadly the rescue packages met the immediate challenge of risk to the international financial system. By late 1983, the central policy question concerned not so much the feasibility of immediate financial rescue (even the Brazilian problems seemed likely to be manageable after limitation of domestic wage indexing paved the way for reinstatement of the IMF package). Rather, the issue increasingly was whether over the medium term the debt problems could be managed as tractable liquidity problems, or whether instead the prospects for debt servicing were so bleak that public policy should be radically revised to treat the debt problem as one of insolvency, using methods analogous to bankruptcy proceedings. The answer to this question depends not only on the domestic political tolerance for adjustment measures but also on the likely international economic environment over the medium term.

3

Debt Prospects Through 1986

The severity of the problem of international debt may be judged best by a close examination of the likely developments in balance of payments and external debt of the principal debtor countries in the medium term. Only such an analysis, rather than recourse to general arguments or extrapolation of past trends, can provide a concrete evaluation of whether systemic risk from international debt is likely to abate or intensify. The analysis requires projections at the level of individual major countries, because treatment of aggregates tends to mask emerging problems of specific countries. This chapter develops a computer-based projection model that incorporates the influence of varying global economic conditions as well as alternative adjustment efforts by the debtor countries themselves.

Insolvency or Illiquidity?

In debt problems of domestic firms, there exists a classic distinction between a firm that has positive net worth but is illiquid and one that simply has negative net worth, and is therefore insolvent. The most fundamental policy issue today concerning international debt is whether the major debtor countries are illiquid or insolvent: whether their obligations should be viewed as largely sound debt or bad debt. If they are merely illiquid, additional lending is appropriate to tide them over short-term difficulties. If they are insolvent, it may be more appropriate to recognize their debt as bad debt and to attempt to salvage at least some portion of the debt while accepting some loss on face value, analogously to domestic bankruptcy proceedings whereby creditors attempt to secure so many cents on the dollar. The proliferating proposals for write-offs and stretchouts (chapter 7) typically adopt the implicit view that the problem is insolvency, not illiquidity.

To analyze whether the problem of developing-country debt is one of insolvency or illiquidity, it is necessary to examine the prospective path of the balance of payments and debt of the major debtor countries over the medium term. The concept here is the "potential" or "ex ante" balance of payments, given at least minimally acceptable growth rates in the debtor countries. If the prospective external deficits are so large that there is no plausible way they can be financed taking into account the severely shocked state of international credit markets, then the diagnosis must be one of insolvency. However, if instead the projected deficits are of a size that is consistent with reasonable magnitudes of financing, and especially if the prospective deficits relative to exports (and other indicators of debt-servicing difficulty) show an improving trend, then the appropriate diagnosis is one of illiquidity.

The conceptual distinction between illiquidity and insolvency is less clear-cut for a country than for a firm. Unlike firms, countries do not disappear. However, they can reach a point of inability to service debt over an extended time period, thereby becoming much like bankrupt firms from the standpoint of creditors. When applied to countries, the categories of illiquidity and insolvency should be seen as metaphorical rather than absolute. Accordingly, the distinction between the two should be recognized as a broad framework for policy analysis, rather than a uniquely defined classification that can be measured precisely. In particular, the basic approach of the quantitative analysis presented here is to examine whether trends are toward improvement or deterioration. It must remain to some extent ambiguous as to whether projected improvement is sufficient for a clear verdict of illiquidity or projected deterioration so severe as to constitute outright insolvency.

A Projection Model

The approach of this study is to conduct alternative projections of balance of payments and debt for the 19 largest debtor countries for the period 1983–86.[1] These countries account for approximately two-thirds of the total external debt of developing and East European countries, and for three-fourths of the debt of this set of countries owed to private banks.[2] The analysis is conducted at the

---

1. The full exposition of this model appears in appendix B. The model estimates were prepared in April 1983. Accordingly, 1983 figures in the tables of this chapter and appendix B are projected, not actual figures. For final, updated projections using actual 1983 results as the base year, see chapter 8 of this study.

2. The totals here include nonoil developing countries, Eastern Europe, and the following OPEC countries: Ecuador, Indonesia, Nigeria, and Venezuela. The 19 countries examined here, by size of total debt, are: Brazil, Mexico, Argentina, Korea, Venezuela, the Philippines, Indonesia, Israel, Turkey, Yugoslavia, Chile, Egypt, Algeria, Portugal, Peru, Thailand, Romania, Hungary, and Ecuador. Because of inadequate data for analysis, Poland (with external hard currency debt of approximately $24 billion at the end of 1982) is omitted from the analysis. For private banks reporting to the Bank for International Settlements,

level of the individual country, considering that group aggregates tend to disguise the severity of debt difficulties that may arise in individual countries.

The strategy of the model is to calculate the external current account deficit, other balance of payments items, and external debt for each country for each year through 1986 under alternative assumptions about world economic conditions. These alternatives are specified in four areas: the rate of economic growth in industrial countries, the international interest rate (LIBOR), the price of oil, and the real exchange rate of the dollar relative to other major currencies. In addition, the model is driven by assumed internal actions of the developing countries: their growth rates and their exchange rate policy. These influences, domestic and internal, determine the course of individual items in the balance of payments year by year, beginning with actual data for 1982 balance of payments.

The model specification is as follows. For oil-exporting countries, the value of oil exports *equals* the value in the base year (1982) *multiplied by* the ratio of the international price of oil in the year in question to the 1982 price, or $34 per barrel. (Note that this approach makes no allowance for change in volume of oil exports.) Similarly, for oil-importing countries, the value of oil imports *equals* their value in the base year *times* the ratio of price in the year in question to price in the base year.

Nonoil exports depend on the rate of growth in industrial countries and on the real exchange rate adopted by the country. The influence of industrial country growth is twofold: it affects the volume growth of exports as well as their terms of trade. Based on statistical estimates in an earlier study, it is assumed that above a threshold of OECD growth at 1 percent per year (where developing-country export growth is zero) each extra percentage point of OECD growth causes an additional growth of 3 percent in the volume of developing-country exports.[3]

---

the total owed to banks by Latin America, Asia, Africa, Eastern Europe excluding the Soviet Union, and the Middle East (excluding Iran, Iraq, Kuwait, Libya, Qatar, Saudi Arabia, and the United Arab Emirates as capital-surplus OPEC countries) amounted to $379.3 billion in June 1982. The corresponding total for the 19 countries examined here was $291.1 billion. BIS, "The Maturity Distribution of International Bank Lending" (Basle, December 1982). For total debt (including short-term), the 19 countries have aggregate debt of $484.2 billion (end-1982), compared with a total for the broad set of countries described above amounting to $739 billion. Calculated from IMF, *World Economic Outlook*, 1983, p. 200, for nonoil developing countries ($612 billion); *Wall Street Journal*, 8 April 1983, for East European ($53 billion); and the estimates of this study for Algeria, Indonesia, Venezuela, and Ecuador.

3. William R. Cline and C. Fred Bergsten, "Trade Policy in the 1980s: An Overview of the Problem," in *Trade Policy in the 1980s*, William R. Cline, ed. (Washington: Institute for International Economics, 1983). The formulation here is: $g_m = -3 + 3g_{dc}$, where g_m is percentage growth of OECD imports from developing countries, and g_{dc} is OECD growth rate. The constant term -3 is larger than in the original estimate (-4.6) to account for higher trend growth of developing-country exports to the OECD than total OECD import growth.

In addition, the model captures the response of real export prices (terms of trade) to industrial country growth. Commodity prices are sensitive to the business cycle so that, when industrial country growth is high, developing-country exports of commodities tend to experience larger price increases than average world inflation; and when the trough of the cycle arrives, these commodity prices tend to fall by more than the decline, if any, in general world prices. In the model here, "real" nonoil export prices for the country in question increase by a given percentage amount (typically three) for each percentage point change in industrial country growth. (This formulation means that once a stable growth rate plateau is reached there is no further change in terms of trade). The response of terms of trade to OECD growth varies by country and is based on statistical estimates for 1961–81.

The next element in calculating export value is a factor for world inflation. The value of exports increases along with the average rate of world inflation (in national currencies, of major industrial countries) in the year in question. There is also a similar inflator for the effect of dollar depreciation on the dollar price of goods in world trade. Experience in recent years has shown that when the dollar appreciates (or depreciates) relative to other major currencies by a given percentage, the dollar price of exports from industrial countries (a measure of world trade prices) tends to decline (rise) by a similar percentage from the rate of inflation that otherwise would be expected from OECD inflation.[4] This term is important because if the dollar depreciates from its currently high level, the effect will be a rise in the dollar value of developing-country exports (as they parallel world trade prices) and a recuperation of the nominal level of these exports relative to the largely dollar-denominated external debt.

The remaining elements in the calculation of future exports capture the effect

---

Because export growth is negative below a threshold of OECD growth at 1 percent, the formulation here means a marginal elasticity of 3 but an average elasticity of only 2 at an average OECD growth of 3 percent (where developing-country exports would grow at 6 percent). In commenting on the earlier, monograph version of this study, some analysts have recognized that the effective export elasticity used in this study is approximately 2; others have erroneously criticized this model as overly optimistic because of the use of an elasticity of 3. See, respectively, Ronald Leven and David L. Roberts, "Latin America's Prospects for Recovery," *Federal Reserve Bank of New York Quarterly Review*, vol. 8, no. 3 (Autumn 1983), p. 8; and Thomas O. Enders and Richard P. Mattione, "Latin America: The Crisis of Debt and Growth," *Brookings Discussion Papers in International Economics*, no. 9 (1983), p. 68.

4. Thus, in 1979–80 exports of industrial countries rose in dollar price by an average of 14.1 percent; the number of special drawing rights (SDRs) per dollar changed by an average of −1.9 percent (dollar depreciation); and average OECD inflation was 11.4 percent. In 1981–82, industrial country exports had an average dollar price change of −3.2 percent; SDRs per dollar changed by an average of 8.6 percent (dollar appreciation); and OECD inflation averaged 9.0 percent. Using the simple relationship, dollar export inflation *equals* OECD inflation *minus* dollar appreciation, these figures conform relatively well to the expected relationship, especially in 1979–80.

of the country's own real exchange rate on its exports (the amount of domestic currency, for example, pesos, per dollar, deflating both pesos and dollars by home-country and US prices, respectively). Thus, a real depreciation causes the country's exports to rise by one-half percentage point for each percentage point of real depreciation. (This impact is spread over two years.) In sum, nonoil exports are driven by OECD growth, world inflation, dollar strength, and the country's real exchange rate. Total exports *equal* nonoil *plus* oil exports.

The forces influencing nonoil imports are domestic economic growth in the developing country in question, world inflation and dollar devaluation, and the real exchange rate. Nonoil imports grow by a percentage reflecting the long-term growth relationship between real imports and real GDP, assumed to be a one-for-one relationship (1 percent trend growth in GDP causes 1 percent import growth). In addition, there is a shorter run cyclical response of imports to income that is typically greater than the long-run trend response (because of factors such as inventory adjustments and temporary protection). It is assumed that a short-run cyclical increase of GDP by 1 percent increases imports 3 percent.

Like exports, imports rise in dollar value in response to additional world inflation and dollar depreciation. Furthermore, a change in the country's real exchange rate by 1 percent causes 0.6 percent change in the country's imports (spread over two years, as in the case of exports). Thus, the country can adjust by depreciating its real exchange rate to reduce imports. Total imports *equal* oil *plus* nonoil imports.

The parameters chosen to indicate the responsiveness of exports and imports to real exchange rate changes ("trade elasticities") are selected to be consistent with past empirical evidence and to strike a balance between "elasticity pessimism" and "optimism," both of which may be found in the international trade literature. Turning to other elements of the balance of payments, exports and imports of nonfactor services (transportation, freight and insurance, tourism) are calculated, respectively, as constant proportions of nonoil exports and imports, determined from base-year levels. Imports of services are defined to include net profits remittances.

Interest payments are calculated as follows. The fraction of long-term debt that is at fixed interest rates, and the average interest rate paid on fixed interest debt in 1982, are determined. For all remaining external debt—short-and long-term—it is assumed that the interest rate paid *equals* the international rate (LIBOR) *plus* a spread of 1½ percent (or, for Brazil, 2 percent). Interest earnings on nongold reserves are assumed to be earned at a US Treasury bill rate assumed to equal 1½ percentage points below LIBOR. Net interest payments are thus the fixed interest rate *times* the portion of debt at fixed rates, *plus* the variable interest rate *times* the portion of debt at variable rates (including short-term), *minus* the interest earnings on reserves. For these calculations, debt and reserves at the end of the preceding year are applied.

As a final element of the current account, private transfers are estimated on the basis of simple 3 percent real growth as inflated by the path of dollar depreciation. The current account balance is then the sum of the above elements: exports of goods and services *minus* imports of goods and services, *minus* interest payments, *plus* transfers.

Given the current account, the capital account is constructed as follows. The change in reserves is assumed to equal either zero, if imports decline, or one-fifth of the rise in imports if they rise—to maintain an acceptable reserve cushion relative to imports. Direct foreign investment is assumed to grow at a real rate of 3 percent annually, as inflated for dollar depreciation. The total amount of new net lending required to finance the balance of payments then *equals* the current account deficit *plus* the rise in reserves, *minus* the amount of direct foreign investment. Total debt at the end of the year *equals* the previous year's debt *plus* net borrowing, and the composition of debt between short- and long-term is assumed to remain the same as in the base period. Amortization on long-term debt *equals* the country's base period amortization rate (ratio of long-term debt amortization to end-of-year long-term debt in the previous year), applied to long-term debt at the end of the preceding year. Gross borrowing *equals* net borrowing *plus* amortization.

To evaluate trends in debt-servicing burden and creditworthiness, four ratios are calculated: the ratio of debt service to exports of goods and services (DSR); the ratio of net debt to exports of goods and services (NDX); the ratio of the current account balance to exports of goods and services (CAX); and the ratio of reserves to imports of goods and services, excluding interest (RSM). Data used in the model are described in appendix D.

The following values are assumed for the basic model simulations. For developing-country growth, it is assumed that real GDP grows by 2½ percent in 1983, 3½ percent in 1984, and 4½ percent in 1985 and 1986. The 1983 rate reflects zero per capita growth on average, and even the 4½ percent rate for 1985–86 is well below the average of the past decade. Moreover, both Brazil and Mexico are assumed to experience −2 percent in growth in 1983. For country exchange rates, it is assumed that all of the major debtors devalue in real terms by 5 percent in 1983 and by 3 percent in 1984. As exceptions, Mexico is assumed to devalue by 5 percent in 1983 but not thereafter (because the sharp curtailment of imports by restrictions and exchange control in 1982 meant the base year already reflected the potential impact of large devaluation). For Brazil real devaluation is set at 15 percent, for Argentina 10 percent, and for Chile 17 percent, in 1983, given large recent devaluations in these countries.

The basic simulations of the model assume the alternative parameters specified in table 3.1. Given the alternative values in each of the four dimensions (industrial country growth, price of oil, LIBOR, and dollar devaluation), a total of 40 combinations results. The basic set of inflation assumptions is applied to

Table 3.1 Alternative global economic parameters

	1982	1983	1984	1985	1986
Industrial country growth (percentage)					
A	0.0	1.0	1.5	1.5	1.5
B	0.0	1.5	2.0	2.0	2.0
C	0.0	1.5	2.5	2.5	2.5
D*	0.0	1.5	3.0	3.0	3.0
E	0.0	2.0	3.5	3.5	3.5
Oil price (dollars/barrel)					
A*	34.0	29.0	29.0	29.0	34.0
B	34.0	20.0	20.0	25.0	25.0
LIBOR (percentage)					
A*	15	10	9	8	8
B	15	11	13	15	15
Dollar (index)					
A*	1.00	1.05	1.15	1.15	1.15
B	1.00	1.00	1.05	1.05	1.05
Inflation (percentage)	4	5	5	5	5

* Base-case assumption.

all variants. It assumes moderate inflation of 5 percent per year, 1983–86. The base-case assumptions were verified as mutually consistent on the basis of the world economic model of Data Resources, Inc. As shown in this table, the base case assumes a 3 percent rate of OECD growth in 1984–86. Recovery from severe world recession might normally yield growth rates considerably higher. Indeed, in order for 1981–86 growth to equal the average OECD growth rate for 1971–80 (3.2 percent), it would be necessary for 1984–86 growth to average 5.7 percent, considering the low growth of 1981–83. Primarily because of relatively robust recovery in the United States in 1983, where actual growth was 3½ percent, the OECD growth rate achieved in 1983 was 2¼ percent rather than the 1.5 percent assumed in the projections; and the OECD itself has forcast 1984 growth at 3½ percent for its member countries.[5] With respect to the other base-case assumptions, the abnormally high current level of the dollar warrants an assumed depreciation of 15 percent over two years; pressure

5. *OECD Economic Outlook*, December 1983, p. 14.

in US capital markets from large budget deficits indicates that although interest rates may decline they are unlikely to fall very far; and on oil prices, some leaders of OPEC itself are now predicting no change in the official price of $29 per barrel through 1985. The alternative hypotheses provide for even sharper decline in the price of oil (in view of the market's weakness for the past two years), higher interest rates (in light of US budget deficits), and less depreciation of the dollar (considering safe-haven effects and the possibility of higher interest rates).

Results

The results of the basic simulations show three central conclusions. First, under the base case for growth of the world economy (1½ percent in 1983, 3 percent annually in 1984–86), the severity of the debt problem recedes substantially. Second, the problem is responsive to global growth: if growth is 2½ percent or below, the situation remains little improved or deteriorates. Third, there is a strong tendency for the debt situation to improve for the oil-importing countries but to become more severe for the oil-exporting countries.

Detailed results of the simulations are presented in appendix B. For purposes of final analysis, however, the basic results include specific country adjustments, to account for the fact that in the initial estimation of the model with the uniform country assumptions outlined above, a number of countries showed highly favorable trends in current account balances (Brazil, Korea, Turkey, Romania) while others show such large deficits that their financing is implausible (Algeria, Venezuela, Chile). Accordingly, domestic growth rates are increased or devaluations reduced in the first group, while growth rates are reduced and the real exchange rate depreciated further in the second group, to reflect additional scope for growth or need for greater adjustment.[6] The reductions in growth from the standard assumption are sharpest for Venezuela and Algeria; in view of their past exceptional gains from higher oil prices, below-average growth in the 1980s would seem politically feasible.

Table 3.2 and figure 3.1 present the aggregate results of the base case (where industrial country growth is 1½ percent in 1983 and 3 percent thereafter), with groupings into oil-importing and oil-exporting countries and with the adjustments just described for 7 individual countries. For the 19 countries combined,

---

6. The following adjustments are made to the internal policies of these countries, beyond any unique assumptions in the base case. (1) For Korea, Turkey, and Romania, 6 percent growth is assumed for 1983–86, and there is no devaluation. (2) For Brazil, 6 percent growth is assumed for 1984–86. (3) For Venezuela and Algeria, devaluation of 7 percent is assumed in 1983 with another 7 percent in 1984, and growth is set at −2 percent in 1983 and only 2 percent in 1984–86. (4) For Chile, growth is set at zero in 1983, 2 percent in 1984, 3 percent in 1985, and 4 percent in 1986.

Table 3.2   Projections of balance of payments and debt, base case, 1982–86 (million dollars and ratios)

	1982	1983	1984	1985	1986
Oil importers					
Exports	110,536	125,243	158,805	179,936	199,758
Imports	−125,552	−135,360	−159,308	−174,566	−194,848
(Oil)	−34,499	−29,426	−29,426	−29,426	−34,499
Interest	−29,464	−29,256	−30,058	−29,591	−30,187
Current account	−35,451	−30,890	−20,207	−12,564	−12,626
Debt	299,377	327,595	346,638	355,816	365,535
Net debt/exports	1.94	1.88	1.55	1.40	1.28
Debt service/exports	0.39	0.38	0.32	0.28	0.26
Oil exporters					
Exports	76,300	69,783	74,836	78,072	89,813
(Oil)	59,140	50,443	50,443	50,443	59,140
Imports	−64,756	−66,835	−84,013	−92,747	−101,070
Interest	−15,423	−16,520	−16,886	−18,305	−21,284
Current account	−20,989	−19,711	−33,973	−40,933	−40,674
Debt	184,778	201,558	234,702	272,769	310,119
Net debt/exports	1.77	2.04	2.13	2.35	2.36
Debt service/exports	0.34	0.40	0.38	0.40	0.41
Total, 19 debtors					
Exports	186,836	195,026	233,642	258,008	289,571
Imports	−190,308	−202,195	−243,321	−267,314	−295,918
Interest	−44,887	−45,775	−46,944	−47,896	−51,471
Current account	−56,440	−50,602	−54,181	−53,498	−53,300
Debt	484,155	529,153	581,340	628,585	675,654
Net debt/exports	1.87	1.94	1.74	1.70	1.62
Debt service/exports	0.37	0.38	0.34	0.32	0.30

Source: Author's calculations.

the current account deficit declines from $56 billion in 1982 to $53 billion in 1986. In real terms at 1982 prices (adjusting for world inflation—but not dollar depreciation) the decline would be even greater, by 23 percent to $43 billion. The indicators of creditworthiness both show improvement. Thus, the aggregate ratio of net debt (gross debt *minus* reserves) to exports of goods and services falls from 1.87 in 1982 to 1.62 in 1986, and the ratio of debt service (long-term debt amortization and interest on both long- and short-term debt) to exports of goods and services falls from 37 percent in 1982 to 30 percent in 1986. Clearly, the medium-term trend is toward improvement.

There is a sharp difference between oil importers and oil exporters, however. Given the base assumption that the nominal dollar price of oil remains at $29 per barrel in 1983–85 and returns to $34 only by 1986, the dollar value of exports rises by only 18 percent for the oil exporters from 1982 to 1986 (3.3 percent annually), and their current account deficit grows from $21 billion in 1982 to $41 billion in 1986, rising by nearly 60 percent in real terms. The net debt-to-exports ratio for oil exporters rises from 1.77 to 2.36—a high level, comparable to that found today in some of the more indebted Latin American countries; and the debt-service ratio rises from 34 percent to 41 percent.

In contrast, for the oil-importing countries the basic projections show a surprisingly favorable outcome. Their combined current account changes from a deficit $35 billion in 1982 to a deficit of $12.6 billion in 1986. Their net debt-to-exports ratio declines from 1.94 in 1982 to 1.28 in 1986, and their debt-service ratio declines from 39 percent to 26 percent. Figure 3.1 shows the divergent trends for the current account deficits of oil exporters and importers through 1986, as well as the stabilization of their aggregate deficit in nominal terms (and therefore its decline in real terms and relative to exports).

Figure 3.1 Projected current account deficits, 19 major debtor countries (billion dollars)

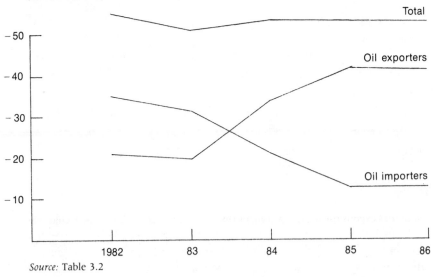

Source: Table 3.2

To a considerable degree this sharply favorable trend for the oil-importing countries is the consequence of substantial increases projected for their exports. For these countries, the dollar value of exports rises by 81 percent from 1982 to 1986, or by an annual average of 16 percent. This rate may appear high, but it is lower than the 20 percent average actually experienced in 1970 to 1980, in dollar terms.[7]

Considering that the dollar depreciates by 15 percent in the base case, and that inflation averages 5 percent, in real terms exports of oil-importing debtor countries rise by 29 percent from 1982 to 1986, or by an annual average of 6.6 percent. This rate is approximately equal to the annual average actually experienced in 1965–80 (6.3 percent),[8] and because the 1982 base is so depressed by global recession, a significantly higher export performance in 1982–86 than the historical average might be expected. In short, sharp increases in the dollar value of exports from the nonoil developing countries should be a prime force in the recovery of their creditworthiness; and the estimated export growth rates are not unduly optimistic when compared with past performance.

Table 3.3 presents the projections for individual countries in the base case. The projections for Brazil are surprisingly favorable; and for 1983–84 they coincide almost exactly with the government's deficit targets, often considered to be on the optimistic side. Thereafter the deficit continues to decline rapidly. Although this profile may be somewhat optimistic, it illustrates the progress that could be made with real devaluation and the possible leeway for relatively brisk growth recovery by 1984 (although anti-inflationary measures could delay recovery until 1985).[9]

The results for Mexico are favorable for 1983—showing a current account deficit somewhat smaller than the $3.4 billion figure originally called for in the IMF-Mexico program. As discussed in chapter 8, the actual outcome for 1983 was even more favorable—a current account surplus of over $5 billion, caused by a precipitous drop in imports.

Results for Argentina resemble those for Brazil, suggesting that for two of the three largest debtors the 1984–86 period holds the potential for considerable

---

7. Calculated from IMF, *International Financial Statistics Yearbook 1981*, p. 67. (The figure here is for the nonoil developing countries.) Note however that the average rate of inflation in OECD countries in the 1970s (9 percent) was also higher than the rate projected through 1986 (5 percent), and by the same differential as for the respective growth rates of dollar export values from nonoil developing countries (20 percent and 16 percent). *OECD Economic Outlook*, 30 December 1981, p. 140.

8. World Bank, *World Development Report 1983* (Washington, 1983), p. 10. The figure includes services exports.

9. Brazil's exports rise by 33.7 percent in 1984. This seemingly high increase is composed of the following (multiplicative) elements: constant, −3 percent; OECD growth effect, 9 percent; terms of trade effect, 6.5 percent; inflation, 5 percent; dollar devaluation, 9.5 percent; current devaluation, 0.8 percent; lagged devaluation, 3.75 percent.

Table 3.3   Current account and debt projections: major debtors, 1982–86[a]
(million dollars and ratios; base case)

		1982	1983	1984	1985	1986
Brazil	CA	−14,000	−7,131	−4,729	−1,041	−647
	D	88,200	93,060	95,843	94,231	92,347
	NDX	3.816	3.463	2.648	2.244	1.965
Mexico	CA	−4,254	−2,321	−5,899	−6,970	−6,005
	D	82,000	82,619	87,573	92,877	96,957
	NDX	2.727	2.817	2.582	2.526	2.316
Argentina	CA	−2,400	−2,476	−825	257	996
	D	38,000	39,752	39,583	38,175	35,898
	NDX	3.720	3.383	2.572	2.146	1.796
Korea	CA	−2,219	−1,720	−334	628	664
	D	35,800	37,826	38,860	38,599	38,524
	NDX	1.060	0.999	0.827	0.725	0.635
Venezuela	CA	−2,200	−4,363	−9,021	−10,681	−10,615
	D	31,285	35,537	45,075	55,781	66,473
	NDX	1.042	1.438	1.910	2.474	2.639
Philippines	CA	−3,500	−4,110	−3,779	−3,581	−3,946
	D	22,400	26,119	29,614	32,796	36,334
	NDX	2.891	3.080	2.724	2.612	2.607

improvement in external debt pressure. For Korea, the adjusted base-case projections indicate a relatively balanced current account even with the assumption of high growth, in part because of a relatively small initial deficit compared to export base. In contrast, even after downward adjustment in growth and substantial depreciation, Venezuela's deficits widen considerably, the consequence of weak oil prices and the virtual absence of nonoil exports.

Among other individual major debtors, Indonesia shows a large deficit emerging, but it begins from a sufficiently strong creditworthiness position that its net debt-to-exports ratio by 1986 is still not implausibly high. The growing debt burden of Israel does raise questions of viability. For its part, Chile shows a relatively large sustained deficit even after country-assumption adjustments, although its exports grow fast enough (because of the sharp response of copper prices to the business cycle) to permit modest improvement in its net debt-to-exports ratio.

		1982	1983	1984	1985	1986
Indonesia	CA	−6,600	−4,568	−7,318	−9,770	−10,160
	D	21,000	25,844	33,611	43,623	53,948
	NDX	0.895	1.159	1.379	1.725	1.900
Israel	CA	−5,100	−6,815	−7,539	−8,593	−9,890
	D	20,400	27,487	35,433	44,322	54,535
	NDX	1.921	2.398	2.504	2.828	3.187
Turkey	CA	−1,100	−1,375	−577	36	−127
	D	19,000	20,329	20,989	20,935	21,163
	NDX	2.406	2.334	1.921	1.677	1.507
Yugoslavia	CA	−464	−551	830	1,350	1,790
	D	18,477	19,359	19,048	18,077	16,698
	NDX	1.136	1.041	0.797	0.653	0.522
Chile	CA	−2,540	−3,911	−3,479	−3,290	−3,865
	D	18,000	21,730	24,872	27,723	31,159
	NDX	3.003	3.096	2.634	2.551	2.594

CA current account; D total debt; NDX net debt (deducting reserves) relative to exports of goods and services.
Source: Same as table 3.2.
a. Eleven largest debtors. For the remaining countries, see appendix table B-2.

Projections in the base case for the other eight countries are shown in appendix table B-2. They show a substantial rise in the deficits and net debt-to-exports ratio of Algeria as well as deterioration for Ecuador; continued deficits and little change in creditworthiness for the Philippines, Egypt, Peru, and Portugal; shift to small deficit or even surplus and improving creditworthiness for Turkey and Thailand; and minimal deficits for Hungary and a surprisingly strong shift to surplus for Romania.

Considering the entire set of individual country projections, discussions with international experts on the specific countries and the emerging patterns of actual performance in 1983 suggest the following directions of bias, if any. The principal cases of overstated deficits and debt appear to be those of Venezuela, Algeria, and perhaps Israel. For the first two, stagnation of oil prices is the principal cause of large projected deficits. However, in the case of Venezuela the model does not capture the sharp cut in imports already in 1983 resulting from rationing of foreign exchange, and accordingly the projections may understate the scope for import compression. The Venezuelan cutback of imports by nearly 60 percent meant that in 1983 there was a current account surplus of $5 billion instead of a deficit of $4.4 billion as projected here.[10] The swing was so sharp that it suggests the possibility for much lower deficits through 1986 than projected in the model here, even after a partial return to more normal practices on import restrictions. For Algeria there may be increased future exports of natural gas, not reflected in the standard methodology. In the case of Israel, the accumulation of debt is overstated because no allowance is made for official grants, which are likely to average $2 billion or more annually, although the estimated current account deficits are not necessarily overstated.[11]

More modest overstatements of future deficits and debt may occur in the projections for Mexico, Indonesia (where devaluation and budgetary restrictions have taken place and future exports of liquified natural gas are likely), the Philippines, Chile, Peru, Ecuador, and Hungary, on the basis of discussions with country experts. For example, for Hungary, the present IMF program called for a modest current account surplus for 1983, rather than a deficit (appendix table B-2), and through the use of import restrictions Hungary appears to have approximated the targeted surplus.

The only notable cases in which the country projections may understate future current account deficits, on the basis of opinions of various country experts, are those of Thailand and Korea (where finance is available for pursuing faster growth) and Brazil (where recent reliance on Third World markets may mean a greater lag in response of exports to OECD recovery than predicted by the model). Thus, the general thrust of these possible individual country biases suggests that in the aggregate the deficits projected here may tend to be overstated rather than understated, meaning that general prospects for improvement in debt-servicing capacity may be even more favorable than indicated here.

The influence of OECD growth on the debt problem is examined in table 3.4, which compares results by ascending growth rates. These results strongly suggest that at least 2½ percent of growth must be achieved in 1984–86 (case C) in order for the debt problem to improve. At this rate, the aggregate ratio of net debt to exports is only slightly improved by 1984–86, and at lower growth it becomes worse in future years than in 1982. In the case of only 1½ percent growth in the period (case A), the current account deficit of the 19

---

10. Naciones Unidas, Comisión Económica para América Latina (CEPAL), *Balance Preliminar de la Economía Latinoamerica durante 1983*, cuadro 7 (Santiago, December 16, 1983).

11. Because the large debtor countries receive little grant assistance as middle-income nations, the model omits such aid. This procedure causes a very modest overstatement of debt accumulation for Mexico, Indonesia, the Philippines, Peru, and Thailand, and negligible overstatement for the other countries. Israel is an extreme exception.

Table 3.4 Sensitivity of projections to industrial country growth, 1986
(million dollars and ratios)

Industrial country growth[a]	Oil importers		Oil exporters		Total	
	Current account	Net debt/ exports	Current account	Net debt/ exports	Current account	Net debt/ exports
A (low)	− 55,730	1.92	− 50,932	2.75	− 106,662	2.20
B	− 39,164	1.64	− 47,008	2.58	− 86,172	1.95
C	− 26,141	1.45	− 43,901	2.47	− 70,042	1.78
D (base case)	− 12,626	1.28	− 40,674	2.36	− 53,300	1.62
E (high)	6,210	1.05	− 36,200	2.20	− 29,990	1.41
Memorandum item						
1982	− 35,451	1.94	− 20,989	1.77	− 56,440	1.87

a. See table 3.1.

countries rises to $107 billion by 1986 and the ratio of net debt to exports from 1.87 in 1982 to 2.20 in 1986. In the event of growth this low, such large potential deficits would be so unlikely to be capable of financing that the diagnosis would have to be one of insolvency rather than illiquidity. Even with the case of 2½ percent growth (case C), the amounts to be financed are sufficiently large that the question of insolvency versus illiquidity would still be open. With growth of 3 percent, however (base case D), there is a sufficiently clear trend of declining relative size of deficits and debt that the situation remains manageable, reflecting illiquidity but not insolvency. At higher growth (3½ percent, case E) the improvement is even sharper.

The strong estimated improvement in developing countries' external accounts in response to higher OECD growth raises the question of whether the projections may be too optimistic because they are based on past relationships that might not apply in the future. Some would argue that terms of trade are unlikely to respond as favorably to OECD growth as in the past, because the inflationary environment of the 1970s has disappeared, and higher real interest rates will work against commodity price recovery. The logic of such concerns is not compelling, however. Higher real interest rates have already reduced commodity inventories, so that the proportionate rise in the amount demanded from this smaller base could be comparable to that found in past experience (or greater if real interest rates subside). Nor is there any reason to believe that the behavior of the general price level (overall inflation) alters the response of relative prices (terms of trade) to OECD growth.

Some analysts contend that because of the greater weight of South-South trade than before, and considering the devastated state of many South-South markets (such as Nigerian demand for Brazilian products), the relationship of developing-country export growth to OECD growth will no longer be as strong as in the past.[12] Considering Brazilian experience as a test case, this concern may be exaggerated. Brazil's exports have already achieved a brisk recovery since the second quarter of 1983 (chapter 2), even before the stimulus they should receive in 1984 as export volumes and commodity prices strengthen in response to OECD recovery and dollar depreciation. More generally, South-South trade should recover as developing-country exports to industrial countries respond to OECD recovery. That is, as country B in the South increases its exports to the OECD it will be able to raise its imports again from country A in the South. Thus, the past relationship should apply, altered at most by a greater time lag.

As noted above, the projections here do show a sharp rise in export value. In the base case, the dollar value of exports from oil-importing countries is projected to rise by 13 percent in 1983 and 27 percent in 1984, averaging 12 percent growth in 1985–86 (table 3.2). The surge in 1984 is attributable to dollar depreciation (and resulting increase in the dollar value of trade). But the projections also show relatively rapid increases in dollar values of imports (18 percent in 1984), whereas experience in Mexico and Brazil in 1983 has shown sharp restraint on imports as a form of adjustment.

In short, there is no reason to depart from past relationships of trade volume and terms of trade to OECD growth in projecting external accounts for developing countries in 1983–86. These relationships hold promise for substantial improvement if 3 percent OECD growth is achieved. And to the extent that the estimates of nominal export growth may be biased upward by factors such as assumed dollar depreciation, any such bias is likely to be offset by similar tendencies in the assumed behavior of imports.

Chapter 8 compares the actual experience in 1983 to the projections of this chapter (which were carried out in April, 1983). The comparison provides an early reading on the validity of the projections through 1986. As discussed in chapter 8, by far the greater tendency in the projections was to overstate external deficits in 1983 rather than to understate them. For the large debtor countries, current account deficits in the aggregate were less than half the size projected. This contrast was especially marked for Mexico and Venezuela. This early evidence suggests that, if there is a bias in the balance of payments projections of this chapter, it is in the direction of caution, not excessive optimism.

The finding that OECD growth must average at least 2½ percent to 3 percent

---

12. Carlos F. Diaz-Alejandro, "Some Aspects of the Brazilian 1982–83 Payments Crisis," *Brookings Papers on Economic Activity,* no. 2, (1983), p. 539.

in 1984–86 for creditworthiness of major debtors to improve may be qualified by possible scope for still further adjustment in developing countries to offset more modest OECD growth. For sensitivity analysis, an alternative calculation assumes that OECD growth is only 2 percent in 1984–86 (case B), but that the debtor countries all carry out an additional 10 percent real devaluation in 1984 beyond the devaluations already assumed in the base case. Because the domestic growth rates are already close to minimum acceptable rates in the base case, it is more appropriate to envision additional adjustment through extra devaluation than through slower growth.

This sensitivity analysis shows that the system is not entirely brittle at a critical OECD growth rate of 2½ percent to 3 percent in 1984–86. Instead, by devaluing an additional 10 percent in 1984 the debtor countries could approximately offset the adverse effects of a decline in OECD growth to only 2 percent in 1984–86. Under these assumptions (with other assumptions as in the base case), the combined current account deficits of the 19 major debtor countries would be 14.4 percent of exports of goods and services by 1986, compared to 14.3 percent in the base case; and the ratio of their net debt to exports of goods and services would stand at 1.66 compared to 1.62 as in the base case. These calculations show that in principle additional domestic adjustment could offset somewhat more adverse OECD growth performance. However, it is appropriate to attach lower probability to the feasibility of this more difficult adjustment than that assumed in the base case. There are already substantial real devaluations assumed in the base case; and adding another 10 percent in 1984 would raise the total assumed devaluations over 1983–84 to 30 percent for Brazil, 25 percent for Argentina, 33 percent for Chile, and 26 percent for Algeria and Venezuela. To achieve real devaluations of these magnitudes would be difficult and would typically cause serious inflationary pressure and, in all likelihood, erosion of real wages.

In short, additional domestic adjustment may provide some leeway for successful global debt management even if OECD growth is somewhat below the 2½ to 3 percent threshold emphasized in this study. But the greater the shortfall in OECD growth, the greater the risk that additional compensating domestic adjustment would be infeasible, economically or (especially) politically.

The alternative results by OECD growth rate once again show the clear distinction between an improving trend for oil importers and a deteriorating trend for oil exporters. The influence of oil price on developing-country debt is examined in table 3.5. Under base-case assumptions about other variables, the scenario of low oil price causes the current account deficits of the oil-exporting countries to surge by $19 billion by 1986, raising their net debt-to-exports ratio from 2.36 in the base case for 1986 to a highly risky level of 3.31. Lower prices for oil cause some improvement for oil importers (about $11 billion in 1986 current account), but not as much improvement as the magnitude of deterio-

Table 3.5   Influence of oil price on balance of payments, 19 major debtor countries, 1982–86ᵃ (million dollars and ratios)

	1982	1983	1984	1985	1986
Expected oil priceᵇ	34	29	29	29	34
Oil importers					
Oil imports	− 34,499	− 29,426	− 29,426	− 29,426	− 34,499
CA	− 35,451	− 30,890	− 20,207	− 12,564	− 12,626
NDX	1.94	1.88	1.55	1.40	1.28
Oil exporters					
Oil exports	59,140	50,443	50,443	50,443	59,140
CA	− 20,989	− 19,711	− 33,973	− 40,933	− 40,674
NDX	1.77	2.04	2.13	2.35	2.36
Total					
CA	− 56,440	− 50,602	− 54,181	− 53,498	− 53,300
NDX	1.87	1.94	1.74	1.70	1.62
Low oil priceᵇ	34	20	20	25	25
Oil importers					
Oil imports	− 34,499	− 20,294	− 20,294	− 25,367	− 25,367
CA	− 35,451	− 21,758	− 10,171	− 6,747	− 1,235
NDX	1.94	1.82	1.46	1.29	1.14
Oil exporters					
Oil exports	59,140	34,788	34,788	43,485	43,485
CA	− 20,989	− 35,366	− 51,041	− 50,644	− 59,906
NDX	1.77	2.70	2.93	2.95	3.31
Total					
CA	− 56,440	− 57,124	− 61,213	− 57,391	− 61,141
NDX	1.87	2.10	1.89	1.79	1.77

CA current account; NDX ratio of net debt to exports of goods and services.
a. Base-case assumptions on industrial country growth, interest rate, and dollar.
b. Dollars per barrel.

ration for the oil exporters. Thus, the net debt-to-exports ratio for oil importers by 1986 improves only from 1.28 to 1.14 as the result of the lowering of oil prices between the two scenarios.

Table 3.6 Oil trade by country, 1982 (million dollars and ratios)

	1982 debt	Oil trade	Exports	Oil/exports
Oil importers				
Brazil	88,200	− 10,759	20,175	−.53
Argentina	38,000	0	7,700	0
Korea	35,800	− 5,962	21,761	−.27
Philippines	22,400	− 2,081	4,908	−.42
Israel	20,400	− 2,000	4,741	−.42
Turkey	19,000	− 3,916	5,807	−.67
Yugoslavia	18,477	− 2,511	10,247	−.25
Chile	18,000	− 730	3,800	−.19
Portugal	12,900	− 1,700	4,044	−.42
Thailand	10,500	− 461	6,860	−.07
Romania	8,200	− 3,359	11,715	−.29
Hungary	7,500	− 1,020	8,778	−.12
Total	299,377	− 34,499	110,536	−.31
Oil exporters				
Mexico	82,000	16,477	21,006	.78
Venezuela	31,285	17,315	18,351	.94
Indonesia	21,000	12,238	19,435	.63
Egypt	18,000	3,000	3,404	.88
Algeria	15,093	8,477	8,504	1.00
Peru	11,100	449	3,200	.14
Ecuador	6,300	1,184	2,400	.49
Total	184,778	59,140	76,300	.78
Total, 19 debtors	484,155	24,641	186,836	n.a.

n.a. Not applicable.
Source: Tables 3.3, B-2; IMF, *International Financial Statistics,* and national sources.

The basic reason for these results becomes clearer in table 3.6, showing the amount of debt and oil trade of the 19 largest debtor countries. As the table shows, oil exports are more vital to the oil exporters (at 78 percent of their exports) than are oil imports to the oil importers (at 31 percent of their imports). To be sure, Turkey, Brazil, and to a lesser extent the Philippines, Israel, and

Portugal have a high weight of oil in imports (varying from two-thirds to two-fifths). But overall the proportionate relief to oil importers from a given decline in the price of oil is considerably smaller than the proportionate increased burden of oil exporters.

This analysis suggests that a major area for possible debt risk to the system is the growing debt of oil exporters, especially if oil prices collapse. The analysis here contradicts the view often expressed, including by some official sources, that sharply lower oil prices would tend to be good for developing countries and their debt problems because they are largely oil importers. That view reflects lack of recognition that the major debtors as a group are oil exporters on balance (table 3.6), and that the effects of oil price changes are much more concentrated for oil exporters than for oil importers. Part of the difficulty with the conventional perception is the tendency to conduct analysis for "nonoil developing countries" while treating OPEC countries separately. Yet the standard classification of "nonoil developing country" includes Mexico, Egypt, and Peru (as well as some other oil exporters); and the OPEC grouping includes countries that are appropriately defined as developing and not in capital surplus: Algeria, Ecuador, Nigeria (omitted here), Indonesia, and Venezuela.

Although a detailed analysis of the impact of lower oil prices is beyond the scope of this study, the question is of sufficient policy importance to warrant carrying the analysis a step further to incorporate indirect effects. A controversial issue preceding the OPEC price reduction in March 1983 was whether a collapse in the price of oil would improve or seriously worsen the problem of international debt.[13] The estimates in table 3.5 indicate that, in terms of direct impact, sharply lower oil prices would tend to aggravate the debt problem, on balance. However, there would be mitigating indirect effects. Lower oil prices would tend to stimulate economic growth in industrial countries and reduce inflation and therefore nominal interest rates. The OECD has estimated that a decline of 10 percent in the price of oil (or $3.30 per barrel, in 1982 when the estimate was prepared) causes an increase in OECD growth by 0.2 percent in each of the two succeeding years.[14] The Congressional Budget Office has calculated that a decline by $8 per barrel in the price of oil would reduce US inflation by an average of 0.75 percentage points, and reduce interest rates by an average of 0.68 percentage points, over four years.[15]

The scenario for low oil prices examined in table 3.5 considers an average reduction of approximately $8 per barrel in 1983–86 from the path in the base

13. See, for example, *Wall Street Journal*, 24 and 26 January 1983.

14. *OECD Economic Outlook* (31 July 1982), p. 139.

15. US Congress, Congressional Budget Office, "Economic and Budgetary Consequences of an Oil Price Decline—A Preliminary Analysis" (Washington, March 1983; processed), p. 15.

case. Applying this reduction to the relationships just cited, the consequence of lower oil prices would be an increase in the OECD growth rate (by 0.48 percent) in 1983 and 1984, lower interest rates, and lower inflation. If the base-case assumptions are adjusted accordingly, it is possible to examine the total impact of lower oil prices after taking account of induced stimulus to OPEC growth and moderation of interest rates and inflation.[16] Incorporation of these feedback effects under lower oil prices causes the 1986 current account deficit of oil-exporting countries to decline by 9.3 percent relative to the estimates with direct effects only (from $59.9 billion, table 3.5, to $54.3 billion) and pushes the oil-importing countries into current account surplus (from −$1.2 billion to +$6.6 billion). After incorporating these beneficial feedback effects, a drop in the price of oil reduces the current account deficit of the 19 countries as a whole in comparison to the base case (from $53.5 billion at expected oil prices to $47.7 billion at lower oil prices after inclusion of feedback effects).

In sum, once indirect effects in OECD growth and interest rates are incorporated, a sharp drop in the price of oil would tend to reduce the current account deficit of the developing countries considered as a group. Nonetheless, such a drop would still tend to aggravate the severity of the debt problem because its adverse effects on oil-exporting countries would be relatively greater than its beneficial effects on oil-importing countries. Thus, in the base case (higher oil prices) by 1986 the ratio of net debt to exports is 1.28 for oil importers and 2.36 for oil exporters (table 3.2). A decline in the oil price alone changes these ratios to 1.14 and 3.31, more seriously aggravating the debt burden of oil exporters than alleviating it for oil importers. Incorporation of beneficial indirect effects from induced OECD growth and lower interest rates only improves these 1986 ratios to 1.03 and 3.15, respectively. Considering that these ratios still show an extremely high burden for oil exporters and only moderate further improvement for oil importers, the conclusion of adverse impact of sharply lower oil prices on the debt burden remains essentially unchanged.

The debt problem is also sensitive to the level of international interest rates. Much of existing debt is at variable interest rates linked to LIBOR. As shown in table 3.7, under a scenario of high interest rates (averaging 13.5 percent in 1983–86 instead of 8.75 percent as in the base case), the total current account deficit of the 19 largest debtors is approximately $29 billion larger by 1986, and the ratio of net debt to exports shows much less improvement (from 1.87 to 1.81) than in the base case (1.87 to 1.62). As the table indicates, with the

---

16. The adjusted scenario applies base-case assumptions except as follows (1983–86, respectively): OECD growth, 1.98 percent, 3.48 percent, 3.0 percent, 3.0 percent; LIBOR: 9.1 percent, 8.3 percent, 7.4 percent, 7.5 percent; inflation: 3.7 percent, 4.2 percent, 4.3 percent, 4.8 percent; oil price: $20, $20, $25, $25.

Table 3.7 Influence of interest rates on balance of payments, 19 major debtor countries, 1982–86[a] (percentage and million dollars)

	1982	1983	1984	1985	1986
Expected LIBOR (percentage)	15	10	9	8	8
Interest	− 44,887	− 45,775	− 46,944	− 47,896	− 51,471
CA	− 56,440	− 50,602	− 54,181	− 53,498	− 53,300
NDX	1.87	1.94	1.74	1.70	1.62
D	484,155	529,153	581,340	628,585	675,654
High LIBOR (percentage)	15	11	13	15	15
Interest	− 44,887	− 48,509	− 59,087	− 72,064	− 80,412
CA	− 56,440	− 53,336	− 66,324	− 77,666	− 82,241
NDX	1.87	1.95	1.79	1.81	1.81
D	484,155	531,887	596,218	667,631	743,641

CA current account; NDX ratio of net debt to exports of goods and services; D total debt.
a. Under base-case assumptions on industrial country growth, oil price, and the dollar.

1982 debt base a 1 percent interest increase (1983) causes $2.73 billion increase in net interest payments by this group of countries.[17]

Comparing tables 3.4 and 3.7, an interest rate 4.75 percentage points higher on average over 1983–86 causes a $29 billion deterioration in current account by 1986, while a 0.75 percentage point decline in OECD growth causes approximately $33 billion deterioration (case B compared with case D in table 3.4). Thus, on average one percentage point change in OECD growth is seven times as powerful as each percentage point change in the interest rate in remedying the debt problem.[18] This relationship varies by country types. For

---

17. For all 19 countries debt is $484.6 billion and reserves are $46.4 billion. Allowing for higher earnings on reserves, the response of interest payments to a 1 percent change in interest, shown in table 3.7, implies that 62 percent of total debt is indexed to LIBOR.

18. Based on the model's equations, 1 percent OECD growth raises exports of goods and services by 3 percent in volume, and by an average of approximately 3 percent in price, for a total of 6 percent export increase. Considering that net debt is 1.87 times exports of goods and services, and that two-thirds of the debt is indexed to LIBOR, a 1 percent reduction in interest rate cuts interest payments by 1.2 percent of exports of goods and services. On the basis of these parameters, without adjustment for differing weights of countries, a 1 percent rise in OECD growth would have an impact equivalent to a 5 percentage point reduction in LIBOR.

countries with especially large debt relative to exports, interest rates have somewhat more effect. Thus, for Brazil and Argentina one percentage point on OECD growth has the equivalent impact of 5.7 and 4.5 percentage points in the interest rate, respectively, somewhat smaller than the average relationship. For oil exporters, whose principal export does not respond to OECD growth (in the model as formulated), the relative growth impact is even smaller; one percentage point in OECD growth is the equivalent of 2.7 percentage points on interest for Mexico and 3.2 percentage points on interest for all oil exporters. Despite these differences, a percentage point increase in growth is much more favorable than a percentage point cut in the interest rate for all of the countries examined (the ratio reaches 10 to 1 for oil importers as a group).

This pattern has major implications for macroeconomic policy in OECD countries. It means that it would be better for the problem of developing-country debt to achieve higher average, sustained growth in industrial countries even at some modest cost in increased interest rates. Moderate expansion would be preferable to hypercautious slower growth even at the price of some rise in interest rates. At the same time, the larger relative impact of one percentage point of growth than of the interest rate also tends to mitigate concern about the mid-1983 upward creep in US interest rates in pursuit of more moderate but sustainable monetary growth (following several months of rapid monetary growth), for the purpose of ensuring more sustainable (and therefore higher average) real growth.

Holding growth rates constant, however, the central thrust of the interest-rate analysis is that higher interest rates would greatly burden the debt situation, pushing it further from illiquidity toward insolvency. A crucial implication of this assessment is that in the choice of macroeconomic tools to achieve recovery, the industrial countries would do far better to choose policy mixes that tend to have lower rather than higher interest rates (looser monetary policy and tighter fiscal policy rather than the reverse), for a given result in terms of real growth.

The final dimension of the model's sensitivity concerns the strength of the dollar. There is widespread sentiment that the dollar has been unduly strong compared with long-run equilibrium, primarily as the result of high US interest rates, "safe-haven" capital inflows, and other factors.[19] In 1983 the US current account deficit increased sharply, and by past experience the consequence will eventually be a decline in the value of the dollar—although higher interest rates caused by fiscal deficits could postpone that decline.

Table 3.8 reports the response of the base-case estimates to a smaller rather than larger dollar depreciation. In the base case the dollar depreciates relative to other major currencies by 5 percent in 1983 and another 10 percent in 1984;

---

19. For example, see John Williamson, *The Exchange Rate System*, POLICY ANALYSES IN INTERNATIONAL ECONOMICS 5 (Washington: Institute for International Economics, September 1983).

Table 3.8 Influence of dollar strength on balance of payments and debt, 19 major debtor countries, 1982–86[a] (million dollars)

	1982	1983	1984	1985	1986
Expected dollar index[b]	1.00	1.05	1.15	1.15	1.15
CA	−56,440	−50,602	−54,181	−53,498	−53,300
NDX	1.87	1.94	1.74	1.70	1.62
D	484,155	529,153	581,340	628,585	675,654
Strong dollar index[b]	1.00	1.00	1.05	1.05	1.05
CA	−56,440	−49,371	−51,123	−50,208	−49,795
NDX	1.87	2.01	1.87	1.81	1.73
D	484,155	527,190	575,091	619,575	663,763

CA current account; NDX ratio of net debt to exports of goods and services; D total debt.
a. Under base-case assumptions about industrial country growth, oil price, and interest rates.
b. Higher index indicates real depreciation.

in the alternative case it does not depreciate until 1984, and then only by 5 percent. A stronger dollar actually causes lower current account deficits in dollar terms and lower dollar debt; but because it reduces the dollar value of exports, it causes a less favorable creditworthiness position as measured by net debt relative to exports. Thus, by 1986, the aggregate ratio of net debt to exports of goods and services declines from 1.87 to 1.62 in the base case, but only to 1.73 in the strong-dollar scenario. Thus, greater precariousness of developing-country debt is another concern that may be added to that of severe US trade imbalances (and resulting macroeconomic sluggishness as well as protectionist pressure) caused by an overly strong dollar. This evaluation reinforces the earlier conclusion that interest rates, at least US interest rates, should be brought down (through reduced fiscal deficits) to facilitate the management of debt, because high US interest rates have contributed importantly to a strong dollar.

Actual experience in 1983 and early 1984 showed a stronger dollar than in the base case projections here. Instead of depreciating by 5 percent in 1983, the dollar appreciated by 5.5 percent, on a trade-weighted basis.[20] The implication of this development for the projections here is that in the near term they are likely to be overoptimistic. In particular, the dollar values of exports (and

---

20. IMF, *International Financial Statistics*, January 1984, p. 453.

imports) are unlikely to be as high for 1984 as projected in the base case, because with less dollar depreciation, dollar prices will not have risen by as much. Thus, ratios of net debt to dollar exports will tend to be less favorable in 1984 than in the base-case projections here.

However, developments in dollar strength in 1983 point primarily to an even sharper subsequent depreciation. Whereas the base case here calls for 5 percent depreciation from the 1982 base in 1983 and another 10 percent depreciation in 1984, after the experience of 1983 it is highly likely that when the dollar's decline does arrive it will be more severe. Accordingly, one might anticipate a decline of the dollar by perhaps 10 percent in 1985, followed by an additional decline of 10 to 15 percent in 1986.

If this outlook proves correct, the main effect of the unexpectedly strong dollar in 1983 will have been to cause a temporary moderation in the improvement of the debt situation but no significant change from its eventual improvement projected for 1986. Considering that for the crucial cases of Argentina, Brazil, and Mexico a return to more normal creditworthiness and borrowing conditions is not predicted to occur before that time in any event (as discussed below), the temporary detour of the dollar to unexpected heights in 1983–84 will have made little difference to the outcome of the debt problem.

Finally, among the 40 possible combinations in the model estimates (5 growth scenarios, 2 oil cases, 2 LIBOR, and 2 dollar cases), it is perhaps worth reporting the best-case and worst-case results. In the best case examined, growth averages 3.1 percent in 1983–86, LIBOR averages 8¾ percent, the oil price holds at $29 per barrel, and the dollar depreciates by 15 percent. Under these assumptions, the aggregate current account deficit falls to $30 billion by 1986, and the net debt-to-exports ratio falls from 1.87 in 1982 to 1.41. In the worst case (average growth of 1.4 percent, average LIBOR of 13.5 percent, oil price falling to $20 in 1983–84, and dollar depreciation of only 5 percent), by 1986 the aggregate current account deficit reaches $138 billion ($75 billion for oil exporters alone) and the net debt-to-exports ratio rises from 1.87 to 2.78 (and reaches 4.11 for oil exporters). Under the worst case the debt clearly cannot be managed and bankruptcy proceedings to deal with insolvency are in order. Clearly, the international debt problem contains major downside risk even though the central analysis here suggests that in the expected, base case it is manageable.

As a summary evaluation of the central projections of this study, it is useful to compare the portion of debt held by those countries whose situations improve by 1986 to that held by those whose situations deteriorate. Judging performance by the trend in the ratio of net debt to exports, this compilation yields the following results. Under base-case conditions (3 percent growth in 1984–86), the following countries register an improvement in their debt situation: Brazil, Mexico, Argentina, Korea, the Philippines, Turkey, Yugoslavia, Chile, Portugal,

Thailand, Romania, and Hungary, with total 1982 debt of $361 billion. The remaining countries show deterioration by 1986: Venezuela, Indonesia, Israel, Egypt, Algeria, Peru, and Ecuador, with a total of $123 billion in 1982 debt. Thus, for 75 percent of outstanding debt the base case indicates improvement over the next four years.

Reviewing those countries that show deterioration, the net debt-to-exports ratios reach the following levels by 1986: Venezuela, 2.6; Indonesia, 1.9; Israel, 3.2; Egypt, 2.4 (almost unchanged from 1982); Algeria, 2.7; Peru, 2.7; and Ecuador, 2.6. Of these countries, Indonesia is the only one with a sufficiently low projected ratio of net debt to exports to suggest scope for avoiding debt difficulties. The others all show projected ratios which, though well below the levels of Brazil and Argentina in their 1982 crises, are not substantially different from the levels of other countries that did experience debt-rescheduling difficulties in 1982 (notably Mexico, 2.7 in 1982, and Ecuador, 2.0). However, as noted above, the projections are almost certainly too pessimistic for Venezuela, and tend to overstate debt for Israel.

Other recent studies have reached the same general conclusions as those found here. Recent studies by Morgan Guaranty bank reach similar conclusions, despite some differences in individual country estimates.[21] The International Monetary Fund has projected that for the nonoil developing countries current account deficits will decline from 19.3 percent of export earnings in 1982 to 14 percent by 1986.[22] While pointing in the same direction as those of the present study, the IMF projections show less improvement than estimated here. Thus, the 19 countries examined here would experience a decline in the ratio of their current account deficit to exports of goods and services from 24.2 percent in 1982 to 14.3 percent in 1986, a sharper reduction than that foreseen by the IMF. On the other hand, the Morgan Guaranty forecasts imply an even stronger reduction in deficits than estimated here (chapter 7, table 7.1). Finally, a more recent projection model for Latin America, prepared by the New York Federal Reserve Bank, comes to conclusions similar to those reached here.[23]

A more precise evaluation of the degree of improvement in the burden of developing-country debt is possible through the application of a statistical model

---

21. *World Financial Markets* (February 1983), pp. 1–11, and (June 1983), pp. 1–15. For 21 major debtor countries, Morgan Guaranty estimates that in 1985 the ratio of debt to exports will be 166 percent; the estimate here for 19 major debtors in 1986 is 162 percent for the ratio of net debt to exports. However, Morgan Guaranty has considerably more pessimistic estimates for Argentina and Brazil (302 percent and 333 percent, respectively, versus 180 percent and 197 percent in this study) and a more optimistic estimate for Chile (187 percent versus 259 percent).

22. IMF, *World Economic Outlook*, 1983, p. 205.

23. Ronald Leven and David L. Roberts, "Latin America's Prospects for Recovery," *Federal Reserve Bank of New York Quarterly Review*, vol. 8, no. 3 (Autumn 1983), pp. 6–13.

Table 3.9   Projections of logit indicator of debt-servicing difficulties,[a] 19 major debtor countries, 1980–86

	1980	1981	1982	1983	1984	1985	1986
Brazil	0.026	0.747	0.810	0.999	0.909	0.402	0.144
Mexico	0.135	0.021	0.435	0.949	0.679	0.241	0.129
Argentina	0.000	0.002	0.311	0.691	0.730	0.121	0.026
Korea	0.027	0.004	0.027	0.004	0.002	0.001	0.001
Venezuela	0.000	0.000	0.000	0.000	0.000	0.000	0.001
Philippines	0.002	0.001	0.050	0.265	0.406	0.133	0.073
Indonesia	0.000	0.000	0.001	0.015	0.010	0.008	0.011
Israel	0.003	0.004	0.033	0.018	0.056	0.042	0.063
Turkey	n.a.	n.a.	0.542	0.189	0.189	0.066	0.031
Yugoslavia	0.009	0.007	n.a.	0.074	0.041	0.011	0.005
Chile	0.000	0.000	0.265	0.650	0.369	0.105	0.051
Egypt	0.049	0.009	0.197	0.604	0.467	0.202	0.148
Algeria	0.003	0.001	n.a.	0.178	0.050	0.109	0.322
Portugal	0.002	0.016	0.164	0.447	0.263	0.073	0.036
Peru	n.a.	0.000	n.a.	0.095	0.220	0.094	0.074
Thailand	0.001	0.001	0.024	0.021	0.011	0.003	0.002
Romania	0.018	0.020	0.054	0.015	0.006	0.002	0.001
Hungary	n.a.	n.a.	n.a.	0.012	0.005	0.002	0.001
Ecuador	0.000	0.000	0.051	0.788	0.669	0.459	0.483

a. Critical level: 0.242.

of debt rescheduling. Using logit statistical analysis, appendix A estimates a model explaining the occurrence of debt reschedulings in the period 1967–82 for approximately 60 countries. The model shows that debt rescheduling is associated with a high debt-service ratio, low ratio of reserves to imports, low rate of amortization, high current account deficit, low domestic growth rates, and a low level of international lending in relative terms. A composite indicator of debt-servicing difficulty using this model yields the projected values shown in table 3.9, with a critical index level of 0.242, such that projected levels in excess of this threshold mean the country's debt-servicing difficulties are likely to be severe and comparable to those of past debt reschedulings.

As shown in table 3.9, the debt-servicing burden is likely to remain above the critical index level associated with reschedulings in Brazil through 1985,

Mexico and Argentina through 1984, Chile through 1984, and Ecuador through 1986. Otherwise the projections show few instances of serious debt-servicing difficulties, especially by 1985–86.

While the projections of the composite indicator of debt-servicing difficulty tend to confirm the analysis here of prospective improvement, they do signal the need for special arrangements for certain major debtor countries over the interim period when borrowing on a fully normal basis of voluntary lending is likely to be infeasible. For this reason, the process of "involuntary lending" analyzed in chapter 4 is of special importance. Banks that already have substantial exposure in Argentina, Brazil, and Mexico are likely to continue providing new lending to them on a quasi-involuntary basis to secure the safety of the previous loans, until there is sufficient improvement that lending can return to a fully voluntary basis.

As a final check on the feasibility of the projections of this study, it is important to consider their implications for domestic savings and consumption potential. A central feature of the base-case projection is that the current account deficit of oil-importing countries declines substantially (from $35.5 billion in 1982 to $12.6 billion in 1986, table 3.2). Yet their interest payments remain high (at approximately $30 billion). Accordingly, the net foreign resource transfer to them declines, implying lower availability of external savings to finance growth. The question arises as to whether this scenario is feasible, given the implication that either domestic growth would have to decline or that domestic savings rates would have to rise as the consequence of lower savings provided from abroad. The feasibility of this projection depends in part on the political sustainability of adjustment programs, and that sustainability depends on the severity of cuts in consumption that might be required by a decline in the resource transfer.

The net resource transfer to a country *equals* its net capital inflow (including direct investment) *plus* its transfers received *minus* its net interest and profits paid abroad. By balance of payments identities, this net resource transfer also *equals* the current account deficit *minus* interests payments abroad *plus* transfers *plus* increases in reserves.[24] From appendix table B-9, for 12 oil-importing countries this calculation shows net resource transfers falling from $11.2 billion in 1982 to $7.0 billion in 1986. Note that the decline in net resource transfer is smaller than would be suspected by examining the declining current account deficit alone; the primary reason is that in 1982 there was a substantial loss of reserves while in 1986 reserves are projected to rise. In other words, a significant

---

24. If RT = resource transfer, K = capital account, I = net interest payments receipts *less* payments, and Tr = private transfers, then $RT = K + I + Tr$. By balance of payments definition, $K = -CA + \Delta R$ where K is capital account balance, CA is current account balance, and ΔR is change in reserves. Therefore $RT = (-CA + \Delta R) + I + Tr = -CA + I + Tr + \Delta R$, as the text states.

portion of the current account deficit in 1982 was financed by reserve loss rather than capital inflow.

In relation to gross national product, the net resource transfer to the 12 oil-importing countries is projected to decline from 1.41 percent of their GNP in 1982 to 0.53 percent in 1986.[25] Assuming standard relations between incremental savings and GNP, a decline of this magnitude (0.88 percent of GNP) would decrease GNP growth by 0.3 percent of GNP annually, unless offset by increased domestic savings. However, these magnitudes are sufficiently modest that adjustment to them should be feasible; as part of concerted efforts to adjust to foreign sector difficulties, it should be possible for countries to raise their domestic savings rates by 0.88 percent of GNP or to accept reduced growth by 0.3 percent annually. Accordingly, the projections of table 3.2 should not prove infeasible from the standpoint of imposing an insurmountable burden of reduced resource transfer. As for the oil-exporting countries, the net resource transfer rises substantially in the base case (from $-\$9.8$ billion in 1982 to $+\$24.6$ billion in 1986), so that the question of feasibility of domestic acceptance of reduction in resource transfer does not arise.

Implications

The estimates of this chapter indicate that a critical threshold for industrial country growth in 1984–86 is 3 percent annually. If this growth rate can be achieved, the debt problems of the developing countries should be manageable and should show considerable improvement. OECD growth as low as 2 percent might conceivably be consistent with satisfactory management of global debt if debtor countries were to take still further, strenuous adjustment measures. The estimates encompass 19 countries accounting for two-thirds of total debt of developing and East European countries. The central result of this analysis is that the debt problem can be managed, and that it is essentially a problem of illiquidity, not insolvency. Thus, the final estimates show the aggregate current account deficit declining from 1982 to 1986 by 23 percent in real terms. The ratio of the current account deficit to exports of goods and services declines from 24 percent in 1982 to 14 percent in 1986, and the ratio of net debt to exports of goods and services declines from 1.87 to 1.62. Countries accounting for three-fourths of the total debt of the 19 countries examined show improving trends toward reduced relative debt burdens.

There could nonetheless be protracted problems in individual countries. Oil

---

25. GNP for 1982 is based on World Bank, *World Development Report 1983*, pp. 148–49, as adjusted for 1981–82 growth and inflation; for 1986 it is based on the growth, inflation, and dollar devaluation assumptions of the model presented in this section.

exporters tend to experience deteriorating debt trends. On a basis of trends in current account and ratio of debt to exports, countries such as Venezuela, Algeria, Israel, and Egypt, could enter into new or more severe debt problems, while Ecuador and Peru could face continuation or intensification of existing debt-rescheduling problems (subject to the qualifications on possible direction of bias in individual country estimates, as noted above).

The analysis of this section is based on the outlook for countries with large external debt. Many smaller countries have experienced debt-servicing difficulties. In the aggregate, nonetheless, the debts of smaller countries with debt-servicing disruptions are small relative to global debt totals. Except for special problems that might arise in individual banks with unusually high exposure in an individual small country, there is little potential systemic threat from even the aggregate debt of the smaller debt countries with debt difficulties.

From another standpoint, however, they could affect the system. Some countries not analyzed in the projections here have gone beyond normal multilateral debt reschedulings and have deferred interest payments, including Poland, Nicaragua, and Costa Rica. It is possible that their actions gradually could build a precedent that could spread to large-debt countries, with systemic consequences. This possibility should remain unlikely, however, as long as the expected improving trends in large-country debt actually materialize. The major debtor countries consistently have shown their desire to demonstrate their superior creditworthiness and unwillingness to be grouped indiscriminately with other developing countries in creditworthiness evaluation, and unless seriously pressed by deteriorating external positions or domestic political unrest, the major debtor countries would be unlikely to imitate the more drastic, nonmarket rescheduling actions and demands of some of the smaller countries.

Some of the implications of this study for industrial country policy are self-evident: the achievement of faster growth and lower interest rates is crucial to resolving debt problems. Other implications are less obvious: a less overvalued dollar would help alleviate the debt problem; and a collapse in oil prices would seriously worsen the debt problem.

The appropriate policy measures to achieve the critical threshold of 3 percent OECD growth should include reduction in out-year budget deficits to permit adequately expansionary monetary policy in the United States, and more expansionary macroeconomic policies of varying mixes in other industrial countries.[26] It is by no means assured that without a shift in macroeconomic policies a growth rate of 3 percent will be achieved. Indeed, simulations with the University of Pennsylvania LINK model show that policy changes of the type just described would raise OECD growth by one-half of a percentage point

---

26. Twenty-six Economists, *Promoting World Recovery: A Statement on Global Economic Strategy* (Washington: Institute for International Economics, December 1982).

annually through 1986, boosting growth successfully above a 3 percent threshold that otherwise might not be met.[27]

The most difficult policy question is whether on balance the results indicate that the system can continue with business as usual, aided by case-by-case rescue packages where needed, or whether the risk of generalized "insolvency" is so great that more sweeping reform is required. The answer to this question must be that, because the chances are good for adequate global recovery, the debt will indeed be manageable, and therefore that it would be counterproductive to adopt, out of unnecessary panic, sweeping debt reform measures that might have adverse effects of their own; but that the underlying risk of insolvency is sufficient that it cannot be ignored and that at least contingency planning should be in progress so that policymakers would be prepared to deal with the less favorable outcomes if they materialized.

---

27. C. Fred Bergsten and Lawrence R. Klein, "Assuring World Recovery: The Need for a Global Strategy," *The Economist,* 23 April 1983.

4

Debt Dynamics: Involuntary Lending, Rescheduling, and Default Incentives

The preceding analysis suggests that, in the medium term under reasonable world economic recovery, the problem of international debt can be managed without serious systemic breakdown. However, the analysis also indicates that for at least some key debtor countries there will be an interim period during which access to capital markets on a voluntary basis will be highly unlikely, requiring instead continued financing on a quasi-involuntary basis by banks that already have a stake in the country. The dynamics of "involuntary lending" are examined in this section to determine whether this process is likely to be viable.

Because reschedulings are currently a major instrument for dealing with debt problems and may remain so during an interim period, the discussion also considers the lessons that have been learned about rescheduling techniques. The discussion closes with an examination of the incentives and disincentives to country default, considering that an option open to borrowers is to declare their unwillingness to continue servicing their debt.

Involuntary Lending

An important element in sovereign lending since August 1982 has been the phenomenon of forced lending. Forced, or involuntary, lending may be defined as the increase in a bank's exposure to a borrowing nation that is in debt-servicing difficulty and which, because of a loss of creditworthiness, would be unable to attract new lending from banks not already exposed in the country. Perhaps the purest example is the case of Mexico. After suspension of its debt-servicing payments in August 1982, Mexico was able to secure an across-the-board 7 percent increase in the exposure of foreign banks as part of a financial package for 1983. The leadership of the International Monetary Fund, indeed, its ultimatum to the banks that in the absence of their increased exposure IMF funds would not be forthcoming, played an instrumental role in this process.

Similar operations of IMF-led bank lending under less than voluntary circumstances have been carried out in Argentina and Brazil, and, to some extent, in Chile, Peru, and Yugoslavia. The total amount of new lending extended in this mode through 1983 was on the order of $15 billion—meaning that for 1983 perhaps half or more of total new net bank lending to developing countries was of the involuntary variety.

Basically, banks are willing to extend new loans in such circumstances because they are in a "lender's trap": they must extend new money in order to shore up the quality of their previous, outstanding loans. Ironically, under current conditions of the international financial market, the lender's trap plays a role that is highly productive in social terms: it helps ensure a source of new lending to countries that are broadly cut off from other sources of private credit because of perceived risk and debt-servicing difficulties.

The basic dynamic of forced lending is that the lender with existing exposure will increase the exposure with new loans as long as the new funds are judged likely to enable a firming-up of the previous exposure rather than to be merely a throwing of good money after bad. Existing lenders will provide new lending if the benefits exceed the costs. The cost of new lending in a risky situation is the risk that it will be lost in default. The benefit of new lending is the value received from shoring up the old loans.

Lenders will provide additional new loans as long as (a) the reduction in the probability of country default thereby achieved, *multiplied by* previously outstanding loans, *exceeds* (b) the terminal probability of default (after the new loans) as *multiplied by* the amount of the new loans. The amount (a) is the expected (probability-weighted) benefit of new lending, while the amount (b) is its expected cost.[1]

The net benefit of new, forced lending, relative to the amount of existing debt, depends therefore on the degree of initial default risk, terminal default risk, and ratio of new loans to previous exposure. Ironically, the incentive for forced lending is greater for a higher initial probability of default, given a specific terminal level of default, because the resulting reduction in default risk is greater. The incentive for forced lending is higher for a lower terminal

---

1. Thus, if the amount of outstanding exposure is D, the initial probability of default is P_0, the amount of the new lending is L, and the probability of default thereafter is P_1 the lender will extend the new loans as long as:

(1) $(P_0 - P_1)D > P_1L$.

That is, new lending will be extended if the reduction in probability of default thereby achieved $(P_0 - P_1)$, *times* outstanding debt (D), *exceeds* the new (lower) probability of default (P_1), *times* the extra capital placed at risk (new lending, L). Expressed as a fraction of outstanding debt, the net benefit from new lending is therefore:

(2) $B = [(P_0 - P_1)D - P_1L]/D = P_0 - P_1[1 + (L/D)]$.

probability of default. And it is higher if the relative increase in exposure required (new lending relative to previous exposure) is smaller.

The case of Mexico perhaps illustrates the process. The probability of default in the absence of new lending was substantial while the probability of default, if the new funds could be mobilized, was low; and the requirement of new lending relative to exposure was moderate (7 percent).

To examine the strength of the incentive for forced lending under alternative conditions, table 4.1 sets forth numerical examples of the net benefits as a fraction of outstanding exposure (equation 2 of note 1), under alternative assumptions about initial default probability, change in default probability achieved, and relative magnitude of new lending compared with previous exposure.

The strong pattern shown in table 4.1 is that under rather extreme conditions it may still be beneficial to extend new loans. Considering first more modest new lending, if banks expand exposure by 7 percent (case A) their expected (probability-weighted) benefit will be between 5 percent and 9 percent of existing exposure if a decline in default probability of only 10 percent is achieved, rising to nearly a 40 percent benefit if a 40 percent reduction in default probability is achieved. Moving to larger new lending, if the improvement in default probability is limited to 10 percent, the conditions for extending new lending become more stringent (lending will occur only at lower original default probabilities) as the size of new lending relative to exposure rises. Thus, banks will not find it beneficial on balance to lend 30 percent beyond existing exposure if the initial default probability is 50 percent and the decline in default productivity thereby achieved is only 10 percent. However, for larger declines in default probability, even large amounts of new lending relative to exposure are beneficial. Thus, there is only one case of net loss at 20 percent reduction in default probability, and for higher achievable reductions, the whole range of new lending and original default risk yields positive expected results from additional lending.

In some of the crucial debtor cases, the absence of new bank lending is likely to trigger extended moratorium, if not once-for-all default. The simple analysis proposed here does not capture moratorium as opposed to default. But an extended moratorium may be conceived of as a partial default—perhaps a 20 percent to 40 percent expected default. The extension of new lending may be thought of as largely eliminating the risk of extended moratorium. Accordingly, it might be proper to think of this reduction of default-equivalent as perhaps 10 to 20 percentage points, the first two columns of the table. As for the amounts of new lending, none of the major rescue operations has involved expansion of bank exposure by as much as 20 percent, and indeed this percentage might be the total expected over a full two- to three-year horizon of involuntary lending. Thus, in practice, the relevant portion of the table is

Table 4.1 Expected net benefit from additional lending under duress (net benefit as a fraction of outstanding exposure)

Case	New lending/ debt	Original default probability	Decline in default probability			
			.1	.2	.3	.4
A	.07	.2	.093	.200	n.a.	n.a.
		.4	.079	.186	.293	.400
		.5	.072	.179	.286	.393
		.6	.065	.172	.279	.386
		.8	.051	.158	.265	.372
B	.15	.2	.085	.200	n.a.	n.a.
		.4	.055	.170	.285	.400
		.5	.040	.155	.270	.385
		.6	.025	.140	.255	.370
		.8	−.005	.110	.225	.340
C	.20	.2	.080	.200	n.a.	n.a.
		.4	.040	.160	.280	.400
		.5	.020	.140	.260	.380
		.6	.000	.120	.240	.360
		.8	−.040	.080	.200	.320
D	.30	.2	.070	.200	n.a.	n.a.
		.4	.010	.140	.270	.400
		.5	−.020	.110	.240	.370
		.6	−.050	.080	.210	.340
		.8	−.110	.020	.150	.280
E	.40	.2	.060	.200	n.a.	n.a.
		.4	−.020	.120	.260	.400
		.5	−.060	.080	.220	.360
		.6	−.100	.040	.180	.320
		.8	−.180	−.040	.100	.240

n.a. Not applicable: default probability cannot be below zero.

probably the first two columns and first three rows. It is striking that in this set of 30 possibilities, in only two cases will the new lending have an expected cost in excess of expected benefits (cases B and C with original probability of default = 0.8 and change in default probability = 0.1).

In sum, a simple model of involuntary lending suggests that over the range of most relevant situations likely to arise—except in cases of relatively clear country insolvency—it will pay the banks to extend additional credit in order to secure the value of existing exposure. The process of involuntary lending should be relatively reliable as a source of continued capital flow during the interim period before the country can return to capital markets on a basis of normal creditworthiness and fully voluntary bank lending.

Free Riders

The above analysis treats all banks that are exposed in a country as a single decision unit. In practice, however, many banks are involved, and especially the smaller ones among them have an incentive to take advantage of the increased quality of their outstanding loans obtained through new lending by the larger banks without incurring additional risk by extending new loans themselves.

This "free-rider problem" is a well-known phenomenon in group action. Principal actors in a group that take action in their own behalf confer an external benefit on other actors that do not themselves carry out similar action. These marginal actors are "free riders" in the sense that they participate in a common benefit without bearing any of its cost. The standard solution to this problem is to find ways of marshalling cooperative action by all beneficiaries. Concentration is helpful: for example, it is easier for a highly concentrated industry dominated by a few large producers to mobilize funds for lobbying efforts than for an industry with many small producers and low concentration.

In the case of bank lending to developing countries, some concentration exists (the 9 largest banks account for 60 percent of US bank loans to developing countries), but there is a sufficient weight of numerous, medium-sized banks in total lending flows that the free-rider problem is not easily resolved by concentration alone. Thus, in the case of Brazil it requires 125 international banks to reach coverage of 90 percent of outstanding loans.

The new role of the International Monetary Fund has been crucial for this reason. In the cases of Argentina, Brazil, and Mexico, the IMF insisted that banks provide additional lending as part of the rescue packages. In a sense, the IMF acted as a unifying vehicle to internalize for the banks as a whole the external benefits that the rescue package would confer on them. It acted as a highly effective coordinator capable of marshalling joint action that the large banks by themselves would have had much more difficulty in securing.

In terms of the model of involuntary lending set forth above, the essential problem is that the small bank perceives that its individual action will have no influence on the probability of default, meaning the condition for new lending is not met. Only a smaller group of large banks will recognize that their individual action (broadly coordinated) will affect default probability. But even for them, there will be a smaller improvement in default probability than would exist under a situation of a monopoly bank or completely coordinated set of banks, because the failure of the smaller banks to cooperate will mean that the new amount lent will be smaller.

The central problem then is to ensure uniform collective action, including by regional and smaller banks. Neither is this goal somehow unfair to the smaller banks. On the contrary, if it is not achieved, the nonparticipating smaller banks benefit at the expense of the larger banks (and the IMF) because they enjoy the benefit of increased quality of their outstanding exposure without bearing their fair share of the burden of increased exposure.

By mid-1983 the experience of involuntary lending had shown mixed results on the feasibility of obtaining coordinated action to overcome the free-rider problem. For Mexico, virtually all 530 foreign banks with exposure had increased their exposure by 7 percent.[2] But for Brazil, even the 125 participating banks had failed to fulfill the package fully—especially in the commitment to maintain interbank deposits in foreign branches of Brazilian banks. In this part of the package erosion was evident in the US regional banks and some European banks. However, by early 1984 the experience of Brazil gave cause for optimism about the process of involuntary lending. Brazil achieved virtually complete bank participation in its revised program of $6.5 billion in new bank lending.[3]

It is unclear how willing the smaller banks will be to repeat involuntary lending in the future. Smaller banks that went along with increased exposure for one or two years may become increasingly reluctant to do so if involuntary lending has to persist for a third, fourth, or even fifth year.

There are three basic ways to enforce joint action and overcome the free-rider problem. The first is through official pressure. The IMF has played an important role. In addition, however, there is the possibility of pressure from central banks. This channel appears to have been exercised the most in the United Kingdom, where there is a strong tradition of moral suasion by the Bank of England in times of crisis. In the United States, perceptions appear to differ sharply on the extent of pressure by the Federal Reserve—with at least some of the regional banks having the impression that the Fed could be uncooperative in future individual bank difficulties if these banks do not cooperate on the debt problem.[4] Nonetheless, there are limits to the use of the

---

2. *Wall Street Journal*, 25 February 1983.

3. On January 27, 1984, Brazil signed a refinancing package that included $6.5 billion in new loans from more than seven hundred banks. *Washington Post*, 28 January 1984, p. D-8.

4. On the basis of comments by participants in "Solvency, Stability and the External Debt of Developing Countries," conference sponsored by the University of Chicago and the Johnson Foundation, May 27, 1983, Racine, Wisconsin.

official channel to pressure new bank lending. The more compulsory such pressure becomes, the more claim banks will have to official compensation if losses do occur.

The second channel for enforcement of collective bank behavior is the network of influence the large banks have on smaller banks. The large banks can impose retaliatory measures such as exclusion from future syndicated loans or termination of correspondent services.

An important third channel, however, may have to be used as well: the particular debt-rescheduling technique of the country itself. As a mild measure, the debtor country might announce that banks refusing to participate in a general program of credit extension would no longer be welcome to participate in future lending to the country once more normal times return. Of course, the country can also exert pressure on banks that have branches within its borders, but such banks in most cases will already be the most avid supporters of a bank-IMF package of new lending (because their stakes in the country's future are the highest).

A more dramatic, but more risky approach would be for the debtor country to announce that it will provide less favorable treatment for banks that do not participate in an extension of exposure that is agreed upon among the country, the IMF, and the major creditor banks. For example, the country could announce that any bank refusing to participate in credit extension under such an officially blessed program would have its loans subordinated to those of the banks that did participate, meaning that in the event of future breakdown in the process the nonparticipating banks would be the last to redeem their exposure. Announcement of loan subordination could involve risk of general erosion of confidence, however. It would probably be a measure for which the country would want to secure official (IMF, central bank) and large-bank support before implementation, in order that adverse psychological effects (even on large banks) not overwhelm the incentive effects for small-bank cooperation.

It should be noted that to some extent the approach of loan subordination is already being applied informally as there is at least some indication that certain countries in arrears are allowing them to accumulate primarily on loans held by banks not carrying out their part of a generally agreed bank strategy of new lending.[5] It is also important to recognize that a more formal process of loan subordination probably could be challenged legally because of cross-default clauses in syndicated loan agreements, whereby all participants agree to call the borrower in default if one participant does so. On the other hand, because the legal basis for such clauses rests on the concept of mutual cooperation to secure repayment, it could be argued by the large banks that small banks calling for default did not warrant fulfillment of cross-default commitments because such smaller banks had violated the spirit of mutual action on behalf

---

5. *Washington Post,* 29 April 1983.

of repayment by their prior unwillingness to bear their fair share of the coordinated new lending.

By coordinated pressure through these three channels of action—official (IMF and central bank), large bank, and debtor country—it may be possible largely to overcome the free-rider problem and to achieve for private banks as a group the basic results indicated by the simple monopoly-bank model of involuntary lending. For nearly two years after the debt crisis erupted in mid-1982, the mechanism of involuntary lending appeared to function relatively well. In the later months of this period a growing reason for effectiveness of the mechanism seemed to be the increasing realization on the part of the banks that the alternative would be significantly worse: the capitalization of interest due, rather than the arrangement of new loans (as discussed in chapter 7).

Policy Implications of Involuntary Lending

The analysis of involuntary lending has major implications for policy on developing-country debt. As table 4.1 suggests, there is a wide range over which banks can be expected to keep lending new money to shore up the security of the old money. This dynamic is crucial because continued bank lending will be essential if the programs for the major debtors are to hold together; the amounts required are too large for the official community to carry without participation by the banks.

Another essential conclusion is that it is important to ensure the dynamics of this lending process by marshalling support from smaller banks that otherwise might try to enjoy a free ride by remaining out of any extension of new credit (while benefiting from the maintenance of the security of their own past loans afforded by the new contributions of the major banks and public sources). Pressure should be brought at three levels to ensure this cooperation: official, bank to bank, and debtor country. In particular, debtor countries might do well to announce that the outstanding debt of uncooperative banks will be subordinated, although this step should only be taken after close consultation with larger banks and public officials in industrial countries.

Two other important interpretations of involuntary lending require explicit clarification. This mechanism is not essentially involuntary in the sense that the government, central banks, or countries force banks to make loans that are against their own interest. Ultimately the free rider problem would probably be overcome even without these pressures because the new lending to avoid default is in the interests of the banks themselves as a group, especially if the alternative becomes more clearly such measures as interest capitalization (chapter 7), especially unilateral. Advocates of the free market need not fear that the banking system is being subverted by official fiat, because in the last analysis the mechanism of additional lending by those banks already exposed is in their own interest. In addition, this process of additional lending does not mean that the banks are "digging themselves in deeper," and that official encouragement of new lending is placing the banking system in even greater jeopardy by raising the stakes. On the contrary, as long as the expansion of exposure is at a rate less than the interest rate being earned, the banks are reducing their real economic exposure in terms of its present discounted value.[6] Thus, in the process of involuntary lending in 1982–83, under the tutelage of the IMF and central banks, the private banks have been digging themselves out in real economic terms, not digging themselves in deeper, because their exposure has grown at a rate well below the interest rate.

Finally, a perhaps surprising implication of this analysis is that it would be a mistake to take banks "off the hook" by having an international agency buy up their claims on developing countries. By so doing, public policy would choke off the most important source of new lending for countries in difficulty: involuntary bank lending. With their claims shifted from the country to an international agency, the banks would no longer have an incentive to provide new loans to the country. The benefit of the new loans constituted by reduced probability of default *times* outstanding debt would no longer enter their calculations. This adverse effect on new bank lending is a central reason why several newly proposed schemes for international debt relief would not appear to be desirable (chapter 7).

The broad conclusion of this analysis of involuntary lending is relatively sanguine: with proper policy measures for enforcement of cooperation among smaller banks (to avoid the free-rider problem), it should be possible to keep enough new bank lending moving to tide over illiquid major borrowers until recovery of the international economy permits them to return to capital markets on a basis of voluntary lending.

Rescheduling Techniques

Debt rescheduling is at once an admission of debt-servicing breakdown and a remedial measure for reestablishing more normal financial conditions. It is

---

6. Suppose a bank has $100 million outstanding in a loan to a country. With market interest rates at 10 percent, the present discounted value of the amount outstanding will decline unless the bank lends an additional $10 million for the next year. Reported exposure must rise to $110 million in that year, to $120 million the next, and so forth, to keep the economically meaningful (present discounted) value of the loan outstanding constant. If instead the bank lends only $5 million new annually, the meaningful value of its exposure declines over time (even though in nominal terms it rises to $105 million the next year and $110 million the following year).

important that the design of rescheduling arrangements be as expert as possible, to avoid subsequent financial disruptions from technical miscalculations.

The rescheduling of official debt has traditionally taken place in "Paris Club" meetings of donor countries. For the major debtors whose debt bulks large in international bank exposure, however, reschedulings of debt owed to private banks are more important. In the past ad hoc meetings of banks (usually in London) have drawn up these reschedulings. In the major new episodes for Mexico, Brazil, and Argentina, rescheduling of bank debt has been orchestrated by the IMF, as described in chapter 2. The discussion here focuses on the technical structure of these reschedulings.

Costs of Rescheduling

One issue in rescheduling is the interest rate on rescheduled debt, and the rescheduling fee. Extra costs to the borrower because of rescheduling have included not only a direct increase in the interest rate spread (for example, from one percentage point to two percentage points or more), and a fee for rescheduling the debt; they have also included a shift in the base rate from LIBOR to the US prime rate, which averages approximately three-fourths of a percentage point higher.[7] There has been considerable outcry (and even self-doubts among bankers) against the typically high interest rates on rescheduled debt and rescheduling fees.[8] Some argue that these charges reduce the chances that the country can regain its economic health. And the US bank regulators, in response to congressional pressure, proposed (and Congress subsequently enacted) that rescheduling fees (and lending fees generally) be taken as income over the life of the loan rather than reported as income fully received in the year of rescheduling—thereby avoiding overstatement of the profitability of rescheduled loans.[9]

Increased costs from higher interest rates and fees have been greatest for Mexico, because its previous spreads were low and because it has formally rescheduled a high proportion of its debt. Mexico rescheduled $19.5 billion in public debt at an interest rate spread of 1¾ percentage points above the US prime rate, or the equivalent of approximately 2½ percent above LIBOR. The average spread on its Eurocurrency borrowings in 1978–80 had been 0.91

---

7. Pedro-Pablo Kuczynski, "Latin American Debt: Act Two," *Foreign Affairs*, vol. 62, no. 1 (Fall 1983), p. 24.

8. Caroline Atkinson and James L. Rowe, Jr., "Debt Terms: Medicine Worse than Disease?" *Washington Post*, 19 June 1983.

9. Federal Reserve Board of Governors, FDIC, and Comptroller of the Currency, "Joint Memorandum: Program for Improved Supervision and Regulation of International Lending" (Washington, April 7, 1983; processed). Note, however, that amortization of rescheduling fees was largely a symbolic issue because the amounts involved are small.

percent above LIBOR, giving an increased cost of borrowing equal to 1.6 percentage points. If this increase is applied to the amount of debt rescheduled (and if private rescheduling of $15 billion is included), the estimated increment in annual interest payments amounts to $560 million. The costs of rescheduling also included a fee of 1 percent, or $345 million (applying the fee to both the public and private reschedulings), or $43 million annually if allocated over the eight-year maturity of the rescheduled loans. Moreover, the new bank lending to Mexico for 1983 was at 2⅛ percent above US prime—equivalent to 2⅞ percent above LIBOR, or approximately 2 percentage points above the average for 1978–80. The extra cost for the new lending was $100 million annually. Total extra costs associated with the debt rescheduling amounted to approximately $700 million yearly. This amount represents 1.75 percent on principal, and approximately 5 percent of the level of imports in 1982.

An important question for the rescheduling process is whether lower additional interest spreads and fees would be appropriate. There is a case for at least some increase in costs on rescheduled loans above their original terms. A higher interest rate partly compensates for increased risk to the lender. A higher rate also serves the positive function of discouraging unnecessary rescheduling attempts—there should be some penalty for rescheduling, although how much is an open question.

More importantly, higher interest rates contribute to the incentive of lenders to continue lending. For larger lenders, the dynamics of involuntary lending discussed above mean that they are locked in and the interest rate is to some extent arbitrary, as long as it is no lower than the rate on the original loan. But, as noted earlier, incentives are clearly needed to induce the smaller lenders to increase their exposure, and for them a higher interest rate on rescheduled loans can be an important factor in going along with an entire debt-rescheduling program that includes new loans.

Moreover, the profit impact of an increased spread is much greater than the cost impact for the borrower. In the Mexican example, an increased spread from 0.9 percentage points to 2½ percentage points above LIBOR nearly triples the profit potential to the lender, as represented by the spread above LIBOR, considering that the lender is highly leveraged and lending on the basis of borrowed funds.

In contrast, for the borrower such an increase raises interest costs only by 15 percent if LIBOR is 10 percentage points. (That is, 1.6/10.9 = .15.) At the same time, it would be awkward, if not impossible, to establish two classes of interest rates: a lower level for large banks locked into new lending and a higher level for small banks that require convincing.

The rescheduling spread has some of the technical characteristics of a price determined in a "bilateral monopoly" (as in wage negotiations between a large firm and a large labor union), whereby there is a range of indeterminacy in the price rather than a single market-clearing level. In such circumstances there is much to be said for a rescheduling spread that both sides consider "fair." To the banks, it would appear unfair for interest rates to be below their original level, or even to remain unchanged (considering that there should be some penalty for rescheduling if the moral hazard of encouraging rescheduling is to be avoided). To the borrowing country, it seems unfair for the interest rate to be increased by a large amount just at the time when it is under the most severe pressure on its balance of payments.

In view of these various considerations, and in light of pressure even within the US Congress for lower interest rates on rescheduled loans,[10] a reasonable reform might be to lower rescheduling costs to perhaps one-half percentage point above the original terms of the rescheduled loans. This spread would still mean that the potential profit would rise by 50 percent for banks borrowing at LIBOR and lending (originally) at LIBOR plus 1 percent (for example), providing some compensation for increased risk. For new lending, the spread would be comparable or perhaps moderately higher to provide additional incentive (considering that new lending is more optional for the bank then rescheduling old loans on which the country is making no payments of principal), especially for smaller bank participation.

By the end of 1983 the banks were tending toward lower interest rate spreads for rescheduling countries. For Brazil, they lowered the spread from 2¼ percent above prime to 2⅛ percent on the $6.5 billion jumbo loan. For Mexico the reduction was much larger, from 2⅛ percent above prime in 1983 to 1⅛ percent for the new lending of $3.8 billion in 1984. Although still approximately 1 percentage point above the spreads paid by Mexico in the late 1970s, this rate was much closer to the modest increment of one-half percent suggested here. The banks cited Mexico's strong external adjustment as justification for the lower spread. However, the banks reportedly resisted pressure from the Federal Reserve to reduce the spreads that had been established for the large block of debt already rescheduled in 1983.[11]

Although a return to lower spreads can help, its impact on the burden of debt servicing should not be overstated. In the Mexican case, if the additional spreads were cut back from the 1.6 percent of 1983 to only one-half percent as suggested here, annual interest costs would decline approximately 1 percent of the principal involved. This reduction would amount to approximately $400

---

10. The House-approved version (but not the final form) of the bill to increase IMF quotas, prohibited "any fee exceeding the administrative cost of the restructuring." That restriction would have gone too far, however, if the problem of mobilizing lending from the smaller banks is taken into account. US Congress, House Committee on Banking, Finance, and Urban Affairs, *International Recovery and Financial Stability Act*, H.R. 2957, sec. 319 (a)(1), 98 Cong., 1 sess., 1983.

11. *Washington Post*, 27 December 1983; *New York Times*, 31 December 1983; *Washington Post*, 30 December 1983; *Wall Street Journal*, 4 January 1984; and *Wall Street Journal*, 20 December 1983.

million, or 3 percent of 1982 imports. This saving would provide only limited benefits in increased domestic growth. The maximum benefit might be perhaps 1 percent additional growth yearly for three years (if GPD is assumed proportional to imports). Considering that there was a sizeable cushion of surplus on the current account in 1983, and that the main constraint to growth by early 1984 was the need to reduce inflation, it is likely that the actual growth benefits from cutting interest rate spreads would be even smaller. Over the life of the loans, the savings in interest payments would be $3 billion, or one-tenth of the face value of the rescheduled principal. As noted earlier, most debtor countries would experience even smaller benefits from reducing spreads back to a modest premium above their original levels, because for most the increase in spread was smaller than in the case of Mexico.

In sum, reducing the interest charges on rescheduled loans would help the economies of debtor nations, but only to a limited degree. Nonetheless, it could make an important contribution to the political viability of the process of international debt management, by conveying a sense of equity in the process to hard-pressed publics in debtor countries. Finally, it should be added that monetary authorities in industrial countries could provide far more interest relief to debtor countries by reducing interest rates to more normal historical real levels (for example, 3 percent above inflation) than the banks could provide by reducing spreads on rescheduled loans.

Coverage and Maturities

A second major aspect of rescheduling concerns coverage. Mexico and Brazil represent sharply different alternatives. Mexico rescheduled all of its public debt owed to banks due from August 1982 through December 1984, including short-term debt, for a total of approximately $20 billion. In contrast, Brazil rescheduled only $4 billion in long-term bank debt coming due in 1983.[12]

Brazil consciously sought to minimize formal rescheduling—for fear of its impact on later creditworthiness—and relied heavily on moral suasion to avoid a decline in outstanding short-term credit. Brazilian authorities also considered their underlying situation to be stronger than Mexico's and apparently felt they could return to the capital market on a voluntary basis later in 1983. The strategy for Brazil, developed with the cooperation of the IMF and private banks, included a four-part program for bank loans: Project 1 involved $4.4 billion in new loans for 1983; Project 2, rescheduling of $4 billion in long-term debt coming due; under Project 3, banks were to keep open short-term trade-

---

12. House of Commons, Fourth Report from the Treasury and Civil Service Committee, sess. 1982–83, *International Monetary Arrangements: International Lending by Banks*, vol. 1 (March 15,1983), and *Wall Street Journal,* 10 February 1983.

credit lines of approximately $9 billion; and in Project 4, banks were to restore short-term interbank deposits in foreign branches of Brazilian banks to $7.5 billion (82 percent of their June 30, 1982, level). But Project 4 failed seriously, because many European banks in particular failed to meet this commitment, and this component of the package remained approximately $1.5 billion short, contributing to growing arrears of nearly $1 billion by mid-1983. Part of the problem was that some European central banks (especially the Swiss) opposed the use of overnight interbank funds for long-term lending. Another element of the problem was that the interest spreads on interbank deposits are much lower than on new lending, giving little incentive to maintain these deposits.[13]

The lesson of the Brazilian and Mexican packages would seem to be that, in the absence of very strong reasons to believe that moral suasion can keep up short-term credit lines, it is better to have a more complete rescheduling (and longer—Mexico's is for two years' principal) than to rely on voluntary maintenance of credit lines combined with a smaller amount of rescheduling. Part of the problem is that Brazil's underlying economic situation did show substantial erosion in 1982 because of low exports, and only under strong fundamentals would a voluntary, market-oriented response, combined with only a limited amount of rescheduling, have much prospect of success.[14] Another lesson is that the interbank market is the least reliable of all as a source of credit-line maintenance. However, as noted in chapter 2, because the complete rescheduling of short-term debt creates a subsequent bulge in amortization, it may be useful to identify a core level of short-term credit likely to be rolled over (primarily, trade credit) and to leave this short-term debt intact while rescheduling other, less reliable short-term debt.

Whether to reschedule a single year's debt coming due or to reschedule several years' debt is another technical issue. The major rescheduling cases have involved restructuring of the principal due, to be repaid over seven or eight years with two to four years' grace period. These reschedulings have been either for one year's principal (Brazil, Argentina, Ecuador, Peru) or two years' principal (Mexico, Chile).[15] The question arises as to whether it would be advisable to restructure debt for three or even more years. The classic issue in rescheduling duration is the choice between keeping lender leverage by keeping the country on a "short leash," on the one hand, and providing a longer term planning horizon for the country, on the other. Once again, the contrast between

---

13. *Wall Street Journal*, 24 February 1983; *Financial Times*, 31 May 1983.

14. In this regard the contrast between Yugoslavia and Brazil is informative. The Yugoslav package involves debt rollover of both short- and long-term debt, rather than formal rescheduling. However, with a net debt to exports ratio of only 114 percent in 1982 compared with Brazil's 382 percent (chapter 3), Yugoslavia was in a stronger fundamental position.

15. House of Commons, *International Monetary Arrangements*, pp. *xxviii-ix*.

the initial experience of Mexico and Brazil suggests that at least two-year reschedulings establish better conditions for orderly adjustment than single-year reschedulings. Brazil (and Argentina) have found it necessary to reschedule principal due in 1984. And although Brazil successfully negotiated this second rescheduling (for $5 billion coming due to banks), there would have been less uncertainty if the initial rescheduling agreement had been for two years. In short, experience in the major rescue efforts suggests that rescheduling of two or even three years' principal is more desirable than a one-year rescheduling. However, much longer reschedulings would not only unduly dilute creditor influence but also perhaps unnecessarily reschedule amounts that could be paid on a timely basis after adjustment and improved international circumstances, needlessly eroding the country's credit rating.

Some proposals for debt reform have called for stretchouts of maturities to the range of 20–25 years, or even to infinity through the conversion of loans to consols that pay interest but never repay principal. However, by itself the "stretchout" issue is largely a red herring. Because principal is being rescheduled, and because it will tend to be rolled over once voluntary lending is reestablished, repayment of principal is not really at issue for the next few years. And as analyzed in chapter 5, it appears that even the maturity bunchings, as repayments on rescheduled loans come due in the late 1980s, seem unlikely to cause serious difficulties. Long-term stretchouts per se cannot provide meaningful debt relief, because it is the *interest*, not the amortization of principal, that determines the true debt burden. With the likely rollover (under whatever degree of creditor volition) of outstanding principal over the next several years, the real issues of debt burden concern the interest rates and the availability of net new financing to help pay the interest, not the choice between 8 years, 25 years, or infinity, as the maturity for rescheduled loans.[16]

Treatment of private debt is another difficult point in rescheduling. Private debt has especially caused problems. In Mexico even interest on private debt was not paid for several months. In Mexico, Venezuela, and to some exent Argentina, the model emerging for private debt has been that the debtor country's government would promise a desirable exchange rate for its repayment only if the creditors would reschedule, facing creditors with the choice of providing rescheduling or seeing their private debtors go bankrupt.[17] This strategy appears to have succeeded but at the cost of considerable frustration on the part of the creditor banks. In the case of Chile, conflict over private debt was substantial. Private debt is high, accounting for approximately 60 percent

---

16. Although at the margin the maturity can usefully be modified to take account of the existing profile of amortization. Thus, in the new bank lending of $3.8 billion to Mexico for 1984, the maturity was raised to 10 years, to help phase in repayments in existing loans after the period of maturity bunching in the period 1986–87.

17. See, for example, *Financial Times*, 8 April 1983.

of Chilean external debt.[18] Credit cutoffs occurred after the government liquidated several large domestic banks and refused to guarantee their external debts. In subsequent negotiations foreign banks insisted that the Chilean government assume responsibility for all private debt; eventually the government agreed to do so only for the debts of Chilean banks, not other private firms.[19]

Although there is no simple solution to treatment of private debt, in the rescheduling process private debt should be more systematically integrated into the total package. At the same time, foreign creditors can hardly expect governments to grant ex post guarantees of loans extended on the basis of private risk; nor can governments completely wash their hands of these loans, considering that there was at least an implicit contract that foreign exchange would be available to permit their servicing. This implicit responsibility is especially relevant where the governments' own policies encourage rapid debt build-up, even if its form was private. In short, private debt should be included as a significant part of the debt renegotiation process in a more systematic manner than in the major recent cases.

To recapitulate, there are technical questions about the best type of rescheduling once debt rescheduling becomes necessary. The evidence of 1982–83 suggests that interest rates on rescheduled debt may have to be increased above original levels to facilitate the process of involuntary lending, although because of political reaction in borrowing countries it may be prudent to limit such increases to modest amounts; that, unless the borrower is truly in a strong fundamental position, formal rescheduling is preferable to disguised, quasi-voluntary rescheduling—especially through the device of maintenance of interbank credit lines; that rescheduling of two years is probably preferable to one, although rescheduling of much longer periods might involve excessive loss of lender leverage; and that private debt should be more formally integrated into the rescheduling process.

Default Incentives

Along the continuum of debt disruptions, the most severe are outright repudiation and extended, unilateral, complete moratorium (indefinite suspension of payment of both principal and interest). These two forms of debt disruption may appropriately be called "default," a term often used rather inappropriately to include even temporary payments disruptions and reschedulings. Because of the growing apprehension that some debtor nations might find adjustment

---

18. *Ercilla* (Chile), 2 February 1983, p. 14.

19. *Washington Post*, 6 May 1983, and discussions with Chilean experts.

programs too onerous to fulfill and might, instead, declare an extended moratorium, it is important to consider the possible incentives and disincentives to default.

In a classic article, Martin Bronfenbrenner argued that a nation would have an incentive to expropriate foreign investment once the sum total of expected future inflows of new investment (appropriately discounted by an interest rate) became smaller than the value of existing investment.[20] More recent theoretical work has emphasized the utility of foreign borrowing to smooth out fluctuations in consumption (for example, because of commodity price fluctuations). This benefit from borrowing enters in the trade-off involved between the attraction of defaulting (to discard the debt burden) on one hand and the cost of thereby being cut off from foreign capital markets into the indefinite future, on the other.[21] In practice the decision about default goes further: it involves considerable risk that even normal trade patterns would be disrupted, beyond denial of access to the capital markets.

Considering the Bronfenbrenner dynamic, there is some cause for concern about growing incentive to default. Several important debtor countries have passed from an early stage in the debt cycle, where interest payments are small relative to new borrowing, to a late phase, where interest payments are large relative to new borrowing or even exceed it. Indeed, this transition may have been largely completed in the aggregate. As shown in table 4.2 and figure 4.1, for the nonoil developing countries the ratio of interest payments to net new borrowing (from all sources) rose from an average of 30 percent in 1975–78 to 55 percent in 1979–81 and 103 percent in 1982, when interest payments actually exceeded new borrowing. Similar trends are shown for four major Latin American debtor countries.[22] The implication of this trend is that the incentive for adherence to the normal rules of international lending has been decreasing because increasingly any cutoff of new lending would be offset by termination of interest payments if developing countries chose to default.

Moreover, the rather extreme relationship of interest to new borrowing in 1982 is likely to continue over the next several years. This point may be seen intuitively by considering that debt is unlikely to continue to grow by a rate higher than the average interest rate on past debt (with LIBOR on the order of

---

20. Martin Bronfenbrenner, "The Appeal of Confiscation in Economic Development," *Economic Development and Cultural Change,* vol. 3 (April 1955), pp. 201–18.

21. Jonathan Eaton and Mark Gersowitz, "Debt with Potential Repudiation: Theoretical and Empirical Analysis," *Review of Economic Studies,* vol. 48 (1981), pp. 289–309.

22. For 1983 the relationships were even more drastic in Brazil and Mexico. Their adjustment programs called, respectively, for current account deficits (i.e., a figure that *exceeds* new borrowing in the form of loans, considering that some direct foreign investment will be received) of $3.4 billion and $6.9 billion, respectively; by contrast, their interest burdens were projected at approximately $11 billion each.

Table 4.2 Relationship of interest burden to new borrowing, nonoil developing countries (billion dollars)

Year	Total debt (A)	New borrowing, net[a] (B)	Interest payments (C)	Ratio, C/B (D)	Ratio, interest/new borrowing: Argentina	Brazil	Mexico	Chile
1974	160.8	...	9.3	...	0.27	0.29	0.19	0.40
1975	190.8	30.0	10.5	0.35	−4.06[b]	0.42	0.27	0.92
1976	228.0	37.2	10.9	0.29	1.27	0.39	0.34	−2.41[b]
1977	278.5	50.5	13.6	0.27	0.36	0.37	0.38	1.03
1978	336.3	57.8	19.4	0.34	0.25	0.25	0.39	0.32
1979	396.9	60.6	28.0	0.46	0.18	0.58	0.52	0.44
1980	474.0	77.1	40.4	0.52	0.27	0.86	0.42	0.45
1981	555.0	81.0	55.1	0.68	0.41	1.08	0.62	0.45
1982	612.4	57.4	59.2	1.03	2.20	0.93	0.79	0.79

Source: IMF, World Economic Outlook, 1983, p. 200, and Institute for International Economics debt data base.
a. Equals debt in year minus debt in previous year.
b. Year in which debt declined.

10 percent) because of contracted capital markets. Thus, the magnitude of new debt is likely to equal or fall short of the magnitude of interest payments. The point is also evident in the simulations of chapter 3. As shown in the appendix table B-9 for the 19 largest debtor countries interest payments are projected to be approximately the same size as new net borrowing in 1983–86, and for the oil-importing countries interest would substantially exceed new borrowing. In short, there is an underlying structural vulnerability in international lending at the present time because, if a judgment is made solely on the basis of simple comparison of the interest burden against net new loans received, the developing countries have little incentive to continue honoring debt-servicing obligations. That is, if they defaulted, their losses in net new loans forgone would approximately equal their gains in interest relief.

In practice, however, the consequences of default could reach far beyond trading the loss of new borrowing in exchange for avoiding interest payments. A defaulting country would risk isolating itself economically from the rest of the world. At best it would forfeit the opportunity to borrow at some future date when foreign capital might be extremely vital to it, because of an export collapse, for example. In addition, even short-term trade credit could dry up, making it impossible for the country to conduct foreign trade at anywhere near normal levels. The denial of short-term trade credits would mean that the

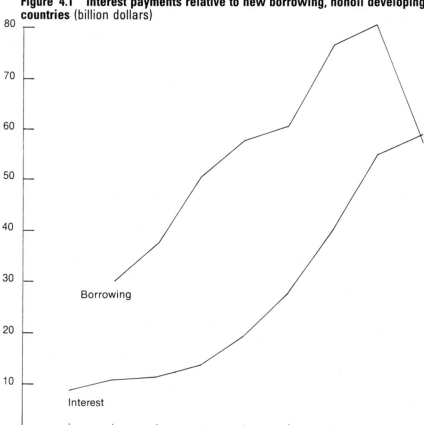

Figure 4.1 Interest payments relative to new borrowing, nonoil developing countries (billion dollars)

Borrowing

Interest

1974   75   76   77   78   79   80   81   82

Source: Table 4.2

country would have to go to a cash basis for its imports. In order to do this it would have to have reserves worth perhaps six months of imports. That is, although in principle a country could continue trade without normal trade credits, it would have to pay cash for imports, and because of the lag in export receipts behind shipments, it would have to expect to wait a number of months between the shipment of exports and the availability of their earnings for spending on imports. In short, only countries with large reserves could continue trade on a cash basis. Ironically, these would be precisely the countries that would not be in serious debt difficulty in the first place.

Because the major opposition party in Brazil called for an extended moratorium on interest and principal in mid-1983, it may be useful to illustrate the limited scope for net gains from such action using relevant financial magnitudes for Brazil. For 1984, the interest payable is approximately $11 billion. An extended, comprehensive moratorium would save this amount annually less the reductions in net new financing caused by the moratorium. For 1984, net new bank financing was scheduled at approximately $3.5 billion at the outset of the year ($6.5 billion in new lending less $3 billion in arrears from 1983). Export credit agencies were to provide approximately $2.5 billion. The IMF and multilateral development banks were to provide perhaps over $2 billion, and direct foreign investment conservatively $800 million. A comprehensive and extended moratorium would almost certainly cut off the financial flows from the banks, export credit agencies, and multilateral agencies, and might cut direct investment by half. The losses in new capital would amount to approximately $8.5 billion. From a potential gross interest savings of $11 billion, Brazil would be left with net savings of only $2.5 billion. And if just one-fourth of short-term trade credits were to dry up, even this net savings would be eliminated. Thus, a unilateral moratorium on interest and principal would bring little if any net financial gain, even before taking into account other adverse repercussions.

Beyond difficulties with access to long-term and short-term credit, defaulting countries could face reprisals. Foreign creditors could attach any of the foreign assets of a defaulting country, as well as its exports abroad (commercial airlines, ships, bank accounts, shipments of commodities, and so forth). For example, in 1972 Kennecott Copper Corporation successfully obtained legal seizure of Chilean copper shipments at a French port, as well as the freezing of Chilean bank accounts in New York, because Kennecott maintained that Salvador Allende had paid inadequate compensation for its expropriated copper mine.[23] Parallel actions could certainly be expected against countries defaulting on external debt. Notably, the only two countries to repudiate debt in recent decades—Cuba in 1961 and North Korea in 1974—did so under conditions that seriously impaired their access to Western (especially US) financial markets.

There is, of course, a wide range of uncertainty about the nature of such international responses. Along the continuum of debt disruption, it is conceivable that if such important countries as Brazil and Mexico declared an indefinite moratorium for reasons of inability to pay, the US government would make no attempt to take reprisals, because of the desire to avoid more permanent jeopardy to political ties. Even in this more benign version of moratorium, however, private parties would have legal access to the type of attachments and interdictions just described, and it would be unlikely that Western governments would actively block the private actors in these efforts. To be sure,

---

23. *New York Times*, 5 October 1972.

in this event the private concerns with truly large interests (especially the major banks) would first seek to reestablish a payment schedule through negotiation before attempting to attach assets, because any assets they could attach would be small relative to their claims on the country. But in the event of extended inability to reestablish negotiations, these private concerns might eventually join in the action of other private creditors to seize assets and shipments.

Under more aggressive circumstances, moreover, such as a moratorium declaration coupled with internal government changes moving significantly to the left (or to the nationalist-right) and announced in terms laying the blame on Western nations, international official reaction might reinforce private reprisals. At the extreme, Western nations might impose trade embargoes on the defaulting country. Such a step would complete the process of moving toward autarky that the country would risk when it first decided on an extended moratorium.

The possibility of international reprisal explains the superficial appeal of the idea of a debtors' cartel. It would be more difficult for industrial countries to impose reprisals such as asset attachments and trade sanctions on a wide coalition of debtor countries taking joint action. A debtors' cartel would be a political coalition to ward off reprisals rather than a traditional economic cartel regulating the supply of a product. The appeal of such a cartel is greatest to the smaller countries and to the less creditworthy countries. If they could enroll large debtors into a common front, small countries seeking to default could greatly reduce the likelihood of foreign reprisals against themselves. Not surprisingly, however, such a cartel has held little appeal for the large debtor countries, even after the sharp deteriorations in their credit positions. They have no desire to tarnish their long-term credit standings further by declaring a common front with certain smaller countries with even more severe debt problems. The very formation of a debtors' cartel would be equivalent to signaling creditors that they could expect aggressive behavior in the future, thereby cutting back even further the availability of new voluntary lending now and in the medium-term future.

On the contrary, there is a strong incentive for individual debtors to attempt to maintain their credit image on a basis of their individual performance. In the late 1970s major borrowers were systematically resistant to calls for general debt relief in the context of North-South negotiations, because they did not want to see their own credit ratings jeopardized. And in late 1982 Brazilian authorities went to great lengths to disassociate themselves from the Mexican financial crisis, maintaining that Brazilian policies had been more prudent. Ironically, by mid-1983 Mexico's adjustment was proceeding more smoothly than Brazil's, and correspondingly Mexico had no desire to be judged on the credit merits of any other Latin American country than itself.

The dynamic of credit-rating self-preservation seems likely to defeat attempts to establish a debtors' cartel. Indeed, the major debtors repeatedly have rejected such proposals. Moreover, the dynamic of individual credit-rating preservation also means that it is by no means axiomatic that if a major debtor such as Brazil or Mexico were to default, or to insist on extreme measures such as interest rescheduling, all other debtor countries would demand the same treatment. Some of the weakest debtors might do so, but other more important debtors very probably would find such an event the occasion to make it clear to creditors that they themselves could be trusted to honor their obligations and were by comparison preferred credit risks. In this way the nondefaulting debtors could not only avoid unnecessary risks of foreign reprisal but would also buttress their future ability to borrow. For all these reasons, an emergence of a meaningful debtors' cartel is unlikely.

In short, the dramatic potential costs of default mean that even if interest somewhat exceeds new borrowing, countries are unlikely to judge it beneficial on balance to default. Moreover, debtors are unlikely to form a cartel and carry out a joint default. Instead, it is much more likely that if normal rescheduling breaks down, a country will go into protracted negotiations, seeking to obtain the equivalent of relief from full market terms on its debt, but in a form that does not proclaim default. Nicaragua is one of the few illustrations. In part because it was in a postwar reconstruction, the new Sandinista regime managed in 1980 to get foreign banks to reschedule not only principal but also all interest in excess of 7 percent. The Polish case also represents an attempt in this direction. In mid-1983 the Polish government stated as an initial negotiating position that it wished to reschedule its entire $25 billion debt to the West over 20 years, with an eight-year period during which no interest would be paid.[24] In both cases, the rescheduling of interest is an extreme step for banks to accept, because it invites the possibility of eventual nonpayment of interest (and, importantly, the failure to pay interest within a specified period of the date due triggers classification of the loan as nonperforming on the banks' books). In the Polish case, acceptance of the proposed terms would have pushed the country further in the direction of de facto default. In this context, it is perhaps not an accident that both Nicaragua and Poland are in political situations that tend to reduce the likelihood of future capital inflows from the United States and some other industrial countries, echoing the political isolation of the former default countries, Cuba and North Korea.

A more significant threat to Western banks than outright default, then, is that some developing countries may seek to obtain reschedulings that substantially depart from normal market terms. The first departure would be rescheduling of interest as well as principal. A more radical departure would be the negotiation of below-market interest rates on rescheduled debt.

---

24. "Polish Officials Seek to Reschedule Debt," *Washington Post,* 15 June 1983.

At the present time even this kind of "radical rescheduling" seems unlikely, because it would seriously damage the country's long-term credit standing. But if world recession were to resume and developing-country export performance remained stagnant, the pressures for this kind of solution would mount. Moreover, considering the high degree of bank vulnerability to developing-country debt, the large debtor countries would appear to have substantial unexploited bargaining potential. If negotiations moved from a cooperative to a confrontational mode, large borrowers might be able to extract substantial debt relief as a bribe or side-payment to keep them from defaulting in a context where there would be some costs to themselves but much greater costs to the creditors and the financial system. (Thus, potentially the amount of "rent" or side-payment they could extract would be the difference between these two costs.) So far, however, the major debtors remain cooperative. Considering the structural weakness of their incentive to continue playing by the rules (with interest exceeding new loans) and their great potential bargaining leverage in view of the heavy exposure of bank capital that they hold, it is to the credit of the long-range judgment of the financial leadership of these countries that they have not yet moved to an adversarial posture relative to the banks nor sought to exploit their bargaining potential in the form of radical reschedulings on nonmarket terms. How long this prudence, and willingness to play by established rules, will continue will undoubtedly depend on whether their economic situations deteriorate further, and by how much.

In sum, despite structural trends that specifically raise the incentives to default, the major debtor countries (except perhaps Poland) still remain far from the point where default or radical rescheduling on nonmarket terms would be an attractive option.

Medium-Term Viability

The projections of chapter 3 suggest that the underlying economic health and creditworthiness of the major debtor countries should show substantial improvement over the medium term, under circumstances of adequate economic recovery in industrial countries. Nonetheless, important obstacles must be overcome for the present international strategy toward external debt to be viable over the longer term.

One potential hurdle is the bunching of maturities of principal payments coming due in the mid- and late-1980s as the consequence of some of the major debt reschedulings. Another critical test will be whether the financial system can return to voluntary capital flows after an interim period of involuntary lending (chapter 4). An even more fundamental issue is whether the present approach of international financial rescue through debt rescheduling and new lending with official orchestration is consistent with political feasibility, or whether the political strains in debtor countries are so severe that major collapses can be expected in the absence of more radical measures.

This chapter examines these three issues of medium-term viability of the current approach to the debt crisis. To confine the scope of the discussion to feasible dimensions, the analysis here concentrates on the three largest debtor countries: Argentina, Brazil, and Mexico. However, similar issues are involved in the instances of other debtor countries.

Maturity Bunching

As discussed in chapter 3, by perhaps 1986, the creditworthiness indicators for Argentina, Brazil, and Mexico should be back to acceptable levels below the critical thresholds associated with past debt reschedulings. Nonetheless, a return to more normal capital market conditions will pose the challenge of dealing with large amortization, because when lending is voluntary, the rollover of past debt coming due cannot be automatically assured.

Table 5.1   Impact of debt rescheduling on amortization profile: Argentina, Brazil, and Mexico (million dollars)

	Original			Revised		
	Long-term	Short-term	Total	Long-term	Short-term	Total
Argentina						
1983	8,000	11,000	19,000	0	—	0
1984	6,436	11,212	17,648	6,036	—	6,036
1985	6,406	11,164	17,570	6,406	—	6,406
1986	6,781	10,767	17,548	13,931	—	13,931
1987	6,400	10,125	16,525	12,150	—	12,150
1988	6,400	10,000	16,400	9,400	—	9,400
1989	6,400	10,000	16,400	9,400	—	9,400
1990	6,400	10,000	16,400	6,400	—	6,400
Brazil						
1983	9,797	16,000	25,747	5,747	16,000	21,747
1984	10,284	16,801	27,165	2,784	16,881	19,665
1985	10,592	17,386	27,978	11,259	17,386	28,645
1986	10,413	17,094	27,507	11,080	17,094	28,174
1987	10,205	16,752	26,957	11,205	16,752	27,957
1988	10,205	16,752	26,957	11,205	16,752	27,957
1989	10,205	16,752	26,957	11,205	16,752	27,957
1990	10,205	16,752	26,957	12,580	16,752	29,332
Mexico						
1983	7,015	16,500	23,515	0	0	0
1984	7,865	16,669	24,536	1,682	169	1,851
1985	7,929	18,022	25,951	7,929	1,522	9,451
1986	8,402	19,471	27,873	11,802	2,971	14,773
1987	8,911	20,586	29,497	17,186	4,086	21,272
1988	9,302	21,676	30,978	17,577	5,776	23,353
1989	9,690	22,766	32,436	14,565	6,266	20,831
1990	10,074	23,856	33,930	14,949	7,356	22,305

Table 5.1 presents the original schedules of amortization due annually for Argentina, Brazil, and Mexico as well as the revised schedules after taking account of debt rescheduling.[1] In addition to the reschedulings in 1982–83, it is assumed that Brazil reschedules $5.5 billion in long-term bank debt coming due in 1984 (in addition to rescheduling $2 billion of official credits due in 1984, through the Paris Club).

The table shows the sharp differences among the three countries in rescheduling strategies. Mexico and Argentina converted all short-term debt to long-term, while Brazil maintained short-term debt intact. The appearance of short-term amortization once again in Mexico in small but growing amounts reflects the assumption that for new debt acquired in the future, the same proportion as in 1982 (27 percent) is in the form of short-term. In Argentina, no new short-term debt arises because there is no projected increase in total debt.

The amortization profiles in table 5.1 are obtained by projecting the original schedules of amortization and then deducting the amounts rescheduled, for the early years, and adding the resulting increments in subsequent amortization to the figures for later years. For example, the Brazilian rescheduling of $4 billion in bank debt due in 1983 was over eight years with two years' grace, leading to deduction of $4 billion in 1983 amortization and annual increments of $667 million to amortization in 1985–90.

The original amortization schedule is taken from the debt projection model described in chapter 3. In that model, amortization is estimated by applying the original amortization rate for long-term debt, calculated as amortization due in 1982 (before rescheduling) as a ratio of long-term debt outstanding at the end of 1981. For Mexico and Brazil this rate was approximately 13 percent; for Argentina, it was 22 percent. These rates are then applied to the projected level of outstanding long-term debt at the end of the year preceding the year of amortization in question. This procedure tends to yield a smooth profile of amortization on long-term debt, while in practice past variations in annual borrowing and maturities mean the actual amortization path is more irregular. Nonetheless, the estimates here appear preferable to other available projections.[2]

The central implication of table 5.1 is that both Mexico and Argentina will have a sharp increase in amortization due by 1986 or 1987, whereas Brazil's amortization profile is much more constant (although at a substantially higher

---

1. The discussion of this chapter treats Argentina's rescheduling as if the terms reached prior to the election of the new government will be followed. In fact the new government has sought a moratorium on principal through mid-1984 and has been engaged in further negotiations on the rescheduling agreements, which were not signed in 1983. The principal practical change for purposes of analysis, however, is that principal due in 1984 as well as 1983 is likely to be rescheduled.

2. World Bank projections of amortization often do not include private debt, are unavailable for debt subsequent to that outstanding at the end of 1981, and do not incorporate the amortization on prospective accumulation of new debt. World Bank, *World Debt Tables, 1982–83 Edition* (Washington, 1983).

level in all years). This contrast is apparent in figures 5.1 to 5.3 which show graphically the amortization profiles reported in table 5.1

The surge in amortization in 1986 for Argentina and 1987 for Mexico suggests that, if at that time economic policies and prospects are not viewed favorably by international lenders, there could be difficulty in refinancing the amortizaton due on a voluntary basis. It might be necessary even then to resort to rescheduling and involuntary lending. However, although these amounts seem large, they are not unmanageable when compared with past magnitudes. Thus, in figure 5.3 the amortization that could have been due in 1983 ($23.5 billion) was larger than the amounts falling due in 1987, and yet financing even greater than the amount originally due in 1983 was accomplished in 1981 when Mexico had not only comparable amortization due but also a massive current account deficit of approximately $12 billion to be covered, mainly by new borrowing from private banks. Thus, if Mexico can return by 1986 to the creditworthiness status it enjoyed as recently as 1981, it should be possible to manage the surge of amortization that will be the legacy of the 1983 rescheduling.[3]

Figure 5.1   Argentina: amortization profile

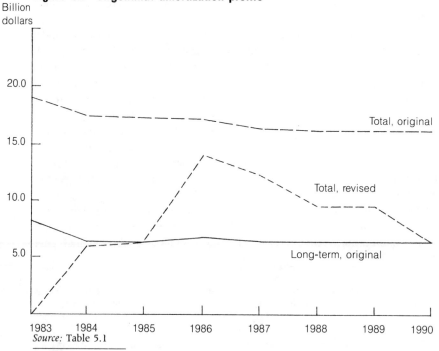

Source: Table 5.1

3. Moreover, Mexico's prospective amortization may be considerably smaller than indicated in table 5.1. Government sources indicate the following amortization on debt outstanding (excluding on $7.5 billion in debt owed by banks), for 1985–1990: $11.1

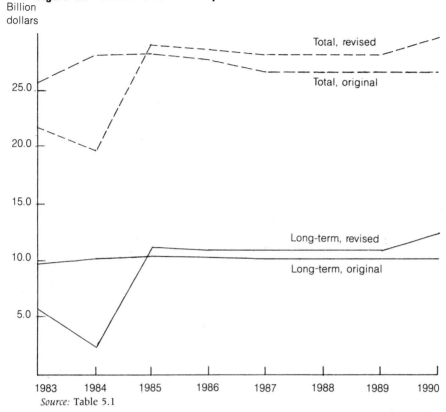

Figure 5.2 Brazil: amortization profile

Billion dollars

Total, revised

Total, original

Long-term, revised

Long-term, original

25.0

20.0

15.0

10.0

5.0

1983   1984   1985   1986   1987   1988   1989   1990

Source: Table 5.1

Brazil's situation is different. Its short-term debt is holding constant at approximately $16 billion, of which about $6 billion is interbank deposits and the rest is primarily trade credit. This short-term debt could be vulnerable to withdrawal in the event of a severe future deterioration in the outlook (for example, in the face of a sharp swing toward economic nationalism). Otherwise, however, this debt should be relatively reliable. The trade debt is closely related to import flows—and is secured by the traded goods as collateral; and the remaining interbank deposits are from a hard core of major foreign banks with a high stake in Brazil.

It is a moot point whether Brazil's rescheduling technique was less or more farsighted than that of Mexico and Argentina. Brazil has avoided the problem of maturity bunching in the late 1980s, as shown in figure 5.2. But its overhang

---

billion, $6.5, $14.8, $14.0, $12.1, and $11.9 billion, respectively. Even with allowance for payments due on new borrowing, these amounts are lower than those estimated here. Leopoldo Solís and Ernesto Zedillo, "A Few Considerations on the Foreign Debt of Mexico" (Washington: World Bank, processed, 1984), p. 57.

Figure 5.3   Mexico: amortization profile

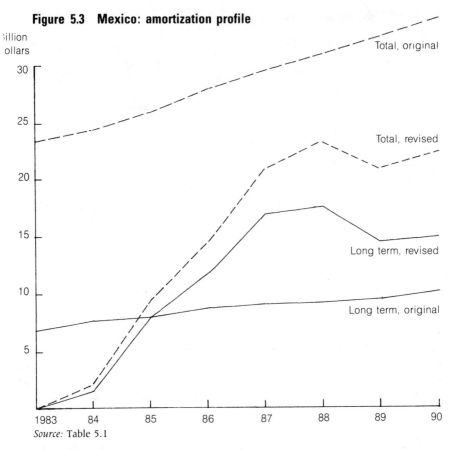

Source: Table 5.1

of short-term debt is at least potentially vulnerable to a sharp deterioration in confidence. On balance, the two rescheduling models—including short-term debt in the amounts rescheduled (Mexico, Argentina) or excluding short-term debt (Brazil)—appear relatively comparable in advantages and disadvantages, judged over the medium-term horizon. In all three countries, however, the maturities due in the late 1980s should be manageable if creditworthiness improves as projected.

Reconversion to Voluntary Lending

Another central question remains about the long-term viability of the recent strategy of international financial rescue: will it be possible to return to the normal process of voluntary lending, and if so, when? It would be difficult to conceptualize the problem as one of only temporary illiquidity if banks could not anticipate conversion back to a voluntary lending basis for decades, if ever.

The transition to voluntary lending will require two conditions. The first is that country-creditworthiness profiles (debt relative to exports, for example) return to acceptable levels. As discussed above, projected improvements suggest that this condition should be met by Argentina, Brazil, and Mexico by at least 1986 (and sooner by several other major debtors). The second prerequisite is that the volume of new lending that can reasonably be expected from the banking community on a voluntary basis be sufficient to meet borrowing needs. The analysis that follows concentrates on the second requirement.

For voluntary bank lending to be sufficient for borrowing needs, external deficits of the debtor countries will have to be moderate. Specifically, net borrowing from banks will *equal* current account deficits, *plus* needed buildup in reserves, *minus* expected direct investment inflows, *minus* finance that may be expected from export credit agencies and other official sources. This amount must be consistent with what the banks as a group are prepared to lend.

The test of transition to voluntary lending is even more rigorous, however. Because some banks—presumably the smaller banks—will want to receive their amortization and reduce exposure under voluntary conditions—*the large banks must be prepared to lend enough not only to cover the balance of payments gap but also to finance gradual withdrawal of those banks that do not wish to lend over the longer run.*

In the 1970s many smaller banks may have become involved in international lending without a real underlying capacity to do so over the longer run, in terms of ability to analyze country risk for example. By contrast, most larger banks are involved in international lending for the long term. Many of them have branches in the debtor countries. Their staffs are large enough to conduct country risk analysis; and they tend to look to the large growth potential of countries such as Mexico and Brazil in the longer run.

If lending is to become truly voluntary, however, at some point in the future it will be necessary for those banks that wish to exit from a country to be able to do so. Ironically, then, while all efforts must be made in the immediate future to ensure that the smaller banks not be free riders but participate in the increased (involuntary) lending required, at the point of conversion back to voluntary lending it will be necessary to allow these same banks not only to abstain from new lending but also to receive amortization payments on past loans. Ideally, at the time of transition back to voluntary lending, many of the smaller banks that currently want out will once again find the prospects of the country attractive and wish instead to remain involved in lending to the country.

As an acid test of the feasibility of return to voluntary lending, appendix tables E-5 through E-7 indicate the increases in exposure of large banks that would be required to finance not only balance of payments deficits but also the orderly withdrawal of small banks at the time of conversion to voluntary lending. The calculations here assume that large banks accounting for 70 percent of exposure continue lending on a voluntary basis, while smaller banks accounting for 30 percent of exposure wish to withdraw. This requirement is perhaps overly rigorous, because in a context of renewed confidence, the exposure magnitude of banks seeking withdrawal might be considerably smaller than 30 percent of the total.

Tables E-5 through E-7 first show the magnitude of total borrowing required, *equal to* the current account deficit *plus* increase in reserves, *minus* direct investment. The expected current account deficit comes from the projection model of chapter 3, with plausible (but less formal) extrapolations for 1987–90. The calculations then assume that net borrowing from banks *equals* two-thirds of total net borrowing required, the remainder being from official sources. Where actual amounts of net bank borrowing are known (as for 1983), the actual figure is used instead.

Total net lending required from large banks would exceed net lending from banks as a whole by the amount of amortization paid out to the smaller, retreating banks. Amortization due to all banks is estimated on the basis of the share of banks in total debt, and it is assumed that 30 percent of amortization due to banks would be paid out (to the smaller banks) rather than rolled over. In the Brazilian case, this payment of amortization includes repayment over three years of short-term debt due to small banks. Total net lending required from large banks thus *equals* net lending needed by the country *plus* amortization to the small banks. The resulting trend in large bank exposure, and its percentage growth, are shown in the final columns of the tables.

These calculations indicate that for Argentina, there would be only small expansion of exposure during the period of involuntary lending (1983–84); that if conversion to voluntary lending occurred in 1985, large banks would have to increase exposure annually by an average of 12 percent in 1985–86; and that by 1988–90, even with transition to voluntary lending, large bank exposure would have to grow only by an average of 6.2 percent annually. This prognosis does depend on the favorable projection of zero net borrowing requirements in 1984–90 because of small deficits or actual surpluses in the current account.

For Brazil, large-bank exposure grows by approximately 9 percent yearly in 1983–84, and by zero in 1985. With conversion to voluntary lending by 1986, large-bank exposure grows again, but solely as the result of financing small-bank withdrawal, and at moderate rates averaging 6.4 percent in 1986–88 and 4 percent in 1989–90. Again, however, the projection of a small current account deficit that can be financed fully out of direct investment is an assumption behind the result of relative ease in conversion to voluntary lending. For sensitivity analysis, an alternative assumption is that the current account deficit would be higher (at $4 billion yearly) and direct investment lower (at $1.5 billion) in 1985–90. Under the alternative scenario (not shown in table E-6), large-bank exposure would need to grow at 5.9 percent in 1985, 15.6 percent in the first year of conversion, 1986, an average of 10.7 percent annually in 1987–88, and 7.2 percent in 1989–90. Even these larger rates would seem feasible, especially taking the slower growth in 1985 together with the surge in 1986.

For Mexico, the combination of a bulge in repayments and a relatively larger projected deficit on current account means that large-bank exposure would have to grow somewhat more rapidly than in Argentina and Brazil to permit conversion to voluntary lending, beginning in 1985. Large-bank exposure would grow by an average of 6.3 percent annually in 1983–84, rise to a rate of 11.5 percent annually in 1985–88, and continue at a rate of 9 percent in 1989–90. However, Mexican economic planners anticipate much lower current account deficits than the $6 billion average in the projections of chapter 3, and the performance on current account in 1983 lends credence to that view. Essentially, they anticipate more robust nonoil exports and lower import requirements. Accordingly, for purposes of sensitivity analysis, an alternative hypothesis would be that the current account deficit is limited to only $3 billion annually, but also that direct investment averages somewhat lower than in the base case, at $2.0 billion in 1985–87 and $2.5 billion in 1988–90. Because the net bank borrowing figures in the base case are almost identical to the actual amounts expected for 1983–84, there is no change for these two years. Under this alternative scenario, again with conversion to voluntary lending by 1985,[4] large-bank exposure would need to grow by 4 percent in 1985, 6.7 percent in 1986, and an annual average of 9.3 percent in 1987–88 and 7.9 percent in 1989–90.

The broad thrust of these calculations is that it should indeed be possible to return to voluntary lending for these key debtor countries by 1985–86. Even if they had to finance the amortization owed to smaller banks accounting for 30 percent of bank exposure, the large banks could assure voluntary lending by expanding their exposure at reasonable rates. The rates might have to be temporarily at what might be considered outer limits—approximately 12 percent annually for Argentina in 1985–86 and Mexico in 1985–88—but would then taper off, and the Mexican expansion would at its peak be a more modest 9 percent (1987–88) under the alternative that assumes smaller future deficits.

The broad implication of these estimates is that it should be feasible to achieve reconversion to voluntary lending. This process will be greatly facilitated if, with a return of general confidence and improved country performance, the smaller banks decide voluntarily to remain active in lending to these countries.

---

4. The conversion years are 1985 for Argentina and Mexico but 1986 for Brazil, based on the year of return to acceptable creditworthiness. See appendix A, "A Logit Model of Debt Rescheduling, 1967–82."

Political Viability

Even though the debt problem should be manageable for most major debtor countries, there remains the risk that political crises in hard-pressed countries may lead to moratoria or defaults before sufficient relief can arrive from international economic recovery. The cases of financial rescue for the largest debtor countries provide concrete test cases for the severity of this risk.

The most successful political acceptance of economic adjustment has been in Mexico. To the surprise of some experts, there has been little social upheaval in response to the austerity program. Real GDP in 1983 declined by approximately 4 percent, following zero growth in 1982. Wage increases, at 25 percent in January 1983 and 16 percent in June, have been far below inflation, and real wages by mid-1983 had fallen perhaps one-third from the levels one year before, yet threatened general strikes failed to materialize.

The broad reason for limited social disruption appears to be Mexico's robust political system. The official party, *Partido Revolucionario Institucional* (PRI), has continued its past success at absorbing dissent from the left. A significant technique has been the use of an anticorruption campaign that has jailed such leading figures as the head of the state oil company under the former administration. This campaign has provided a sense of equity about the adjustment process, giving the impression that former profiteers will not escape while the public bears the burden of adjustment. Similarly, the populace is well aware that sharp reductions in living standards for the middle and upper classes are also taking place, again giving a sense of equity. The price paid by traditional elites was most conspicuously evident in the nationalization of the banks in September 1982, but the collapse in availability of luxury imports is another manifestation.

The mild political response to painful adjustment in Mexico also reflects the fact that for several years growth had been rapid because of the oil bonanza. From 1976 through 1981 real growth of GDP averaged 7.5 percent and per capita growth 5.8 percent.[5] With zero growth of GDP in 1982 and -4 percent in 1983, per capita real GDP fell approximately 10 percent from its 1980 level by 1983 but was still as high as in 1979, while in other Latin American countries per capita income by 1983 had plummeted to levels of far earlier years.

Significant doubt remains about the continuation of political acquiescence to economic adjustment in Mexico. Continued decline in per capita income into 1984 and beyond would pose a much more severe test for the system.

---

5. Growth rates discussed in this section are from IMF, *International Financial Statistics*, October 1983; Inter-American Development Bank, *Economic and Social Progress in Latin America: 1983 Report* (Washington, 1983), p. 116, and Naciones Unidas, Comisión Económica para América Latina (CEPAL), *Balance Preliminar de la Economía Latinoamericana durante 1983* (Santiago, December 16, 1983).

Correspondingly, a failure of the international economy to sustain adequate recovery could eventually force such slow growth that social unrest could explode in Mexico. The central expectation, however, must be that Mexico will gradually restore economic growth and successfully avoid serious political disruption.

The political underpinnings to debt management in Brazil have proved to be considerably weaker. The essential reasons are that Brazil's political system, in transition from military rule back to democracy, is less robust than Mexico's; and that recession started earlier and has caused larger income losses in Brazil than in Mexico, in part because Mexico's bloated import bill was easier to cut than Brazil's, where import restraint has been successively tightened since 1974. Because of recession associated with adjustment measures begun in 1981, following a decade of per capita GDP growth averaging 6 percent, Brazil's per capita growth was −4.3 percent in 1981, −2.4 percent in 1982, and perhaps −6 percent in 1983. From its peak in 1980 per capita GDP fell by 12 percent through 1983 to a level last experienced in 1976. Moreover, because of a severe decline in external terms of trade, Brazil's per capita real income has fallen even more than per capita gross domestic product, adding perhaps another 4 percent to the decline.[6]

In this environment violent social unrest erupted in 1983. In April, a week of rioting and looting occurred in Sao Paulo. By the fall of 1983 sackings of food stores had occurred in the Northeast and in Rio de Janeiro. These outbreaks were a new phenomenon for the military regime.

Similarly, overt political opposition to the strategy of adjustment and management of foreign debt has been relatively high in Brazil. In August 1983 the opposition party (Partido do Movimento Democrático Brasileiro, PMDB) formally called for a three-year moratorium on all interest and principal; a prestigious leftist economist advocated the moratorium; and even some important business groups approved some form of moratorium.[7] The real strength of opposition to the adjustment strategy became clear when in October 1983 the opposition party and several members of the government's own party defeated a centerpiece of the program—the law decreed in July limiting wage indexation to 80 percent of inflation. The defeat jeopardized reinstatement of the IMF loans and bank loans suspended since late May.

By early November the political prospects for economic management improved sharply, as Brazil's official party reestablished an alliance with a small labor party and successfully passed a compromise law that on average limited wage

---

6. Carlos F. Diaz-Alejandro, "Some Aspects of the Brazilian 1982–83 Payments Crisis," *Brookings Papers on Economic Activity*, no. 2 (1983).

7. *Journal do Brasil*, 18 August 1983, and Celso Furtado, *Não a Recessão e ao Desemprego* (Rio de Janeiro: Paz e Terra, 1983).

indexation to 87 percent of inflation but applied a sliding scale that guaranteed 100 percent indexing for low-income workers.[8] This measure paved the way for prompt IMF approval, resumed bank lending, and successful mobilization of $6.5 billion in new bank lending. In turn, this demonstration that the international financial community could deliver on its part of the package seemed likely to undercut the demands for moratorium.

The Brazilian political balance remains tenuous. Serious failure of the adjustment program to succeed in 1984 could conceivably lead to a radicalization of even the government's strategy. Candidates for the 1984 election could be tempted to gain support through nationalist-populist positions on debt, especially if the elections are direct. The greater likelihood, however, is that the November 1983 resolution of the acute impasse on wage indexing will have marked the trough of the Brazilian crisis, and that with international funding moving again, the broad political perception within Brazil will be that it is better to muddle through with the existing strategy than to risk economic damage of unknown dimensions through a debt moratorium.

The crucial element in the political equation is the resumption of economic growth. Critics of the IMF and of the current debt strategy insist that imports, which fell by 27 percent in value from 1981 to 1983, must be allowed to grow sharply to permit economic reactivation; hence the appeal of moratorium. The critics do not take account of the likely loss of new lending and short-term credit that could freeze up trade following a moratorium, quite apart from foreign legal seizure of export shipments. They thereby overestimate the increase in net foreign exchange availability that might be obtained by a moratorium (chapter 4). Moreover, domestic growth for 1984 seems likely to be constrained by measures necessary to avoid hyperinflation. With inflation running at an annual rate of nearly 300 percent in the third quarter of 1983, implementation of IMF-agreed budget cuts seemed prudent even taking into account the fact that much of the inflation was from cost-push factors (drought and floods especially). The demand effects of budget deficit cutbacks by 3 percent of GDP could be approximately offset by stimulus from export expansion and import substitution, the reversal of crowding out in the credit market, and the inertial growth tendency in the Brazilian economy, leaving perhaps zero or slightly positive net growth for 1984. If political patience can withstand another year of recession, Brazil should then be well positioned for recovery in 1985.

The Argentine political environment has produced less formal opposition to the current debt strategy than in Brazil but has nonetheless been widely regarded as subject to erratic swings. Because of its self-sufficiency in both oil and food, Argentina is better positioned than most debtor countries to withstand the economic isolation that could follow default. Growth performance has been

---

8. *Washington Post*, 10 November 1983.

extremely poor, with real growth of GDP averaging only 2.1 percent in 1976–80 and declines in GDP by approximately 6 percent annually in both 1981 and 1982. With growth of 2 percent in 1983, real GDP per capita in 1983 was 14 percent below the level of 1977.

Like Brazil, Argentina is returning to civilian rule. Unlike the Brazilian case, the Argentine democratization was imminent in 1983. Perhaps because of the sobering effect of having a serious expectation of taking control in the immediate future, neither the Peronists nor the Radical party called for an extended and comprehensive debt moratorium, in contrast to the position of the opposition party PMDB in Brazil—although both candidates in Argentina's October 30, 1983, election spoke in general terms about seeking tough negotiating terms.[9]

The potential fragility of the political context for debt management was highlighted in early October 1983, when a local judge temporarily jailed the central bank president on charges of violating Argentine law by signing an agreement renegotiating the debt of the state airline. But the resounding electoral victory by Raúl Alfonsín of the Radical party, with 52 percent of the vote to the Peronists' 40 percent, seemed to inaugurate a new era of potentially more stable politics. A victory of this magnitude seemed likely to give Alfonsín a relatively free hand in economic policy despite potential obstruction by Peronist labor unions.

On external debt, the new Alfonsín regime pressed for reduction of interest rate spreads above LIBOR, longer maturities, and sufficient magnitudes of new lending and rescheduling in 1984 to permit a rise in imports to achieve an all-important reactivation of the economy. However, there is little reason to anticipate a more radical shift toward extreme measures such as an extended moratorium on interest. Because a new IMF agreement was required prior to a rescheduling of 1984 principal, however, difficulties arose as the new regime sought to convince the IMF to accept a policy package that left the budget deficit as high as 10 percent of GDP and planned to raise real wages by 6 percent to 8 percent, even though by mid-1984 inflation was running at an annual rate of nearly 600 percent.[10]

The case of Yugoslavia illustrates that adverse political repercussions of economic adjustment occur in socialist as well as developing countries. The IMF adjustment program includes unpopular austerity measures such as cuts in subsidies on flour and bread. The adjustment measures involve cutbacks in federal loans to the poorer regions of the country, an unpopular act in a country where the regional republics and provinces have great strength relative to the federal government and where latent tensions between ethnic groups (Serbs, Croats, Albanians, Montenegrins) persist. Considerable political unrest appears

---

9. *La Nación*, Buenos Aires, 31 October 1983, Edición Internacional, p. 6.

10. For further discussion of the Argentine case at mid-1984, see chapter 8.

to have developed in Yugoslavia's poorest province, Kosovo, as reflected by the seeming increase in arson and a sharp rise in work stoppages.[11]

Among other major debtors, perhaps the most notable case of political disruption is that of Chile. In mid-1983, despite the regime's gesture of permitting the return of over 100 political exiles, the Democratic Alliance of five parties opposing the Pinochet regime began a monthly series of national days of protest and the protests brought violence. The government responded with the announcement of a plebiscite to revise the constitution for the acceleration of congressional elections, and maintained an intermittent dialogue with the Democratic Alliance.

Although this opposition group has insisted that only a return to democracy will give Chile the international support required to deal with the debt problem, external debt is a less central issue in the Chilean political process today than in Brazil. Instead, political conflict is focused on the establishment of a timetable for return to democracy. Nonetheless, extremely adverse conditions, including a 14 percent decline in GDP in 1982 (associated with restrictive policy to reduce foreign deficits), have contributed to the extent of national discontent with the Pinochet regime.

Considering these cases together, the pattern that emerges is one of severe strain to the political fabric as a consequence of the adjustment measures required by the debt problem.[12] How well political institutions bear up under this strain depends on their underlying strength, and much of international debt is owed by countries whose political regimes are in stages of transition (Brazil, Argentina, possibly Chile, and prospectively the Philippines). There are signs of synergism between the debt problem and transition to democracy. In Brazil, the opposition used the debt problem as a lever to assert more power than it had ever been able to achieve before during the 20-year history of military rule. In Chile, Pinochet's opponents may try to do the same.

An important point to keep in mind about the economic environment for political response is that the external constraint does not necessarily mean economic stagnation over the medium term. External adjustment means a need to shift resources from the nontradables sector to tradables (exports and import substitutes). After an initial period of recession—caused by an immediate reduction in activity in nontradables while activity picks up in tradables only after a time lag—there should be renewed economic dynamism from the tradables sector.[13] Accordingly, it would be a serious mistake to project into

---

11. *Wall Street Journal*, 10 November 1983.

12. For further discussion of these strains, see Riorden Roett, "Democracy and Debt in South America," *Foreign Affairs*, vol. 62, no. 3 (1984), p. 69.

13. Anne O. Krueger, "Interactions Between Inflation and Trade Regime Objectives in Stabilization Programs," in William R. Cline and Sidney Weintraub, eds., *Economic Stabilization in Developing Countries* (Washington: Brookings Institution, 1981), pp. 83–118.

the indefinite future the conditions of economic recession recently experienced in countries such as Mexico and Brazil, and correspondingly wrong to predict political collapse from such stagnation.

Despite political strains and the somewhat unpredictable chemistry mixing debt and political reform, so far the often-predicted collapse of international debt because of domestic political explosion has failed to occur. As analyzed in chapter 8, however, by mid-1984 a sharp divergence existed between the impressive performance in external economic adjustment and the escalation of political perceptions of the need for major debt relief, spurred by the lagged political effects of severe domestic recessions in 1983 and by the upturn in international interest rates in the second quarter of 1984. Nonetheless, with the possible interim exception of Argentina, the major debtor countries remained in a mode of political cooperation with industrial country creditors (as reflected by the mild outcome of the Cartagena meeting of economic and foreign ministers of major Latin American countries), and their internal political bases for carrying out successful debt management appeared to remain broadly viable.[14] Over the medium term political tolerance to the present rules of the game on debt servicing and rescheduling could be even more severely tested, and this tolerance could easily rupture in at least some important countries if the global economy fails to sustain sufficient recovery.

---

14. A glaring and tragic exception was the Dominican Republic, where rioting against IMF austerity measures led to scores of deaths in April. *Washington Post,* 30 April 1984.

6

Adequacy of Banking Institutions

The external debt disruptions of 1982–83 have raised new doubts about the adequacy of present banking arrangements. In particular, in considering whether to approve increased International Monetary Fund (IMF) quotas, many legislators objected that higher quotas would be a bailout for the banks, and that the banks got themselves into difficulty through excessive and irresponsible lending abroad.[1] The result of this wave of criticism of bank behavior has been congressional pressure for tighter regulation of banks, and a response by the regulatory authorities proposing somewhat heightened regulation of external lending. At the same time, many academic critics have questioned whether the organization of central bank responsibility for the "lender-of-last-resort" function has been adequate for international lending.

This chapter first examines whether structural flaws in the organization of international bank lending contributed to debt crises. It then reviews the proposals for new regulation of external loans. The discussion concludes with an examination of the argument that central bank coverage of international lending is inadequate, thereby posing a risk to the system.

Organization of Foreign Lending

Many critics hold that in the 1970s bank lending to developing countries was excessive, and that it departed from past standards of prudence.[2] However, as was widely recognized in the mid-1970s and again in 1979–80, bank lending played a socially valuable role in facilitating the financial recycling of OPEC

---

1. For a statement of this viewpoint, see *Wall Street Journal*, editorial, 9 March 1983.

2. See, for example, David Lomax, "Sovereign Risk Analysis Now," *The Banker* (January 1983), pp. 33–39.

surpluses to nonoil developing countries in the process of adjustment.[3] Official lending responded only sluggishly, especially to middle-income countries, so that it was primarily bank lending that met the sharply increased need for financing. Moreover, as was repeatedly pointed out at the time, if this lending had not been forthcoming, developing countries would have been forced to cut back their imports from industrial countries, causing an even sharper world recession after the first oil shock.[4]

There were of course market forces inducing heightened bank lending abroad. As was recognized by international agencies, both the surge of deposits "from oil exporters' surpluses" and the "dampening effect of the international recession on competing demands for bank loans in the industrial countries" caused an expansion in the supply of bank lending to developing countries.[5] It should be added that the innovation of variable interest loans greatly contributed to bank willingness to lend in an inflationary environment.

In short, a substantial rise in the relative magnitude of bank lending to developing countries in the 1970s was not only to be expected from international macroeconomic developments but was also broadly socially desirable. None-theless, by the late 1970s and early 1980s many qualified observers questioned whether the dynamic response of banks had not become too much of a good thing. Henry C. Wallich of the Federal Reserve Board of Governors criticized the growth of bank lending to developing countries as unsustainably rapid, and at an average pace of 25 percent from 1975 to 1980 it was rapid indeed.[6]

After the rash of debt disruptions in 1982–83 it became fashionable, especially among conservative-populists to charge that banks had acted irresponsibly. The demonstration in chapter 1 of this study that international economic forces contributed extremely large amounts to indebtedness, especially in 1980–82, should be sufficient evidence to dispel the notion that bank irresponsibility, and for that matter, country irresponsibility, has been the sole or primary cause

---

3. Although it would be wrong to imply, as has often been done, that developing-country deficits were largely caused by OPEC surpluses. In a statistical examination I have found that from 1973–81 a change in the OPEC surplus by a given magnitude translated into a corresponding change only 14 percent as large in the deficits of nonoil developing countries, and that in addition the developing countries had a high ongoing deficit as well as a sharp response in their deficits to changes in OECD growth. William R. Cline, "External Debt: System Vulnerability and Development," *Columbia Journal of World Business*, vol. 17, no. 1 (Spring 1982), pp. 4–14.

4. John A. Holsen and Jean L. Waelbroeck, "The Less Developed Countries and the International Monetary Mechanism," *American Economic Review*, vol. 66, no. 2 (May 1976), pp. 171–76.

5. IMF, *Annual Report* (Washington, 1976), p. 21.

6. Henry C. Wallich. "Banks, LDC's Share Concern For Viable System," *Journal of Commerce*, 30 July 1981, p. 4A; and BIS, *Annual Report* (Basle, 1978), p. 92 and 1981, p. 105.

of today's debt problem. Nonetheless, it is important to consider whether flaws exist in the organization of international bank lending that have contributed to the problem.

In 1979 I suggested, based on the Peruvian experience, that banks might be lending excessively because they tended to assume that international institutions and governments of industrial countries would come to the country's aid in case of trouble, and that banks thereby "externalized" the risk in foreign lending.[7] While any such bias toward excess lending surely could not account for the bulk of increased developing-country debt in recent years (again, considering the large external shocks in recent years enumerated in chapter 1), this influence may nonetheless be a factor to address. Similarly, in the late 1970s, the desire of European, Japanese, and regional US banks to enter more actively into international lending appears to have contributed to increased lending supply at low spreads above LIBOR as new and traditional lenders competed for market shares.[8]

These various supply factors, including ample availability of funds from OPEC deposits, in some important cases led to continued bank lending to countries that ideally would have borrowed less while adopting adjustment measures under IMF auspices but instead availed themselves of bank financing. A conspicuous case was Peru in 1976; Mexico and Argentina in 1981 to early 1982 also would fit this description. Thus, from December 1981 to June 1982 when Mexico was in the last phase of budgetary and other policy excess before its August crisis, US banks increased their exposure in Mexico at an annual rate of 34 percent. And from December 1979 to December 1980, as Argentina pursued a policy of extreme overvaluation, US banks increased their exposure in Argentina by 42 percent.[9]

The experience of international lending in the last decade suggests a need for better discipline and organization of bank lending. There is a need not only to avoid excessive lending, and some excessive lending undoubtedly did occur in the 1970s, but also to avoid severe cutbacks in lending, such as occurred in 1982. Some analysts have advocated that the International Monetary Fund formally adopt the role of mentor to bank lending, and that it provide a "traffic signal" showing a green light for lending to countries pursuing desirable policies but an amber or red light warning against bank lending to countries not doing

---

7. William R. Cline and Sidney Weintraub, eds., *Economic Stabilization in Developing Countries*, (Washington: Brookings Institution, 1981), pp. 40–41.

8. Thus, the average spread above LIBOR for Eurocurrency loans to developing countries was about 1 percentage point in 1973–74, 1.5 percent in 1975–77, down to 1.2 percent again by 1978, and only 0.9 percent in 1979–81. IMF, *International Capital Markets, Recent Developments and Short-Term Prospects*, September 1980, p. 26, and July 1982, p. 15.

9. Federal Financial Institutions Examination Council, *Country Exposure Lending Survey*, various issues.

so. Indeed, the IMF already acts as a moderator in the other direction: as outlined above, it has pressed banks to combine new lending in countries where they might otherwise hold back and undermine a financial recovery package.

An IMF traffic signal would involve difficult political problems. Intense lobbying of the more powerful members would accompany any case where an amber or red light was about to be activated. Yet if the IMF had officially maintained a green light for a country that subsequently had debt difficulties, at the least official credibility would be undermined and at the most banks might claim official responsibility for their difficulties.

A more promising vehicle for improving the organization of bank lending is the new Institute for International Finance (IIF). This organization, formed by international private banks, has as its primary mandate the provision of improved information about borrowing countries. The "information gap" hypothesis holds that a major contributing factor in the debt crises of 1982 was that individual banks did not know how rapidly their competitors were expanding lending, especially short-term, and that by the time the true magnitude of increased debt was known the situation was out of control. Although this view surely overstates the role of information per se, a better information system could make a modest contribution, especially because the central source of data on bank exposure—the Bank for International Settlements—provides these data only after a six-month lag.

The Institute for International Finance has a much more important potential agenda, however: the evaluation of country risk. The institute is expected to prepare periodic reviews of economic policies and performance in debtor countries, and these evaluations could be helpful to banks in signaling incipient problems as well as registering major improvements. Although member banks have ruled out for the time being the announcement of explicit country credit ratings by the IIF, it could conceivably develop such a rating system in the future.

Existing private rating firms are paid by the countries (or firms) they rate, and countries tend not to finance a rating unless it is likely to come out favorably. A country-rating mechanism by private banks would avoid the drawbacks of imposing an official straight jacket on the market. It could of course be subject to bias from banks with existing exposure in a given country, although it might be possible to design sufficient staff independence that such bias could be minimized (for example, through liaison with international agencies).

The Institute for International Finance could also help moderate downswings in capital flows by assisting in the mobilization of lending support from otherwise free-riding banks (chapter 4).

In sum, although it is inaccurate to attribute the debt problem chiefly to past bank irresponsibility, the experience of the last decade has shown the need for bringing more order to bank lending so that it does not swing from excessive expansion to excessive contraction. The Institute for International Finance could play an important institutional role (well beyond merely providing information) in addressing the problem of organizing international lending. Some analysts have expressed concern that any such institutional change could have adverse effects on developing countries through the cartelization of credit markets.[10] But at least in the medium term, following the events of 1982–83, it is likely that a more organized credit market would increase the supply of credit rather than restrict supply in classic cartel fashion.[11]

Bank Regulation

Beyond institutional innovation in the private market, the official regulators are also moving to introduce more discipline in foreign lending, in part because of congressional pressure on them to do so as a quid pro quo for increased IMF quotas (in view of the political argument against bailing out banks).

It is important to recognize that tightened bank regulation will not solve any immediate problem; at the moment the problem is too little new bank lending to developing countries, not too much. Nonetheless, it would be imprudent to delay longer in taking necessary steps to strengthen the system for the long run.

The basic problem regulatory reform needs to address is the overextension of sovereign lending beyond limits that are prudent for the system. The system now appears too vulnerable to loans extended to developing and East European countries, as illustrated by the loan-capital ratios and default scenarios examined in chapter 2. Similarly, it appears that at present the US system seems to have generated relatively modest provisioning, or setting aside of reserves, for loans to countries in difficulty. Thus, in 1982 the nine largest US banks had an estimated total provisioning of $614 million attributable to foreign loans, or about 1.7 percent of the value of their total loans outstanding to countries that have experienced significant debt disruption recently.[12] Although provisioning

---

10. Edmar L. Bacha and Carlos Diaz-Alejandro, "International Financial Intermediation: A Long and Tropical View," *Essays in International Finance*, no. 147 (Princeton, NJ: International Finance Section, Department of Economics, Princeton University, May 1982).

11. Moreover, the lending market is so competitive that achievement of a cartel that could extract monopoly rent would be highly unlikely, quite apart from antitrust enforcement.

12. The provisioning figure is based on the banks' annual reports. The total loans referred to amounted to $36.7 billion for 11 countries (Argentina, Brazil, Chile, Costa Rica, Mexico, Nicaragua, Peru, Sudan, Zaire, Poland, and Romania). Federal Financial Insti-

means short-run nuisance in lower reported profits, inadequate provisioning risks shock to international banks and the system under unfavorable scenarios.

The Federal Reserve, Comptroller of the Currency, and Federal Deposit Insurance Corporation (FDIC) have explicitly recognized the "transfer" risk in sovereign lending caused by the possible inability of a country to raise enough foreign exchange to service debt.[13] This recognition is important in itself, because in the past some prominent bankers have asserted that sovereign lending has no risk at all because countries do not disappear. The three agencies have proposed a five-point program of regulation. It involves (a) a stricter examination of country exposure, including expectation of higher capital-to-loan ratios for banks with greater concentration of country exposure; (b) more public disclosure of the country exposure of banks; (c) the definition of new loan classifications: Loss, Reservable, and Debt-Service Impaired, with requirements for write-off or provisioning into reserves in the first two cases, respectively; (d) stretchout of reported income from loan fees; and (e) increased cooperation with bank regulators abroad and, possibly, greater sharing of IMF information.

These proposals are highly desirable reforms. They generally strike the proper balance between sufficient reform to increase prudence in the system and avoidance of overkill that would cut off foreign lending. They may tend to err in the direction of leniency by not requiring any loan provisioning for rescheduled loans as long as the new terms of the loans are met. Under this approach there would be no required provisioning of loans to Mexico and Brazil currently, and would have been none for Poland in 1981 or 1982, even though in some countries with more conservative banking practice (for example, Switzerland) considerable provisioning has been taking place for these countries (although typically with encouragement, rather than requirement, by central banks). Unfortunately, however, the application of normal provisioning rates (10 to 15 percent of face value annually, up to an eventual 50 percent) would be far in excess of the amount needed for rescheduled loans and would impose a severe burden on banks. Loans to countries that have rescheduled in the last year account for perhaps 150 percent of capital of the large banks, meaning that provisioning of up to 15 percent of capital annually might be required, wiping out bank profits. Such provisioning could be regulatory overkill. Thus, the recommendation of provisioning of rescheduled loans, contained in the House

---

tutions Examination Council, "Country Exposure Lending Survey: December 1982" (Washington, 1983; processed). However, capital positions have been improving. The 17 largest banks raised their capital-to-loan ratio from 4.39 percent at the end of 1980 to 5.02 percent at the end of 1982. Communication with Federal Reserve staff, April 1983.

13. Federal Reserve Board of Governors, FDIC, and Comptroller of the Currency. "Joint Memorandum: Program for Improved Supervision and Regulation of International Lending" (Washington, April 7, 1983; processed).

of Representatives version of the bill for the IMF quota increase,[14] was highly undesirable. In the event, the final bill omitted provisioning of rescheduled loans, adhering instead to the proposal by the regulators themselves that special reserves be set aside only on loans to countries with "protracted inability . . . to make payments on their external indebtedness" as indicated by failure to pay interest, to meet the terms of restructured debt, or to comply with an IMF or other adjustment program.[15] More generally, any future provisioning of rescheduled loans should be set at a much lower level than for generally doubtful loans (for example, only 2 percent to 3 percent per year). Alternatively, it might be appropriate to provision only against that amount of principal actually postponed, rather than against the full loan.

Conceptually a challenging question is whether the reforms should include country ceilings. The joint memorandum argues that country differences, political pressures, and the current high exposure of some banks in some countries rule out country ceilings. Broadly, the position of the regulators appears correct, as discussed below. Nonetheless, it is perhaps useful to conceptualize possible theoretical approaches to country limits.

Domestically a US bank cannot lend more than 15 percent of its capital to a single borrower, whether it is General Motors or the corner drug store. If this domestic regulation is valid, some corresponding ceiling on country loans might also follow logically.[16] Specifically, if the domestic probability of default in general is at a given level, A, and the probability of default on country loans is at another level, B, then the same logic that gives a 15 percent loan ceiling to domestic loans would imply a loan ceiling of 15 percent *times A/B* in country lending. Thus, if the probability of default by a borrowing country is one-fifth the probability of default for a domestic borrower, the country loan ceiling should be 15 percent *times* 5, or 75 percent. In that way the expected or probability-weighted damage to the bank from a single country borrower would be the same as that from a single domestic borrower. In the past some thought that the probability of country default was zero, so that conceptually the loan ceiling would be infinite (A/B = infinity, when $B = 0$). Today the probability of country default no longer appears to be zero. And it must be kept in mind that unlike domestic loans, country loans have no tangible collateral.

In practice, there appears at present to be little firm basis for determining the

14. US Congress, House Committee on Banking, Finance, and Urban Affairs, *International Recovery and Financial Stability Act*, H.R. 2957, 98 Cong., 1 sess., 1983.

15. *Supplemental Appropriations Act*, PL 98–181, 1984, sec. 905.

16. The 15 percent limit does apply to a single central government, but considering state firms and private borrowers there is no corresponding country ceiling. Note, however, that there is no ceiling domestically on interrelated loans—such as loans to different oil companies—yet the interrelatedness risk bears some resemblance to transfer risk.

risk of country as opposed to domestic default (*B* relative to *A*), making it difficult or impossible to apply the above approach operationally. One recent study concluded that the real cost to creditors of all debt rescheduling (based on the difference between original and adjusted terms on a present-value basis) between 1956 and 1980 amounted to $2 billion, compared with total loans to developing countries of $400 billion in 1980.[17] Even in the terminal year this amount was only half of 1 percent of principal, implying that over a 24-year period the average loss rate was only 0.02 percent annually. And even this loss was confined to official creditors, who had motives of concessional assistance in the cases where loss was significant (Indonesia, Ghana, India, and Pakistan). By contrast, the recognized losses on private debt reschedulings have been negligible, because reschedulings have been at market terms. To judge from past experience, then, the probability of country default *B* would not be far from zero and an infinite country ceiling would not be far wrong.

However, to assess country risk as zero under today's circumstances would be naive. Considering perhaps the most severe cases of country risk, loans to Poland, Zaire, and Sudan might reasonably be judged to be worth no more than two-thirds their face value. If this valuation were accepted, the implied, aggregate losses to Western banks would amount to $5.3 billion. Assuming these losses were realized over five years, and comparing them to total bank loans to developing countries and Eastern Europe, the average loss rate on country lending would be 0.28 percent annually. By comparison, for the nine largest US banks average domestic loan losses were 0.72 percent of loan value in 1982.[18] Thus, a forward-looking analysis might place the ratio *A/B* at approximately 260 percent, implying a country limit at approximately 40 percent of capital.

Nonetheless, the determination of the probability of country default is clearly imprecise, and in a legalistic approach it might be necessary to make the assessment of relative country default risk on actual past losses—meaning near-zero realized losses and near-infinite country ceilings. Accordingly, the approach outlined above is not operational in practice, and it is probably best to accept the regulators' conclusion that establishing country ceilings would be a mistake. Pragmatically, a serious problem is that some banks have such high single-country exposure (such as Citibank with 74 percent of its capital in Brazil) that specifying a limit would either leave them in violation (and unable to bear their share of "involuntary lending") or establish an uncomfortably high limit

---

17. Chandra Hardy, "Rescheduling Developing-Country Debts, 1956–1980: Lessons and Recommendations," Overseas Development Council Working Paper No. 1 (Washington, February 1982), p. 26.

18. From annual reports, total loans were $398.8 billion, and domestic charge-offs were $1.4 billion in 1982. From the Federal Financial Institutions lending survey, total foreign loans were $205.3 billion. Thus, domestic loans of the nine largest banks were $193.5 billion, giving a domestic loss rate of 0.72 percent.

that might lead other banks to excess. There is also the question of whether two classes of countries would have to be differentiated, with country ceilings applying to developing (and East European) but not industrial countries. Nonetheless, examination of the logic of country ceilings leaves less room for complacency about their absence today than in the past—because of the higher probability of future country default than in the past. Accordingly, the other prudential reforms proposed by the regulators are all the more welcome.

A reform that should be added to the regulators' list is more liberal income-tax treatment of reserves. It is paradoxical that at a time when the regulatory authorities seek increased provisioning, the Internal Revenue Service is attempting to reduce the share of bank loans that can be deducted when provisioned to only 0.6 percent of total loans instead of 1 percent. Surely for system stability the IRS should be making revisions in the opposite direction. Indeed, a major reason for the greater extent of provisioning on loans to developing and East European countries by European banks (and in particular German banks) appears to be the more lenient tax deductibility of the amounts set aside in reserves (and therefore the attraction of maintaining "hidden" reserves in the form of undervalued assets).

Overall, the proposals by the Federal Reserve, Comptroller of the Currency, and FDIC warranted strong support, and they became the principal basis for that final form of the IMF quota bill that passed Congress in November 1983. It is safer to adopt this strategy now, and evaluate the results in one or two years, than to risk further aggravating the liquidity problem by enacting regulatory overkill. In the longer run it is crucial to reduce bank exposure to developing countries as a fraction of bank capital. The Western financial system now is too vulnerable to developing-country debt.

Lender of Last Resort

Another area of concern about adequacy of banking institutions is that central bank "lender-of-last-resort" coverage may be inadequate for international lending. Under the traditions of central banking, a bank in difficulty borrows from its central bank if it is illiquid, although if it is insolvent the remedy involves either merger with a stronger bank or dissolution, with protection guaranteed only to insured depositors.

In international lending, however, there is ambiguity about whether the host-country central bank or that of the parent country bears the lender-of-last-resort (LLR) responsibility for a subsidiary of a foreign bank, and some observers consider this ambiguity dangerous.[19] In the case of foreign branches,

---

19. See, for example, Jack Gutentag and Richard Herring, "The Lender-of-Last-Resort Function in an International Context," *Essays in International Finance*, no. 151 (May

there is no ambiguity: because the parent bank is legally responsible for its branches, a branch in trouble would appeal to its parent, which in turn would appeal to the parent central bank.

For subsidiaries, some confusion has existed because major central banks have agreed in the "Basle Concordat" of 1975 that supervisory responsibility for subsidiaries lies with host-country central banks; yet a subsequent recommendation of the same group of central banks provided that banks should be supervised by home-country authorities on a globally consolidated basis.[20] Moreover, the Bank of England has specifically stated that "there should not necessarily be considered to be any automatic link between acceptance of responsibility for ongoing supervision and the assumption of a lender-of-last-resort role."[21] In 1983 the Basle group updated the 1975 concordat, clarifying that both host-country and parent-country central banks jointly shared responsibility for supervision of branches and subsidiaries with respect to liquidity; and that with respect to solvency, parent central bank supervision applied to branches while joint parent-host supervision applied to subsidiaries. The new policy also explicitly stated, however, that this allocation of jurisdiction applies only to supervision, not lender-of-last-resort responsibility.[22] The LLR loophole thus remains.

To some extent concern about LLR coverage may have been exaggerated. Most US loans through the Eurocurrency market are handled through London branches of US banks, not subsidiaries.[23] Subsidiaries do play a significant role in some cases, such as subsidiaries of German banks operating in Luxembourg.

The simplest way conceptually, but not necessarily politically, to cover possible gaps in LLR coverage would be to obtain joint agreement by all offshore lending countries (United Kingdom, Luxembourg, Panama, Singapore, the Bahamas, and so on) that they would make it a legal requirement that the parent bank stand behind its foreign subsidiary. The Bank of England already requires nonbinding letters of comfort to this effect. Making the requirement legally binding would ensure the same chain of backing that exists in the case of branches: subsidiary to parent, parent to its home central bank. Parallel

---

1983). By contrast, the Group of Thirty has judged the international LLR network to be adequate. Group of Thirty, *Balance of Payments Problems of Developing Countries* (New York, 1981), pp. 11–12.

20. Richard S. Dale, Statement Before the US Congress, House Committee on Banking, Finance, and Urban Affairs, US House of Representatives, 98 Congress 1 sess. (April 20, 1983).

21. W. P. Cooke, "Developments in Cooperation Among Banking Supervisory Authorities," *Bank of England Quarterly Bulletin*, vol. 21, no. 2 (June 1981), pp. 234–44.

22. *IMF Survey* (July 11, 1983), pp. 201–4.

23. Based on interviews with private bank officials, London, June 1982.

action by all offshore countries could avoid central bank unwillingness to adopt this measure because of fear of loss to competitive centers.

Some authorities maintain that a legally binding obligation of parents to subsidiaries, or more generally a clarification by central banks of exactly who would bear LLR responsibility in the case of subsidiaries, would pose the problem of "moral hazard," encouraging reckless action by providing excessive assurance of backing. This argument is not persuasive: any domestic US bank knows that if a central bank is to support it, the Federal Reserve is that central bank; yet the knowledge of this designation causes no moral hazard because the parent bank cannot be assured of support regardless of its actions. While the moral hazard argument appears unfounded, closer supervision of foreign subsidiaries by parent-country banks would be necessary under a binding parent-bank responsibility; however, the recent approach of global consolidation in supervision is already moving in this direction.

A different type of objection to mandatory parent backing of subsidiaries is that it might be viewed by host governments as infringement on their sovereignty over the subsidiaries. Foreign central banks of parent companies could hardly be expected to be the LLR of the subsidiaries without exercising substantial supervision over them (a trend already in process under global consolidation of capital adequacy tests). Yet, despite the newly reformulated concordat, that supervision might be seen by the host country as undermining the principle of its sovereignty over the subsidiaries (an already sensitive principle in view of issues arising in the area of economic sanctions against the Soviet Union, for example). As an alternative to mandatory parental backing, therefore, a host country could insist that foreign bank subsidiaries be converted to branches, for which there would be no problem of either parental backing or potential undermining of host-country sovereignty (because in the case of branches host countries do not assert sovereignty in the first place).

For some observers, the collapse of the Banco Ambrosiano subsidiary in Luxembourg is evidence of the danger of inadequate LLR coverage. However, because it was a holding company rather than a fully owned subsidiary, and because malfeasance rather than normal business loss appears to have been involved, the Luxembourg Banco Ambrosiano case is not a pure test of the problem of LLR coverage of subsidiaries.

More generally, it would indeed appear that loopholes exist in lender-of-last-resort coverage. However, experience to date suggests that the international financial system has less to fear from a series of bank failures attributable to such loopholes than from straightforward exposure risk of banks whose LLR coverage is not in doubt but whose country loans are. Moreover, the events of 1982–83 illustrate a willingness of central banks to work together in crisis, suggesting that if necessary they could agree on the division of LLR responsibility for currently ambiguous cases.

7

Policy Strategy

Since August 1982 the industrial and debtor countries have groped toward the right policy response to the international debt crisis. As this response evolves, the international financial community will have to choose between either a consolidation of the case-by-case approach of financial rescue applied to date—incorporating debt rescheduling and new lending on market-related terms together with official support—or toward more radical restructuring of debt, planned or accidental.

The viability of developing-country debt over the medium term will depend importantly on the availability of new lending from abroad. The discussion of this chapter first examines the prospective financing needs in comparison with prospective availability of funds from the international financial institutions and other sources to provide an idea of the feasibility of debt management in the next few years. The analysis then considers a range of recent proposals for more radical debt reform. The policy synthesis then concludes with observations on possible contingency measures and an overview of the best strategy to pursue in international management of the debt crisis.

IMF Quotas

The policy debate in the United States in 1983 centered on whether there should be an increase in International Monetary Fund (IMF) quotas, which provide the primary basis for its lending capacity. Although many countries had called for a doubling of quotas, until the fall of 1982 the Reagan administration opposed a substantial increase.[1] Then, after the dimensions of the debt problem became evident in the Mexican crisis, the administration advanced a proposal it had been considering, to raise the amount available for

---

1. *Washington Post,* 7 September 1982.

lending in the IMF General Arrangements to Borrow (GAB) and to open eligibility for its use as an "emergency fund" for all members of the IMF. Eventually the administration agreed to an increase of 47 percent in IMF quotas (from a base of SDR 61 billion, or approximately $67 billion to SDR 90 billion) combined with an increase in the General Arrangements to Borrow from $6 billion to $19 billion.[2] By August of 1983 both the US Senate and the House of Representatives had passed separate versions of the proposal, but the final bill still required resolution of differences in conference between the two houses as well as passage of appropriations legislation. The House bill passed only narrowly, and only after the inclusion of several restrictive amendments, many of them aimed at tightening regulation of banks. Finally, in November 1983, Congress passed the IMF quota increase, in part because the administration accepted authorization of spending on domestic housing as part of the package.[3]

Throughout the 1950s up to the early 1970s, IMF quotas amounted to about 10 percent of world trade. Before the new quota increase, however, they had fallen to 4 percent.[4] It would be important to raise IMF quotas even if there were no debt problem. In the current environment, it is doubly important to raise IMF resources. If the IMF is to have the influence it needs to induce countries to adopt appropriate policies, it must have sufficient resources to make their participation in such programs attractive. Moreover, with smaller IMF resources banks must bear a higher share of lending and countries must adopt more drastic measures to compensate for lower resource availability. Furthermore, industrial countries as well as developing countries have borrowed from the IMF; the United States itself did so in 1978, and the United Kingdom and Italy have also been large borrowers. In a historical perspective, then, there is an acute need for increased IMF resources.

A more specific evaluation of the inadequacy of IMF resources can be made by comparing its available resources with potential needs.[5] In mid-1983 the IMF had approximately $35 billion in available, lendable resources ($15 billion in lendable currencies, unused credit lines of $6 billion in the General Arrangements to Borrow, $2 billion in the supplementary financing facility, $8 billion in the enlarged access facility financed largely by borrowing from Saudi Arabia, and $4 billion in SDRs in the General Account). The amount available to lend varies, depending not only on loans made but also on whether particular

---

2. Agreement in principle was reached in November 1982. *Washington Post,* 21 November 1982.

3. *New York Times,* 19 November 1983.

4. IMF, *International Financial Statistics,* various issues.

5. The data for the following analysis are drawn primarily from IMF, *International Financial Statistics,* various issues. Note that an analysis reaching similar conclusions on IMF resource availability appears in Group of Thirty, *The IMF and the Private Markets* (New York, 1983).

currencies are considered sufficiently strong to be made available for lending. Outstanding commitments not yet drawn upon (including the large recent programs for Argentina, Brazil, and Mexico) amounted to $19 billion. Thus, the IMF's remaining available resources amounted to approximately $16 billion, of which $6 billion was available only for GAB industrial countries. The remaining $10 billion probably should be held largely in reserve, and it could have been more than exhausted by just three countries borrowing 450 percent of quota (before the quota increase): Venezuela, Indonesia, and Nigeria. The increase in IMF quotas by nearly 50 percent plus expansion of the General Arrangements to Borrow added approximately $29 billion to resources available for lending, giving a total of nearly $40 billion.

US congressional reaction to the proposed IMF quota increase was mixed. Many legislators argued that the funds could be better used to address unemployment at home, and that the measure would be a bailout for the banks.

But an international financial collapse would cause far more unemployment inside the United States than might be caused by allocation of resources to the IMF. Indeed, the true cost of the contribution is extremely low. The US contribution will be $8.4 billion. Of this amount, $5.6 billion would be for the quota increase and $2.8 billion for the increase in the GAB. Of the quota increase, 25 percent will be paid in SDRs or other currencies (nondollar, for the United States) specified by the IMF, at zero interest. The other 75 percent will be provided only as called upon, and when called, it would earn remuneration at 85 percent of the SDR interest rate. At current interest rates, the net interest loss on the quota contribution should average about 3.6 percent, for an annual cost of $200 million—an extremely low price for international financial insurance.[6] There would be minimal interest losses on funds lent through the GAB because borrowers would pay rates comparable to US borrowing costs.

As for the argument that the IMF "bails out the banks," it is by now clear that the IMF has been successfully pressuring the banks to continue lending, far from financing their withdrawal. If this charge is meant to convey that without IMF action the banks would experience losses, then the more relevant question becomes whether the general public would truly benefit if the absence of IMF action precipitated avoidable debt collapses that caused such bank losses. It is difficult to conceive of scenarios in which the banks would be forced to absorb large losses during financial crisis without causing losses as well for the general public outside of bank stockholders, indeed, probably much larger losses

---

6. In January 1984 the Executive Board of the IMF announced that remuneration on quota amounts borrowed would, over three years, be raised from 85 percent to 95 percent of the SDR interest rate. Accordingly, the prospective costs to the United States will be even lower than the estimate here.

than those of the banks themselves considering the effect of bank leveraging. In addition, some legislators have criticized bank irresponsibility, but the analysis of chapters 1 and 2 should make clear that the bulk of today's external debt problem is much more attributable to international economic shocks than to irresponsible behavior of banks.

Even with the 47 percent increase in IMF quotas, and even with the $19 billion emergency fund, IMF resources may prove to be too small. Policymakers should be prepared to support IMF borrowing in private capital markets if necessary,[7] and from individual governments such as those of Saudi Arabia, Germany, Japan, and the United States. In addition, the IMF must be prepared to go beyond its own internal ceilings on lending to individual countries, in the cases of the "super debtors" that must be kept on track if the system is not to be in severe jeopardy.

Opponents also argue that the IMF should sell its holdings of gold, worth approximately $40 billion at market prices, or borrow in private capital markets, to raise resources rather than receive additional quota contributions from member countries. Compared with quota increases, however, either of these options would tend to reduce the financial strength of the IMF. While that result is undoubtedly consistent with the agenda of some political groups, it is difficult to see how movement in this direction could avoid erosion of the already limited infrastructure for addressing international economic problems.

Finally, critics of IMF adjustment programs sometimes charge that by telling each country individually to reduce imports, the IMF pursues a fallacy of composition, because not all countries' imports can decline at the same time, and their collective attempt to make imports fall will cause world recession. This critique contains two flaws. The first is the implicit assumption that countries in difficulty have any alternative to reducing their trade deficits. They do not, because their financing is limited.[8] Indeed, these critics should favor larger IMF resources, not smaller, because with more lending capacity the IMF could recommend more gradual adjustment programs consistent with slower reductions in external deficits. The second flaw in the critique is the failure to recognize that the magnitude of the trade cutback required—$25 billion to offset decreased bank lending—is small relative to aggregate OECD trade (about

---

7. Group of Thirty, *The IMF and Private Markets*.

8. If the IMF typically lent considerably less than its quota-based ceiling to borrowing countries, and if it had large unused resources, the critique would have more force. The IMF could then vary its practice to require more stringent adjustment with less lending for an individual country during global business cycle expansion, but to permit less stringent adjustment with more financing for the same country when it was borrowing along with many other countries in the midst of global recession. But in practice the IMF has been lending its full limit to countries in difficulty and its resources are slim, ruling out the option of more moderate adjustment with higher lending despite justification on global cyclical grounds.

$1.5 trillion), and that such a cutback need not induce world recession if there is even a modicum of shift of macroeconomic policy toward expansion in industrial countries.

Financing Requirements

In 1982 severe strain on the international financial system occurred as private banks cut back their net new lending to developing countries outside the Organization of Petroleum Exporting Countries (OPEC), from $43.2 billion in 1981 to only $26.5 billion. The flow of new lending seems to have declined somewhat further in 1983.[9] The central question is whether there will be sufficient new bank lending, in the medium term, to finance even reduced developing-country deficits that are consistent with acceptable domestic growth.

Table 7.1   Current account balance of nonoil developing countries, 1982–86 (billion dollars)

Projections	1982	1983	1984	1985	1986
IMF projections	−86.8	−68.0	n.a.	n.a.	−93.0
This study					
16 countries	−44.7	−39.3	−33.0	−27.4	−27.0
Nonoil LDCs[a]	−86.8	−76.3	−64.1	−53.2	−52.5
Morgan Guaranty					
8 countries	−33.3	−19.4	n.a.	−13.3	n.a.
Nonoil LDCs[a]	−86.8	−50.6	n.a.	−34.7	n.a.

n.a. Not available.
Source: IMF, *World Economic Outlook,* 1983, p. 205; chapter 3, this study; and *World Financial Markets,* June 1983, p. 9.
a. Applying 1982 ratio of subgroup to total.

---

9. Calculated from BIS, *The Maturity Distribution of International Bank Lending,* (Basel, July 1983, June 1982, and June 1981). The BIS data also show that new bank lending to noncapital-surplus OPEC countries rose from $2.1 billion in 1981 to $5.6 billion in 1982, while the banks actually reduced exposure to Eastern Europe (excluding the Soviet Union) by $1.8 billion in 1981 and $5.8 billion in 1982. For 1983 available data indicate new lending of only $6 billion in the first half. However, lending tends to be seasonally lower in the first six months of the year; and approximately $11 billion was committed, though not fully disbursed, in involuntary lending for 1983 to the three largest debtors alone. BIS, *The Maturity Distribution,* December 1983.

The adequacy of financing may be examined by comparing projected deficits with prospective sources of financing. The International Monetary Fund has projected that the current account deficit of nonoil developing countries will decline from $86.8 billion in 1982 to $68 billion in 1983 and then rise again, to $93 billion by 1986. However, as shown in table 7.1, on the basis of projections for 16 major nonoil developing countries (including Mexico) in chapter 3 of this study the total deficit would be considerably less by 1986, only $53 billion. A recent study by Morgan Guaranty bank implies even lower nonoil developing country deficits by this period (table 7.1).

The analysis of chapter 3 of this study would suggest that in addition to nonoil developing countries (including Mexico and Ecuador, following IMF definitions), some OPEC countries will need to borrow substantial amounts. For 1986 the base-case estimate of the current account deficit just for Algeria, Indonesia, and Venezuela is $26 billion (a figure that is probably too high because actual adjustment in all likelihood will have to be greater than assumed in the projections). Considering these various estimates, a central figure for developing-country borrowing needs (including the three OPEC countries just mentioned) would be on the order of $75 billion to $80 billion on average in each of the next few years (although the figure would be higher if the IMF estimates are accepted, and lower if the Morgan Guaranty estimates are adopted).

Possible levels of average annual financing for 1983–86 are shown in table 7.2, by source. Official transfers, concessional lending, and net direct investment are all based on 1982 levels with a small allowance for inflation.[10] Levels of multilateral lending and official export credits are similarly based on recent levels and some allowance for inflation and real expansion.[11] In the table, the high alternative, case A, assumes that banks maintain modest net lending of $25 billion, equivalent to annual expansion of exposure by approximately 7 percent. Case B assumes instead that new bank lending is only $10 billion yearly (an extremely low level that would go little beyond ''involuntary lending'' for a few major debtor countries). In optimistic case A, with approximately $40 billion in lendable resources and a normal period of five years between increases, the IMF lends $7 billion net per year. In pessimistic case B, despite the quota increase the IMF follows conservative policies, including sparse use of the GAB emergency fund, and lends only $4 billion per year.

The hypothetical levels of financing shown in table 7.2 indicate that with higher IMF lending, and if private bank lending reverts to a slightly higher but

---

10. IMF, *World Economic Outlook*, 1983, p. 194.

11. OECD, *Development Cooperation 1982*, pp. 206, 233. Note that the World Bank (excluding IDA) accounts for the bulk of multilateral net disbursements. As discussed below, its net lending reached $4.5 billion in 1982, and for 1983–86 the level might be on the order of $6 billion annually.

Table 7.2 Prospective annual net financing, selected OPEC[a] and nonoil developing countries, 1983–86 (billion dollars)

	Case A	Case B
Official transfers	14	13
New direct investment	12	10
Official lending		
Concessional	10	10
Nonconcessional		
Multilateral development banks	8	7
IMF	7	4
Official export credits	4	3
Private lending	25	10
Total	80	57

OPEC Organization of Petroleum Exporting Countries.
a. Noncapital-surplus.

still moderate rate, it should be just barely possible to secure the approximately $75 billion to $80 billion in capital that should be required by nonoil developing countries and noncapital-surplus OPEC countries annually in this period. However, if bank lending slows still further and lending from official sources (including the IMF) is smaller (case B), financing will be inadequate to cover even the moderate capital needs of developing countries despite their adjustment efforts and their improved positions during world recovery. Thus, the stakes are high for securing adequate official capital flows and for pursuing policies that enhance rather than cut off private bank flows.

This analysis also has implications for multilateral development lending. If the capital of the multilateral development banks could be expanded so that their lending rates could rise by 50 percent over this period, they could contribute approximately $4 billion additional net lending annually, or between 5 percent and 7 percent of total net capital flow. Such an increase would be a valuable contribution, especially if private bank financing were low. Accordingly, expansion of multilateral bank lending warrants early attention, although mobilizing the necessary political support will not be easy.

The multilateral banks could also provide more capital in the next three to five years by accelerating the disbursement rate on their loans. Because of long lags in project-loan disbursements, net flows from these agencies are significantly below loan commitment levels. Thus, in 1982 the World Bank made new loan commitments of $10.3 billion and received principal repayments of $1.8 billion.

But its net disbursements were only $4.5 billion, far less than the difference between commitments and repayments, because of the multiyear lag in disbursement schedules. Gross disbursements were only $6.3 billion, or 61 percent of commitments.[12] There is a strong case, at least until the firm establishment of international economic recovery, for acceleration of World Bank disbursements. For this purpose a more pronounced movement toward program lending through structural adjustment loans, rather than project lending, would be desirable. Accelerated disbursement does transfer resource availability from the future to the present, but this reallocation would be highly desirable in light of the current global financial situation (and the still shocked credit markets), especially in those countries where substantial improvement in the external sector is anticipated over the medium term (such as Brazil, chapter 3). The World Bank could more consciously use variations in its disbursement rate and structural adjustment loans to play a countercyclical role in the world economy. (At present its role may even be pro-cyclical, aggravating recessionary effects, because its disbursements are linked to tandem funding by the recipient country, and this funding tends to dry up during financial stress.)

Proposals for Radical Reform

Most analysts agree that orderly servicing of external debt of developing and East European countries will be contingent on world economic recovery in future years. But a number go further: they argue that the debt is already unmanageable and that, either regardless of the extent of world recovery or because they expect it to be weak, the only way to defuse the systemic threat of the debt is to reduce its real burden for developing countries. Their plans typically involve an internationally coordinated stretchout of the debt and reduction in its interest burden.

The principal reform proposals under discussion in the United States are those by Peter B. Kenen of Princeton University, Senator Bill Bradley (D-NJ), Congressman Charles E. Schumer (D-NY), and financier Felix Rohatyn. A unique proposal has also been suggested by Norman A. Bailey of the National Security Council. In addition, some British bankers have been calling for new institutional changes, and some other academics and statesmen have proposed variants on the major reform schemes.

The proposal by Peter Kenen[13] (and in many regards the approach advocated by Senator Bradley) would establish a new International Debt Discount

---

12. World Bank, *Annual Report 1982*, pp. 10–11, 53, 148.

13. *New York Times*, 6 March 1983. A variant on this theme appears in Leslie Weinert, "Banks and Bankruptcy," *Foreign Policy*, no. 50 (Spring 1983), pp. 138–49.

Corporation. This agency would buy up developing-country debt held by banks at a discount of 10 cents on the dollar. It would pay the banks in long-term bonds against itself. It would become the creditor of the developing country, taking over the debt in question. It could afford to grant a modest reduction in the interest rate payable by the developing country, because of the 10 percent discount at which the debt would be purchased from banks. In addition, the agency would renegotiate the debt to longer maturities.

Under Kenen's plan, all banks would be given a limited period of time to decide whether to participate. Once the closing date was reached, subscribers would have no choice among country loans to be sold off: they would exchange all loans for any countries participating in the program. (Otherwise banks would sell off only the weakest loans.) Banks that did not choose to participate by the closing date would not be eligible thereafter to sell their loans to the corporation.

Felix Rohatyn has proposed a related reform measure. Drawing on the analogy of a worldwide Municipal Assistance Corporation—the entity created to revive New York City from bankruptcy—he proposes that developing-country debt be stretched out to long-term maturities of 15 to 30 years, and its interest reduced to perhaps 6 percent.[14] The schedule of principal repayments would be designed so that interest plus principal payments would be no more than 25 percent or 30 percent of exports annually. The vehicle for this conversion would be the International Monetary Fund, the World Bank, or a totally new agency. Such an agency would buy the claims of the banks with long-term bonds it would issue. Rohatyn recognizes that the conversion to long-term, low-interest loans would impose a loss on banks, and that the divison of the loss between bank stockholders, taxpayers, and countries would have to be resolved. He argues that against this loss, banks would achieve greater security of their assets, and that regulators could permit them to spread out their write-downs over a long period of time. Rohatyn also envisions the need for the US government to be prepared to purchase preferred shares in banks as a means of providing them with an infusion of capital in the event that foreign countries seek to intimidate the United States with financial blackmail by threatening outright repudiation of debt.

Congressman Schumer has proposed the conversion of bank loans to long-term, low-interest loans, with the guidance of the IMF.[15] This conversion would be managed directly by the banks and debtor countries, with no new international intermediary: the banks would still be the creditors. Where such

---

14. Testimony by Felix Rohatyn before the US Congress, Senate Committee on Foreign Relations, 98 Cong. 1 sess. (January 17, 1983).

15. See, for example, *Journal of Commerce*, 13 April 1983, and *New York Times*, 10 March 1983.

conversion is not agreed between the banks and the country, the US executive director in the IMF would be instructed to vote against any IMF loans. The conversion program would set repayments at a manageable fraction of export earnings. Schumer's plan also calls for increased loan-loss reserves when debts are not paid on time—unless restructuring is part of an IMF-negotiated conversion of short-term to long-term loans; establishment of an insurance fund with a small surcharge on renegotiated debt; and country ceilings on short-term loans.

Norman Bailey, formerly of the US National Security Council has proposed that developing-country debt be replaced with a form of equity asset ("exchange participation note") entitling the holder to a specified share in the country's export earnings.[16] Congressman Andrew Jacobs, Jr., (D-Ind.) has proposed the "Reckless Risk Recovery Act of 1983," which would require that banks owning loans to countries that do not meet payment schedules and which subsequently receive loans from the US government or the IMF reimburse the US Treasury for a pro rata share of such loans.[17]

Certain British bankers (including officials of Barclays Bank and Morgan Grenfell) have advocated a discounting device whereby banks could sell off their rescheduled developing-country debts to central banks or other agencies in order to obtain liquidity for use in other lending, domestic and foreign.[18] Such purchases by central banks could be in the form of bonds issued to the private banks, eligible for discounting for cash if the banks experienced illiquidity. In some versions those bonds would bear no interest so that their eventual sale would only be at a significant discount, causing a loss for the bank—and reflecting the sentiment that banks should pay the price for mistaken loans.

Gutentag and Herring of the University of Pennsylvania have proposed a package of reform measures.[19] Banks would be forced to "mark to market" the foreign loans on their books, making banks more cautious about foreign lending. They could sell off loans at a market rate to the IMF, World Bank, or a new entity, which would combine them with similar loans of other banks and resell

16. Norman A. Bailey, "A Safety Net for Foreign Lending," *Business Week*, 10 January 1983, p. 17; and in *The International Financial Crisis: An Opportunity for Constructive Action*, T. de Saint Phalle, ed. (Washington: Georgetown University Center for Strategic and International Studies, 1983), pp. 27–36.

17. US Congress, House, *Reckless Risk Recovery Act of 1983*, H.R. 2069, 98 Cong., 1 sess. (March 11, 1983).

18. Janet Porter, "Answers to Liquidity Crisis Sought," *Journal of Commerce*, 17 March 1983; Barnaby J. Feder, "The World Banking Crisis: Phase Two," *New York Times*, 27 March 1983.

19. Jack Gutentag and Richard Herring, "Overexposure of International Banks to Country Risk: Diagnosis and Remedies," testimony before the US Congress, House Committee on Banking, Finance, and Urban Affairs, Subcommittee on International Trade, Investment, and Monetary Policy, 98 Cong., 1 sess. (April 26, 1983).

to the public participations in the pool (similarly to the Federal Home Loan Mortgage Corporation). Countries in difficulty could convert their loans to consols (where principal is never repaid) at market interest rates. If they missed interest payments, the value of the loan would be marked down in the banks' book by 1 percent for each month's interest missed.

A different genre of proposals would provide insurance for new international lending rather than converting existing debt.[20] Some of these proposals seek to build on the relative popularity of export credit by developing new insurance vehicles based on existing official export credit agencies. Although insurance mechanisms warrant consideration, a fundamental question remains as to whether the public would be prepared to make available through insurance schemes funds that it is unprepared to provide in more traditional forms such as multilateral lending.

Evaluation of Radical Reform

Most of the proposals for sweeping debt reform share the following flaws.

Diagnosis

The proposals typically diagnose the current debt situation as unmanageable. In effect, they judge the developing countries to be insolvent, not just illiquid. But unless world economic conditions are depressed for the next three or four years, this debt should be manageable, as analyzed in chapter 3.

---

20. Financier Minos Zombanakis has proposed that rescheduling countries make 13-year agreements with the IMF, and that after 10 years a country unable to service its debt, despite complete adherence to the IMF program, would have its payments guaranteed by the IMF for years 11 through 13. However, the great uncertainty concerning country adherence to IMF programs for a decade, in light of the experience of difficulty of adherence even for months, raises considerable doubt that lenders would take such a program seriously, even if the IMF were prepared to accept such responsibilities. *The Economist* (30 April 1983), pp. 7–16. British ex-minister Harold Lever has proposed that the official export credit agencies establish an international agency to insure new bank lending, with IMF advice. He suggests large magnitudes of insured lending: $40 billion to $60 billion annually. *The Economist* (9 July 1983), pp. 14–16. William H. Bolin of the Bank of America and Jorge del Canto, formerly of the IMF, have similarly proposed a new Export Development Fund, loosely linked to the World Bank, to make long-term loans to developing countries for capital equipment imported from industrial countries. The loans would be guaranteed by the official export credit agencies of industrial countries. William H. Bolin and Jorge del Canto, "LDC Debt: Beyond Crisis Management," *Foreign Affairs* (Summer 1983), pp. 1099–1112.

Adverse Impact

Most of the proposals constitute a counterproductive, panic-based action that would tend to turn good debt into bad debt. Several of the schemes would tend to choke off new bank lending to LDCs. Few banks will be prepared to lend new money if the likelihood is high that such money will be subsequently mandated into a program requiring the loss of 10 cents on the dollar, or converted into a low-interest asset. This risk would exist for any bank subscribing to Kenen's International Debt Discount Corporation, because countries currently not suspected to be in trouble could subsequently sign up for the corporation's debt discounting. Perhaps even more important in the current context, *the transfer of bank claims from countries to an international agency would eliminate the incentive for new involuntary lending* as analyzed in chapter 4. Thus, banks holding claims on Brazil and Mexico are presently lending more to shore up the security of their outstanding loans. But if these claims were transferred to an international agency, this incentive for lending new money to Brazil and Mexico would disappear. Yet the choking-off of new loans would precipitate precisely the crisis that the authors of such proposals fear. Countries such as Brazil need more than a stretchout of existing loans: they need infusions of new loans to cover at least a major portion of the interest due on old loans. Most of the reform proposals would make sense only in an environment in which no new loans whatsoever are expected but maturities are being lengthened; they do not address the need for new lending.

Impact on Bank Capital

Several of the proposals appear naive in that they do not address their dire implications for bank capital. Even a 10 percent write-off of developing-country and East European debt would mean a 30 percent cut in capital for the large banks (or somewhat less, allowing for profits and tax effects). More ambitious debt relief such as Rohatyn's and Schumer's would quite likely cause bank losses to exceed capital.

Requirement of Public Capital

New international agencies would have to have massive capital to take over significant developing-country debt. If only half the approximately $700 billion debt were taken over, and if capital backing were full, and if paid-in capital were 10 percent of total, industrial countries would have to authorize contingent liability for $350 billion and actually pay in $35 billion to give an international agency capital backing to take over the debt. Such magnitudes are far beyond any contributions made to multilateral institutions in recent years. As for

Schumer's proposal, which does not involve an international agency, it is extraordinary in requiring an outright loss by banks, without providing them in return even the increased security that would be achieved by switching their claims from developing countries to an official entity.

Moral Hazard

The establishment of a new international entity to stretch out maturities of developing-country debt and reduce its interest burden would inevitably pose serious "moral hazard" problems of inducing changes in action that are to the self-interest of the debtor at the expense of the creditor and taxpayer. With such an entity in place there would be a strong incentive for any developing country to seek debt relief even when it would be possible with appropriate adjustment policies to continue to meet orderly debt payments. Such an incentive would result even from maturity stretchout, which would be less injurious (if at all) to banks; it would be extremely strong if in addition there were substantial reduction in the interest rate owed (by far the more damaging feature for creditors). It would be a structural flaw in the system to build in an incentive to debt-servicing disruption. It is for this reason that debt reschedulings have typically been carried out only when the alternative was imminent default.

Some of the specific proposals vary from the central theme of the Kenen-Bradley-Rohatyn-Schumer approaches but involve other difficulties. Bailey's exchange participation notes would seem unlikely to receive much acceptance in markets because of the limited credibility of being able to enforce a claim on a certain fraction of the country's export earnings. In the Gutentag and Herring approach, it is unclear why banks voluntarily would sell off sovereign loans at a deep discount as long as chances remained for greater recovery, and in the absence of a wide market for such sales it would be arbitrary for regulators to impose a low market valuation to which these assets would be marked. As for converting country loans to consols, it is unclear why countries should be given an infinite leash, even if the typical rescheduling leash of one to two years is too short.

Contingency Planning

Given the current outlook for the world economy and developing-country debt, it would be far better to have emergency plans in reserve than to set up sweeping new reform mechanisms that could make the problem worse than need be. The general strategy of contingency planning should be something along the following lines. Debt problems should continue to be handled case by case. When a country gets into trouble there should be negotiations between it and its private and public creditors. It is quite possible that some of the negotiated reschedulings already concluded will come unstuck, perhaps including one or more of the rescue packages arranged for the super-debtors.

If the conventional reschedulings and rescue packages are insufficient, the first line of defense would be to repeat the package but with an additional round of support from the key participants: private banks, industrial country governments (through such instruments as Federal Reserve swap loans, agricultural credits, and export agency loans), and the IMF. In even more extreme cases it may be necessary to have banks capitalize some portion of the interest otherwise due into additional principal due in future years. The national regulatory authorities could treat such capitalized interest as not causing classification of the loans as nonperforming, provided that there were a coherent, IMF-supported adjustment program. However, the banks in this case might appropriately set aside provisions for the amount of interest rescheduled, rather than reporting it as accrued income available for distribution to shareholders. In even worse cases, it could be necessary for creditors to enter some arrangement analogous to bankruptcy proceedings, whereby creditors would seek to collect only some fraction of the debt over a prescribed period.

The central point is that the resolution of such contingency cases would be addressed in a negotiating context case by case without setting up international machinery that would cause perverse incentives for unnecessary default.

One possible innovation that warrants consideration is the use of "zero coupon bonds" as an instrument for lending without imposing an immediate interest burden. Like US savings bonds, zero coupon bonds pay no interest until maturity. They are redeemed at a fixed, stated value and their initial sales price is discounted accordingly, so that they yield a market rate of return (but pay the return only at maturity). Zero coupon bonds have the merit of being a normal capital-market asset that would nonetheless accomplish the delay of interest payment to a later date when a country's external position is expected to be much stronger. The alternative of rescheduling interest on existing loans would accomplish the same economic effect but would raise problems of market psychology as well as of regulatory response.

The preferable use of zero coupon bonds would be as the vehicle for new loans to a country in difficulty. Thus, instead of making new loans to a country for seven years at annual interest of LIBOR plus 1½ percent (for example), banks could instead purchase zero coupon bonds from the country in comparable amounts.[21]

---

21. Because the bond would bear a fixed payment, this innovation would involve moving the banks back to the fixed-interest basis of their lending before the advent of variable-interest loans (linked to LIBOR) in the mid-1970s. Conceivably zero coupon bonds could be designed to bear variable interest, but for purposes of applying accepted capital market instruments it would probably be preferable merely to revert to bank assumption of the risk of interest fluctuation.

A less attractive alternative, but one that might have to be considered in more extreme circumstances, would be to convert existing loans into zero coupon bonds (technically, by simultaneously having the country prepay the loans and issue zero coupon bonds). The disadvantage of such conversion of past loans is that it would be extremely close to the deferral of interest on existing loans, a step that triggers classification of loans as nonperforming. Of course, it would be even better to remain with the normal types of bank financing; but as a contingency strategy, when the alternative might be moratorium, zero coupon bonds warrant attention.

Interest Capitalization and Forgiveness

Among the alternative contingency possibilities, by early 1984 it appeared increasingly that the most likely to be chosen (if any) was the capitalization or even relief of interest. Some banks, particularly in Europe, reportedly were beginning to argue that interest capitalization might be desirable (although again their tax incentive for such an approach must be kept in mind). Accordingly, this approach warrants special examination. Broadly, it would appear that although there are some advantages to interest capitalization there are more serious disadvantages.

The capitalization of interest, which is equivalent to rescheduling of interest, lessens the problem of free riders. Whereas the smaller banks might refuse to provide additional new lending, it probably would be more difficult for them to oppose the capitalization of some of the interest owed to them. They would merely be informed by the country and the lead banks that a specified portion of interest would be added to the principal of the loan due in the future rather than paid currently. However, even under these circumstances banks not wishing to go along might be able to cause difficulties for the arrangement by pursuing opposing legal action. Ironically, the capitalization or rescheduling of interest would be easiest when the banks in question considered it less onerous to accept a seeming fait accompli (interest capitalization) than to make new loans. Some smaller banks allegedly would be in this situation because of the reluctance of their boards of directors to take responsibility for making new loans to risky clients, even though in economic terms there would be little difference from making new loans (and, as developed below, the net result of interest capitalization could well be to expand bank exposure even more rapidly than under the regime of coordinated new lending).

The qualified advantage of circumventing the free-rider problem would come at a price. At an operational level, it would be necessary for a package of interest capitalization to receive the blessing of bank regulators. It is unclear what the position of regulators would be on this issue. A considerable body of opinion assumes that regulators might have to declare loans with capitalized interest subject to some form of loan-loss reserves. That is, when new loans are made simultaneously with the receipt of interst on old loans, both sets of loans are legally unimpaired. But the nonreceipt of interest on old loans might qualify them as not only nonperforming for purposes of interest accrual (in accounting terms), but also as subject to loan-loss reserves, even with an agreement to treat the interest as being added onto the principal (capitalized). The effect of imposing loan-loss reserves on loans to major debtor countries would be devastating to bank earnings (except perhaps in Europe where larger reserves have been set aside). However, it is also possible (and likely, if there were official support for this approach) that regulators could decide that such reserves were not required because the ultimate collectibility of the loans had not been impaired.

A second operational problem with interest capitalization is that the stock market could react adversely regardless of regulatory interpretation. Investors could decide that any loans requiring such extreme action must be worth considerably less than had been assumed previously. And although the price of bank stock is not directly a concern of public policy, further deterioration from already low levels (compared to normal price-earnings relationships with the overall market) would make it still more difficult for banks to improve their capital base, adding another element of instability in the financial structure.

These operational complications are not the most significant drawbacks to interest capitalization, however. It is the possible induced effect of this approach on debtor-country behavior that is potentially more serious. Interest capitalization could encourage the country not only to act more unilaterally but also to increase substantially the net rate of accumulation in its debt. As practiced in the first two years of the debt crisis, the process of involuntary lending (or, as official parlance has come to call it, "nonspontaneous lending") has retained a significant element of voluntariness, in the sense that banks still had to take the conscious decision to make new loans in the light of a proposed package of country adjustment. Shifting to the basic mode of interest capitilization would tend to erode this last degree of voluntariness in the lending process. Hundreds of banks would merely receive a cable informing them of their rescheduled interest payments instead of going through the decision-making process of making new loans.

Even the mechanics of interest capitalization, compared with those of continued new lending, would tend to lead to further loss of influence by banks over economic policy in the debtor country. At present the new bank lending is disbursed on a phased basis, typically quarterly. If country policy seriously deteriorates, banks can suspend disbursements (usually at the same time as a suspension of IMF disbursements). But under an agreement to capitalize a portion of the year's interest, it is unlikely that a counterpart to suspending disbursements would exist. Having made the decision to capitalize the interest, the banks would be without further influence over country policy during the course of the year, or even longer if the interest capitalizations were for a multiyear period.

The counterpart of the further decline in voluntariness of lending is that debtor countries would be tempted to take on considerably larger additional debt than could have been mobilized under the approach of coordinated (involuntary) new lending. Conceivably some form of IMF supervision could be designed to avoid this result (as discussed below), but the structural tendency of this approach would be in this direction. That is, if under the previous approach banks would have made new loans equal to half of interest due, under interest capitalization the country might seek to achieve net increase in principal exposure equal to the entire amount of interest owed (capitalizing all interest). But doing so would further postpone the day when the country's creditworthiness could be established, because future debt/export and debt-service ratios would be considerably higher than otherwise.

The case of Brazil provides an illustration. Consider the possibility that Brazil would over a five-year period capitalize all of its approximately $10 billion in annual interest.[22] If Brazil used the net resources thereby obtained to increase imports (and there would be little likelihood that authorities determined to capitalize interest would do so merely to follow a cautious strategy of building reserves), by the end of five years total debt would be nearly $50 billion higher than otherwise (increasing debt by approximately 50 percent). (While net additional debt accumulation would be less than the full $10 billion initially, considering that new lending would have occurred to pay part of the interest, an additional interest burden would accumulate on the more rapidly growing debt over the period.) By 1988 Brazil's debt/export ratio would be far above 200 percent instead of well below this important threshold as in the projections of this study (chapter 3). As a result, the return to creditworthiness and voluntary lending would be considerably less likely. Essentially, the problem is that achieving larger net increase in debt through interest capitalization merely postpones the problem of unsustainable debt burden into the more distant future.

It is possible that this effect could be avoided by having the IMF approve the amount of interest that would be capitalized as part of an overall adjustment package. Similarly, bank acquiesence in interest capitalization might be conditional on such an IMF-oriented program, to address the problem of unilateral country action. It might even be possible to have a mixed mode of new lending,

---

22. Professor Rudiger Dornbusch of MIT has proposed a program along these lines. His approach would involve a sharp devaluation, an incomes policy, and avoidance of further reductions in budget deficits. Rudiger Dornbusch, presented at a seminar held by Corporación de Investigaciones Económicas para Latinoamerica, Santiago, October 24, 1983.

whereby the larger banks would make new loans while smaller banks (and some European banks) would carry out the same proportional increase in exposure by capitalizing a portion of their interest.

Even with IMF orientation, however, the fundamental dynamic of greater unilateralism would seem likely to be present in negotiations once the general principle of interest capitalization were accepted. The drawbacks of unilateralism and temptation toward excessive debt accumulation might be mitigated but probably could not be eliminated through controls such as prior IMF approval. Through the first several months of 1984, moreover, the existing practice of involuntary lending appeared to be holding up, making the need for interest capitalization doubtful. Brazil successfully mobilized its $6.5 billion jumbo loan and Mexico its $3.8 billion credit from the banks. The uncertain gains of enforcement against the remaining small fringe of free riders hardly seemed to warrant the risks involved of a widespread shift to the mode of interest capitalization. Instead, this option seemed best left to the reserve of contingency mechanisms for reconsideration if the international debt situation once again took a serious turn for the worse.

A more extreme measure than interest capitalization would be the actual forgiveness of some portion of interest. Many critics contend that while the debtor countries have undertaken their fair share of the painful adjustment process, foreign banks have not done so, and that it is time for them to take losses, presumably in the form of granting interest rate relief that actually reduces the interest rate well below their cost of capital (a rate substantially below LIBOR). Even some US congressmen appear to hold this view (chapter 7). Without digressing to the ethics of burden-sharing (although it may be noted that by extending new loans under risk the banks do incur a burden, and in addition they have experienced declining stock prices), it is important to consider the possible benefits and costs to debtor countries and banks from interest forgiveness.

The basic dilemma in interest relief is that only a small amount of positive growth effects for debtor countries could be achieved by even crippling losses for the banks. This dilemma exists because the banks are leveraged institutions; most of the money they lend is not their own but borrowed, and modest reductions in their lending rates would cause substantial losses without major relief to the debtor countries.

Total debt owed by nonoil developing countries to foreign banks is approximately $330 billion (chapter 2, table 2.3). Reducing interest rates by half from, for example, 11 percent to 5.5 percent, would save approximately $18 billion on the annual interest bill. This amount corresponds to approximately 4 percent of the imports of goods and services (excluding interest) of the nonoil developing countries.[23] Accordingly, the level (but not the growth rate) of imports could

---

23. IMF, *World Economic Outlook*, 1983, p. 188.

experience a one-time rise of 4 percent if banks forgave half the interest on outstanding loans. If this gain were not to be reversed in subsequent years, this amount would have to be forgiven year after year for the life of the loan. Even if there were no adverse induced effects on debtor countries (through reduced lending, which almost certainly would occur), over a five-year period the average impact on domestic growth would be an increase in the growth rate of 0.8 percentage points, under the assumption that GDP is proportional to imports.

Even though cutting bank interest rates in half would at best provide a very modest increase to developing-country growth (0.8 percent over five years only), this amount of interest forgiveness would cause extreme damage to bank capital. It would sharply reduce the real value of the loan assets. Thus, a seven-year loan at 11 percent would lose 30 percent of its (present discounted) value if the interest rate were cut to 5.5 percent. If interest were entirely eliminated, the value of a seven-year loan would be cut in half. Yet with loans to developing and East European countries standing at nearly three times the capital of the large banks, a reduction of just one-third in the outstanding value of these loans would be sufficient to push these banks near to technical bankruptcy. It would seem a poor bargain indeed to bankrupt much of the banking system to purchase 0.8 percent additional growth in developing countries over five years.

But the bargain would probably be even worse, because there would be adverse indirect effects for the debtor countries themselves. Almost certainly even an agreed forgiveness of interest would cut off new bank lending to the debtor country. And a unilaterally declared cut or elimination of interest could prompt the cutting off of short-term trade credit and other retaliatory responses examined in chapter 4. In the former case, the decision to seek interest forgiveness would mean that the country expected to receive less new borrowing than its interest payments into the indefinite future, perhaps one to two decades. Yet while it is currently true that interest exceeds new lending, this condition seems unlikely to be permanent through the end of the century. Indeed, because historically more normal real interest rates would mean far lower nominal rates than recently experienced, it would be likely that by at least the 1990s new lending once again would exceed interest payments.

Banks have been expanding exposure in developing countries at approximately 5 percent to 7 percent annually since the outbreak of the debt crisis.[24] Because interest forgiveness would be likely to cut off all new lending, forgiveness of just half the interest would leave the debtor country no better off at all (assuming interest rates are in the range of 10 percent to 14 percent).

In sum, forgiving just half of the interest on bank loans would practically bankrupt the major banks but at best would increase debtor-country growth rates by only a small amount (less than 1 percent annually over five years)

---

24. IMF, *World Economic Outlook*, 1984, p. 18.

and, under more realistic assumptions, the net effects for borrowing countries would be much smaller or even negative because of induced cutbacks in new bank lending. The advocates of bank sacrifice through sharp reductions in interest far below the cost of money would appear not to have calculated the costs and benefits of such measures to the system and to the debtor countries themselves.

Interest forgiveness also raises issues of transfers. With interest cut in half or less, there would be a transfer from industrial countries to debtor countries. It is unlikely that the cost of this transfer could be limited to the shareholders of banks. Even if the losses did no more than exhaust the capital and equity of the banks, there would be adverse induced effects in the economies of industrial countries that would affect the population at large (even with skilled intervention by central banks). The public in these countries would be even more vulnerable to bearing the transfer costs if interest forgiveness were larger than the illustrative halving described above, because then the losses would exceed bank capital by a large amount.

The transfer from bank shareholders and the general public in industrial countries to debtor countries would not follow patterns normally associated with intentional transfers, because the principal debtor countries are not normal recipients of grant aid, which is limited to the poorer countries. The transfer would still be progressive (tending to reduce inequality of world income), of course, because citizens in the debtor countries are poorer than those in industrial countries. Practical adverse consequences rather than considerations of international equity are the reason for avoiding interest forgiveness.[25] The essential risk is that widespread interest forgiveness could cause such severe dislocations to the financial system and the world economy, and such permanent damage to the debtor countries' future ability to borrow, that both the aggregate economic effects and those for the debtor countries themselves would be adverse.

A balance must be maintained between interest relief and the need for incentives to new lending (chapter 4). Considering the likely effects of interest forgiveness reducing rates below the cost of money to the banks, the best strategy would appear to be the negotiation of lower spreads above LIBOR, particularly as progress toward adjustment is achieved. To go further to the radical measure of interest forgiveness would do long-term damage to the credit standing of the country. By contrast, squeezing spreads above LIBOR would be perfectly consistent with maintaining the country's long-term credit rating.

---

25. Similarly, pragmatic considerations of adverse effects warrant more attention than equity arguments such as the idea that recent interest rates have been usurious because they are far higher in real terms than those at the time the loans were contracted. This argument, incidentally, ignores the gains to borrowers from negative real interest rates in the 1970s (although it may be argued that those tempting rates themselves induced debtor countries into excessive borrowing).

To recapitulate, interest capitalization runs the risk of making the financing process even less voluntary, more unilateral, and biased toward overborrowing and excessive delay in the reattainment of creditworthiness. IMF supervision would be unlikely to eliminate these drawbacks entirely. Accordingly, the capitalization of interest should be avoided if possible and applied only as a contingency measure in extreme cases. The more radical measure of interest forgiveness would cause major damage to the banks, obtain at best only modest growth benefits for debtor countries, and more probably damage even these countries themselves because of the resulting long-term cessation in new lending.

A Balanced Strategy

The central conclusion of this study is that with reasonable recovery in the global economy, the problem of international debt should prove manageable and the degree of its current risk to the international system should decline. The adoption of appropriate macroeconomic policies to ensure global recovery is therefore important not only in its own right but also because of the debt problem.

The external debt situation clearly poses a potential risk to the international financial system. The nine largest US banks have nearly 300 percent of their capital exposed in loans to developing and East European countries. One of the two largest US banks has 74 percent of its equity capital exposed in Brazil and another 55 percent in Mexico. Approximately two-thirds of the value of outstanding bank loans to developing and East European countries is owed by countries that have experienced some form of disruption in their debt servicing within the last year. And even under the broadly favorable base-case outlook (chapter 3), capital flows of $75 billion to $80 billion annually will be required and countries accounting for one-fourth of total debt (primarily oil exporters) will experience deterioration in their debt-servicing burden.

Despite this systemic risk, a measured policy response is the best course. Overreaction by banks, public officials, or borrowing countries could make matters far worse. In particular, some of the more sweeping policy proposals for global debt reform could prove counterproductive.

The basic policy strategy recommended in this study is as follows. The root cause of the current debt problem is global recession. Country adjustment programs with IMF and other official support—such as the rescue programs for Argentina, Brazil, and Mexico in 1982–83—should continue to be the basic approach to interim management of the debt problem until the natural improvement associated with international economic recovery can take effect. Progress under the key rescue packages has been impressive to date, although in Argentina a potential impasse with the International Monetary Fund over an appropriate adjustment package posed a special (if temporary) threat to the basic international strategy of adjustment cum external financial support of illiquidity, not insolvency, and if sufficient financial packages can be arranged to tide over debtor countries temporarily, they should be able to return to a sound financial footing within two to four years.

However, some major borrowers are unlikely to be able to return swiftly to financial normalcy. Detailed debt projections applying a statistical model based on past debt reschedulings suggest that it may not be until 1985 that Mexico and Argentina can return to normal borrowing from the capital market, or until 1986 for Brazil. Until that time it is essential that continued new lending be extended by banks already exposed, although in relatively moderate amounts (such as 7 percent of exposure annually). Fortunately, the analysis of chapter 4 suggests that the banks have a strong incentive to continue lending, because modest new lending can ensure that their outstanding loans do not go sour.

To ensure new lending by banks already exposed, the "free-rider" problem, whereby smaller banks seek to avoid bearing their share of extra lending, should be addressed through moral suasion by central banks, pressure from large banks, and incentives by borrowing countries—possibly including subordination of loans of uncooperative banks.

It is central to this broad strategy that the official international financial agencies have sufficient means not only to address the problem but also to provide a psychological climate of competent international management of the debt problem. For this purpose the recent increase in the quotas of the IMF and resources of the General Arrangements to Borrow was a vital measure. Moreover, this increase was ultimately unaccompanied by threatened regulatory requirements that would have choked off new lending. The final version of the US legislation increasing the IMF quota appropriately rejected the more punitive measures contained in the earlier House version of the bill, such as a requirement to set aside reserves on all rescheduled loans.

More generally, bank regulatory overkill should be avoided. Regulatory reforms proposed by the Federal Reserve, Comptroller of the Currency, and FDIC, and incorporated in the legislation increasing US quotas in the IMF, strike the appropriate balance between increased prudence and excessive regulatory restrictions. It must be kept in mind that, because new international bank loans have fallen from $43 billion in 1981 to $26 billion in 1982 and perhaps less in 1983, the current problem is too little lending, not too much. It is misguided to see the debt problem as primarily the result of excessive or irresponsible bank lending; the analysis of chapter 1 shows the overwhelming role of exogenous shocks in the world economy in creating the current situation (oil price shocks, sharply higher interest rates, and declining export prices and volumes caused by global recession).

In the basic strategy of treating external debt problems as ones of temporary illiquidity rather than insolvency—meaning that public policy adopts temporary lending rather than write-offs or other actions analogous to bankruptcy proceedings—it must be recognized that there may nonetheless be new disruptions ahead. Policymakers should be prepared to deal with such contingencies, including large disruptions. The basic plan for such contingencies should be to remain in a negotiating process with the country. This process should in each case involve additional efforts on the parts of all parties: the country in its adjustment measures, the banks in their additional lending, and industrial country governments and the IMF in their support. In some cases the IMF may have to exceed its quota-based ceiling on loans to a given country (as it has occasionally done in the past, as in the case of Jamaica). Correspondingly, it is desirable that, under the new, higher level of IMF quotas, the country ceiling as a percentage of quota not be proportionately reduced (at least not fully), to permit some increase in the absolute amounts of IMF resources available to individual countries.[26]

It is essential to this strategy that the creditor-debtor relationship remain in a cooperative mode. Some of the largest debtor countries have large unused bargaining leverage because of their weight relative to bank capital. As long as the basic dynamics of negotiation are cooperative, however, debtors are unlikely to exploit this leverage because of longer run costs of damaging their creditworthiness. Indeed, each country's concern for its own creditworthiness should be a relatively secure safeguard against the emergence of a debtors' cartel with demands for concessional renegotiation.

For this general strategy to work, it will be important that official financing flows be as substantial as possible. Through the 1970s capital flows to developing countries were shifting in composition from official to private, with the result of shortening maturities and rising interest rates. The sluggish response of official lending and strong response of private lending to increased borrowing needs (driven by the oil shock and global macroeconomic conditions) caused this shift, but after the abrupt contraction in private lending associated with debt disruption in 1982–83, it is time for the pendulum to swing back again. Accordingly, the chances for the basic strategy to work will be increased if, in

---

26. At the annual meetings of the IMF in 1983, US officials proposed not only that the access to IMF resources be reduced as a percentage of quotas to offset the quota increase, but also that the access percentage be cut back even further in future years. In a compromise solution, the IMF's Interim Committee agreed to cut back normal access from 150 percent to 102 percent of quota (per year for three years), exactly offsetting the 48 percent rise in quotas; but it is also agreed that in individual cases of serious balance-of-payments problems the access ratio could be 125 percent. The compromise applied only to 1984, and was to be subject to review for subsequent years. *Washington Post*, 27 September 1983.

addition to the IMF quota increases, larger volumes of lending are provided through the World Bank and other multilateral financial agencies.

It would not appear essential to the strategy recommended here that new institutions be invented. As analyzed earlier in this chapter, proposals for stretching out debt and reducing its interest rate through a new international agency would probably be counterproductive, because the result would be to choke off new bank lending (even if the large requirements for public capital could be mobilized). Even a new vehicle for "bridge lending" prior to IMF agreements seems unlikely to be essential, because central banks can act on a case-specific basis (as they have done) when a large debtor country is involved, and if the country is small it can merely go into arrears without jeopardizing the system.

The greatest unknowns in this general strategy are twofold: will international economic recovery be sufficient, and will the political tolerance to austerity programs in developing countries be sufficient to provide time for adjustment measures to work? As is argued in chapter 3, the prospects seem relatively favorable that the critical threshold of 3 percent OECD growth in 1984–86 will be achieved, although additional macroeconomic policy changes would be desirable to help ensure this outcome.

With respect to political stability, analysts such as Henry A. Kissinger have warned against political breakdown in hard-pressed debtor countries.[27] So far, however, the political response in critical cases has been encouraging, as discussed in chapter 5.

Successful pursuit of the basic strategy outlined here should alleviate the severe economic recession that has hit the developing countries harder than any since the Great Depression. Largely because of debt and balance of payments pressures, economic growth rates are abysmal. However, under conditions of reasonable world recovery, the calculations of chapter 3 suggest that the major debtor countries should be able to return to growth rates on the order of 3 percent to 5 percent in 1984–86. Successful orchestration of the lending process outlined here will be a requirement for this outcome, however. Effectively managing the debt crisis will mean not only that jeopardy to the financial system and economies of the North is avoided but also that a return to crucial long-run growth in the South can be achieved.

Summary Recommendations

The analysis of this study leads to several concrete policy recommendations.

---

27. Henry A. Kissinger, "Saving the World Economy," *Newsweek,* 24 January 1983.

Strategy

Global economic recovery is essential. More expansionary policies would be desirable in key countries such as Germany, the United Kingdom, and Japan. In the United States, the massive budget deficit looming for several years should be reduced, paving the way for a monetary policy that can reduce interest rates and thereby avoid recessionary spillovers to the rest of the world and undue debt-servicing burdens for developing countries in particular. Similarly, a better fiscal-monetary match is required to reduce overvaluation of the dollar, which also aggravates the debt burden (chapter 3).

Sweeping debt reform, such as comprehensive programs to stretch out debt and reduce interest rate obligations, should be avoided as counterproductive. New forms of capital flows should be sought to replace declining bank lending in a context where large increases in offical lending will be difficult.

Official Capital

Efforts should nonetheless be made to increase lending through multilateral development banks, on an accelerated basis through structural adjustment loans instead of project loans. It was of paramount importance that the proposed IMF quota increase be adopted, and the approval of legislation for this purpose by the US Congress in November 1983 was a crucial, if belated, policy response. Substantial expansion of World Bank capital and lending by official export credit agencies should be the next major step in the response of official lending to the debt problem.

Trade Policy

Another longer term policy implication of this study is that it will be crucial to avoid new protection in industrial country markets against the exports of developing countries. The prospect of improvement in the relationship of external debt to exports hinges on growing exports from developing countries. If a wave of new protection depresses exports from levels they might otherwise be expected to attain as global recovery proceeds, the prospects for improvement in the problem of international debt will be much more bleak. Tighter import restrictions on textiles and apparel, sugar, and steel are among the disturbing signs of increased protection in industrial countries within the last two years, and these measures have affected the exports of developing (as well as industrial) countries. Nonetheless, industrial country markets currently remain relatively open to exports from developing countries, and this continued market opportunity will be essential for a favorable resolution to the debt problem. This fact must be kept in mind in all decisions concerning national policy response to new pleas for protection—at a time when protectionist demands are high because of high unemployment and (in the United States) an overvalued dollar that makes domestic production less competitive.[28]

Banking

The new banking regulations on foreign lending suggested by the Federal Reserve, Comptroller of the Currency, and FDIC, and embodied in the final IMF quota bill are appropriate. More restrictive banking regulations (such as the earlier House version of the bill, making all rescheduled loans subject to provisioning) should be avoided because of the severe risk of regulatory overkill that would restrict lending even more at a time when the need is for its recovery.[29] Country lending limits for banks should probably be avoided, although not because country lending is without risk. Lender-of-last-resort capacity should be strengthened by a joint agreement of offshore banking centers to require legally that foreign parent banks stand behind their subsidiaries. Serious consideration should be given to a much higher ceiling on the amount of loan loss reserves (relative to total assets) that may be set aside on a tax-deductible basis under US regulatory practice, to provide incentives for more adequate voluntary provisioning on loans to countries in protracted debt-servicing difficulty.

Private banks should continue new lending at modest rates to countries in adjustment. The IMF should continue its important new role of mobilizing bank lending actively. Central banks, large private banks, and borrowing countries should take measures to overcome the "free-rider" problem and ensure that smaller banks continue to lend as well.

The new Institute for International Finance should prepare country credit ratings as well as provide banks with information, in order to provide more discipline to the bank-lending process.

Rescheduling

Formal rescheduling should generally be relied upon rather than moral suasion unless the borrower is in a strong fundamental position, and reliance on

---

28. C. Fred Bergsten and William R. Cline, *Trade Policy in the 1980s*, POLICY ANALYSES IN INTERNATIONAL ECONOMICS 3, (Washington: Institute for International Economics, November 1982).

29. The final bill was not completely free of dubious amendments, however. It included the Schumer amendment calling for banks to reduce interest rates and stretch out short-term loans and to limit a country's debt service to 85 percent of exports, with US opposition to IMF loans to countries where such softening of terms does not occur. However, the provision is subject to waiver under "extraordinary circumstances." *Supplemental Appropriations Act*, PL 98–181, 1984, sec. 805.

interbank deposits as a form of indirect rescheduling is especially ineffective. Rescheduling for two years or even more is probably preferable to single-year reschedulings. While higher interest rates and fees in rescheduling probably facilitated rescheduling by helping mobilize bank support, such increases should be more modest than in the recent past because of political reaction in borrowing (and some lending) countries. There is considerable scope for reduction of spreads back to levels of, perhaps, one-half percentage point above the spread originally specified in the loan, especially for those countries that have made strong progress in external adjustment (although it should be recognized that the resulting relief for the debtor country would be modest in economic terms). In cases of breakdown in initial rescheduling packages, a contingency approach should be to maintain a cooperative creditor-debtor relationship and to make additional adjustments on the part of each party to the package.[30]

By pursuing the basic strategy outlined here and adopting specific elements recommended for its implementation, it should be possible for the international community to overcome the systemic strains posed by the debt crisis of 1982–83 and to restore more complete stability to the international economy.

---

30. For a discussion of related policy recommendations from the vantage point of mid-1984, and in particular the concept of a "cap" on interest rates to even out their fluctuation over time, see chapter 8.

8

Current Prospects for International Debt

The quantitative projections of chapter 3 were completed in April 1983 and first published in September 1983.[1] The book version of this study neared completion in June 1984, nearly two years after Mexico's suspension of payments had inaugurated the international debt crisis. By mid-1984, additional evidence had become available on the evolving process of international debt management. This chapter provides an early evaluation of the projections of chapter 3 by comparing them with actual experience in 1983. It also highlights the principal trends through the first half of 1984 in the economic dynamics of the debt problem and in the issues confronting policymakers.

In broad terms, actual experience through June 1984 tended to confirm the basic analysis and policy strategy set forth in the earlier chapters of this volume. In strictly economic terms, external deficits of major debtors in 1983 were far below the levels originally expected, indicating external adjustment ahead of schedule (although in part at the cost of serious domestic recessions). By mid-1984 economic growth in countries in the Organization for Economic Cooperation and Development (OECD) was running at a rate of 4 percent, well above the expected level of 3 percent. On the other hand, the dollar failed to depreciate in 1983 and again through mid-1984, and the interest rate began to climb again. The powerful influence of higher-than-expected OECD growth offset the strong dollar and higher interest rates, however; and, combined with a sharply improved 1983 base, these macroeconomic influences implied trends for 1984 and beyond that were at least as favorable as those originally projected (in chapter 3) for the major debtor countries as a group. Moreover, domestic economic recovery was beginning in the major debtor countries.

Political perception appeared to diverge from this emerging economic reality,

1. William R. Cline, *International Debt and the Stability of the World Economy*, Institute for International Economics POLICY ANALYSES IN INTERNATIONAL ECONOMICS 4, September 1983. An earlier public report of the results of the projections appeared in Lawrence Rout, "New Study Indicates World Debt Crisis May be Solved as World Economy Spurts," *Wall Street Journal*, 26 May 1983, p. 34.

however. Largely because of the lagged reaction to recessions in debtor countries in 1983, and because of frustration over the upward reversal in interest rate trends, by mid-1984 the political atmosphere was one of heightened concern among debtor countries about the viability of continuing to service their debt according to the new regime of rescheduling, adjustment, and coordinated lending that had prevailed since August 1982. The inability of Argentina and the International Monetary Fund (IMF) to reach agreement during the first half of 1984 further added to the sense of political erosion. Thus, a paradox dominated the international atmosphere on debt: underlying economic trends on balance were favorable while political perceptions seemed to deteriorate. This chapter traces these emerging economic and political trends, and, as a supplement to chapter 7, examines their policy implications.

Experience Through Mid-1984

From mid-1983 to the second quarter of 1984 the international economy experienced major improvement and the debt crisis showed important signs of amelioration. The most important development was the emergence of a strong international economic recovery. Industrial country growth of real GNP rebounded from −0.1 percent in 1982 to 2.3 percent in 1983 (year-over-year). Led by robust recovery in the United States, the industrial countries were widely expected to achieve real growth near 4 percent in 1984, a percentage point higher than in the base-case assumption of chapter 3.[2] The centerpiece for recovery from the global debt problem appeared to be falling into place.

Some major debtor countries also made dramatic external adjustments that were considerably greater than expected. Mexico had pledged in its IMF program to reduce its external deficit on current account (which includes interest paid) from approximately $5 billion in 1982 to $3 billion in 1983. Instead, Mexico achieved a current account *surplus* of $5.5 billion. Venezuela, which could have been expected to have a sizeable current account deficit in 1983, achieved a surplus of $5 billion. As discussed below, in the aggregate the large debtor countries experienced much lower external deficits in 1983 than projected in chapter 3. As a group their external adjustment was ahead of schedule.

The international economic environment showed other favorable signs in addition to the rise in growth in industrial countries. Commodity prices began

---

2. The International Monetary Fund anticipated 3.6 percent growth for industrial countries in 1984. Project LINK, an international group of academic forecasters based at the University of Pennsylvania, expected growth for the OECD countries to be 4.3 percent in 1984. IMF, *World Economic Outlook* (Washington, April 1984), p. 1 (hereafter referred to as *World Economic Outlook*, 1984) and Eric W. Bonwit, Lawrence R. Klein, et al., *Project LINK: World Outlook*, March 12, 1984 (Philadelphia, Pa.: University of Pennsylvania; processed).

to show improvement. For a broad range of commodities excluding oil, dollar prices rose by an average of 6.7 percent from 1982 to 1983 and by an additional 8.7 percent (for a total of 16 percent) through the end of the first quarter of 1984, after having declined by 25 percent from 1980 to 1982. The only exception to this trend was in metals; dollar prices of copper, iron ore, nickel, and tin were no higher by the first quarter of 1984 than they had been in 1982. In contrast, prices of beverage commodities and nonfood agricultural raw materials rose by approximately one-fourth from 1982 to the first quarter of 1984.[3]

Exports of nonoil developing countries rose significantly in 1983. The value of their exports to industrial countries rose by 12 percent. Their total exports rose 2.9 percent in dollar value and by 5.3 percent in volume, after having fallen in 1982 (by 4.7 percent in value, despite a rise of 1.7 percent in volume). This performance meant a rise in the share of nonoil developing countries in total world exports, which rose only 2 percent in volume (after a decline of 2½ percent in 1982). Moreover, it meant higher export growth than predicted by the general relationship of exports to growth in industrial countries applied in chapter 3, by which exports from nonoil developing countries would have been expected to grow by only 3.9 percent in volume. The improvement showed an accelerating trend, as export value for these countries rose by 5.2 percent from the fourth quarter of 1982 to the same period in 1983. For Latin America, the export turnaround was slower, as the dollar value of total exports declined by 1.2 percent in 1983 following a reduction by 8.5 percent in 1982. Brazil was an exception, however, as it achieved export growth of 8.5 percent.[4]

The external balance of the nonoil developing countries (including Mexico) showed sharp adjustment in 1983. After having surged from $42 billion in 1978 to $109 billion in 1981, the current account deficit of nonoil developing countries declined to $82 billion in 1982 and then continued to fall to $56 billion in 1983. This reversal was achieved by a reduction in the trade deficit from $83.4 billion in 1981 to $29.4 billion in 1983, achieved in turn wholly through a reduction in imports (from $412.8 billion in 1981 to $361.1 billion in 1983).[5] Given the major adjustment in current account deficits in 1982–83, the great bulk of the reduction expected in future years had already been telescoped into these two years. Thus, the ratio of current account deficit to exports of goods and services fell from 23.9 percent in 1981 to 12.6 percent in 1983, compared to a stable threshold of approximately 10 percent expected by

---

3. IMF, *International Financial Statistics*, May 1984, p. 73.

4. *World Economic Outlook*, 1984, pp. 6, 7, 180; IMF, *International Financial Statistics*, May 1984, p. 68; United Nations Economic Commission for Latin America, *Adjustment Policies and Renegotiation of the External Debt*, E/CEPAL/G.1299 (Santiago, 1984), p. 4; and Central Bank of Brazil, *Brazil Economic Program: Internal and External Adjustment*, vol. 2 (March 1984), p. 22.

5. *World Economic Outlook*, 1984, pp. 10, 189, 192.

the IMF beginning in 1984 and persisting through 1990.[6] The large adjustment made in 1983 meant that for 1984 and beyond the principal need was not for further increases in trade balances but rather for a parallel rise in both exports and imports, so that higher import levels compatible with reactivation of growth would be available without recourse to higher borrowing.

Even stronger signs of favorable external sector performance were evident in early 1984. In the first four months, nonoil exports from Mexico rose by 56 percent over the same period in 1983, and the trade surplus was running at an annual rate of $15 billion. In Brazil, manufactured exports were 68 percent higher in the first four months of 1984 than in the same period of 1983, and by June the cumulative trade balance surplus was $6 billion, far ahead of the rate required to meet the target of $9 billion for the year as a whole. Moreover, the domestic economies of both countries showed signs of recovery from their severe recessions of 1983. In 1984 industrial production was 3.8 percent higher than in 1983 in Mexico for the first quarter, and 2.2 percent higher in Brazil for the first six months.[7]

Despite many signs of improvement in 1983 and the first half of 1984, two negative factors had led to continued or even mounting concern about the debt problem. First, economic recession in 1983 had been severe in many major debtor countries. Nonoil developing countries experienced average growth of only 1.6 percent (following 1.5 percent in 1982). In Latin America real gross domestic product fell 3.3 percent, giving a cumulative decline in per capita income of 9 percent from 1980 to 1983.[8] It was unclear how soon significant domestic recovery could occur if import levels were to avoid sharp increases once again (although, as argued below, there is reason to believe that substantial growth rates can be established again with considerably lower ratios of imports to GDP than in previous years). The severe debtor-country recessions of 1983, combined with the lag in political perceptions, meant that in several countries the rhetoric insisting on some form of debt relief continued or escalated, even as exports began to rise and industrial production showed signs of a turnaround. The second unfavorable development was the rise in US and international interest rates, as the US prime rate reached 13 percent in the second quarter of 1984. Although much of the additional debt-servicing costs would be offset by higher export earnings associated with higher growth than originally expected

---

6. Ibid, pp. 9, 218.

7. News agencies as reported in *Daily Report: Latin America* (Washington: Foreign Broadcasting Information Service), 6 and 22 June 1984, p. M2; *Journal of Commerce*, 26 June 1984; *Financial Times*, 5 July 1984; and *Gazeta Mercantil*, International Edition, 25 June 1984.

8. *World Economic Outlook*, 1984, p. 1, and Naciones Unidas, Comisión Económica para América Latina (CEPAL), *Balance Preliminar de la Economía Latinoamericana durante 1983*, cuadro 1 (Santiago, December 1983).

in industrial countries (nations in the OECD), the reversal in interest rate trends served as a catalyst for escalation in debtor-country demands for more favorable terms.

Moreover, to some extent the abrupt reduction of external deficits in 1983 was attributable to reduced availability of financing; debtor countries had little alternative to lower deficits. Nonetheless, financing did not collapse. Bank exposure to debtor countries grew by an estimated 5 percent to 7 percent during the year, although the bulk of this lending was involuntary.[9] And of the $26 billion reduction in the current account deficit of nonoil developing countries from 1982 to 1983, approximately half was attributable to the unexpected surpluses run by Mexico and Venezuela, outcomes not caused by financing constraints.

In sum, experience through early 1984 showed the successful realization not only of expected international growth recovery but also of external adjustment by debtor countries. The dark side of this broadly favorable outcome was the rise in interest rates by the second quarter of 1984 and the severe recessions in debtor countries in 1983. Increasingly it was apparent that domestic economic recovery by 1984 or at the latest 1985 was likely to be a precondition for political viability of debt management.

Actual Versus Projected Performance

The availability of preliminary data on external sector performance in 1983 provides a basis for an initial evaluation of the validity of the projections set forth in chapter 3. Table 8.1 compares those projections with the actual economic outcome for the 19 largest debtor countries in 1983. The basic trend shown in the table is that external adjustment in 1983 was much more rapid than had been predicted, reinforcing the policy conclusion of this study that the debt problem is manageable. For these countries as a group, the actual current account deficit was approximately half as large as originally projected, giving an aggregate current account deficit of $23 billion instead of $50 billion for these countries in 1983.

The principal source of the unanticipated adjustment came on the side of reduced import values. Total imports for the large debtor countries were 12.4

---

9. *World Economic Outlook*, 1984, p. 11. For US banks, final data showed an increase of only 2.6 percent for end-1983 over end-1982 in exposure to Eastern Europe, nonoil developing countries, and five OPEC countries (Algeria, Ecuador, Indonesia, Nigeria, and Venezuela). For nonoil developing countries the rise was 3.5 percent, and if new lending scheduled for Brazil for late 1983 but received in early 1984 is included, the rise for nonoil countries was 4.6 percent. Federal Financial Examinations Council, *Country Exposure Lending Survey: December 1983* (Washington, 24 May 1984).

Table 8.1 Comparison of projected and actual performance, 1983 (billion dollars)

	Projections			
Country	Percentage growth	Exports	Imports	Current account
Brazil	−2.0	23.50	17.44	−7.13
Mexico	−2.0	19.18	14.43	−2.32
Argentina	2.5	8.82	6.18	−2.48
Korea	6.0	24.32	24.75	−1.72
Venezuela	−2.0	15.95	12.22	−4.36
Philippines	2.5	5.42	8.31	−4.11
Indonesia	2.5	18.58	17.14	−4.57
Israel	2.5	5.37	11.75	−6.82
Turkey	6.0	6.40	8.78	−1.38
Yugoslavia	2.5	11.52	14.99	−0.55
Chile	0.0	4.48	4.88	−3.91
Egypt	2.5	3.02	8.47	−2.56
Algeria	−2.0	7.26	7.70	−2.40
Portugal	2.5	4.53	8.92	−1.74
Peru	2.5	3.42	4.27	−2.26
Thailand	2.5	7.60	7.95	−0.51
Romania	6.0	13.24	11.89	0.41
Hungary	2.5	10.04	9.53	−0.96
Ecuador	2.5	2.38	2.61	−1.24
Total	2.07[a]	195.03	202.20	−50.60

Source: Chapter 3; *Gazeta Mercantil,* 5 March 1984; Banco de Mexico, *Indicadores Económicos;* CEPAL, *Balance Preliminar 1983;* IMF, *International Financial Statistics,* May 1984; Institute of International Finance; and selected estimates by experts of international financial agencies and foreign ministries.
a. Weighted by imports.

percent lower in dollar values than projected in chapter 3. Export values were also slightly lower than anticipated, by 0.8 percent. The continued rise of the dollar in 1983, rather than a decline as anticipated in the projections of 1983, played a role in the lower-than-expected values of both imports and exports. The real exchange rate of the US dollar on a trade-weighted basis rose by 5.8

Percentage growth	Actual		
	Exports	Imports	Current account
−3.3	21.90	15.41	−6.50
−4.7	21.40	7.72	5.55
2.0	7.71	4.56	−2.57
9.3	24.44	24.27	−1.60
−2.0	14.67	5.34	5.06
1.4	4.78	7.62	−3.10
2.0	19.60	21.10	−4.20
0.9	5.50	8.60	−4.00
3.0	6.21	8.39	−1.75
−2.5	10.16	11.45	0.26
−0.5	3.84	2.84	−1.09
7.0	3.60	8.70	−1.30
4.0	12.00	10.00	−1.80
−0.5	4.56	7.60	−1.70
−12.0	2.96	2.83	−1.34
5.8	6.35	10.20	−2.84
3.0	12.76	10.40	1.16
0.8	8.77	8.42	−0.31
3.5	2.30	1.63	−0.59
1.02[a]	193.51	177.08	−22.66

percent in 1983 instead of declining by 5 percent (chapter 3). Dollar prices of traded goods correspondingly declined (by 3.2 percent, as measured by the unit value of exports from industrial countries) rather than rising as anticipated.[10] The projection model assumed dollar-price increases of traded goods generally would rise in 1983 by 10 percent, from world inflation of 5 percent and dollar depreciation of 5 percent. Because dollar prices declined by 3 percent, the actual

10. IMF, *International Financial Statistics*, May 1984, pp. 458, 470. Note that the contrast indicates that prices of internationally traded goods appear to have risen by less than world inflation even without accounting for dollar depreciation. With industrial country inflation averaging 5 percent in 1983, the 5.8 percent rise in the dollar should have meant a decline of only 0.8 percent in dollar prices, instead of a decline by 3.2 percent.

nominal trade figures for 1983 could have been expected to be 13 percent below the projections of chapter 3. Thus, the real magnitude of 1983 imports was almost the same as that projected (12.4 percent lower in nominal terms, consistent with prices 13 percent lower than expected), while 1983 real exports were actually about 12 percent higher than projected (0.8 percent lower in nominal terms, in the face of prices 13 percent lower than expected).

In the aggregate, then, real imports in 1983 were almost identical to those projected and real exports were 12 percent higher; but falling instead of rising dollar prices made dollar values of imports well below predicted levels. Thus, the experience of 1983 suggests that in real terms the model applied here was accurate in the aggregate on the side of imports and conservative on the side of exports.

For an important subset of debtor countries, the decline in imports was considerably greater than anticipated. For the seven Latin American countries examined here, imports in 1983 were 35 percent below the level projected in chapter 3, a difference of 25 percent in real terms. Declining domestic growth and a return to less exaggerated import levels were the driving forces. In Mexico and Venezuela imports (in dollar values) declined by 46.5 percent and 59.4 percent, respectively from 1982 to 1983.[11] Compared to the forecasts here for 1983, actual imports were 46.5 percent and 56.3 percent lower for these two countries, respectively. In Mexico, part of the difference was attributable to lower growth than expected (−4.7 percent instead of −2.0 percent), but in Venezuela growth was −2 percent as predicted.

For the Latin American countries excluding Peru (where the collapse in growth was extreme), growth was 1.16 percentage points lower than projected (weighting by imports; table 8.1). On the basis of the cyclical elasticity of imports with respect to income used in the projection model (3.0), this divergence would imply real imports 3.5 percent lower than originally projected. Yet real imports were 25 percent lower than projected (as just described). Accordingly, import adjustment in Latin America in 1983 far exceeded the amount that could be attributed to reduced domestic income. Some of this unexplained reduction in imports was attributable to tighter protection and, in the cases of Mexico and Venezuela, limitations on availability of foreign exchange at the controlled exchange rate combined with an extremely costly free exchange rate. Nonetheless, it also seems highly likely that much of the reduction in imports reflected a return to less exaggerated levels than during the oil bonanza, for Mexico and Venezuela, and growing success in new import substitution (especially in Brazil). Thus, it is probable that future income recovery need not balloon imports up once again to their previous levels. The issue of structural reduction in import requirements is discussed below.

---

11. Banco de Mexico, *Informe Anual 1983* (Mexico City, 1984), p. 239; CEPAL, *Balance Preliminar 1983*, cuadro 6.

On the side of exports, only a portion of the additional real exports could be explained by OECD growth higher than expected. Industrial countries achieved growth of 2.3 percent in 1983 instead of 1.5 percent as assumed in the projection model.[12] Applying the marginal export elasticity of 3.0 and an average terms of trade elasticity of 1.5 in the first year, the additional 0.8 percent in OECD growth could account for 3.6 percent extra real export earnings, less than one-third the excess of actual over projected real exports for 1983.

The implications of these comparisons are as follows. First, with external deficits only half as large in 1983 as projected, external adjustment was taking place at an impressive rate, well ahead of schedule. Second, in real terms the model came extremely close to actual results for imports, and relatively close (11 percent below actual) for exports, suggesting general reliability of the model in the aggregate. Third, projected results are sensitive to assumptions about nominal values as driven by the dollar exchange rate and world inflation. And fourth, in individual countries large divergences can arise from projected values (Mexico, Venezuela). The broad thrust of these observations is that the 1983 results provide support not only for the model itself, but also for its qualitative conclusion that the debt problem is manageable.

Updated Projections

The availability of actual data for 1983 and the emerging evidence on likely trends in global macroeconomic variables provide the basis for new projections of balance of payments and debt. While the full range of analyses and sensitivity tests conducted in chapter 3 is unduly extensive for purposes of this chapter, it is appropriate to present a new set of base-case estimates to reexamine the central conclusions reached in chapter 3.

The projection model applied here is the same as that used in chapter 3 (as set forth in appendix B). The actual 1983 trade and current account balances, real exchange rates, and other values are applied for this base year, and thereafter debtor-country growth rates are as assumed in chapter 3 (adjusted basis).[13] For the macroeconomic assumptions, the updated projections apply the average between forecasts of the commercial firm Data Resources, Inc. (DRI), and project LINK.[14] These forecasts call for the following growth for industrial countries in 1984–86: 4.2 percent, 2.7 percent, and 2.4 percent. As

---

12. *World Economic Outlook*, 1984, p. 1.

13. Except for Korea, whose 1984–87 growth rate is set at 7.5 percent in light of its high 1983 growth.

14. Ron Napier, "The International Overview: A Most Unusual World Recovery," Data Resources, Inc., May 23, 1984; and Eric W. Bonwit, Lawrence R. Klein, et al., *Project LINK: World Outlook*.

in the base case in chapter 3, average growth is 3 percent annually. However, the expected time path involves considerably more robust growth in 1984, followed by some deceleration. To extend the projection period, the analysis here assumes 3 percent in 1987.

For 1983–87 as a whole, these assumptions imply the absence of a major recession over a five-year period following the recession of 1981–82. This performance implicitly assumes that the problem of the US budget deficit will be reduced to manageable proportions, and that the United States will not be forced into sharp recession either because of high interest rates or as a means of reducing its large external current account deficits. More generally, the average growth rate of 3 percent in 1983–87 should be attainable in the absence of oil shocks (which contributed heavily to the unusual severity of the 1974–75 and 1981–82 world recessions), on the basis of post-war experience. Nonetheless, a serious shortfall in OECD growth from this range would make a return to creditworthiness by distressed debtor countries much more problematical, as analyzed in chapter 3.

For interest rates, these forecasters anticipate a London Interbank Offer Rate (LIBOR) at 10.5 percent in 1984 (following 10 percent in 1983), 11.3 percent in 1985, and 10.4 percent in 1986. LIBOR is typically ¾ percentage point below US prime. By late June 1984 prime had reached 13 percent, and many observers expected it to rise further into early 1985. The projections here assume prime of 13 percent in the second half of 1984, 13.5 percent in the first half of 1985, 12.5 percent by 1985:III and a decline of ½ percentage point quarterly through 1986:II. The corresponding LIBOR rate applicable (with the six-month lag typical of international lending) is 10.5 percent for 1984, 12.5 percent in 1985, and 11 percent in 1986. For 1987 the DRI–LINK rate for 1986 is applied (9.4 percent), and a rate of 9 percent is assumed for 1988.

The projections here apply the DRI–LINK average inflation rates of 5 percent in 1984, 5.8 percent in 1985, 6.2 percent in 1986, and 6 percent thereafter. For the dollar, the two forecasters expect an average depreciation by 0.4 percent in 1984, 4.4 percent in 1985, and 3.8 percent in 1986. However, because of the large imbalance in the US current account for 1984–85, perhaps a more likely scenario is 10 percent depreciation in 1985 and another 10 percent in 1986 (although this depreciation could be concentrated in a short but sharp adjustment rather than phased in gradually over the two years). These values are used for the base case here, while the DRI–LINK depreciation forecasts are applied as an alternative case. However, in both cases the model is altered to apply a ratio of 0.8 (instead of 1.0) to obtain the increase in dollar prices caused by a dollar depreciation of 1 percent, making the expected depreciation of the dollar somewhat less powerful in alleviating the debt burden than in the calculations of chapter 3.[15]

---

15. Intuitively the parameter relating dollar price increase to dollar depreciation should

For oil prices, DRI projections call for stability at $29 per barrel in 1984–85 and $30 in 1986. Forecasts are not available from Project LINK. The DRI projections are approximately the same as those used in chapter 3 of the study, and for this chapter no change is made in those projections ($29 per barrel in 1984–85, $34 in 1986). Intensified hostilities between Iran and Iraq, including air attacks on oil tankers, had failed to increase oil prices by mid-1984, and many analysts anticipated continued weakness in the market despite uncertainty caused by the war. For 1987 the projections here assume that oil prices rise by 5 percent (to $36 per barrel), slightly below inflation. It should be noted that, because of dollar depreciation and world inflation anticipated through 1987, the price of $36 in that year implies a reduction by 18 percent in real terms from the 1983 level.

The projections here incorporate more detailed analysis for the four largest Latin American countries. Special treatment is warranted not only because of the central importance of these countries to the aggregate debt picture, but also because of major special circumstances that preclude unrefined extrapolation from the 1983 base. Thus, in both Mexico and Venezuela, 1983 imports were unsustainably low. Such extreme reductions are possible temporarily (through inventory reductions, for example) but not on a permanent basis. At the same time, imports in 1981 were at bloated levels as the consequence of the oil bonanza and exchange rate overvaluation.

To obtain the appropriate benchmark level for sustainable import levels, the ratio of real import values to real GDP was calculated for the period 1970–82.[16] The three years with lowest values of this ratio were chosen as indicative of the minimum import requirements characteristic of the period before the oil bonanza (for Mexico: 1971, 1977–78; for Venezuela, 1970–71, 1973). On the basis of these ratios, sustainable import levels were 38 percent higher than actual imports in Mexico in 1983 and 29 percent higher than actual in Venezuela. Using these hypothetical sustainable levels as the base for import calculations, the general model was applied to obtain new forecasts for these two countries.[17]

---

be less than 1.0 because for that portion of world trade composed of US exports, dollar prices would be expected to rise by much less than the amount of the depreciation.

16. From IMF, *International Financial Statistics, Yearbook 1983* and May 1984.

17. Other assumptions include the following. Domestic growth is 2 percent in Mexico in 1984, 4 percent in 1985, and 6 percent thereafter; in Venezuela it is 2.5 percent in 1984 and 4.5 percent thereafter. In Venezuela, nonoil exports grow at 15 percent annually in real terms from their extremely small base; interest earnings are $1.5 billion annually in excess of the amount calculated by the general model based on official reserves alone (reflecting the large role of foreign assets of the private sector and state firms, beyond official reserves, as is evident in detailed analysis of recent balance of payments data); service exports grow at 7 percent annually in real terms in response to a devalued exchange rate; and service imports in tourism and oil-related services grow at 3 percent annually in real terms while transportation services grow proportionately with imports.

For Brazil, an important structural change in oil imports requires adjustment from the standard model. Because of large increases in domestic oil production (and increased replacement of oil by alcohol), Brazil was expected to reduce its oil import requirements in 1984 by nearly one-fourth.[18] The oil import projections are premised on this reduced base. In addition, the projection here incorporates detailed forecasts for several individual commodities (including coffee and soybeans) in light of world market prospects, and adopts a more conservative elasticity of exports with respect to industrial country growth in light of new research on Brazilian trade.[19] Domestic growth is projected at 1.5 percent in 1984, 3 percent in 1985, and 6 percent thereafter.

For Argentina projections for individual commodity exports (beef, wheat, corn) assume that by 1985 terms of trade return to their 1971–80 average (excluding the exceptionally favorable years of 1973–74), and that export volume grows at 5 percent annually (with no additional response to OECD growth, considering the large weight of grain exports to the Soviet Union). Manufactured exports are assumed to grow at 4 percent in volume plus an elasticity of 0.8 times OECD growth.[20] An examination of Argentine imports indicates that although they declined by 54 percent from 1981 to 1983, the 1983 ratio of real imports to real GDP was still above those for 1976–78. Accordingly, imports are projected using the standard model, without upward adjustment in the base (unlike the cases of Mexico and Venezuela). Domestic growth is assumed to be 3.5 percent in 1984 and 5 percent thereafter.

The updated projections appear in tables 8.2 through 8.4. The dominant feature of these projections is that they retain through 1987 much of the sharp improvement in the external balance achieved in 1983, as the aggregate current account deficit of the 19 major debtor countries remains in the range of $30 billion—$40 billion rather than the range of $50 billion—$55 billion originally projected through 1986 (chapter 3). This continued lower deficit is achieved despite the assumption of restoration of adequate domestic growth in debtor countries by 1984 or, at the latest, 1985. The essential dynamics are that the strong OECD growth of 4.2 percent in 1984 boosts export earnings by a substantial amount (13 percent), permitting a sizeable rise in imports (15 percent) to accommodate higher domestic growth. Export earnings also rise

18. *Gazeta Mercantil*, International Edition, 23 January 1984.

19. For commodities the elasticity is set at 1.0, and for manufactures at 2.0, a parameter consistent with the estimate by Fishlow for noncoffee exports (1.83). Note however that no constant growth term is used here, so that the projected export growth rate is actually considerably lower than implied by Fishlow's statistical tests (which indicate a constant growth rate of 5.8 percent in addition to the impact of industrial country growth). Albert Fishlow, "Coping with the Creeping Crisis of Debt," (Berkeley: University of California, 1984; processed), appendix table A.

20. This elasticity is the long-run estimate found in Inter-American Development Bank, *External Debt and Economic Development in Latin America* (Washington, 1984), p. 134.

Table 8.2 Updated projections of balance of payments and debt, 1983–87
(million dollars and ratios)

	1983	1984	1985	1986	1987
Oil importers					
Exports	116,979	136,849	163,975	193,844	217,402
Imports	−119,762	−134,721	−156,833	−189,649	−210,058
(Oil)	−28,649	−26,869	−27,309	−31,680	−33,477
Interest	−30,021	−33,616	−39,768	−38,563	−36,880
Current account	−24,040	−21,220	−19,444	−20,023	−13,625
Debt	322,013	344,023	364,980	387,885	401,295
Net debt/exports[a]	2.05	1.86	1.63	1.45	1.32
Oil exporters					
Exports	76,529	81,066	86,995	102,545	111,262
(Oil)	51,334	51,334	51,334	60,185	63,418
Imports	−57,320	−69,491	−83,053	−99,256	−109,619
Interest	−14,643	−16,743	−19,374	−19,302	−18,956
Current account	1,376	−9,733	−20,705	−22,906	−24,396
Debt	199,232	209,167	229,758	252,409	274,947
Net debt/exports[a]	1.84	1.78	1.78	1.67	1.67
Total, 19 countries					
Exports	193,508	217,915	250,970	296,389	328,664
Imports	−177,082	−204,212	−239,886	−288,905	−319,677
Interest	−44,664	−50,359	−59,142	−57,865	−55,836
Current account	−22,664	−30,953	−40,149	−42,929	−38,021
Debt	521,245	553,190	594,738	640,294	676,242
Net debt/exports[a]	1.96	1.83	1.68	1.52	1.44

a. Exports of goods and services.

briskly in 1985 and 1986 (by 15 percent and 18 percent), as dollar depreciation adds a boost that compensates for the moderating OECD growth rate.

The updated estimates show smaller accumulation of debt through 1986 than estimated in chapter 3, with the total reaching $640 billion instead of $676 billion. Combined with a slightly higher dollar value of exports by 1986 (associated with slightly higher world inflation assumed), there is a modest improvement in the trend of the ratio of aggregate net debt to exports of goods and services: from 1.87 in 1982 to 1.52 in 1986, as opposed to 1.62 estimated before (tables 3.2 and 8.2).

It should be noted that the accumulation of debt in the updated projections is not as much smaller than that estimated in chapter 3 as would be expected from the reductions in current account deficits. The reason is that in the new projections, much more conservative estimates are applied for direct foreign investment. For the 19 countries as a group, direct investment is projected to average $5.8 billion annually in 1984–86 rather than the $11.1 billion in chapter 3.[21] Even the revised estimates assume considerable recovery of investment from the depressed levels of 1983. Correspondingly, the requirements for bank lending and official capital flows in this period are not as greatly reduced as the updated projections of current account deficits might imply.

For the oil-exporting countries, the net debt-exports ratio declines from a base of 1.77 in 1982 to 1.67 in 1986, instead of rising to 2.36. The much more favorable prospects for Mexico and Venezuela in the updated projections account for most of this change. For oil importers, the updated projections show more gradual improvement than in the original estimates. Their aggregate ratio of net debt to exports of goods and services declines from 1.94 in 1982 to 1.45 in 1986 (rather than 1.28 as projected in chapter 3) and to 1.32 by 1987. Delayed dollar depreciation and somewhat higher interest rates than assumed in the base case in chapter 3 account for the slower (but still strong) pace of improvement for oil-importing countries as a group.

At the aggregate level, the central implication of the updated projections is that they reinforce the judgement of chapter 3 that the debt problem is one of illiquidity, and not insolvency. The broad and pronounced trend in external balances and debt is toward improvement through the mid- and late-1980s. Major debtor countries should be able to reestablish their creditworthiness over this period, as their exports grow in an environment of international economic expansion.

Tables 8.3 and 8.4 report projections for individual debtor countries. As shown in table 8.3, the updated projections are much more favorable than the original estimates for Venezuela, substantially more favorable for Mexico, marginally less favorable for Brazil, and significantly less favorable for Argentina. The improvement for Venezuela and Mexico stems from the persistently lower level of imports, as analyzed above. For Brazil, although the updated export projections are modestly lower than before (especially in 1984 as the consequence of delayed dollar depreciation), and interest payments are higher because of a less favorable trend for LIBOR, considerable savings on oil imports approximately compensate (compare tables 8.3 and appendix table B-7). For

21. For Brazil, direct investment averages $1 billion in this period; for Mexico, $750 million; and for Argentina, $180 million. These estimates are considerably lower than those in tables B-6 to B-8.

Table 8.3 Updated projections of balance of payments and debt: four major debtor countries, 1983–87[a] (million dollars and ratios)

	1983	1984	1985	1986	1987
Argentina					
Exports	7,710	8,516	10,403	12,594	14,132
Imports	−4,564	−5,183	−6,498	−7,826	−8,710
Interest[b]	−4,979	−5,098	−6,205	−5,994	−5,549
Current account	−2,570	−2,612	−3,341	−2,426	−1,446
Debt	44,000	46,577	50,001	52,493	53,891
Net debt/exports[c]	4.86	4.65	4.08	3.52	3.21
Brazil					
Exports	21,899	25,713	29,469	34,978	39,341
Imports	−15,408	−16,220	−18,194	−22,695	−24,918
(Oil)	−8,400	−6,620	−7,060	−7,940	−8,340
Interest[b]	−9,600	−10,958	−12,999	−12,383	−11,471
Current account	−6,500	−4,528	−5,083	−4,365	−1,667
Debt	91,913	96,003	100,481	104,346	104,658
Net debt/exports[c]	3.66	3.22	2.94	2.55	2.27
Mexico					
Exports	21,399	22,630	23,611	27,775	30,006
(Oil)	16,002	16,002	16,002	18,761	19,699
Imports	−7,720	−11,418	−13,466	−16,187	−17,968
Interest[b]	−8,796	−9,526	−10,693	−9,912	−8,852
Current account	5,546	628	−1,982	−434	885
Debt	87,632	87,244	88,886	88,864	87,136
Net debt/exports[c]	3.08	2.84	2.71	2.30	2.06
Venezuela					
Exports	14,670	14,869	15,232	18,081	19,324
(Oil)	13,712	13,712	13,712	16,076	16,880
Imports	−5,340	−7,427	−9,400	−11,267	−12,480
Interest[b]	−800	−1,734	−1,958	−1,749	−1,470
Current account	5,060	1,810	−884	−667	−936
Debt	34,000	32,508	33,667	34,567	35,586
Net debt/exports[c]	1.46	1.32	1.33	1.15	1.11

a. Base case: dollar depreciation 10 percent in 1985, 10 percent in 1986.
b. Net.
c. Exports of goods and services.

Table 8.4 Updated projections of balance of payments and debt, selected countries, 1983–87 (million dollars and ratios)

	1983	1984	1985	1986	1987
Korea					
CA	−1,600	392	1,001	1,428	2,263
D	40,100	39,839	39,617	39,350	37,818
NDX	1.204	1.036	.838	.671	.556
Philippines					
CA	−3,100	−3,300	−3,152	−3,771	−3,747
D	24,600	27,693	30,589	34,119	37,414
NDX	3.085	2.854	2.501	2.409	2.369
Indonesia					
CA	−4,200	−7,200	−10,856	−13,608	−15,869
D	25,000	32,762	44,349	58,855	75,183
NDX	1.02	1.264	1.572	1.782	2.113
Israel					
CA	−4,000	−4,153	−3,879	−4,832	−5,177
D	24,200	28,592	32,735	38,000	43,444
NDX	2.338	2.297	2.158	2.153	2.215
Turkey					
CA	−1,750	−1,435	−832	−1,069	−958
D	17,000	18,526	19,468	20,793	21,823
NDX	2.056	1.983	1.676	1.508	1.406
Yugoslavia					
CA	260	−1,882	−1,500	−1,625	−1,254
D	20,500	22,992	24,971	27,256	28,921
NDX	1.313	1.251	1.104	1.001	.940
Chile					
CA	−1,090	−338	−107	−201	369
D	17,900	18,089	18,045	18,097	17,474
NDX	3.172	2.522	2.063	1.799	1.521
Egypt					
CA	−1,300	4	−38	−106	78
D	18,600	17,806	17,209	16,557	15,467
NDX	2.099	1.694	1.378	1.109	.909

	1983	1984	1985	1986	1987
Algeria					
CA	−1,800	−609	−1,429	−1,175	−753
D	15,400	15,682	17,036	18,119	18,558
NDX	.815	.768	.737	.651	.601
Portugal					
CA	−1,700	−2,548	−2,691	−3,158	−3,290
D	14,300	16,999	19,786	23,115	26,395
NDX	2.242	2.220	2.096	2.060	2.101
Peru					
CA	−1,340	−3,167	−3,834	−4,856	−5,512
D	11,800	15,113	18,868	23,632	28,947
NDX	2.827	3.093	3.216	3.578	4.030
Thailand					
CA	−2,840	−1,621	−1,312	−1,968	−2,016
D	11,000	12,369	13,652	15,605	17,380
NDX	1.024	.966	.839	.818	.817
Romania					
CA	1,160	1,454	2,209	2,789	3,760
D	8,400	7,268	5,445	3,232	−155
NDX	.588	.412	.229	.066	−0.093
Hungary					
CA	−310	−650	−757	−825	−461
D	8,100	9,078	10,191	11,479	12,232
NDX	.642	.606	.566	.525	.491
Ecuador					
CA	−590	−1,199	−1,682	−2,060	−2,290
D	6,800	8,052	9,742	11,814	14,070
NDX	2.398	2.507	2.678	2.815	3.067

CA current account; D external debt; NDX ratio of net debt to exports of goods and services.

Mexico, Brazil, and Venezuela the trend over time is unambiguously favorable, as the ratio of net debt to exports of goods and services declines between 1983 and 1987 from 308 percent to 206 percent in Mexico, 366 percent to 227 percent in Brazil, and 146 percent to 111 percent in Venezuela. Using a threshold of approximately 200 percent for creditworthiness, the 1987 estimates broadly indicate reestablishment of creditworthiness for all three countries (and by 1988 the ratio of net debt to exports declines further to 198 percent for Brazil and 183 percent for Mexico).

In Argentina the trend is also strongly positive. Nonetheless, more comprehensive estimates of outstanding debt raise its total to $44 billion at the end of 1983, and the actual export base of 1983 was smaller than anticipated. Accordingly, the ratio of net debt to exports in 1983 was extremely high (486 percent), and despite continued improvement over the next four years the projected level will still stand at over 300 percent in 1987 (versus 180 percent in the projections of chapter 3).

The results here generally confirm the conclusion in chapter 5 that Mexico and Brazil could return to voluntary lending by perhaps 1986 or 1987. In comparison with the estimates of chapters 3 and 5, the deficits to be financed virtually disappear for Mexico (except in 1985) and increase only modestly for Brazil. For Argentina, however, the updated estimates suggest that reconversion to voluntary lending may take longer. Nonetheless, the clear trend toward improvement in creditworthiness indicates that it should be possible to continue the recent process of rescheduling and extension of new, orchestrated bank lending for Argentina, even though the return to voluntary lending may be significantly delayed because of the higher relative level of indebtedness.

Table 8.4 reports updated projections for other major debtors individually. In general these estimates are similar to the earlier estimates (table 3.2 and appendix table B-2). The updated projections are more favorable than those of chapter 3 for Israel, Chile, Egypt, and Algeria. Sharp import adjustment in Israel and Chile had occurred by the updated base year of 1983 (table 8.1). For Algeria the original 1982 data base seriously underestimated actual exports in that year.[22] For Egypt, actual nonoil exports in 1983 were a much larger share of total exports than originally predicted, providing the base for larger export growth despite stagnant oil prices. The only significant cases of deterioration in the updated projections, compared to those of chapter 3, are for Argentina (discussed above), Portugal, and Peru. In both of the latter countries, however, special circumstances in the new, 1983 base suggest that over the longer term it may be more reliable to use an average of the original and updated projections than the updated forecasts alone.[23]

---

22. Because of sharp upward revisions in later issues of *International Financial Statistics.* Compare the issues of April 1983, p. 64, with June 1984, p. 78.

23. In Portugal, preliminary estimates indicate unusually low transfers (workers' remit-

The updated projections using more modest dollar depreciation (based on the DRI–LINK projections) are somewhat less favorable than the base case, but not fundamentally different in policy implications. (Chapter 3 discusses how a stronger dollar affects trade values and debt-export ratios.) From a 1982 base of 187 percent, the ratio of net debt to exports of goods and services declines to 151 percent by 1987 instead of 144 percent as in the base case of this chapter. The impact of a stronger dollar is minimal or even favorable for oil exporters (because oil prices are assumed to be independent of dollar strength). The erosion in improvement is concentrated among oil-importing countries, whose aggregate ratio of net debt to exports stands at 145 percent in 1987 in the strong-dollar case, instead of 132 percent in the base case (table 8.2). However, the clear trend toward improvement in creditworthiness of these countries still remains, even in the strong-dollar scenario.

For the largest debtors, the impact of smaller dollar depreciation is as follows. In comparison with the base case of this chapter, the stronger dollar causes the ratio of net debt to exports by 1987 to stand at 251 percent instead of 227 percent, for Brazil, and 334 percent instead of 321 percent, for Argentina, registering a modest deterioration. For Mexico there is a small improvement (197 percent instead of 206 percent), as is also the case for Venezuela (97 percent instead of 111 percent). In short, both in the aggregate and for major individual countries, the basic conclusion of a strong trend toward improved creditworthiness remains unaltered by the assumption of significantly smaller depreciation of the dollar.

In summary, updated estimates using actual 1983 data as the base confirm the conclusion of chapter 3 that for most major debtor countries the debt problem is manageable and will be alleviated over time as international economic recovery progresses. This confirmation is reached despite the adverse developments of somewhat higher interest rates and greater delay in dollar depreciation than originally anticipated. The higher than expected OECD growth for 1984, the sharp curtailment in 1983 of imports from an inflated base in Mexico and Venezuela, and the coming to fruition of major import substitution projects in Brazil (especially in oil), all contribute to the still broadly favorable outcome.

Alternative Studies

The debt crisis has prompted a wave of new research. It is beyond the scope of this chapter to provide a comprehensive review of this emerging economic

tances) in 1983; note, however, that the original 1982 base used for the projections of chapter 3 had overestimated exports of services. In Peru, the extreme change in income following the 12 percent decline in 1983 tends to give a sharp subsequent rise in imports (because of the high cyclical elasticity), and application of the ratio of service imports to goods imports based on 1983 tends to overstate future imports of services as a result.

literature on external debt. However, certain alternative studies warrant special comment because their general approach to the analytical problem of insolvency versus illiquidity resembles that of this study, and they provide a basis for comparison with the results found here.

As noted in chapter 3, studies by the Morgan Guaranty Bank and the Federal Reserve Bank of New York have come to conclusions similar to those of this study.[24] Both studies present projections of balance of payments and debt for major debtor countries, using models that take account of the same basic variables considered in this study (growth rate in industrial countries, interest rate, oil price, and terms of trade, although only one study includes the impact of dollar depreciation on dollar prices of traded goods). Importantly, both studies assume approximately the same average growth rate of OECD economies as that used in the base case in chapter 3 of this study, 3 percent in 1984 and after. The two studies show significant improvement over time in creditworthiness indicators such as the debt-exports ratio, reaching the conclusion that the debt problem is one of temporary illiquidity.[25]

A recent projection analysis by the staff of the International Monetary Fund also reaches conclusions similar to those of this study.[26] The IMF staff assume industrial country growth of 3.6 percent in 1984 and 3¼ percent in 1985–90, inflation of 4 percent in dollar prices, a reduction in nominal interest rates by 3 percentage points from 1986 to 1988, oil prices constant in real terms, and no improvement in developing-country terms of trade after 1984. Commercial bank exposure is assumed to hold constant in real terms (grow at 4 percent nominal rate) from 1985 to 1990, while direct investment is assumed to grow more rapidly. In this base case, the ratio of debt to exports of goods and services declines from 150 percent in 1983 to 124 percent in 1990, for all nonoil developing countries, and from 194 percent in 1983 to 150 percent for the 25 countries with the largest external debt at the end of 1982.[27] These estimates parallel the decline in the debt-export ratios projected in this study for the 19 largest debtor countries, from 196 percent in 1983 to 148 percent in 1987 (table 8.2). Moreover, the IMF calculations similarly find a reactivation of developing-country growth, to 4.6 percent annually in 1985–90 for the nonoil developing countries.

---

24. Morgan Guaranty Trust Co., "Global Debt: Assessment and Long-Term Strategy," *World Financial Markets* (June 1983), pp. 1–15; Ronald Leven and David L. Roberts, "Latin America's Prospects for Recovery," Federal Reserve Bank of New York, *Quarterly Review*, vol. 8, no. 3 (Autumn 1983), pp. 6–13.

25. Although the timing is modestly different; like chapter 3 of this study, Leven and Roberts find that by 1987 debt ratios characteristic of the late 1970s should be reestablished (p. 11), while Morgan Guaranty emphasizes that even by 1990 several major borrowers would still have debt-export ratios of 200 percent or higher (p. 10). Ibid.

26. IMF, *World Economic Outlook,* 1984, chapter 4 and Supplementary Note 7.

27. Ibid, p. 219.

Some observers have criticized the IMF projections as overly optimistic because of the assumptions of 3¼ percent OECD growth and a decline in interest rates by 3 percent after 1986. However, by past experience these assumptions are not unreasonable, considering that current real interest rates are extraordinarily high by historical standards. Moreover, the IMF model is conservative in its assumptions on terms of trade and in its omission of any impact of prospective dollar depreciation on dollar prices.

The IMF analysis does call attention to the subject of maturity bunching; for the 25 largest debtor countries amortization rises from 10 percent of exports in 1984 to 19 percent in 1987.[28]

In short, alternative studies by Morgan Guaranty Bank, the Federal Reserve Bank of New York, and the International Monetary Fund obtain quantitative projections similar to those in this study. However, another set of studies comes to less favorable conclusions. This group of studies includes those by the Brookings Institution, the Overseas Development Council, and the Inter-American Development Bank.

Enders and Mattione of the Brookings Institution apply country models of Data Resources, Inc., to project balance of payments and debt for major Latin American countries.[29] Although the authors make assumptions on international macroeconomic conditions similar to those of this chapter, they obtain considerably more pessimistic projections. From 1982 to 1987 the aggregate external debt of Argentina, Brazil, Chile, Colombia, Mexico, Peru, and Venezuela rises by 21 percent; the rise for these same countries (excluding Colombia) is a broadly comparable 19 percent in this study. However, the aggregate debt-export ratio for these countries declines only from 291 percent to 252 percent (seven countries) in Enders–Mattione, compared with a decline from 297 percent to 232 percent for these countries in this chapter (ratio of gross debt to exports of goods and services). The estimates here involve more rapid export growth in dollar value terms.

Nonetheless, the Enders–Mattione study does not differ widely from the conclusion here that Latin American external debt is manageable in terms of external adjustment, given declining debt-export ratios. Instead, the sharpest difference is in the estimation of Latin American growth. Enders and Mattione conclude that by 1987 real GDP will be only 5.6 percent higher than in 1982 for the seven Latin American nations, giving annual growth of only 1.1 percent.[30] In contrast, the rise of real GDP over this period for the six Latin American countries considered here (weighting by GDP) is assumed to be 14.2

---

28. For these countries, amortization rises from $35 billion in 1984 to $85 billion in 1987. Ibid, p. 70.

29. Thomas O. Enders and Richard P. Mattione, *Latin America: The Crisis of Debt and Growth*, Studies in International Economics (Washington: Brookings Institution, 1984).

30. Ibid, pp. 36–37.

percent (1982–87), for average annual growth of 2.7 percent (with negative growth in Brazil and Mexico in 1983 pulling down the averages).

The divergence stems wholly from extremely pessimistic growth forecasts in the Brookings study for Brazil (− 4.9 percent cumulative growth from 1982 to 1987, versus 13.6 percent here) and Mexico (6.6 percent, versus 13.6 percent). The authors project much higher growth for the other five major Latin American countries (averaging 19.4 percent cumulative). Yet this dispersion would not appear justified by the authors' own projections of external debt, which show the Brazilian debt burden not greatly different from that of other countries with much higher projected growth (Argentina, Chile) and the debt burden for Mexico considerably lower. Moreover, the growth forecasts for Mexico and Brazil, which were made in the second quarter of 1983, would appear to have been superseded by somewhat more favorable subsequent forecasts by DRI itself, which in the second quarter of 1984 expected cumulative growth from 1982 to 1987 to be + 1.4 percent for Brazil (instead of − 4.9 percent) and 8.3 percent for Mexico (instead of 6.6 percent).[31]

Another relatively pessimistic study has been prepared by the Inter-American Development Bank (IDB).[32] The IDB model assumes that industrial country growth averages 2.5 percent annually through 1990. It applies an export elasticity of 1.5, with real exports growing at 4.5 percent (including the effect of individually projected export earnings for principal commodities in each country). The model assumes that the ratio of imports to GDP returns from a depressed level of 10.6 percent in 1982–83 to 13 percent by 1990, still below the 1981 level of 16.4 percent. Import requirements are then driven by the assumed growth of GDP. International interest rates are assumed to average 11 percent and inflation 7 percent.

The results of the IDB model are not encouraging. If 1985–90 growth in Latin America averages 2.7 percent—meaning constant per capita consumption—external debt rises from $353 billion in 1984 to $429 billion in 1990 (a decline of 19 percent in real terms), the current account deficit is a small $8

31. Data Resources, Inc., *Latin American Review* (June 1984). Moreover, other commercial forecasters are less pessimistic. Wharton Econometric Forecasting Associates and DIEMEX–Wharton anticipate cumulative growth of +4 percent from 1982 to 1987 in Brazil and 10.9 percent in Mexico. [By communication.] With respect to the more modest differences between the present study and Enders–Mattione regarding external balances and debt, the chief difference appears to be the absence, in the latter, of any impact of dollar depreciation on dollar prices of traded goods. The elasticities of exports with respect to OECD growth do not differ significantly between the two studies at the assumed average OECD growth rate of 3 percent, as recognized by the two authors in the final version of their study. Enders and Mattione, *Latin America: The Crisis of Debt and Growth*, p. 37. Note, however, that the two studies differ somewhat more than is apparent on external sector projections. If the same domestic growth rates were assumed the divergence in projected external deficits would be greater.

32. Inter-American Development Bank, *External Debt and Economic Development in Latin America* (Washington, 1984), pp. 59–97.

billion on average in 1988–90, and the ratio of interest payments to exports declines from 35.8 percent to 21 percent. But in the higher growth alternatives permitting significant growth of per capita income (with GDP growth averaging 5.4 percent), the current account deficit for Latin America mushrooms to an average of $53 billion in 1988–90, debt rises to $617 billion by 1990 (an increase of 17 percent in real terms over the 1984 base), and the ratio of interest to exports declines by considerably less, to 27.3 percent by 1990.[33] The implicit finding is that the growth of 5½ percent will be unsustainable in the 1980s because of resulting external deficits that cannot be financed.

These results contrast sharply with those of the present study. Domestic growth for 1985–88 averages 5.2 percent for the Latin American countries here, approximately the same as the high-growth variant in the IDB study. Yet the external accounts estimated here do not careen out of control; instead, improved creditworthiness is generally achieved.[34] The chief differences in the two sets of results appear to be as follows.

First, the real growth rate of exports is considerably lower in the IDB study. For the four largest Latin American debtor countries, nonoil exports grow in real terms at an average rate of approximately 6 percent in 1984–88 in the present study. This growth rate is supported by Albert Fishlow's statistical estimate of 5.6 percent growth for real exports of oil-importing Latin American countries at industrial country growth of 3 percent.[35]

Second, the IDB makes no allowance for the impact of prospective dollar depreciation on dollar values of traded goods. This effect raises dollar export values by 8 percent in 1985 and another 8 percent in 1986 (base case), and while it also raises import prices, the overall impact is favorable (except for exporters of oil, whose price does not respond to the dollar) because the countries are in trade surplus and export gains exceed import increases.

Third, the IDB study assumes that the ratio of imports to GDP must rise by nearly one-fourth from its low 1982–83 base. But the analysis here of individual

---

33. Ibid, p. 71.

34. Thus, for 1988 (not reported here) the aggregate current account balance is estimated here as −$645 million for Argentina, Brazil, Mexico, and Venezuela, while the figure is −$38.7 billion in the high-growth variant of the IDB study. Ibid, pp. 74–80.

35. Albert Fishlow, "Coping with the Creeping Crisis of Debt," appendix table A. Note that the low export growth rate in the IDB study is partly attributable to a low elasticity with respect to industrial country growth. The IDB elasticity is approximately 1.5 over the long run but it involves lengthy lags and the initial-year elasticity is only 1.0. IDB, *External Debt*, p. 136. By contrast, the elasticities used in the studies initially reviewed above are: Federal Reserve, 1.7; Morgan Guaranty, 3.0; and IMF, 2.0. Ronald Leven and David L. Roberts, "Latin America's Prospects for Recovery," p. 8; *World Financial Markets* (June 1983), p. 9; and IMF, *World Economic Outlook*, 1984, p. 71. In this study the marginal elasticity is 3.0; at average OECD growth of 3 percent the average elasticity is 2.0; and some lower elasticities are used in the estimates for major Latin American countries, as discussed above.

Latin American countries indicates that only in Mexico and Venezuela were 1983 imports at unsustainably low levels relative to GDP, on the basis of 1970–82 experience. The IDB approach thus would appear to overstate the increase in imports required by GDP growth, especially in light of the large real devaluations that have taken place in the region.

In another study, Fishlow sees "merit" in the conclusion of projection models that diagnose the debt problem as one of illiquidity rather than insolvency, although he emphasizes export growth at rates higher than the interest rate as the essence of this distinction.[36] But Fishlow casts doubt on the reliability of a favorable debt outcome as global recovery proceeds. Doubting the assumption that dollar depreciation and OECD recovery can have an additive effect on export prices as large as assumed in my own model (chapter 3),[37] Fishlow reduces my 1984 increase in export earnings of oil-importing, major-debtor countries from 27 percent to 19 percent and finds that the effect is a more moderate decline in the debt-export ratio by 1986 than in the original projections.[38] However, as the new calculations of the present chapter indicate (including the alternative case with considerably smaller dollar depreciation in 1985–86), even the deferral and downscaling of dollar-depreciation effects do not alter the basic trends and conclusions identified earlier in this study. Moreover, the only evidence available on the debate so far—1983 experience—strongly points toward conservatism rather than excessive optimism in the calculations of this study, considering that actual 1983 deficits were only half as large as had been projected, and that this overperformance was only partially attributable to more severe domestic recession than expected (as analyzed above).

In sum, several recent quantitative studies provide additional evidence on the prospective path of developing-country debt. Certain of the studies generally confirm the estimates here. Others tend toward greater pessimism, although for the specific reasons cited they are perhaps less persuasive. However, it is important to recognize that all of these studies have a considerable common ground in terms of policy implications. They all show that the debt problem is substantially more manageable if growth in industrial countries is robust and interest rates are not excessive. And even the more pessimistic studies show a trend of at least some improvement in debt-export and interest-export ratios

---

36. Albert Fishlow, "The Debt Crisis: Round Two Ahead?" in Richard E. Feinberg and Valeriana Kallab, eds., *Adjustment Crisis in the Third World* (Washington: Overseas Development Council, 1984), chapter 1.

37. Although Fishlow presents no contrary theoretical argument, and his empirical example of experience in 1978 would seem to be biased by the sharp decline in coffee prices in that year for reasons unrelated to the dollar.

38. From the base level of 1.88 in 1983 to 1.54 in 1986, instead of the 1986 level of 1.28 estimated in chapter 3. Ibid, p. 43.

over time. The broad implication of this whole set of studies is that the debt problem is manageable as one of temporary illiquidity, with the caveat from Enders–Mattione and the IDB that debtor-country growth may be more stagnant than generally expected; and the admonition from Fishlow that the relief from dollar depreciation, terms of trade recovery, and OECD growth may be smaller (and the relative weight of interest rates greater) than generally assumed.

Emerging Issues

In mid-1984 as the international debt crisis approached its second anniversary, several issues were becoming dominant, some widely recognized and discussed and others, equally or more important, only faintly perceived in the policy debates.

Resource Transfer

One of the more fundamental issues is whether heavily indebted countries can or should make outward resource transfers, as assumed in the projections of this study. Thus, the Economic Commission for Latin America (ECLA) criticized the "perverse transfer of resources" whereby in 1982 and 1983 Latin America made payments of interest and profits that exceeded net capital inflow (including unrecorded capital flight) by $20 billion and $29 billion, respectively. It should be noted at the outset that in the absence of capital flight, these transfers would have been much smaller: $10 billion in 1982 and $22 billion in 1983. Thus, 35 percent of the net outflow of resources in 1982–83 was attributable not to interest payments to foreign creditors but to decisions of Latin American citizens to send capital abroad.[39]

The basic concept that must be recognized, however, is that for an interim period the excessively indebted countries must indeed make outward transfers of resources if their debt levels are to be reduced relative to exports and if their creditworthiness is to be restored, as noted in chapter 3. While it is true that the normal flow of capital is from developed to developing countries, and although the net flow of capital *principal* will still remain in this direction, for most of the 1980s the interest due on past debt is likely to exceed net new capital inflows.

This process need not spell domestic economic stagnation. Outward resource transfer means that exports substantially exceed imports. An increased trade surplus can occur painlessly to the extent that the external terms of trade improve, so that price movements rather than greater export quantities are

---

39. CEPAL *Balance Preliminar 1983*, p. 9; and Economic Commission for Latin America, *Adjustment Policies and Renegotiation of the External Debt* (Santiago, 1984).

involved. Ironically, the trade surplus can also come at relatively low cost to the extent that underemployed resources can be mobilized to increase exports; and there would appear to be considerable excess industrial capacity in Latin America today that could be used for exports or import substitutes. It should be recalled that Keynesian analysis points out that in the presence of idle resources, outward resource transfer is a benefit rather than a burden; in the national accounts equation, a larger trade surplus means a larger level of demand and resource utilization in the economy. And indeed, the expansionary effect of export growth is precisely the needed measure to prevent budgetary cutbacks and monetary restraint from causing recession for lack of aggregate demand. Nonetheless, much of the outward resource transfer will come at a real cost.

The level of the interest rate has a crucial influence on the size of the outward resource transfer required to restore creditworthiness. Consider a country whose debt-export ratio is 350 percent, and suppose the government seeks to reduce this ratio to 200 percent over five years (a case not unlike that of the heavily indebted Latin American countries). For this progress to be made, export growth must exceed debt growth by 12 percent annually.[40] For simplicity, and because 12 percent export growth (in nominal terms) is perhaps feasible but ambitious, assume nominal debt remains constant and exports grow at 12 percent. Zero growth in debt requires a trade surplus equal to interest payments (abstracting from noninterest services). In the third year of the period (for example), at an interest rate of 12 percent the trade surplus would have to be 30 percent of exports (or, imports would have to be 30 percent smaller than exports) to remain on the adjustment path. If instead international interest rates average 7 percent (for example, 4 percent for inflation, 2 percent real interest rate, and 1 percent spread), the trade surplus required to adhere to the adjustment path would be only 17.5 percent of exports (imports would have to be only 17.5 percent below exports).[41] Interest rates matter vitally; the Federal Reserve and the US government will bear major responsibility in the coming years for the required size of outward resource transfers from debtor countries.

Even with lower interest rates, however, some outward transfer of resources is likely to be required if heavily indebted countries are to reduce their debt-export ratios sufficiently to regain creditworthiness in this decade. The transfer would shrink to zero only if net capital inflows equaled interest. But this

---

40. That is, in this example the magnitude of exports relative to debt must grow by a multiple of 1.75 (or, 350/200) over 5 years, meaning a compound growth rate of 12 percent for exports relative to debt.

41. That is, after three years debt is still equal to 350 and exports equal 140 (having risen from 100 in the base year). With zero capital inflow (unchanged debt), the trade surplus must equal .12 x 350 = 42 or 30 percent of exports in the high interest rate case, but only .07 x 350 = 24.5 or 17.5 percent of exports in the lower interest rate case.

condition would mean that external debt would grow at the interest rate.[42] In the example above, where the debt-export ratio is 350 percent, an export growth rate of 12 percent would mean that it would take almost 12 years to reach the target debt-export ratio of 200 percent even at the favorable interest rate of 7 percent.[43]

The critics of outward resource transfers implicitly contend that sufficiently more financing should be available so that at the least the resource transfer is zero, but not negative. However, consider the consequences if this goal is achieved for Argentina, Brazil, and Mexico in 1984 through 1987. For these countries cumulative interest payments are projected to total $109.6 billion (table 8.3), for a cumulative net outward resource transfer of $77.6 billion (taking account of total current account deficit, private transfers and increased reserves). If instead their net resource transfers were zero, their total debt by 1987 would be higher by this amount, raising the ratio of net debt to exports of goods and services from a projected average of 234 percent to one of 313 percent. Instead of approximately achieving a threshold associated with credit-worthiness (200 percent) the three countries would remain at relative debt levels far above this target.

It is reasonable to ask, nonetheless, whether a more sustainable balance might be struck by accepting slower external adjustment in return for a smaller outward transfer of resources. As noted below, the balance might usefully have been shifted in that direction in 1983, when domestic recessions were severe. But the domestic growth rates postulated in the projections here (and consistent with their outward resource transfers) are already relatively robust for 1985 and after (in the range of 4½ to 6 percent annually). Because of "speed limits" on growth, higher foreign borrowing and lower outward transfer of resources would be likely to have only limited impact in raising growth further, and instead would tend to reverse the composition of growth away from tradables to nontradables.

Furthermore, because the outward transfer of resources is declining as a share of GDP, domestic absorption (consumption plus investment) can rise even faster than GDP. Thus, for Argentina, Mexico, and Brazil, the nominal dollar value of outward resource transfers is projected at $16.3 billion in 1984 and $22.2 billion in 1987. Allowing for world inflation and dollar depreciation, this outward transfer declines by 6.8 percent in real terms over this period, while

---

42. That is, interest payments, R, would equal: $R = iD_{t-1}$ where i is the interest rate and D_{t-1} is debt in the previous year. At zero resource transfer, net capital inflow, K, would offset this amount, or: $K = iD_{t-1}$. Thus, $i = K/D_{t-1}$. Considering that K is the increase in debt, this result means that debt grows at the interest rate.

43. As before, exports relative to debt must grow by a multiple of 1.75. However, with debt growing at 7 percent (because, by zero resource transfer, debt must grow at the interest rate), exports are growing only 5 percent faster than debt (rather than 12 percent), and it requires 11½ years, rather than 5, to achieve the target debt-export ratio.

real GDP rises by 16 percent for the three countries. In per capita terms, adding (or subtracting) real net resource transfers to (from) real GDP, domestic real absorption (consumption and investment) per capita should rise by 8.6 percent from 1984 to 1987, after having declined by 14.5 percent from 1980 to 1984, in the three largest Latin American debtor countries. Despite the decline in 1980–84, the future improvement should contribute to political viability of the debt strategy described here despite the pressure of net outward transfers of resources. Accordingly, it would seem more prudent to pursue the return to creditworthiness than to accumulate larger debt (and reduce outward resource transfer) over this period.

In sum, the heavily indebted countries would be risking a dangerous perpetuation of their excessive relative debt, and would postpone into the distant future the reestablishment of creditworthiness, if they sought to borrow amounts large enough fully to cover their interest payments and eliminate outward resource transfers, even if somehow sufficient international capital were available from private and public sources for them to do so.[44] These countries can either regain creditworthiness in the medium term or avoid outward resource transfer; they cannot do both. At great cost, these countries have already erred on the side of excessive borrowing in the last decade; it would be poor advice to recommend that they do so again in the remainder of this one.

Import Requirements for Growth

An underlying reason for the concern of critics who decry outward resource transfers is their explicit or implicit assumption that increased imports are critical to the resumption of domestic growth. While there is considerable truth to the assumption that import availability affects growth, it would be wrong to attach excessive rigidity to the relationship between the two.

As discussed above, in the major cases of Mexico, Venezuela, Argentina, and Brazil it is unlikely that the ratio of imports to GDP characteristic of the period 1979–81 need be restored to achieve future growth. Mexico and Venezuela had bloated import bills as the result of easy availability of foreign exchange at overvalued exchange rates during the oil bonanza. Because of its ill-fated attempt to use the exchange rate as an anti-inflationary device, Argentina had a severely overvalued exchange rate that encouraged excessive imports. In Brazil, major import substitution projects begun in the 1970s have now started to come on stream. The importance of increased domestic oil production has

---

44. This conclusion assumes that large amounts of new grants or concessional (low interest) loans will not be available to these middle-income countries, considering that despite their balance of payments difficulties they remain less poor than low-income Africa and Asia, and concessional funds are scarce.

been outlined above. Other sectors have shown comparable developments; thus, whereas Brazil imported 5 million tons of steel in 1974, it now exports 5 million tons annually.[45]

More generally, the issue of import requirements turns on the conceptual framework of the development model. For two decades the dominant model in this respect has been the "two-gap model" first proposed by Chenery and Strout.[46] In this model, the special characteristics of imports—their provision of raw materials and capital goods considered not to be available domestically—make them essentially a unique factor of production. In a programming approach, imports came to be treated as related to GDP by a fixed coefficient, and if the available imports were fully exhausted before other scarce inputs (domestic capital, labor, and national resources), imports were the "binding constraint" that set the upper limit on domestic GDP.

While the two-gap model has provided a useful framework for development planning, its basic insights must be supplemented with the recognition that changes in the price signals affecting imports can alter the import coefficient, especially over the medium term as time is allowed for reallocation of resources. Whereas the two-gap model implies that domestic recession is the only alternative when an external crisis reduces import capacity the literature has increasingly stressed that this "expenditure reducing" form of external adjustment is less desirable than "expenditure switching"—the reallocation of resources away from production of nontradables to the production of tradable goods and services.[47] Depreciation of the real exchange rate is the primary instrument for changing price signals to induce this reallocation of resources (expenditure switching). One consequence is an increase in exports, and therefore import capacity. But another is a reduction in import requirements per unit of GDP as import substitution replaces some imports by domestic goods and in addition the composition of demand shifts away from imports because of the increase in their relative price.

In policy terms the intense political reaction in debtor countries against domestic adjustment to the debt crisis has implicitly been based on the conceptual framework of expenditure reducing as the only basis for adjustment, identifying adjustment with recession. Underlying this view is the dominant two-gap construct which assumes a rigid ratio of required imports to GDP. But in the actual context of adjustment by major debtor countries today, it is clear that

---

45. Angelo Calmon de Sa, former minister of industry, trade and commerce, Brazil. Remarks presented at the Fourteenth Annual Meeting of the Latin American Association of Development Finance Institutions, Fortaleza, Brazil, May 18, 1984.

46. Hollis B. Chenery and Alan M. Strout, "Foreign Assistance and Development," *American Economic Review*, vol. 56 (September 1966), pp. 680–733.

47. See for example John Williamson, *The Open Economy and the World Economy* (New York: Basic Books, 1983), chapter 8.

expenditure switching already has begun to play a major role and is likely to be the principal vehicle for adjustment in the future. Reliance on expenditure switching makes possible adjustment without recession. It also makes possible the interim shift to outward transfer of resources needed to regain creditworthiness, without requiring the permanent recession that might be anticipated as the consequence in a more rigid two-gap framework.

Reliance on expenditure switching does pose the issue of its timing. It takes time for new investments in exports and import substitutes to take place and to achieve production results. During this interval external finance can help avoid excessive expenditure reduction and recession as the primary instrument for immediate external adjustment. The severe recessions in 1983 in Brazil and some other Latin American countries suggest that on balance the cutback in external finance was excessive relative to the ideal path of adjustment, which would have involved less immediate cutback in borrowing, less immediate expenditure reduction, and less initial recession, smoothing the transition toward adjustment through expenditure switching. However, this observation on the abruptness of timing in external adjustment in 1983 does not reverse the more fundamental point that, over the medium term, new borrowing must indeed be much lower than in 1980–81 and, probably, lower than interest payments.

Domestic Versus External Constraints

A related conceptual issue concerns the understandable tendency in debtor countries to blame domestic economic recession solely on the debt crisis even though other domestic constraints may contribute as well. By 1984 in Mexico, Brazil, and even Argentina, the external constraint had become sufficiently alleviated that the more serious constraint on growth was the need to bring down domestic inflation. With inflation running at over 200 percent annually in Brazil and nearly 600 percent in Argentina early in 1984, these countries faced a severe problem of economic stabilization even without considering the external sector (and, at least in Brazil, trade performance in the first half of 1984 was developing comfortably in excess of the trade balance target of $9 billion). By 1984 it was the need to reduce inflation, rather than a need to reduce imports still further, that required fiscal and monetary restraint, posing at least some short-run contractionary pressure on demand and growth (alleviated in an important degree by the demand stimulus from export expansion).

Ideal policies for reducing inflation without recessionary consequences are elusive, and the dearth of such policies even in industrial countries was the basic cause of the severe global recession of 1980–82. But the joint occurrence of the debt crisis and extreme inflation have led the public in several important debtor countries to attribute the full range of problems of domestic inflation and recession to the debt problem. Perhaps worse, this contemporaneous set of events tends to lead the domestic public to condemn measures essential for controlling inflation in the belief that they are being imposed by the International Monetary Fund for the purpose of adjusting to the debt crisis. Yet in Argentina, for example, expansionary fiscal and monetary policies in the face of hyperinflation would lead to ultimate economic collapse even abstracting entirely from the aspect of external debt.

In short, by mid-1984 it appeared more and more that domestic inflation, not the debt problem, was the central constraint on near-term growth, at least in Argentina, Brazil, and to a considerable degree Mexico. Correspondingly, the political appeal of calls for massive debt relief, while fully understandable, were based on erroneous perceptions about the potential impact that relief on the external sector could provide in a context of high domestic inflation as the main factor inhibiting growth.[48]

Interest Rate Pressure

The economic and political climate for external debt suffered a setback in the second quarter of 1984 when, within the space of a few weeks, the US prime interest rate rose by 2 percentage points to 13 percent. This adverse shift acted as a catalyst to unite the presidents of Argentina, Brazil, Colombia, and Mexico in a strong statement opposing the rising interest rate and calling for measures to lessen the debt burden (as discussed below). However, few commentators made the parallel observation that OECD growth of 1984 was rising strongly and above expectations, providing additional export earnings.

Because of its growing importance, the trade-off between benefits of additional exports from higher OECD growth, on the one hand, and additional costs from higher interest rates, on the other, warrants another look. In the model of chapter 3, 1 percent additional growth in industrial countries causes the following changes. In the first year, exports rise by 3 percent in volume and, on average, 1½ percent in terms of trade (with another 1½ percent on terms of trade delayed until the second year). On this basis, 1 percent additional growth causes 4½ percent additional export earnings in the first year.

In 1983, nonoil developing countries (including Mexico) had total debt of $668.6 billion. Of this amount, 31.7 percent was long-term debt owed to official creditors. Assuming that the rest was at floating interest rates tied to international

---

48. As a technical matter there is of course an impact of import availability and exchange rates on inflation itself. But with total imports on the order of 10 percent to 15 percent of GDP, even large external relief measures that might permit a rise of imports by, for example, one-fifth, would add only 2 percent to 3 percent of supply availability to the entire economy. With inflation of 200 percent to 600 percent, increased supply of this magnitude would be unlikely to provide a dramatic resolution of the inflationary problem.

interest rates, a total of $457 billion debt is interest-sensitive. These same countries had foreign exchange reserves of $76 billion in 1983, merchandise exports of $331.7 billion, and services exports of $115.5 billion.[49]

Applying the above OECD-growth elasticity to exports of goods and services, and the first-year terms of trade elasticity to merchandise exports alone, 1 percent increase in OECD growth would raise export earnings of nonoil developing countries by $18.4 billion in the first year. In contrast, 1 percent increase in LIBOR applied to $381 billion in interest-sensitive net debt costs the nonoil developing countries $3.81 billion additional annually. In the first year, each percentage point in OECD growth can compensate 4.8 percentage points on the interest rate. Considering that in 1984 OECD growth is likely to be higher by at least a full percentage point than projected in chapter 3 (approximately 4 percent instead of 3 percent), a rise of up to 5 percentage points in the interest rate could be accommodated with no change in net payments, well above the 2 percentage point rise by mid-1984.

Several caveats are in order. First, the effect of higher interest rates on commodity prices is not examined specifically (but should be already incorporated in the estimates of the impact of OECD growth on export prices); nor is their impact on the dollar (although they should delay its decline rather than strengthen it further—from 1983:IV to June 1984 the dollar rose only 0.4 percent while LIBOR rose 2 percentage points).[50] Second, for heavily indebted countries the relationship is less favorable. Brazil's debt-export ratio is approximately 2½ times as high as that for nonoil developing countries, so for Brazil the trade-off is approximately 1 percentage point in OECD growth for 2 (rather than 4.8) percentage points on LIBOR. On this basis the rise in interest rates to mid-1984 canceled most of the export gains from higher than expected OECD growth in 1984, in the case of Brazil. Third, the elasticities in chapter 3 are toward the favorable end of the range among various studies. If instead the elasticities estimated by the Federal Reserve Bank of New York are used (OECD growth elasticity = 1.7), and using Fishlow's estimates of the terms of trade response to higher OECD growth (an elasticity of 1.21 in the first year and 1.53 in the second), the first-year effect of 1 percent additional OECD growth is a rise of export earnings by $11.6 billion for nonoil developing countries.[51] The corresponding trade-off between OECD growth and LIBOR is 3.0 to 1 (instead of 4.8 to 1) in the first year. Even by this criterion experience to mid-

49. IMF, *International Financial Statistics*, May 1984, p. 38, and *World Economic Outlook*, 1984, pp. 189, 206–07.

50. *World Financial Markets*, July 1984, pp. 12–13.

51. Ronald Leven and David L. Roberts, "Latin America's Prospects for Recovery," p. 12, and Albert Fishlow, "Coping with the Creeping Crisis of Debt," appendix B.

1984 would show the export earnings gain from higher than expected OECD growth in excess of the extra costs of 2 percentage points run-up in interest rates, for nonoil developing countries as a group.

These effects are for one year only, however. If higher growth and higher interest rate scenarios are sustained over time (as in the contrasting cases in chapter 3), the favorable growth effect begins to dominate interest effects even more. The reason is that the growth rate effect is cumulative while the interest effect is approximately constant. That is, each year the export base grows from the OECD-growth elasticity by an additional layer above the original projection (although for its part the terms of trade increase is completed after the second year), while the higher interest rate continues to be applied to a debt base not greatly different from the projected level. As noted in chapter 3, for these reasons the model here finds that by the fourth year the relative power of 1 percent higher OECD growth compared to 1 percent change in LIBOR is even greater: 7 to 1, for nonoil developing countries (the ratio is similar using the Federal Reserve and Fishlow elasticities), and approximately 5 to 1 for Argentina and Brazil.

In sum, in the first year additional export earnings from an extra percentage point of OECD growth compensate for extra interest costs from 3 to 5 extra percentage points on LIBOR for nonoil developing countries as a whole, and by the fourth year the ratio is as high as 7 to 1. Accordingly, with industrial country growth in 1984 likely to be 4 percent instead of 3 percent, the extra interest costs from a 2 percent rise in interest rates by mid-1984 were likely to be more than offset by extra export earnings (and approximately just offset for the most heavily indebted countries). And this comparison concerns only the deviations from the original projections of underlying improvement (higher OECD growth, higher interest rates). Those basic trends toward improvement appeared, at mid-1984, to be on course. Thus, as illustrated at the beginning of this chapter for the case of Brazil, exports appeared to be rising far in excess of the prospective increase in interest costs. Nonetheless, the alarm of debtor countries over rising interest rates appropriately served notice that any further escalation of rates could become more burdensome in economic terms and frustrating to debtor countries in political terms. Furthermore, if high interest rates ceased to be the consequence of high OECD growth and became instead the cause of lower OECD growth, the combined impact on debtor countries would be severe.

Interest Cap and Contingency Lending

In the second quarter of 1984 the rise in US interest rates evoked an innovative proposal, primarily associated with Anthony M. Solomon, president of the

Federal Reserve Bank of New York.[52] This proposal would set a ceiling on interest rates on both new and rescheduled loans. If market interest rates then rose above this ceiling, the difference between the market rate and the ceiling rate would be added to the loan's principal due upon final maturity (that is, the increase in interest would be capitalized). If subsequently the market interest rate fell below the ceiling rate, the ceiling rate would continue to be paid and the difference from the market rate would be deducted from that additional principal that had been accumulated earlier as capitalized interest. Presumably, after that amount was exhausted, the interest payments would then move down paralleling the decline in market rates.[53]

The basic idea of this mechanism would be to average out interest rates over time. Any interest deferred during a period of increasing interest rates would be repaid during periods of lower rates. Considering that interest above the "cap" rate is capitalized for future repayment, not simply forgiven, and that the mechanism averages out the interest rate, it may be helpful to refer to this concept as the "reimbursable interest-averaging cap" (RIAC). This type of interest cap offers considerable relief from the cash-flow problems associated with temporarily higher interest rates. As shown in chapter 3, a surge of 5 percentage points or so in international interest rates can halt progress toward improved creditworthiness. If the interest rate surges for three years, for example, and then falls correspondingly below its initial level for the following three years, the debtor country may be forced into wrenching cutbacks in imports and growth in the first period, while being unable to recoup its losses fully by higher-than-average imports and growth in the second period. The underlying rationale of the RIAC is that it is cheap insurance against this sort of roller-coaster impact on the debtor country. Its cost would be expected to be especially low if it were adopted under conditions of mid-1984, when interest rates were extremely high and over a longer term period lower rates would be expected (unless there were a reemergence of persistent inflation at double digit levels). Importantly, because the amounts capitalized would be limited and would be set by a fixed rule rather than negotiation, this mild form of interest capitalization

---

52. As reported in *Journal of Commerce*, 10 May 1984.

53. A more extreme interest cap has been broached—but not proposed—by Henry C. Wallich of the Federal Reserve Board of Governors. Wallich has noted that loans could be treated such that any interest in excess of inflation plus a normal real interest rate would be capitalized. But with inflation of only 5 percent and a real interest rate historically at 3 percent, only 8 percent would be paid currently, and perhaps another 5 percent capitalized (under typical current conditions). Capitalization this large would classify the scheme in the family of major interest capitalization approaches, with the shortcomings (in this case, primarily inducement to greater imports and slower adjustment) discussed in chapter 7. Henry C. Wallich, "The Problems of the World Banking Community—A Central Banker's View," remarks at the *Financial Times* World Banking Conference, London, December 8, 1983.

would not suffer from the drawbacks of adverse induced changes in debtor-country behavior discussed in chapter 7.

A possible drawback of the interest cap in economic (as opposed to institutional) terms is that it makes no distinctions about the environment surrounding an interest increase. Implicitly it assumes all else remains unchanged. Historically, however, interest increases have tended to be accompanied by increased inflation. Considering that higher world inflation would tend to boost prices of the country's exports and imports, under such circumstances the need for additional financing might be less than implied by the interest increase (if the country were in trade surplus, so that export value rose by more than imports as the result of inflation). Or again, the situation of 1984 was one of higher interest rates caused in considerable part by high economic growth in the United States; and, as analyzed above, increased exports from higher-than-expected OECD growth seemed likely to equal or exceed increased debt servicing costs from higher-than-expected interest rates. The RIAC would tend to defer interest unnecessarily under these conditions. It would be the most helpful in the case of higher interest rates combined with no rise in inflation or OECD growth.

Operational and institutional questions would need to be resolved before the RIAC could become a reality. Regulators would have to be prepared to treat its deferred interest favorably, not declaring loans nonperforming and interest in arrears. The accounting profession would need to bless the mechanism rather than treating deferred interest under nonaccrual status. A judicious prognosis of stock market reaction would be required, to determine whether investors might have an adverse psychological reaction to the RIAC, fearing that any interest capitalization at all meant lower quality of the asset. Another institutional consideration is that the cap could distract attention of monetary authorities in industrial countries from the more basic need to reduce the underlying level of market interest rates, as noted by at least one prominent European banker.[54] And there is reason to believe, indeed, that a major reason for the appeal of the interest cap to Federal Reserve officials is that they anticipate possible future rises in the interest rate as the US recovery proceeds and the clash between private borrowing and heavy government borrowing associated with large fiscal deficits becomes even more pronounced.

As an alternative to the RIAC, it would be possible for the banks to undertake a commitment to contingency lending to be mobilized during periods of a surge in interest rates, with the expectation of a reduction of new lending once interest rates declined. If even 50 or 100 large banks internationally accepted such a commitment, much of the benefit of the more formal RIAC could be accomplished. Accounting and regulatory obstacles would probably be avoided

---

54. *Journal of Commerce*, 5 June 1984.

in this approach. Ideally the IMF would act as the coordinator of contingency bank lending, indicating the amounts required. This approach would also provide the flexibility for determining an appropriate amount of additional lending on the basis of a more comprehensive evaluation of changes in international circumstances (including inflation and world growth) rather than basing extra lending solely on interest rate increases.

The final choice between the reimbursable interest-averaging cap and contingency bank lending would depend on the credibility of mobilizing extra bank lending. Because many doubt the viability of involuntary lending more generally, contingency bank lending might inherently lack the psychological assurance provided to debtor countries by the more formal RIAC; and it might also be considerably less likely to circumvent the problem of free-rider banks.

Under the circumstances of 1984, a crucial benefit of either the RIAC or a new arrangement for contingency lending would be that such a mechanism would go a long way towards addressing the political frustration of debtor countries in the face of increasing international interest rates. The Cartagena consensus of eleven Latin American debtor countries (discussed below) called for some arrangement to lessen the impact of temporarily higher interest rates. Higher interest rates seemed to be the primary risk to the emerging scenario for successful debt-management, and public perceptions in hard-pressed debtor countries about the viability of continued debt servicing could be considerably improved if this risk were addressed.[55]

Ideally private sector efforts to help stabilize the cash flow of debtor countries in the face of interest fluctuation would be supplemented by official measures. The International Monetary Fund could initiate a mechanism of Compensatory Finance for Interest Fluctuation, analogous to its mechanism for fluctuation in export earnings.[56] While the IMF probably could not mobilize sufficient funds to bear the entire burden of such lending, it could finance a considerable portion of prospective fluctuations. Indeed, a commitment by the official community along these lines could be helpful in mobilizing banks to undertake a similar commitment.

Floating interest-debt of developing countries, net of reserves, is approximately

---

55. Ironically, the interest cap seemed not to be high on the list of objectives of at least the Brazilian and Mexican authorities. The President of the Central Bank of Brazil stated that it would merely postpone the burden of higher rates; and in the new round of Mexican negotiations at mid-1984 the cap was reportedly not on the agenda. *New York Times*, 24 May 1984; *Journal of Commerce*, 14 June 1984; and *Wall Street Journal*, 11 July 1984. It is likely that lower interest rate spreads are a higher priority because they provide a permanent gain for the debtors. However, the appeal of the RIAC or a contingency lending commitment would surely become much greater if the prospect of sizeable, additional interest increases were more imminent.

56. As proposed earlier in "Statement of William R. Cline," US Congress, Joint Economic Committee, *International Economic Policy*, Hearing, May 4, 1981, p. 64.

$380 billion, as noted above. The interest cap probably would not be appropriate for countries with no current debt-servicing difficulty. If, for example, half of interest-sensitive net debt were to be covered, a rise of 4 percentage points in the interest rate would require $7.6 billion in additional finance each year. If private banks provided half of this amount, the funds required for an IMF compensatory finance window for interest rates would amount to $11.4 billion over three years. This amount could be accommodated by the emergency fund in the General Arrangements to Borrow, perhaps supplemented by special borrowing from governments or even the private capital market. Implementation of the mechanism under the GAB would also be consistent with limiting availability of the mechanism to countries with debt-servicing difficulties and with IMF adjustment programs, in view of the new orientation of the GAB toward use for payments problems posing difficulties for the international financial system.

In addition, this new IMF facility could be designed to take account of any other offsetting international influences (such as inflation or growth) so that the net impact of higher interest rates (rather than their gross effect) could be the criterion for financing. Together with compensatory financing for export fluctuations, this instrument would give the IMF a broad capacity to finance temporary liquidity needs caused by international economic shocks.

Overall, a reimbursable interest cap as described here could be a useful innovation, and it warrants pursuit. It would help avert economic losses in debtor countries from temporary surges in the interest rate. It would avoid the need to obtain additional rounds of involuntary lending as the consequence of temporary increases in the interest rate; but it would also avoid the unfavorable incentives associated with broader interest capitalization schemes.[57] If institutional considerations preclude its formal adoption, an informal understanding by at least the major banks to increase new lending to offset increased interest rates (contingency lending) would be a helpful alternative. Moreover, the development of compensatory finance for interest fluctuation within the IMF would be a desirable parallel measure in the official sector.

Bank Confidence

Finally, a sobering development in mid-1984 was the nervousness in financial markets about the reliability of major banks. In May, Continental Illinois bank in Chicago experienced serious difficulty with large withdrawals associated with market rumors based on perceptions of its losses on, primarily, domestic energy and other corporate loans. The bank had been heavily involved in losses

---

57. This favorable judgment does not apply to schemes that would set ceilings far below market rates (requiring much greater capitalization), or (especially) to approaches that would simply forgive any interest above a specified ceiling.

associated with the earlier failure of Penn Square bank. Continental Illinois had relied heavily on volatile deposits by large foreign interests, which withdrew deposits as rumors mounted. A large support package from the Federal Reserve and major private banks calmed the financial run on Continental Illinois. But within a week investors staged a one-day siege on Manufacturers Hanover Trust, selling off its stock and avoiding its certificates of deposit, on the basis of unfounded rumors that the bank was having difficulty raising funds through normal channels. The widely cited reason for the market's nervousness about Manufacturers Hanover (which was in a considerably sounder situation than Continental Illinois in terms of problem loans) was that the bank was heavily exposed in Latin America and, especially, Argentina (table 2.1). And although the drain of withdrawals was stemmed from both banks, it appeared likely that a merger or other solutions would be required for the weakened Continental Illinois. Moreover, stock prices for several of the large US banks continued a decline to levels far below their normal relationship to the stock market averages. Many analysts attributed low stock prices to public perception that much of international debt was worth well below its book value.[58]

The reaction of the Federal Reserve in the case of Continental Illinois provided evidence that the Fed would not permit a financial run to cause a bank collapse, and US banking authorities even took the unusual step of pledging that large depositors not covered by insurance of the Federal Depositors' Insurance Corporation would not experience losses. But the market nervousness about large banks was a new factor that had to be taken into account in the determination of US monetary policy. Moreover, market apprehension appeared to linger for a long time. Immediately after the Contential Illinois and Manufacturers Hanover episodes in late May 1984, the spread between interest paid on bank certificates of deposit and US Treasury bills rose from its normal level of approximately 50 to 60 basis points (hundredths of a percentage point) to 172 basis points; and by mid-July the spread remained at 163 basis points, indicating continued pressure for "flight to quality" in the security of government financial assets.[59] Erosion in market psychology was also potentially a factor in ongoing negotiations with major debtor countries. On one hand, it might make some major debtors more cautious about statements that could disturb markets. On the other hand it could lead other major debtors to believe that their negotiating position was strengthened because the US banking system was too vulnerable to risk an extreme confrontation.

---

58. *New York Times*, 25 May 1984, and *Wall Street Journal*, 8 June 1984. In early June 1984, stocks of the money-center banks sold for an average price-earnings ratio of 4.5, compared to the stock market average of 10.7. Ibid. Normally these bank stocks carry a price-earnings ratio of 85 percent of the stock market average, on the basis of discussion with bank stock analysts.

59. *Wall Street Journal*, 25 May 1984; 12 July 1984.

Trends in Negotiations

By mid-1984 the process of international debt management stood at a juncture of acute divergence between the positive emerging performance on external adjustment and heightened political perception of crisis. At the economic level, as set forth above, the recovery of external equilibrium and progress toward renewed creditworthiness was well ahead of schedule. But in some dimensions the political environment involved escalation of crisis perception and undertones of a possible drift toward confrontation.

Two phenomena seemed to lie behind this paradox. First, political perceptions involved long lags, and the painful domestic recessions of 1983 were being translated into increasingly frequent political statements in international forums on the need for debt relief, even as modest signs of domestic economic recovery in 1984 within debtor countries began to appear. Second, the brisk rise in US interest rates in the second quarter of 1984 served as the catalyst to mobilize the political leaders of major Latin American debtor countries into joint expressions of a need for change. In turn, statements favorable to the improvement of terms came from banking leaders, the International Monetary Fund, and chiefs of state at the London summit conference.

Calls for debt relief had already been frequent in preceding months. Thus, in Quito, Ecuador, at the Latin American Economic Conference in January 1984, Latin American countries called upon creditor banks, governments, and agencies to share the responsibility for the debt burden through debt negotiations consistent with recovery in domestic economic growth. In addition to reduction of spreads and commissions, and longer maturities, the Quito Plan of Action advocated the limitation of debt servicing to a "reasonable" percentage of export earnings, such as 15 percent to 25 percent. Furthermore, it recommended that interest rates be reduced to levels below commercial rates, in exchange for new official guarantees placed on the debt by existing or new international agencies.[60]

A more dramatic evolution of the institutional and negotiating framework occurred in late March 1984, when, to enable Argentina to bring interest payments within the 90-day limit that determines whether US banks can continue to accrue interest arrears into earnings, Mexico, Venezuela, Colombia, and Brazil extended an unprecedented loan of $300 million to Argentina. Although the US Treasury pledged a back-up bridge loan in this amount that would become available once Argentina reached an agreement with the International Monetary Fund through a letter of intent (permitting reimbursement of the four other Latin American nations at that time), the initiative was novel for its coordinated action among Latin American nations. Importantly, it

---

60. Latin American Economic System (SELA), "Renegotiation of Latin America's External Debt: Prospects for the Implementation of the Quito Declaration and Plan of Action" (Caracas, 1984; processed).

marked a vivid statement of support of these major debtor countries for the lending process rather than the long-feared formation of a debtor's cartel designed to carry out coordinated default. Indeed, adverse spillover from Argentina's difficulties onto Mexico's efforts to mobilize its $3.8 billion in new loans from the capital markets appeared to play a major role in prompting Mexican leadership of the initiative.

Latin American cooperation on debt entered a new phase in May 1984 when, primarily in response to the rapid rise in US interest rates, the presidents of Argentina, Brazil, Colombia, and Mexico issued a joint statement condemning higher interest rates and protectionism, and calling for a meeting of foreign and economic ministers of the four countries.[61] Eventually the ministers of 11 Latin American nations participated at this meeting, in Cartagena, Colombia, in June 1984.

The presidential statement reflected political frustration that adjustment efforts were being offset by adverse international economic developments (although, as analyzed above, the statement made no corresponding reference to export gains from higher international growth). Significantly, by explicitly naming the foreign ministers as parties to the forthcoming meetings, the statement signaled a shift in gravity from dominance of the issue by the more pragmatic economic ministries to the more political foreign ministries. The declaration seemed to be a step toward making the debt problem a "political issue" (an increasingly common call that, nonetheless, tends to ignore the fact that debt is primarily owed to the private sector, not governments).

The four-country initiative seemed unlikely to lead to a radical shift in debt strategy, however. Of the four participants, Mexico, Brazil, and Colombia were in relatively favorable positions in terms of successful management of external debt. Indeed, Venezuela—the other logical party in view of its participation in the March loan to Argentina—refused to participate in the declaration, apparently in the belief that its strong position on international reserves placed it in a different situation that would not be helped by association with a statement that might be interpreted as a drift toward radicalism.

Moreover, there was evidence that at least some of the economic ministers in question considered the debt problem to be manageable. At virtually the same time as the declaration of four presidents, the Brazilian Planning Minister Antônio Delfim Netto presented to the Brazilian congress an upbeat analysis of success in external adjustment, which included projections of future recovery.[62]

---

61. "Joint Presidential Statement Calling for a Meeting of Latin American Foreign Ministers and Financial Authorities to Discuss the International Debt Crisis," Embassy of Argentina, Washington, May 19, 1984. The presidents expressed their "concern that the hope for the development of our peoples, the progress of the Democratic tendencies of the region and the economic security of our continent are being seriously undermined by facts that are foreign to our countries and beyond the control of our governments."

62. The analysis pointed out, among other considerations, that domestic production of

An important objective of the presidential statement was to lobby the industrial nations prior to the June 1984 London summit conference to take action on global debt and on interest rates in particular. The lobbying effort had at least some impact, as the summit leaders included in their communique the recommendation that for debtor countries that had taken "successful efforts to improve their positions there should be more extended multiyear rescheduling of commercial debts" and similar arrangements for the debt owed to governments.[63] The summit leaders adhered to the "case by case" approach to debt problems that they had adopted in their meeting a year earlier. They took no decisions, however, that would address the more fundamental macroeconomic issues, including high international interest rates and an overvalued dollar in particular.

At the same time, both the International Monetary Fund and the leading private banks were voicing expressions of the need for accommodating adjustments in the terms of lending and rescheduling. Jacques de Larosière, managing director of the IMF, called for commercial banks to reschedule over "a longer time frame" for countries that have made progress in adjustment but face heavy amortization schedules. He also advocated improved terms on interest rates for countries that have demonstrated good performance and reduced the risk involved in lending to them.[64] For their part, major private banks publicly stated their intention to negotiate longer term solutions to the debt problems of Mexico and perhaps Brazil, including significant reductions in interest rate spreads as well as rescheduling in advance of maturities falling due for perhaps up to five or six years.[65]

The actual outcome of the Cartagena meeting of ministers from Latin American debtor countries was one that provided reassurance that the countries had no intention of forming an aggressive debtors' cartel for default. At the same time, however, the Cartagena consensus set in motion a series of periodic meetings and review by these countries that represented an open-ended possibility for evolution of debtor cooperation. It also set forth a list of proposals that, on the whole, were relatively pragmatic.

---

petroleum and its substitutes had risen from 16 percent of consumption in 1979 to 60 percent in 1984. The document concluded that "Today there is a consensus that even under relatively pessimistic hypotheses, appropriate management of its economic policies will enable Brazil to obtain significant economic development as well as order in its external accounts." Secretária de Planejamento da Presidência da República, "CPI Da Divida Externa e do Acordo FMI/Brasil," Depoimento do Ministro-Chefe Antônio Delfim Netto (Brasilia, 10 May 1984); processed, pp. 5, 8.

63. *New York Times*, 11 June 1984.

64. *IMF Survey*, 18 June 1984, pp. 180–81.

65. *New York Times*, 6 June 1982; *Journal of Commerce*, 14 June 1984.

The Cartagena consensus[66] called for: international policies that would reduce interest rates; a shift in reference rates to the cost of capital to banks; reduction to a minimum in loan spreads above cost and elimination of commissions; temporary mechanisms to reduce the impact of high interest rates, including a new IMF facility; improved terms of lending through longer maturities and grace periods, and, for some debtor countries, multiyear rescheduling. The countries agreed that treatment of debt should depend on each country's specific circumstances. In extreme cases, consideration should be given to deferral of part of interest, on a noninterest-earning basis, to be repaid subsequently with a specific proportion of increased exports. The group called for: an end to creditor demands that private sector commercial risk be transferred to the public sector; more flexibility on the part of financial regulatory authorities in industrial countries; increased resources for international agencies, and a new allocation of Special Drawing Rights. The meeting enjoined the IMF to shift toward greater priority on production and employment, exclude external interest rate shocks from fiscal targets, and adjust monetary targets when required by unforeseen increases in inflation. It called for the World Bank and the IDB to increase program lending and accelerate disbursements. The group advocated more favorable terms on reschedulings of loans from foreign governments, and it called for elimination of trade barriers in industrial countries as well as efforts to stabilize commodity prices. In all, the proposals bore the imprint of finance ministers more interested in concrete results than in dramatic declarations.

The overall effect of these developments in May–June 1984 was a distinct shift in the negotiating climate, toward greater politicization and, conceivably, aggressiveness on the part of the major debtors, and toward greater accommodation (but always within the framework of a market-related solution rather than debt forgiveness) on the part of the banks, Western governments, and the IMF. The seeming drift of the negotiating environment in the direction of the debtor countries was reflected by Argentina's insistence in negotiations with the IMF on substantially raising domestic real wages; and even in the willingness of Bolivia to declare formally a four-year extension of its de facto moratorium as a condition for ending domestic labor strikes.[67]

The emerging strategy of banks and international financial institutions at mid-1984 appeared to be one of rewarding those countries with good economic performance while strictly resisting pressure to provide new financial support without strings attached to countries with poor performance. The implication was that it was necessary to confer some tangible reward in the form of more favorable terms to provide positive reinforcement for adherence to adjustment

---

66. As reported by international press agencies. *Daily Report: Latin America* (Washington: Foreign Broadcast Information Service), 25 June 1984, pp. A1–A5.

67. *New York Times*, 12 June 1984; *Journal of Commerce*, 31 May 1984.

programs. Such a reward would not only strengthen the hand of economic policymakers in the well-performing debtor country but also, perhaps more importantly, would serve as an incentive for other countries to bring their own economies into more successful adjustment programs to qualify for similar improvements in terms. This nascent "rewards" strategy had not yet evolved to the incorporation of mechanisms for "punishment" of noncooperating countries. However, the willingness of Manufacturers Hanover and other banks to accept reductions in reported profits on interest in arrears on Argentine loans, rather than make major new loans in the absence of an IMF program, was a signal of a move in the direction of negative reinforcement for poor performance.[68]

At mid-year 1984, Argentina posed the most serious uncertainty for the continued functioning of the international mechanism for dealing with debt problems. That mechanism, as developed over the preceding two years, contained as an integral part the condition of agreement between the International Monetary Fund and the debtor country on the country's adjustment program. Without an IMF program, new bank loans were not provided, placing in jeopardy the continued servicing of interest on old loans. Yet through the second quarter of 1984, Argentina had not reached agreement with the IMF. The Argentine government released announcements implying that its demand for an increase in real wages by 6 percent to 8 percent was not negotiable. Yet this strategy appeared incompatible with the need to temper a virulent inflation running at nearly 600 percent annually.[69]

---

68. Regulatory changes in June 1984 provided that loans would go on a non-accrual basis immediately after 90 days in arrears on interest, rather than at the end of the quarter in which that event occurred. This measure promised to defuse the tense negotiating context at the end of each quarter caused by having the concentration of non-accrual decisions at that time. Although the new practice was not mandatory until the third quarter, most banks that were not already using this approach adopted it in the second quarter. Overall, the impact of nonperforming Argentine loans on second quarter profits was limited, reducing these profits by 22.5 percent for Manufacturers Hanover, 12.6 percent for Chase Manhattan, 5 percent for Citibank, and 6.2 percent for Morgan Guaranty, from levels that would have been achieved otherwise. *New York Times*, 18 July 1984; *Washington Post*, 20 July 1984.

69. *Wall Street Journal*, 15 June 1984. The government's insistence on continued real wage increases was understandable from the standpoint of its political pledges but more questionable on economic grounds. At least some measures suggested that the rise in real wages had already reached the limits of prudence in view of the risk of accelerating inflation. Primarily because of rapid wage increases in the last quarter of 1983 as labor and business anticipated a possible wage freeze, by January 1984 average real wages for industry were 45 percent higher than in May 1983, and 15.5 percent higher than their previous peak in 1974 even though real per capita income had declined by 13 percent from 1974. Calculated from Fundación de Investigaciones Económicas Latinoamericanas, *Indicadores de Coyuntura*, Abril 1984, pp. 35, 42; Alejandro Foxley, "Stabilization Policies and Their Effects on Employment and Income Distribution: A Latin American Perspective," in William R. Cline and Sidney Weintraub, eds., *Economic Stabilization in Developing*

At the beginning of the third quarter of 1984 it remained unclear whether a compromise could be worked out between the IMF and Argentina. The greater likelihood remained that some agreement would be reached, even if after significant delay, because the incentive to do so was great for all parties. There was also a growing possibility, however, that Argentina could enter a financial limbo as banks declared its obligations nonperforming and, subsequently, even value-impaired (requiring the setting aside of loan-loss provisions). If such a situation could be confined to Argentina (in addition to a handful of smaller countries such as Bolivia), the damage to the financial system would remain tolerable.[70] However, in the unlikely event that political considerations led Mexico and Brazil to follow Argentina—in this already less than likely scenario for Argentina itself—the dimensions of stress on the financial system would escalate to much more dangerous levels (as examined in chapter 2).

More generally, the Argentine case potentially raised a basic issue in the system-wide management of debt: could an important debtor be "quarantined" if it reached an impasse with the international financial community, so that its actions would not precipitate a chain reaction that would include other major debtors? The emerging system of rewards and (possibly) punishments might help achieve such a quarantine. Nonetheless, domestic political attitudes in several countries (including Brazil, Peru, and others) were sufficiently volatile that it would be far safer to avoid testing the quarantine hypothesis. Early in the third quarter of 1984 there was evidence that the Argentine government was beginning to take anti-inflationary measures and that it might be moving toward agreement with the IMF.[71]

The Lost Decade

As analyzed above, the emerging evidence by mid-1984 indicated that, at least on economic grounds, the major debtors were successfully on or ahead of

---

Countries (Washington: Brookings Institution, 1981), p. 202; and IMF, *International Financial Statistics*, various issues. More fundamentally, it is doubtful that the government could in fact achieve a target increase in real wages by rapid escalation of nominal wages; instead, inflation would be likely to accelerate still further, frustrating the wage increases.

70. At the end of 1983, the nine largest US banks had $5.35 billion outstanding in exposure to Argentina, or 17 percent of their capital. Federal Financial Institutions Examination Council, "Country Exposure Lending Survey: December 1983." If these loans were all on a nonaccrual basis, the reduction in earnings would be approximately $640 million (assuming 12 percent average interest), or 11.6 percent of 1982 before-tax profits. If in addition 10 percent of face value were set aside into loan loss reserves, the total reduction in earnings would rise to $1.18 billion. Even in the more severe case the effect would be a reduction of about one-fifth in before-tax profits, not enough to cause structural damage to the banks (as long as the Federal Reserve acted to stem any bank runs that might be prompted by the adverse psychological impact).

71. *Journal of Commerce*, 6 July 1984.

Table 8.5 Real GDP per capita in selected countries, 1980–90
(1970 = 100)

	1980	1983	1990	Average Per capita growth (percent) 1970–80	Average Per capita growth (percent) 1980–90
Country					
United States	122.3	123.7	144.0	2.0	1.6
United Kingdom	119.0	125.9	147.2	1.8	2.1
Germany	130.2	130.0	153.8	2.7	1.7
France	135.0	136.2	157.1	3.1	1.5
Italy	128.0	127.9	148.0	2.5	1.5
Japan	144.2	156.4	198.5	3.7	3.2
Average,[a] six industrial countries	128.9	132.7	158.0	2.6	2.0
Brazil	178.5	160.0	184.5	5.9	0.3
Mexico	138.4	131.0	153.7	3.3	1.1
Argentina	109.2	94.7	117.5	0.9	0.7
Venezuela	110.8	99.1	111.7	1.0	0.1
Chile	108.3	92.9	109.6	0.8	0.1
Peru	105.5	89.5	102.0	0.4	−0.3
Philippines	141.0	141.8	161.7	3.5	1.4
Korea	192.1	241.7	358.9	6.7	6.4
Average,[a] eight developing countries	152.6	147.2	179.3	4.1	1.3
Average,[a] seven developing countries[b]	147.8	135.7	157.4	3.8	0.7

Source: IMF, *International Financial Statistics, Yearbook,* 1983 and June 1984.
a. Weighted by population.
b. Excludes Korea.

schedule in carrying out external adjustment to the debt crisis, and that they were poised for a return to domestic economic recovery as well. However, this assessment should not obscure the fact that the early 1980s had been a period of profound disruption to their domestic economic growth, in considerable degree because of their debt problems.

The losses in growth in this period set back the major debtors so far that even with return to substantial growth in 1985–90, the 1980s as a whole seem likely to be a lost decade in terms of economic growth for the major debtor countries that have been in debt-servicing difficulty.

Table 8.5 presents data on real per capita GDP for 1970–90, in the form of index numbers and average growth rates. Data through 1983 are actual results. For 1990 the projections are based on the assumptions used earlier in this chapter.[72] For the major industrial countries, these data indicate that by 1983 per capita income was only 3 percent above the 1980 level; but for seven major debtor countries that have experienced debt-servicing difficulties (that is, excluding Korea in the table), 1983 per capita income was 8.2 percent below the level in 1980.

For the decade 1980–90 as a whole, the poor start through 1983 combined with the assumed recovery for the rest of the decade will mean average growth in per capita income of only 2 percent for industrial countries, compared to 2.6 percent in the decade 1970–80. But for the troubled debtor countries the slowdown is much more severe: from 3.8 percent per capita growth in 1970–80 to 0.7 percent in 1980–90. At this rate the entire progress of the 1980s will amount to no more than two years' growth at rates of the previous decade, for these countries.

In the 1970s the international distribution of income could be said to have been improving as developing countries grew more rapidly in per capita terms than the industrial countries. For the 1980s the reverse is almost certain to be true, at least for the subset of countries considered in table 8.5.

On economic grounds the prospect of a lost decade for the 1980s does not imply likely default on debt. Default could make growth still lower (chapter 4). Moreover, table 8.5 shows important differences among countries that help explain why at least Mexico and Brazil might not be pushed to default: their growth was so rapid in the 1970s that even with the setback of the early 1980s their cumulative growth for 1970–90 is impressive, exceeding that of all industrial countries except Japan. In contrast, the dismal growth performance

---

72. In addition, in 1988–90 industrial country growth is assumed at 3 percent; a growth rate of 6 percent is assumed for Mexico and Brazil, 7.5 percent for Korea, and 5 percent for other developing countries. Population growth is assumed to continue at 1977–82 rates. Industrial country growth is allocated by country on the basis of OECD forecasts for 1984–85 and assuming identical per capita growth thereafter (except for Japan, which is assumed to grow 1 percent faster than other OECD countries in per capita terms). *OECD Economic Outlook* 35, (July 1984), p. 14.

of Argentina, Chile, Peru, and Venezuela even in the 1970s indicates a more fundamental inability to achieve rapid growth that goes beyond the adverse experience of the early 1980s (although the data for Venezuela do not include the favorable terms of trade effect from higher oil prices). The sharp deceleration of growth for these major debtor countries does suggest pressure on their domestic political systems. However, it is likely that by 1985 the worst of these strains will have been overcome, if domestic growth on the order of 4½ to 5 percent occurs as anticipated here.

The growth patterns shown in table 8.5 do imply the heightened need for policies in industrial countries that will increase the chances of a return to buoyant growth in debtor countries. Notwithstanding the exception of Korea, whose growth performance has demonstrated that domestic recession was not inevitable in the face of international recession, the fact remains that much of the cause of the dramatic setback for debtor countries in the early 1980s lay in international economic shocks, and misguided policies in industrial countries played a significant role in these shocks. It is incumbent on industrial countries, then, to correct those policy distortions that have adverse effects on developing countries (as well as themselves). The two most important distortions are monetary-fiscal policies that cause unusually high interest rates internationally, and trade protection.

Protection

By mid-1984 the possibility of higher protection continued to pose a significant risk for the process of debt management. In this period protection against exports from developing countries had crept forward in industrial countries. Even more severe new protection had arisen in the markets of developing countries themselves as they sought to deal with acute external imbalances, yet inadvertently made matters even worse for their heavily indebted trading partners.

Industrial country protection grew noticeably tighter in textiles and steel, and new protection seemed imminent in copper. In December 1983 the Reagan administration tightened protection on textiles and apparel by instituting a mechanism of automatic "calls" for consultations on bilateral quotas whenever certain indicators (such as imports as a share of consumption) exceeded critical target levels in individual products. More generally, the new extension of the Multi-Fiber Arrangement negotiated at the end of 1981 is widely regarded as more restrictive than its predecessor.[73] Other new protection in 1982 had

---

73. *Wall Street Journal*, 6 January 1984; and Martin Wolf, "Managed Trade in Practice: Implications of the Textile Arrangements," in William R. Cline, ed., *Trade Policy in the 1980s* (Washington: Institute for International Economics, 1982), pp. 455–82.

included quotas on sugar imports into the United States, which (for example) reduced Brazil's quota from 1 million tons to 400,000 tons yearly, at a cost of approximately $150 million annually.

Other industries took advantage of an election year in the United States to seek new protection. Producers of steel, copper, and footwear submitted petitions in early 1984 for protection under the safeguard mechanism (section 201) of US trade law. By mid-year the International Trade Commission (ITC) had ruled that domestic industry was being injured in both steel and copper. The ITC recommended new protection in both cases, although the final decision would be up to the President.[74]

Tighter protection on steel poses difficulties for Brazil, Mexico, and to some extent Argentina, while new protection on copper would be a serious blow to Chile. Rapidly rising steel exports were a source of export gains for major debtor countries in 1983. Mexico raised its exports of steel to the US market from 112,000 tons in 1982 to 650,000 tons in 1983. Brazil had doubled its steel exports to the US market to over 1 million tons in 1983. Imports from developing countries accounted for nearly 15 percent of the US market in the first quarter of 1984, with imports from Japan and Europe each providing approximately an additional 5 percent of the market. In a protective effort in Congress, the steel industry sought legislated quotas cutting total imports to 15 percent of US consumption, with most of the cutbacks focused on developing countries. In addition, prospective application of US penalties on subsidies of steel imports further threatened imports from Brazil, Mexico, and Argentina. By mid-year both Brazil and Mexico had offered voluntary restraints cutting steel exports by one-third to one-half.[75]

The value of exports potentially lost from new protection in steel and copper appeared to be substantial, though not devastating. In copper, Chile stood to lose perhaps $120 million (3 percent of total exports) in annual exports to the United States if protection proposed by some of the ITC commissioners were imposed. In steel, Mexico was likely to lose on the order of $90 million annually and Brazil $180 million annually from likely cutbacks in the US market, or one-half of 1 percent of total exports for Mexico and two-thirds of 1 percent for Brazil.[76] In addition, there would be losses in the European markets, where new restraints on Brazil and other suppliers were also under negotiation.

---

74. *New York Times*, 12 July 1984; *Wall Street Journal*, 28 June 1984.

75. *Washington Post*, 14 June 1984; *Gazeta Mercantil*, 6 February 1984; *Journal of Commerce*, 9 March 1984; *New York Times*, 2 May 1984; *Washington Post*, 27 April 1984.

76. Copper imports to the United States would be cut by 24 percent or 134,000 tons in one proposal; *Wall Street Journal*, 28 June 1984. Chile's share of the cost would probably be about 60 percent, and at 70 cents per pound this reduction would be $120 million annually. The estimates for steel assume a cutback of 250,000 tons annually for Mexico and 500,000 tons for Brazil, at an average price of $350 per ton.

Despite their obvious damage to debt-servicing prospects, the impact of possible new protection in steel and copper was likely to be modest in economic terms, as suggested by the estimates just cited when considered relative to total exports. In political terms their potential impact could be much worse, adding to the perception in Latin America that the debt problem was becoming unmanageable. The four Latin American presidents who originated the Cartagena initiative singled out increasing protectionism, along with higher interest rates, as the reason for their new demands for more favorable terms on debt.

Ironically, heightened protection still played a limited role in the debt problem. Only a minimal share of the debt disruption of 1982 and after could be attributed to export losses caused by new protection in industrial countries. On the contrary, the markets of the industrial countries remained relatively open to exports from developing countries. Not even all of the trends were toward new protection, as shown in the rejection by the US International Trade Commission of the petition for safeguard protection in the footwear industry.[77]

In sum, overwhelming protection remains a threat rather than a reality, and if markets in industrial countries can be kept approximately as open as they currently are, it should be possible for the debtor countries to achieve the export growth projected in this chapter. It is nonetheless critically important that policymakers in industrial countries resist new protectionist pressures, and incorporate possible risks to the financial system along with other considerations such as health of the industry and consumer costs of protection, in their decisions on trade policy. The launching of a new round of global trade negotiations, one that would include on its agenda protection affecting both sides of North–South trade, could be a helpful force for forestalling demands for new protection against developing countries.

Conclusion

The evidence reviewed in this chapter, and the updated projections of balance of payments and debt, confirm the basic conclusions reached earlier in this volume. The problem of international debt is likely to recede as international economic recovery proceeds, and it remains appropriate to manage the problem as one of illiquidity, not insolvency, and on a case-by-case basis. In 1983 major debtors experienced much faster external adjustment than anticipated, and the emerging external performances of Mexico and Brazil are particularly impressive.

---

77. *Wall Street Journal,* 6 June 1984. Moreover, statistical models of protection, when applied to projections of manufactured exports from developing countries, do not predict a large rise in protection through 1990. William R. Cline, *Exports of Manufactures from Developing Countries* (Washington: Brookings Institution, forthcoming).

Overall, external adjustment is ahead of schedule, not behind schedule. Moreover, internal recovery is beginning to occur.

Nonetheless, political strains remain intense. There is a growing dichotomy between favorable economic adjustment to the debt problem and political escalation of pressure for debt relief. The political pressure reflects not only a lagged response to severe domestic recessions in 1983 but also frustration over the upturn in US interest rates in the second quarter of 1984.

As demonstrated in the analysis of chapter 3, a surge of interest rates to the range of 15 percent or higher could abort the improvement in debt-export ratios and raise the likelihood of moratoria. For this reason and for the sake of sustainable recovery in the US economy itself, it is imperative that US policymakers achieve a reduction in fiscal deficits that will ease the pressure on capital markets and interest rates.

To date, however, higher than expected growth in industrial countries in 1984 has compensated, or more than compensated, for the upward drift in interest rates, as higher export earnings offset larger interest costs. The underlying trend toward improvement from international economic recovery remains on course. The central expectation still remains that OECD growth will achieve the critical threshold of 2½ percent to 3 percent annually identified earlier in this study as necessary for major debtor countries to return to creditworthiness over the medium term, and that the parallel condition of avoiding an explosion in interest rates will also be met.

The updated projections reinforce the earlier projected trends of a return to creditworthiness for major debtors. The new estimates suggest modestly lower capital needs in the medium term than those found in the original estimates, although the same broad conclusions about capital requirements remain valid, especially if greater allowance is made for the need to rebuild reserves and for the likelihood that leakage to capital flight cannot be avoided entirely. Substantial official flows of capital will be required, and it is important that the successful increase of IMF quotas in 1983 be complemented by expanded lending progams in the World Bank, regional development banks, and export credit agencies of industrial countries. In addition, continued flows of bank capital will be necessary, in the range of 5 percent to 7 percent annual expansion of exposure.

At mid-1984 the negotiating environment appeared fluid and contained significant elements of openness to more favorable terms, on the part of creditors, but at the same time vulnerability to political escalation on the part of certain debtor countries (with the Argentine case posing the greatest uncertainty for the time being).

Among concrete reforms, the most promising were continued reductions in interest rate spreads above market rates; a shift back from prime to LIBOR as the base rate; and a possible formal or informal cap to neutralize fluctuations in interest rates, ideally accompanied by a new compensatory finance mechanism within the IMF for interest rate fluctuations. The incipient move toward multiyear rescheduling, while offering psychological reassurance to debtors, was perhaps less urgent (in view of the analysis in chapter 5, suggesting that a somewhat earlier return to voluntary lending would be feasible, and considering that interest levels matter more than maturity terms in view of the general expectation that debt already outstanding must be refinanced rather than drawn down in net terms).

The problem of international debt continues to pose a severe challenge to policymakers in both industrial and developing countries for judicious economic management. Both groups deserve full credit for prompt and imaginative action in near-crisis situations and, in the case of many developing countries, for the courage to adopt measures that are painful and unpopular in the short run but essential to external adjustment and domestic growth in the medium term. Ultimately, however, no array of interim bridge loans, interest rate caps, stretchouts, and so forth can replace sustained economic growth in industrial countries, combined with more normal interest rates, as the centerpiece to resolution of the problem of international debt. As the brief financial siege on two of the largest US banks in May–June of 1984 demonstrated, the stakes are high. If the political leaders of developing countries are to be asked to demonstrate the courage to adopt unpopular adjustment measures, no less should be asked of the leaders of industrial countries in correcting budgetary and other disequilibria so that sustained, balanced international growth may be achieved.

Appendices

A   A Logit Model of Debt Rescheduling, 1969–82

The evaluation of a country's creditworthiness remains an imprecise process. The debt crisis of 1982 made it abundantly clear, however, that there are high stakes for both public policy and private market decisions in knowing when countries are nearing the range of breakdown in normal debt-servicing ability. For this purpose a quantitative behavioral model affords a summary measure for judging the evolution of creditworthiness over time and across countries. It can help track the deterioration of creditworthiness in recent years. It can help classify the relative importance of various factors in a deterioration. And it can serve as a criterion for evaluating whether and when in the future countries currently in rescheduling situations might return to voluntary borrowing, emerging from the current mode of new borrowing that is essentially involuntary on the part of lenders.

The previous statistical studies of this nature have tended to follow relatively similar approaches.[1] They use statistical techniques—typically discriminant or

---

1. Early studies of debt-servicing capacity tended to be based on *a priori* models of economic growth in which domestic saving plus capital inflows provided the impetus to growth, and the analysis was oriented toward examination of the behavior (and sustainability) of foreign debt relative to domestic income given savings behavior, capital productivity, and growth targets. See Dragoslav Avramovíc, et al., *Economic Growth and External Debt* (Baltimore: Johns Hopkins Press, 1964); and, for a later reformulation, Robert Solomon, "A Perspective on the Debt of Developing Countries," *Brookings Papers on Economic Activity,* no. 2 (1977), pp. 479–501. Perhaps the earliest statistical analysis of debt-servicing capacity was in Charles R. Frank, Jr., and William R. Cline, "Measurement of Debt-Servicing Capacity: An Application of Discriminant Analysis," *Journal of International Economics,* vol. 1 (August 1971), pp. 327–44. Subsequent statistical models include those in: Pierre Dhonte, "Describing External Debt Situations: A Roll-Over Approach," IMF *Staff Papers,* vol. 22, no. 1 (March 1975), 159–86; Gershon Feder and Richard Just, "A Study of Debt-Servicing Capacity Applying Logit Analysis," *Journal of Development Economics,* vol. 4, no. 1 (March 1977), pp. 25–38; Nicholas Sargen, "Economic Indicators and Country Risk Appraisal," Federal Reserve Bank of San Francisco, *Economic Review* (Fall 1977), pp. 19–35; Krishnan Saini and Philip Bates, "Statistical Techniques for Determining Debt-Servicing Capacity for Developing Countries: Analytical Review of the Literature and Further Empirical Results," Federal Reserve Board of New York, Research Paper, no. 7818 (September 1978).

logit analysis—that apply continuous independent variables to explain a dichotomous dependent variable—typically, debt rescheduling versus no rescheduling. Thus, if a country reschedules, its dependent variable is "1" for the year; otherwise it is zero; and this dependent variable is explained by independent variables considered to affect debt-servicing capacity, such as the ratio of debt service to exports of goods and services, ratio of reserves to imports, and so forth.

Experience has shown that the statistical models estimated in the early 1970s tended to over-predict the incidence of debt-rescheduling problems in the late 1970s.[2] The recycling of the oil surplus appeared to occur in a context in which the entire capital market experienced an outward shift in supply, permitting market financing of deficits that in earlier circumstances would have precipitated default. The key innovation of indexing interest rates to world levels, the increase in loanable deposits coming from members of the Organization of Petroleum Exporting Countries (OPEC), and governmental encouragement of the recycling process, may all have played a role in this shift.[3] Whatever the explanation, these analyses suggest that direct application of the earlier model results to recent country data would not prove a useful approach, and that instead new analysis using contemporary data is required, ideally incorporating the influence of the changing environment in the international capital market. The following analysis is an attempt to meet this need.

Other studies of creditworthiness have approached the problem from the theoretical standpoint of optimal borrowing. New insights have emerged from this literature, such as the point that countries may make borrowing decisions on the basis of seeking to smooth out fluctuations in consumption over time that otherwise would be forced by export fluctuations.[4] The analysis here attempts to incorporate such insights.

---

2. In his 1979 study, Gordon W. Smith applied the earlier Frank-Cline and Feder-Just models and found that, when applied to data in the mid-1970s to 1977, both predicted many rescheduling problems that in fact did not occur. Gordon W. Smith, "The External Debt Prospects of the Non-oil-exporting Countries," in *Policy Alternatives for a New International Economic Order: An Economic Analysis*, William R. Cline, ed. (New York: Praeger Publishers for the Overseas Development Council, 1979), pp. 287–329.

3. Indeed, some bankers diagnose this period as having shown an unsafe deterioration in the standards considered acceptable in creditworthiness judgments by international banks, and urge a return to tighter creditworthiness standards. David Lomax, "Sovereign Risk Analysis Now," *The Banker* (January 1983), pp. 33–39.

4. Rudiger Dornbusch, "Real Interest Rates, Home Goods and Optimal External Borrowing," *Journal of Political Economy*, vol. 91, no. 1 (February 1983); Jonathan Eaton and Mark Gersowitz, "Debt with Potential Repudiation: Theoretical and Empirical Analysis," *Review of Economic Studies*, vol. 48 (1981), pp. 289–309.

Causes of Debt-Servicing Difficulty: A Model

Debt-servicing difficulty usually involves the following sequence of events: inability of the country to borrow enough in new funds to be able to cover external deficits, a decline in reserves, the emergence of arrears on debt payments, some form of formal or de facto temporary moratorium on payments of principal (although interest payments are typically continued because their termination would classify foreign loans as "nonperforming"), and eventually a rescheduling agreement between the debtor and its creditors. Official debt is rescheduled at creditor meetings in the "Paris Club"; private debt is rescheduled by meetings of the major banks involved, frequently in London.

There are gradations of debt-servicing difficulty. Countries may not actually reach rescheduling or even arrears, but instead may adopt an International Monetary Fund (IMF) stabilization program or arrange other special financing. Countries may go into arrears for a time and then reestablish payment on a timely basis. At the same time, some debt disruptions are more severe than rescheduling. An extended moratorium on principal without a rescheduling agreement is worse for creditors than a rescheduling; a moratorium that includes interest is even worse; and at the extreme end of the spectrum there is outright debt repudiation.

For the purpose of assessing financial system stability, a debt rescheduling represents the appropriate threshold of severity for analysis. IMF stabilization loans are far too common to pose a threat to capital market stability, and indeed they typically have acted as the signal to the capital market that creditworthiness was improving. Arrears in themselves, especially if minor or temporary, pose no special systemic problem. Debt reschedulings, however, mark a major qualitative break in the spectrum of erosion. Although in the past reschedulings have usually avoided any direct loss to creditors and have often meant higher profits because of rescheduling fees, there is no denying the fact that reschedulings tie up capital that creditors might otherwise wish to reallocate, and lock resources into assets that have a *prima facie* deterioration of their quality because of the failure to have met original payment schedules. Indeed, rescheduling fees are justified by banks on grounds of increased risk. Another piece of evidence that rescheduled loans are not considered worth full face value is that they have virtually no secondary market. Whereas banks often sell off participations in normal loans, they rarely do so in the case of rescheduled loans.

Debt reschedulings are therefore of sufficient concern that they serve as a meaningful criterion for classification of cases as having serious debt-servicing difficulties. Of course, more extreme disruptions—such as extended moratorium or outright repudiation—are also appropriate criteria for such a classification. For purposes of the analysis here, the following discussion will use the term "rescheduling" as a summary term that also encompasses more severe forms of debt disruption.

Considering the anatomy of a typical debt rescheduling episode as outlined earlier, it is clear that there are two sides to a rescheduling. There is a "demand" side, reflecting the decision of the country to seek rescheduling. Because rescheduling tarnishes a country's credit rating, potentially raising the future cost of borrowing, countries will not seek rescheduling lightly. Instead, they will be likely to enter into the sequence of arrears, temporary moratorium, rescheduling only if the opportunity cost of continuing normal debt servicing has risen to levels perceived by policymakers to be prohibitively high. At that point their "demand" for debt rescheduling will shift discontinuously from zero to positive.

For its part the "supply" of rescheduling is really the obverse of the supply of additional foreign finance on a basis of business as usual. The "nonsupply of credit" is essentially the state at which the "supply of rescheduling" comes into play.

Foreign Credit Market

Because the alternative to rescheduling is merely that the country borrows more funds abroad to cover its needs and debt-servicing obligations, debt reschedulings may be conceptualized as a breakdown in the normal process of achieving equilibrium in the market for foreign credit. The theory of credit rationing helps explain why such breakdowns can occur.[5] Unlike most commodity markets where the price can merely rise until an equilibrium is found between the quantity demanded and that supplied, in credit markets the price—the interest rate—is subject to a ceiling beyond which even lenders do not wish to go. Where lenders have imperfect information about borrowers—and for developing countries lending information has typically been even more limited than in domestic credit markets—the lenders will interpret the interest rate the borrower is prepared to pay as an informational proxy for the severity of the borrower's situation. Accordingly, beyond some ceiling established by normal practice, the lender will be unwilling to lend more in return for a higher interest rate because a higher rate would merely be proof of the desperate straits of the borrower and therefore of the unacceptable risk of the loan. In international (and especially sovereign) lending, in recent years the effective ceiling on the interest rate appears to have been in the vicinity of a 2½ percentage point spread over the London Interbank Offer Rate (LIBOR).

It is useful to interpret debt reschedulings, then, as the consequence of the

---

5. Joseph Stiglitz and Andrew Weiss, "Credit Rationing in Markets with Imperfect Information," *American Economic Review*, vol. 71, no. 3 (June 1981), pp. 343–410.

disequilibrium that occurs in the international credit market when the amount the country seeks to borrow (perhaps even after an array of domestic austerity measures, devaluation, and so forth) exceeds the amount that foreign banks are prepared to supply at the upper ceiling interest rate. The international credit market thus fails to clear. A nonmarket solution must be established, and it is arrived at in a bargaining process: debt rescheduling.

The process of credit market breakdown is illustrated in figure A-1. In part A of the figure, the supply of new loans (or alternatively, net new lending deducting the amount of previous loans banks no longer wish to roll over) is shown in schedule SS, relating the amount of capital flow (K) to the interest rate (i). The quantity supplied is zero if the interest rate is below i_0 (LIBOR plus a minimum spread for transactions costs); it increases in response to the interest rate the country will accept. At the credit-rationing interest rate ceiling, i^*, however, supply of capital becomes totally inelastic: no more than the amount K^* will be offered regardless of how high an interest rate the country offers.

Demand for foreign lending is shown in curve DD. It reflects the scarcity of foreign capital to the country, which in turn reflects not only the scarcity of domestic capital but also the scarcity of foreign exchange.[6] At a lower interest rate the amount of foreign borrowing demanded increases, so that DD is downward sloping. In panel A of figure A-1, the credit market is in equilibrium at amount K_t of new lending and interest rate i_t.

In panel B of the figure, however, the credit market is in disequilibrium. The capital supply curve has shifted to the left $(S'S')$—for example, because of a general contraction in international capital markets (as occurred for Eastern Europe in 1981 and for Latin America in 1982).[7] The demand for borrowing has increased, however, as the curve $D'D'$ has shifted outward and to the right. Domestic crop failures, a collapse in world markets, higher world interest rates, and resulting claims on foreign exchange, are examples of factors shifting outward the demand curve for foreign borrowing. As a result of the high demand for borrowing and the low supply of loans, the market is in disequilibrium. At the interest rate ceiling of i^* (caused by the credit-rationing phenomenon), the amount of borrowing demanded is K_D while the amount supplied is only K_S. There is a disequilibrium gap between the two equal to G.

Under normal circumstances the country can take adjustment measures to

---

6. For the classic distinction between capital scarcity and the special role of foreign exchange scarcity in developing countries, see Hollis B. Chenery and Alan M. Strout, "Foreign Assistance and Development," *American Economic Review*, vol. 56, no. 4 (September 1966), pp. 680–733.

7. In practice, when confidence collapses, the shift of the supply curve of lending can be even more extreme than shown in figure A-1, to the left of the origin such that creditors are seeking actually to reduce their outstanding exposure.

Figure A-1 Credit market breakdown

A. Equilibrium

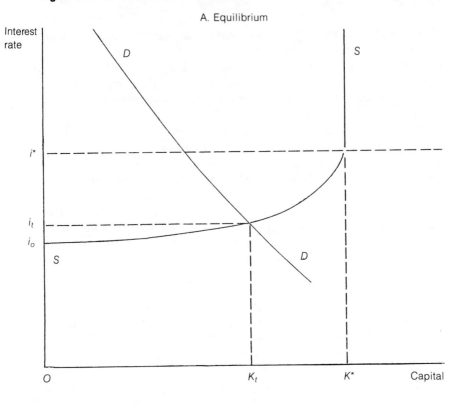

B. Disequilibrium

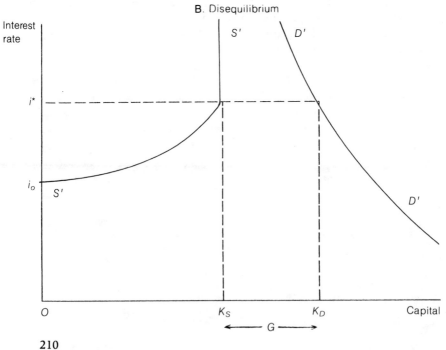

shift the demand for foreign borrowing backward to the left, often with IMF guidance. Indeed, the announcement of an adjustment package (especially one with IMF participation) may serve to shift the supply curve of international loans outward to the right, because other things being equal it will give foreign lenders more confidence.

But under severe circumstances it may be impossible to shift the demand curve for foreign funds, $D'D'$, sufficiently to the left, or to induce sufficient rightward shift in the supply curve, $S'S'$ to eliminate the gap "G." For example, an abrupt leftward shift in $D'D'$ might require such severe contractionary measures that they would be politically impossible. Or, because of an unusually nervous international climate for lending, the supply curve $S'S'$ might fail to shift outward even in the face of adoption of corrective measures. Under such circumstances a debt rescheduling may occur. Essentially, in the bargaining context of a rescheduling the borrower and lenders will reach an agreement over how to divide up the gap G; if the borrower's leverage is high the full amount of the gap G will tend to be covered by the extension of new, involuntary lending and postponement of maturities otherwise due. If the lender's leverage is stronger, a smaller portion of G will be covered and the country will be forced to take additional painful measures to shift demand curve $D'D'$ even further to the left.

Demand for Rescheduling

The demand for rescheduling is an induced demand that exists when the country is in the credit market disequilibrium position shown in panel B of figure A-1. Perhaps the most fruitful way to view the demand for rescheduling is as a probabilistic phenomenon. Thus, because a rescheduling is in the first instance a binary ("on" or "off") event—either a rescheduling problem arises or it does not—it is useful to consider the probability that a rescheduling will be demanded.[8] In terms of figure A-1 (panel B), any force that shifts the demand for capital curve outward to the right will tend to increase the probability that a rescheduling will be demanded.

Consider the debt-service ratio, a traditional indicator for creditworthiness. The higher the ratio of debt service to exports of goods and services, the greater will be the likelihood that in the event of a severe decline in export earnings the country will no longer be able to meet debt-service obligations. Suppose for example that one country devotes 10 percent of exports to debt service while another devotes 50 percent.[9] Then if both countries experience a 20

---

8. It is also possible to think of the amount of rescheduling demanded, in addition to the probability that a rescheduling will be demanded.

9. The discussion here does not distinguish between interest and amortization of principal.

percent reduction in exports, the first country would have to cut back imports by only 22 percent (the share of imports that would be represented by 20 percent of exports), while for the second country imports would have to be cut back by 40 percent.[10]

Other things being equal, with a higher debt-service ratio the situation of a disequilibrium such as that shown in figure A-1, panel B, is more likely to arise if the debt-service ratio is higher, because (as just illustrated) the chances are greater that a large surge in borrowing demand (shifting $D'D'$ rightward) will occur from a given shortfall in exports, given the greater proportionate reduction in imports that would be required in the absence of the extra borrowing.

Figure A-2   The debt-service ratio and the probability of rescheduling

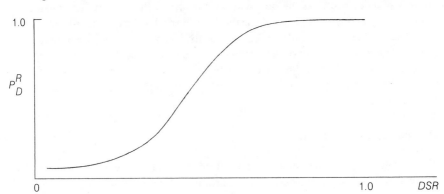

In terms of the probability of demand for rescheduling, figure A-2 illustrates the influence of the debt-service ratio. In the figure the probability that the country will seek a rescheduling (P_D^R) rises as the debt-service ratio rises. Above a certain low range of debt-service ratio where there is little risk of rescheduling, the relationship rises more rapidly; it then tapers off again because the maximum probability of demand for rescheduling is 1.0. (Note that the diagram suggests that a debt-service ratio of 1.0 would be highly likely to provoke demand for debt rescheduling; yet frequently, reported debt-service ratios exceed 100

If the country can count on principal rollover, all that matters in the comparison is interest. However, principal rollover is not assured. In the discussion, use of foreign exchange *equals* imports *plus* debt service. The source of foreign exchange is limited to exports for simplicity (meaning no new borrowing).

10. Thus, in the first country exports = 100, debt service = 10, imports = 90. In the second country, exports = 100, debt service = 50, imports = 50. A cut by 20 in funds available for imports represents 22 percent in the first country and 40 percent in the second.

percent. Such ratios treat all short-term debt as being paid off each year and included in amortization. Instead, the basic concept of debt-service ratio used in this study includes interest on short-term debt but not its principal, on grounds that short-term debt traditionally has been rolled over. For this definition, the debt-service ratio rarely even approximates 100 percent.)

As a first factor in explaining debt rescheduling, then, there is the influence of the debt-service ratio (DSR) on the probability of demand for debt rescheduling, where the superscript $+$ ($-$) indicates a positive (negative) impact:

(1) $\qquad P_D^R = f_1 (\overset{+}{DSR}).$

A second and related factor is the level of reserves relative to imports. When reserves are high—perhaps 50 percent of imports or above—it is likely that export shortfalls can be met through drawdowns of reserves. Export declines are therefore less likely to shift the demand curve for foreign borrowing sufficiently outward to the right that the disequilibrium condition of figure A-1, panel B will arise. Accordingly, turning to the induced probability of demand for rescheduling, this probability will be lower, the higher the ratio of foreign reserves to imports (RSM):

(2) $\qquad P_D^R = f_2 (\overset{-}{RSM}).$

A third influence on the demand for rescheduling is the country's domestic rate of economic growth. In terms of the classic "absorption" approach to the balance of payments,[11] the change in the trade balance *equals* the change in the country's output *minus* the change in its absorption. Thus, the higher the growth of output, the greater the exportable surplus is likely to be and the further to the left the underlying demand curve for foreign borrowing (figure A-1) to cover a trade deficit is likely to be. Perhaps even more important (considering that absorption may rise along with output growth), the rate of economic growth also indicates the scope for consumption cutback. In the light of a Duesenberry "ratchet" consumption function, for example, whereby consumption tends to fall less than proportionately when income falls because consumers have become accustomed to a given level of consumption, a reduction in per capita income (or even a slowdown from normal growth) will be likely to raise the ratio of consumption to income and output, causing a deterioration in the trade balance under the absorption approach. Furthermore, the more severe the decline in national income, the closer the consumption level (which will fall to some extent even with a ratchet effect) will be to levels considered minimally acceptable, and the greater will be resistance to austerity cutbacks

---

11. Sidney S. Alexander, "Effects of a Devaluation on the Trade Balance," *IMF Staff Papers*, vol. 2 (April 1952), pp. 263–78.

in an adjustment program—meaning that in terms of figure A-1 it will be less likely that equilibrium can be reestablished by a corrective leftward shift of demand curve $D'D'$ in panel B. Thus, for example, a 5 percent cutback in consumption for purposes of balance of payments adjustment will be less painful and more feasible politically if it occurs in the context of, say, a 5 percent trend in income and consumption growth (meaning no change in consumption from the previous year's level) than if it must be imposed in addition to cutbacks already occurring because of a trend of -5 percent per capita growth and consumption (meaning a total cutback of 10 percent from the previous year's consumption level).

In terms of recent theoretical work on external debt,[12] when a decline in growth occurs, especially negative growth per capita, increased demand for borrowing can be expected, because of the desire to smooth the path of consumption over time. Thus, the demand curve in figure A-1 shifts to the right when the growth rate declines, increasing the likelihood of a credit market disequilibrium.

On the basis of these various approaches, the probability of induced demand for rescheduling will be negatively related to the rate of (per capita) economic growth (g):

$$(3) \qquad P_D^R = f_3 (\overline{g}).$$

A related influence on the demand for rescheduling will be the level (as opposed to growth rate) of per capita income itself. Assuming that there is declining marginal utility of consumption, poorer countries may have a stronger resistance to reductions in consumption than richer countries. They may thus be less able to resolve a potential disequilibrium situation (figure A-1, panel B) by austerity programs that cut back consumption than are richer countries.[13] Thus:

$$(4) \qquad P_D^R = f_4 (\overline{y}),$$

where y is per capita income.

A final variable that influences the demand for rescheduling is the ratio of the current account deficit to exports of goods and services (CAX). Referring to figure A-1, the current account deficit broadly equals the full amount of new financing required (aside from the amount of capital provided by direct foreign

---

12. Eaton and Gersowitz, "Debt with Potential Repudiation."

13. Note however that this contrast would require not only that the marginal utility of consumption be declining—or that the elasticity of utility with respect to consumption be below unity —but also that this elasticity itself be declining as income rises. For a constant elasticity, the proportionate change in utility would be identical from a proportionate decline in consumption for both rich and poor countries.

investment), or, the amount K_t, in panel A of figure A-1. Normalizing the current account deficit for the country's economic size may appropriately be done by dividing by the exports of goods and services. In figure A-1, a rightward shift in DD means a larger current account deficit until the point where the maximum capital flow set by credit rationing, K_s, is reached and exceeded by the demand curve (panel B). Thus, the larger the current account deficit before actual rescheduling, virtually by definition, the closer the credit market is to the point of breakdown. However, as suggested by panel A of figure A-1, the relationship may be nonlinear. Over a fairly wide range the current account deficit may increase without approximating the credit-rationing ceiling. But as the deficit gets closer to the ceiling, the probability of induced demand for rescheduling would be expected to rise rapidly. Accordingly, and using a quadratic specification to capture the nonlinearity, it would be expected that:

(5) $P_D^R = f_5\,(h\;\overline{CAX^2})$,

where h is an adjustment to retain the information of whether the current account is in deficit or surplus.[14]

Supply Side

In addition to the factors influencing the demand for rescheduling, there are forces affecting the "nonsupply" of foreign credit, or the "supply of rescheduling." In terms of figure A-1, factors that tend to shift the supply curve of foreign credit to the left tend to raise the probability that a disequilibrium will arise between the amount of foreign capital demanded and that supplied, leading to a rescheduling.

There are two basic sets of supply-side influences. The first includes a number of variables that act as screening criteria whereby creditors judge the strength of the country's borrowing capacity. Other things being equal, an adverse movement of these screening criteria shifts the supply of foreign credit to the left, increasing the probability of rescheduling from the supply side. The second type of influence concerns the international economic environment rather than country-specific factors. If there is a general cutback in international lending as occurred in 1982, there exists a supply-side shock giving an impetus to rescheduling for reasons beyond the country's control.

Within the first cluster of screening criteria, some of the same variables that apply on the demand side are also relevant on the supply side. Thus, the debt-

---

14. If $CAX < 0$, $h = -1$. If $CAX > 0$, $h = 1$. This device is necessary because squaring the current account/exports ratio turns all signs positive, failing to distinguish between deficits and surpluses. The negative expected coefficient means that a larger deficit increases the probability of rescheduling.

service ratio is an important criterion on the supply side, one that has traditionally been used by lenders in creditworthiness decisions. It is relevant to the lender in the same way that the ratio of mortgage payments to household income is relevant for a home loan: it represents a claim on the relevant income stream (in this case export earnings), and the higher that claim relative to the income stream, the greater its burden and thus the greater the likelihood of inability to continue meeting the debt obligation. On the supply side, a higher debt-service ratio will tend to dry up credit supply, raising the probability of rescheduling from the supply side (P_S^R):

$$(6) \qquad P_S^R = f_6 \, (\overset{+}{DSR}).$$

It is of fundamental importance that some of the same factors that raise the probability of rescheduling on the demand side also do so on the supply side. In terms of figure A-1, certain influences, such as a high debt service ratio, tend to shift the demand curve for credit to the right and the supply curve to the left. This phenomenon means that the private capital market can be especially unstable as a country nears a rescheduling situation. In particular, it has frequently been observed that private creditors often supply abundant capital when the balance of trade is relatively strong but actually seek net repayments when it is weak, so that swings in the capital account exacerbate those in the current account.[15] In short, the fact that a credit market gap tends to develop from both the demand and supply sides tends to make debt-rescheduling situations develop abruptly and dramatically.

The screening criteria also include certain variables that reflect the country's real international balance sheet. A lender will be more willing to lend to a borrower with a higher real net worth. Three additional variables reflect the country's net worth: net debt relative to exports, inflationary erosion of debt, and amortization rate.

The ratio of net debt (gross debt *minus* reserves) to exports of goods and services is an alternative screening measure of the burden of the country's debt, paralleling the debt-service ratio. It is a longer term measure, examining the "stock" concept of the country's balance sheet rather than the "flow" concept of the current rate of debt service—which may be distorted by differences caused by bunching of maturities (at present or later). Use of the net debt to exports ratio will be distorted, however, unless it is applied only to countries relying mainly on nonconcessional loans, because the real burden of a 30-year debt at 3 percent interest (for example) is much lower than that of a debt of 8 years maturity with interest at LIBOR plus 1½ percent. Because the net debt

---

15. See for example, William R. Cline, "Economic Stabilization in Peru, 1975–78," in William R. Cline and Sidney Weintraub, eds., *Economic Stabilization in Developing Countries* (Washington: Brookings Institution, 1981), p. 325.

to exports ratio is essentially an alternative to the debt-service ratio as a screening criterion for relative debt burden, it is listed as an alternative to the previous equation:

$$(6') \qquad P_S^R = f_6 \, (N\overset{+}{D}X),$$

where NDX is the ratio of net debt to exports of goods and services.

A more distinct screening criterion for lenders is the inflationary erosion of outstanding debt. Especially in the 1970s higher interest rates mainly reflected higher inflation. But higher inflation provided a compensatory erosion of the real value of debt. The net effect was a cash flow pressure as, in effect, loans were forced to be repaid ahead of schedule in real terms—because the higher interest payment was immediate but the inflationary erosion of debt was not to be paid off until the future. Despite the cash flow pressure, the real long-term burden of the debt was overstated, as long as the real interest rate (nominal *less* inflation) remained unchanged while the nominal interest rate and observed debt-service ratio were rising. Because lenders may tend to take account of the inflationary erosion of the country's debt as a factor improving its real balance sheet, greater inflationary erosion of debt should mean less likelihood of rescheduling from the standpoint of credit supply. Thus:

$$(7) \qquad P_S^R = f_7 \, (\dot{p}\overset{-}{D}/X),$$

where $\dot{p}$ is a measure of world inflation, D is total outstanding debt, and X represents exports of goods and services. The term $\dot{p}D$ is the amount of inflationary erosion of debt, and the larger this erosion, as normalized by exports, the more favorable the country's real balance sheet.

Similarly, lenders consider the influence of amortization on a country's net worth. Higher amortization means that the country is more rapidly eliminating a liability, and more rapidly increasing its net worth. *For a given debt-service ratio*, a country with a higher amortization rate will appear to have a stronger balance sheet to a lender, because the country will have a higher component of debt service that is liquidation of liability (amortization) than another country with the same debt-service ratio but a lower amortization rate. Thus, in an extreme case where a country paid zero interest on all loans, its debt service would be wholly amortization, and other things being equal the lender would judge the country's net worth as being improved by the act of reducing its liabilities by paying amortization on debt.

The positive influence of a higher amortization rate *given* a certain debt-service ratio may also be seen in the following way. If, among countries, interest rates are broadly comparable, then the fact that country A has the same debt-service ratio as country B but a higher amortization rate means that country A has lower total debt (otherwise its interest payments relative to exports would be the same as those for country B and its total debt-service ratio would be *higher*), giving it a more favorable balance sheet position. For these reasons, the supply of credit is more likely to be forthcoming, and the probability of rescheduling induced by credit supply problems lower, if the country's amortization rate is higher:

$$(8) \qquad P_S^R = f_8(\bar{A}),$$

where A is the amortization rate, or the ratio of amortization to debt.

Beyond factors reflecting net worth, there are other screening criteria affecting credit supply. One is the level of per capita income. Because international lending involves imperfect information, certain basic economic measures take on an important role as summary evidence of creditworthiness. Past practice in international lending has tended to treat low-income countries as not creditworthy for market-based loans, consigning these countries to concessional official lending. As noted earlier, poor countries may be less able to cut income to achieve foreign adjustment when necessary. However, considering that low-income countries can have high rates of return on capital and sound management of the external sector just as well as medium-income countries, the real influence of per capita income is perhaps more ambiguous. There has probably been a confusion of positive and normative analysis, with the supposed lack of creditworthiness of low-income countries driven more by the normative judgment that they deserved grants and concessional loans than by the positive assessment that they could not manage hard-term loans. Indeed, in recent years private lenders have discovered profitable opportunities in low-income countries such as India. Nonetheless, because of its "summary evidence" role in a market seriously lacking in information, the level of per capita income serves as a screen on creditor supply. Of two countries with otherwise similar external sector profiles, the country with the lower per capita income will tend to have a greater perceived likelihood of foreign credit disequilibrium and debt rescheduling. Thus:

$$(9) \qquad P_S^R = f_9(\bar{y}).$$

Another screening criterion on the side of credit supply is the country's savings rate. Lenders will judge a country as a sounder risk if it is generating a high level of domestic savings, so that lenders can have greater assurance that funds borrowed from abroad will not go simply to replace domestic savings and permit high rates of consumption. Thus, on the credit supply side the probability of rescheduling is lower if the savings rate is higher:

$$(10) \qquad P_S^R = f_{10}(\bar{s}),$$

where s is the ratio of domestic savings to GNP.

A final screening indicator affecting creditor attitudes is the country's recent record in export growth. Other things being equal, creditors will tend to judge the country's ability to service debt in the future as stronger if the level of future exports is expected to be higher, and past export growth is a simple basis for the formation of expectations about future export growth. Thus:

(11) $P_S^R = f_{11}(\bar{g}_x)$,

where g_x is the recent growth rate of exports.

A final supply-side variable concerns the global supply of lending rather than country-specific conditions. In 1981 and 1982 shocks to the confidence of capital markets tended to reduce lending to entire regions: Eastern Europe and Latin America. In such a situation any individual country tends to face a leftward shift of the credit supply curve (figure A-1) because of global conditions rather than because of its own performance. Similarly, the large surge in international lending in the mid-1970s, associated with the recycling of petrodollars, meant that any individual country tended to face a credit supply curve that had shifted rightward toward more abundant supply of capital. Indeed, the favorable shift of credit supply generally in the mid-1970s may explain why by the late 1970s many countries were able to sustain debt-servicing levels that on the basis of previous experience would have precipitated debt reschedulings (as discussed earlier). And the rash of Latin American debt reschedulings in 1982 can similarly be attributed in part, perhaps, to the shrinkage of global credit supply to developing countries and Latin America in particular. Thus:

(12) $P_S^R = f_{12}(\bar{L})$,

where L is a measure of global credit abundance. For this measure, this study applies total net external borrowing by all nonoil developing countries as a fraction of total imports of these countries: $L = B/M$.

Other variables that have on occasion been used in previous empirical studies of debt rescheduling are omitted here. Thus, Feder and Just included export fluctuation, the ratio of imports to GDP (a measure of dependence on imports), and the ratio of capital inflow to debt service, as explanatory variables.[16] However, they found incorrect signs on the first two of these variables. As for the third, it raises questions of simultaneity. As set forth above, capital inflow is the obverse of debt rescheduling. It would not be surprising to find a negative statistical relationship between them (as Feder and Just do). But high capital inflow should be construed more as a consequence of creditworthiness than a cause of it, and this variable therefore would not appear to belong on the right

---

16. Feder and Just, "A Study of Debt-Servicing Capacity."

hand side of the equation as an explanatory variable. This point is even clearer when considering the use of the model for purposes of projection: future projections of exports, debt-service ratio, and so forth can be done on the basis of exogenous influences. But a future projection of capital inflow would make little sense without first determining, separately, the country's future credit-worthiness. Accordingly, the analysis here does not include a capital inflow variable as an explanatory factor.

Another variable sometimes included in analyses of debt rescheduling is inflation (or, alternatively, the rate of growth in the money supply).[17] Inflation may act as a proxy variable for the quality of economic management, at least as perceived by creditors. And its performance in past models has been relatively strong. However, for purposes of the analysis of this study inflation is not a satisfactory explanatory variable. It is not necessarily a good indicator of economic management; thus, Argentina and Chile entered broadly similar balance of payments and debt difficulties in 1979–82 because of policies leading to overvaluation, even though Argentina's inflation was near 200 percent and Chile's reached less than 10 percent. Similarly, the fact that Brazil's inflation was high in 1980–81 does not mean that creditors perceived its management at that time as having been of poorer quality than that in Mexico where inflation was substantially lower. An even more compelling reason for omitting inflation is that one of the major purposes of the model is for use in projections, and there is little firm basis for projecting country-by-country inflation rates in the future.

Reduced Form

When these various factors on both the demand and supply side of credit market breakdown and rescheduling are taken into account, a reduced form of the model relating the probability of debt rescheduling to the several economic variables is obtained. Note that there are no variables in which both demand and supply influences exist but with opposite signs; in the two cases where effects on both sides are expected—the debt-service ratio and per capita income—both the demand and supply of debt rescheduling have the same sign in their relationships to the variables.[18]

In many econometric applications, the presence of both demand and supply influences stemming from a given variable causes difficulties of interpretation.

---

17. Sargen, "Economic Indicators and Country Risk Appraisal," and Saini and Bates, "Statistical Techniques for Determining Debt-Servicing Capacity."

18. There is inevitably some arbitrariness in classifying an influence as on the demand or supply side. For example, reserves relative to imports could arguably be called a credit supply determinant because it is a relevant indicator for lender screening.

In the present case, however, the fact that where they overlap on individual variables the demand and supply influences run in the same direction means that there is no risk of obtaining an invalid statistical relationship (in terms of the sign) from at least this source of econometric complication ("simultaneity").[19] Instead, the "reduced form" equation used for the statistical estimates incorporates the joint effect of both demand and supply influences. Estimation just of the reduced form does mean that it is not possible to distinguish between the relative roles of the demand and supply sides where both are present, even though being able to make that distinction might be helpful in terms of policy implications.[20]

The reduced form equation does tell an overall probability of debt rescheduling, considering both demand and supply factors. The equation is a "logit" model, of the form:

$$(13) \qquad z_t = b_1 DSR_{t-1} + b_2 RSM_{t-1} + b_3 g_t + b_4 y_t + b_5 (h\ [CAX]^2_{t-1})$$

$$+ b_7 \left(\frac{pD_{t-1}}{X_{t-1}} \right) + b_8 A_{t-1} + b_{10} s_{t-1} + b_{11} g_{x,t} + b_{12} L_t.$$

In the equation, z_t is the variable indicating the presence of a rescheduling in year t. Its value is unity for a rescheduling and zero otherwise. The independent variables are those enumerated above, with the subscript of the coefficient "b" in each case corresponding to the individual equation. Except for the current account deficit relative to exports, all variables are specified in linear form, in the absence of any particular theoretical reason to expect nonlinear influence.

The subscript $t-1$ indicates that the data are for the previous year. Where these lagged variables are used, it is assumed, that because of time lags in data, decisions taken in a given year are broadly determined by data pertaining to the end of the previous year (debt, reserves) or the flows for the full previous year (for example, debt-service ratio). The variables having a contemporaneous impact are per capita income growth (g_t) and global lending (L_t). Thus, if income is declining sharply there can be immediate effects on the country's

---

19. The problem of "simultaneous equations" arises when more than one relationship is active at the same time. Thus, in the demand for and supply of a commodity, there may be ambiguity in interpreting a statistical relationship of amount sold to price, because it is unclear whether the relationship being observed is on the supply side (in which case the quantity increases as price rises) or the demand side (in which case the quantity decreases as price rises).

20. In the case of per capita income, for example, if the supply side influence dominates, capital supply might be increased by a systematic effort to provide accurate data on developing-country economies and management, so that creditors relied less on summary screening measures such as per capita income for lack of other information. But if the demand side dominates there would be little policy change that could affect the influence of this variable, because the lack of resiliency in consumption associated with low income would not be subject to policy change.

willingness to sustain normal debt servicing; and, as the experience of 1982 showed, a contraction in global lending can have an immediate effect in precipitating debt-servicing difficulties. As for the level of per capita income, y, the broad variation occurs across countries, not within one country over time, and it makes little difference whether the specification is contemporaneous (year t) or lagged $(t-1)$.

As an alternative to equation (13), the same equation can be estimated but instead replacing the first term $(b_1 DSR_{t-1})$ with the alternative indicator of debt burden, the ratio of net debt to exports $(b_6 NDX)$.

In the logit method, once an equation of the form in (13) is statistically estimated (using maximum likelihood techniques), the resulting dependent variable z may be transformed into a indicator of the probability of rescheduling, as shown in equation (14):

$$(14) \qquad P_C^R = \frac{1}{(1 + e^{-z})},$$

where P_C^R is the composite indicator of the probability of rescheduling, and e is the base of the natural logarithm. This probability indicator can vary from zero (as z approaches negative infinity) to unity (as z approaches positive infinity).

Data

The data used to estimate the statistical model of debt rescheduling are as follows. Appendix D describes the measurement of, and data sources for, the debt-service ratio, total debt, and net debt. For reserves relative to imports of goods and services, the value of nongold reserves is taken from *International Financial Statistics* (IFS). Although exclusion of gold may understate reserves substantially in some cases, it facilitates international comparison, given varying national practices on gold valuation.[21] The denominator of the reserves variable—imports of goods and services—excludes interest payments from services imports, because the influence of the interest burden is already captured in the debt-

---

21. In the aggregate, gold reserves accounted for only 5.4 percent of total reserves of nonoil developing countries at the end of 1982, in the official IMF valuation at SDR 35 per ounce. Using a relatively conservative market valuation of gold of SDR 300 per ounce, however, gold would account for 33 percent of total reserves. IMF *International Financial Statistics* (April 1983), pp. 37–41. The exclusion of gold reserves may therefore tend to bias the coefficient on the reserves variable. If gold reserves were always proportional to other reserves, the estimated reserves coefficient would be biased toward overstatement (by the ratio of total to nongold reserves). However, because the fraction of reserves held in gold varies by country, the result may be to introduce random error in the reserves variables, with a resulting tendency to reduce its significance and, perhaps, its size. Note that the alternative of including gold causes its own problems of assessing a meaningful valuation.

service ratio. The data sources are IFS for imports of goods and services and *Balance of Payments Yearbook* (BOPY) for interest payments. For Venezuela, the data on reserves include external assets held by the national petroleum company and the national investment fund, from national sources. (These reserves were large in the late 1970s and were in fact consolidated into reported reserves in 1982.)

The amortization rate is calculated as follows. Amortization of medium- and long-term debt is taken from BOPY. For each year, this amortization is divided by total long-term debt outstanding at the end of the previous year (with long-term debt estimated as described in appendix D).

For the ratio of current account deficit to exports of goods and services, IFS data on the current account balance are applied. For the savings rate, IFS data on private consumption and government consumption are *summed, divided* by gross domestic product, and the result *subtracted* from unity. The growth rate of per capita income is obtained using IFS data on real GDP and population. For the most recent years in which IFS data remain unavailable, regional and national sources are used.[22]

The level of per capita income is based on IFS data and international purchasing power comparisons conducted by the United Nations. For each country the real 1975 per capita income (in dollars) is obtained from the UN international comparisons.[23] For all other years, IFS data on real GDP per capita relative to the IFS figure for 1975 are applied to the 1975 cross-country estimates to obtain annual real per capita income. Because the resulting estimates adjust the data on per capita income in dollars by the differing purchasing power of the dollar across countries, they show a smaller variation in real per capita income than do unadjusted data. (International evidence shows a systematic tendency for the exchange rate to understate the real value of domestic income in lower income countries, largely because the labor-intensive goods and services in which they have lower-cost production tend not to be traded goods and the exchange rate is set by traded goods only.)

The variable on global external borrowing measures total net external borrowing, from private and official sources, by nonoil developing countries.[24] It is normalized by dividing by total merchandise imports for these countries (IFS). For 1969–72 the data series on total borrowing is not available. For this

---

22. UN Economic Commission for Latin America, *Preliminary Balance of the Latin American Economy in 1982,* January 1983; Asian Development Bank, *Annual Report 1982.*

23. Irving B. Kravis, Alan W. Heston, and Robert Summers, "Real GDP *Per Capita* for More than One Hundred Countries," *The Economic Journal,* no. 88 (June 1978), pp. 215–42; and Kravis, Heston, and Summers, *World Product and Income: International Comparisons of Real Gross Product* (Baltimore: Johns Hopkins University Press for the World Bank, 1982).

24. IMF, *World Economic Outlook* 1983.

period, total borrowing is estimated by multiplying the ratio of total borrowing to the trade deficit in 1973, by the trade deficit for nonoil countries in 1969–72.

The export growth variable is calculated as the ratio of average real exports in years t and $t-1$ to that average for years $t-2$ and $t-3$. Real exports are calculated by *dividing* the dollar value of exports by the unit value index of exports of industrial countries (thereby reflecting the real purchasing value of export earnings rather than an index of export quantity). A four-year growth period is sufficiently long to avoid extremes of annual fluctuation, and sufficiently short to be considered relevant by creditors for evaluation of recent performance. IFS data are used for this variable.

Table A-1   Debt rescheduling cases included in logit analysis

Country	Year(s)	Country	Year(s)
Argentina	1976, 1982	Mexico	1982
Bolivia	1981	Peru	1976, 1978
Brazil	1982	Philippines	1970
Chile	1972, 1974	Romania	1982
Costa Rica	1982	Sierra Leone	1977, 1980
Gabon	1978	Togo	1979
Ghana	1970	Turkey	1978, 1982
Jamaica	1978, 1981	Zaire	1976

The dependent variable records debt reschedulings. It is zero in the absence of a rescheduling and one in the presence of a rescheduling. Table A-1 lists the countries and years in which reschedulings occurred. The key cases of Argentina, Brazil, and Mexico in 1982 are included as instances of rescheduling even though formal rescheduling agreements were not reached until 1983. The meaningful economic event of suspension of payment and interim payments crisis occurred in 1982 in these cases. The frequent cases of rescheduling in India and Pakistan (as well as nonscheduling years in these countries) are omitted from the analysis because they were primarily designed to confer development assistance rather than being the consequence of developments in private capital markets. For the same reason, reschedulings in Indonesia in 1970 and Ghana in 1974 are omitted.

In the analysis, in the year following a rescheduling the observation is omitted. From the standpoint of the logit model, in a year following rescheduling there could be a tendency to predict rescheduling because the underlying conditions had not yet reversed sufficiently (for example, reserves might still be low). And in an economically meaningful sense the situation would not be normal (i.e., a representative year of nonrescheduling) because debt payments for the year would have been substantially revised. But there would not necessarily be a new rescheduling following the one the previous year. Alternatively, the country could be in a situation where a rescheduling does occur as a follow-up to an earlier rescheduling that only rescheduled debt due immediately. In this case the actual debt-service ratio in the previous year (which had been rescheduled) would seriously understate the debt service that would be due in the current year in the absence of rescheduling, and the standard model could predict no rescheduling when one was in fact necessary. Past empirical studies have indeed found a tendency for erroneous predictions to be concentrated in years immediately following rescheduling.[25]

The logit model is estimated using data for 60 countries over a period of 15 years (1968–82). As shown in table A-2 the earliest year for the dependent variable is 1969. After taking account of missing data and deletion of observations in the year following rescheduling, there are a total of approximately 670 country-year observations in the central estimates. Among these, there are only 22 cases of rescheduling, or only 3 percent of the sample. This extreme imbalance between the frequency of nonscheduling and rescheduling has implications for proper interpretation of the econometric results, as discussed below.

Results

The initial results of the estimation of the logit model of rescheduling appear in table A-3. The variables in the table refer, respectively, to the debt-service ratio, the ratio of reserves to imports, inflationary debt erosion relative to exports, the amortization rate, the square of current account balance relative to exports (with negative sign for deficit), the savings rate, the growth rate, real per capita income, global external borrowing relative to imports, net debt relative to exports, and the growth of exports. The abbreviations for those variables that are specified with a one-year lag begin with "L."

The estimated results broadly confirm the hypothesized influences on debt rescheduling and succeed in a relatively high degree of explanation of rescheduling and nonrescheduling. The debt-service ratio ($LSDR$) is highly significant (high "t" statistic)[26] and has the correct sign: a higher debt-service ratio causes

---

25. Frank and Cline, "Measurement of Debt-Servicing Capacity"; and Feder and Just, "A Study of Debt Servicing Capacity."

26. A t-statistic of above 1.96 indicates that the coefficient is significantly different from zero at the 5 percent level of significance.

Table A-2   Countries included in logit analysis of debt rescheduling

Country	Period included	Country	Period included
Algeria[a]	1970–81	Mauritius	1969–76
Argentina[a]	1969–76, 1978–82	Mexico[a]	1969–82
Bolivia[a]	1969–81	Morocco[a]	1970–80
Brazil[a]	1969–82	Nicaragua	1969–79
Burma	1969–81	Nigeria[a]	1969–77
Chile[a]	1969–72, 1974,	Paraguay	1969–82
	1977–82	Peru[a]	1971–76, 1978, 1981
Colombia[a]	1969–71, 1973–82	Philippines[a]	1969–70, 1972–82
Costa Rica	1969–82	Portugal[a]	1974–82
Cyprus	1969–80	Romania[a]	1980–82
Dominican Republic	1969–81		
		Rwanda	1972, 1974–80
Ecuador[a]	1969–82	Senegal	1972–79
Egypt[a]	1969–82	Sierra Leone	1969–73, 1975–77,
El Salvador	1969–81		1979–80
Ethiopia	1969–76	Spain[a]	1972–82
Gabon	1969–70, 1973–78	Sri Lanka	1969–81
Ghana	1970, 1972–73,	Sudan[a]	1969–78
	1976–78	Syria[a]	1969–76, 1978–81
Greece[a]	1969–81		
Guatemala	1969–82	Tanzania	1970–80
Guyana	1969–76	Thailand[a]	1969–82
Haiti	1976–82	Togo	1970–79
Honduras	1969–82	Trinidad and Tobago	1969–78
Indonesia[a]	1972–82	Tunisia[a]	1969–81
Israel[a]	1969–82	Turkey[a]	1969–78, 1982
Ivory Coast[a]	1971–78	Uganda	1969–78
Jamaica	1969–78, 1981	Upper Volta	1970–79
Jordan	1973–81	Uruguay	1969–82
Kenya	1969–74, 1976–80	Venezuela[a]	1969–82
Korea[a]	1969–82	Yugoslavia[a]	1969–81
Madagascar	1970–79	Zaire[a]	1969–76
Malaysia[a]	1971–82	Zambia[a]	1969–81

a. Also included in large-debtor analysis (model L).

Table A-3 Estimates of logit model of debt rescheduling[a]

Model	A	B	C	D	E
Variable					
LDSR	10.000 (3.45)	—	11.029 (5.45)	—	12.405 (5.24)
LRSM	−15.523 (3.85)	−12.148 (3.38)	−15.063 (4.18)	−10.189 (3.12)	−16.554 (4.19)
LINX	−2.102 (.43)	9.450 (2.41)	—	—	—
LAMZ	−12.172 (2.18)	−1.532 (.43)	−12.772 (2.70)	−1.157 (.36)	−12.875 (2.48)
LSQCA	−1.304 (2.04)	−1.074 (1.69)	−1.201 (1.99)	−.932 (1.60)	−1.383 (2.16)
LSAV	.424 (.16)	−.508 (.21)	—	—	
GRO	−.123 (3.10)	−.129 (3.16)	−.130 (3.36)	−.139 (3.58)	−.135 (3.25)
GDP	.00014 (.43)	.00032 (1.17)	—	—	—
EXBOR	−15.374 (3.04)	−23.496 (4.40)	−13.874 (3.72)	−21.466 (4.43)	−15.025 (3.74)
LNDX	— —	.734 (1.92)	—	1.273 (4.15)	—
XGR	—	—	—	—	−1.424 (.94)
Observations	640	640	670	670	574
Reschedulings	22	22	22	22	20
Chi-squared	772	762	812	795	700
Error (percentage)[b]					
Type I	9.1	18.2	9.1	13.6	10.0
Type II	13.6	14.6	13.0	16.1	12.5

— Not included.
a. T-statistic in parentheses.
b. Type I: failure to predict actual rescheduling. Type II: prediction of rescheduling when none occurs. Cutoff = .041.

a higher indicator of rescheduling. The same is true of the ratio of reserves to imports (*LRSM*), which has the expected negative sign (higher reserves mean lower likelihood of rescheduling). The amortization rate (*LAMZ*) has the expected negative sign (faster amortization means less likelihood of rescheduling) and is statistically significant in the three cases where it is included jointly with the debt-service ratio. As might be expected, the amortization rate is not significant when the debt-service ratio is replaced by the ratio of net debt to exports (*LNDX*).[27]

The current account deficit relative to exports (*LSQCA*) has the correct sign. It is statistically significant at the 5 percent level in three of the five models and at the 10 percent level in the other two. The growth rate of per capita GDP (*GRO*) also has the correct sign, and it shows strong statistical significance in all cases.

The weakest variables in the analysis are the inflationary erosion of debt (*LINX*), the savings rate (*LSAV*), and the level of GDP per capita (*GDP*). The variable for inflationary debt erosion has the wrong sign, and curiously it is statistically significant in one of the models (B).[28] For its part, the savings rate shows very low significance, and its sign fluctuates. The level of real per capita GDP also shows no statistical significance, and it carries the wrong sign. The weak results for the level of per capita income suggest that the underlying ambiguity of this variable, as discussed above, is dominant, and that the conventional perception that low-income countries are not creditworthy may be unwarranted. Because of the weakness of these three variables—inflationary debt erosion, savings rate, and per capita income—they are excluded in all but the first two versions of the model.

The variable for global borrowing (*EXBOR*) shows the correct sign (negative: higher level of lending globally means there is less likelihood of rescheduling for individual countries) and its level of significance is high, in all of the models estimated. This result is especially important because the variable provides a way of overcoming a major limitation of previous models: their inability to capture the changing conditions in the 1970s, when a sharp increase in international lending prevented reschedulings that would have been expected

---

27. When the debt-service ratio is included, a higher amortization rate implies lower total debt for a given debt-service ratio, as discussed above. However, when the debt to exports ratio replaces the debt-service ratio, a higher amortization rate does not imply lower debt burden—because the influence of total debt is already being captured.

28. Because inflationary debt erosion is higher when the interest rate is higher strictly as the result of higher inflation, this variable to some extent parallels the debt-service ratio itself. That is, higher interest payments associated with inflation cause both a high debt-service ratio and a high value of the variable for inflationary debt erosion. When the debt-service ratio is not itself included in the analysis, as in model B, its influence appears to be picked up by the variable *LINX*, giving the result of an incorrect sign with statistical significance.

on the basis of earlier model estimates. This variable is also important in explaining the wave of reschedulings in 1982, when capital availability reversed sharply.

When the ratio of net debt to exports (*LNDX*) is applied in place of the debt-service ratio (models B and D), it is found to have the right sign and to have strong statistical significance. On the other hand, the variable for export growth (*XGR*) (model E) is not statistically significant, although it does carry the correct sign.

The five alternative models shown in table A-3 represent alternative combinations when some variables are excluded. Because the export growth variable requires additional years of data, its inclusion (model E) requires the deletion of approximately one-seventh of the observations. Considering that this variable is not statistically significant, the sacrifice of observations is unwarranted, and this version of the model is less useful than the others.

Model versions A through D result from choice between debt-service ratio (A, C) and ratio of net debt to exports (B, D), on the one hand, and inclusion of the variables for inflationary debt erosion, savings rate, and per capita income (A, B) or exclusion of these variables (C, D), on the other.

The overall statistical performance of the models is more difficult to gauge than in the case of normal regression analysis, where the "adjusted R-squared" represents the percentage of variation explained (as adjusted for the number of variables used relative to the number of observations).[29] One measure of statistical performance is the Chi-squared statistic for overall significance. This criterion shows strong performance for the estimates; it is typically in the range of 700 or more, far above the value (approximately 50) required to indicate overall statistical significance at the 1 percent level.[30]

The best indicator of the model's performance, however, is the degree of its success in predicting the occurrence and absence of rescheduling. For the purpose of converting the model's estimate of the logit function, z (equation 13), into a prediction of rescheduling or nonrescheduling, it is necessary to transform the logit measure "z" into a composite probability of rescheduling (P_C^R) using equation (14) above. Moreover, it is necessary to choose a threshold probability, P_C^{R*}, above which a country is predicted to reschedule and below which no rescheduling is predicted.

The first of these two steps simply applies equation (14) to the estimates of

---

29. Because the dependent variable is either 0 or 1, the R^2 has little meaning. For example, even if the logit model enabled perfect prediction of all rescheduling and nonrescheduling cases, the R^2 would be substantially below unity, because the predicted "z" value is a continuous variable while the dependent variable is either 0 or 1, meaning that the measure R^2 would always show "unexplained variance."

30. That is, where the chances would be only one out of one hundred that purely random processes would provide the measured relationships.

table A-3. The second step is more complicated. One possible approach in logit analysis is simply to choose 0.5 as the critical probability threshold, the implication being that if the composite probability exceeds 0.5 the probability of a rescheduling is greater than 50 percent and accordingly rescheduling should be predicted. However, in the results presented here this procedure would result in an extremely unbalanced distribution of errors: only a small percentage of nonrescheduling cases would be falsely predicted as rescheduling, but practically all of the rescheduling cases would be falsely predicted as nonrescheduling.

The procedure adopted here draws upon the well-established tradition in dichotomous statistical analysis—discriminant analysis in particular—of choosing the critical threshold for classification such that a "good" distribution of errors across the two classes is achieved.[31] Specifically, the critical threshold P_C^{R*} is chosen so that the total error is minimized subject to a relatively equal percentage rate of error in the two classes of observations. That is, it is essential that not all of the error be concentrated in either one direction or the other. High overall explanation but failure to predict most rescheduling cases (i.e. predicting nonrescheduling almost uniformly) would be especially misleading for policy purposes, considering the crucial focus of concern on those conditions that lead to actual rescheduling.

The critical threshold that best achieves the objectives of overall explanation and balance in distribution of error between rescheduling and nonrescheduling cases is a level of P_C^R equal to only 0.041. This low level would appear to reflect the large imbalance between nonrescheduling cases (97 percent of country-year observations) and rescheduling cases (3 percent) in the underlying population.[32] Using this threshold for prediction, the alternative models in table A-1 correctly explain an average of approximately 86 percent of nonrescheduling cases and 88 percent of rescheduling cases. The best overall performance is achieved by model C, for which only 9.1 percent of actual reschedulings are

---

31. See for example T.W. Anderson, *Introduction to Multivariable Statistical Analysis* (New York: John Wiley, 1958), pp. 127–134.

32. Note that in a previous application of logit analysis—explanation of the presence of major nontariff barriers—I have found a similar relationship of the critical threshold to the sample distribution. In that case, with approximately 8 percent of US manufacturing sectors (by number) covered by major nontariff barriers (including all textile-apparel sectors as a single large sector), the best critical threshold for the logit probability was 30 percent. William R. Cline, *Exports of Manufactures from Developing Countries: Performance and Prospects for Market Access* (Washington: Brookings Institution, forthcoming). The implication of the threshold found here and that used in the earlier study is that when the sample is heavily distributed toward nonevent cases (for example, nonrescheduling, here), the critical threshold for balanced percentage distribution of error will be considerably below 50 percent. This result is not surprising in light of the fact that the logit estimation process is blind to the distribution of errors and, when there is a high preponderance of nonevent cases, will naturally tend to estimate parameters that predict a low incidence of error in those cases.

unpredicted (type I error) and only 13.0 percent of nonrescheduling cases are falsely predicted as reschedulings (type II error). This incidence of error compares favorably with that obtained in previous studies of this nature,[33] especially considering that this study includes a more recent time period than did previous studies, which, in most cases, would involve considerable error if the original models were extrapolated (as discussed above).

In sum, the central results of the logit analysis are those shown for models C and D. These models correctly explain rescheduling or nonrescheduling in over 85 percent of country-year cases. They find that the key influences on rescheduling are the debt-service ratio, ratio of imports to reserves, amortization rate, current account deficit, growth rate, and the global environment for financing—all variables suggested in the theoretical analysis proposed earlier. In addition, comparable explanation is achieved if the net debt to exports ratio is used in place of the debt-service ratio as the measure of debt burden.

Large Debtor Countries

The results just described are the best estimates obtained for the entire population of 60 countries examined. An examination of the detailed predictions shows a systematic difference between the larger and smaller debtor countries, however. Considering the 31 countries with the largest debt, the average value of the predicted probability of rescheduling (P_C^R) in model C is 0.32, for those country-years in which rescheduling occurred. In contrast, for the other countries with smaller debt, this average is 0.20. Thus, the results appear to indicate that the smaller debtors reach rescheduling situations at lower levels of underlying debt burden than the larger debtors. This conclusion is not surprising when the actual countries in question are reviewed. The larger debtors with reschedulings include Argentina, Brazil, Mexico, the Philippines, Chile, Peru, Turkey, Romania, Bolivia, and Zaire. The rescheduling cases among smaller debtors include Ghana, Costa Rica, Jamaica, Gabon, Sierra Leone, and Togo. Most of the countries in the first group (with the notable exceptions of Bolivia and Zaire) would be judged on an informal basis by international creditors to be able to sustain relatively higher levels of debt than those in the second group because of past debt performance and level of development (the lack of statistical significance of the per capita income variable notwithstanding).

Because the vulnerability of the international financial system is primarily affected by the viability of the debt held by the larger debtor countries, it is useful to have a more refined analysis for this class of countries. For this

---

33. For a comparison of the degree of explanation achieved in earlier studies, see Robert Z. Aliber, "A Conceptual Approach to the Analysis of External Debt of the Developing Countries," World Bank Staff Working Paper, no. 421 (October 1980), p. 24.

purpose, a second logit model is estimated using only the 31 largest-debtor countries. The adjusted large-debtor model includes a dummy variable for Mexico, considering that in the initial models Mexico tends systematically to be predicted as rescheduling in the 1970s when it did not reschedule.

Table A-4   Estimates for logit model of rescheduling:[a] large debtor sample (model L, 31 countries)

Variable	Coefficient	Variable	Coefficient
LDSR	12.769 (3.63)	EXBOR	−15.835 (3.08)
LRSM	−16.742 (3.02)	DMEX	−.971 (.72)
LAMZ	−15.724 (2.25)	Observations	362
LSQCA	−2.228 (1.92)	Reschedulings	14
		Chi-squared	442
GRO	−.235 (2.93)	Errors (percentage)[b]	
		Type I	21.4
		Type II	2.6

a. T-statistic in parentheses.
b. See table A-3, note b.   Cutoff probability = .242.

The results of the large-debtor model (named "model L") are shown in table A-4. In general the same variables as before are statistically significant and only these variables are included in the final, reported version: debt-service ratio, reserves relative to imports, amortization rate, current account deficit, growth rate, and global lending rate. Although the dummy variable for Mexico (DMEX) is not statistically significant, its inclusion definitely improves the degree of explanation (by eliminating several type II errors for Mexico).

Overall the results of model L are comparable to those of model C for the entire set of countries, in terms of significance (t-statistics, Chi-squared). Moreover, the critical probability threshold for prediction is now 0.24— suggesting that when the sample is more homogeneous it is possible to obtain a relatively balanced distribution of error with a probability closer to the intuitive 50 percent than might be expected from the underlying sample distribution (which is still only 4 percent rescheduling, 96 percent nonrescheduling). At this threshold, model L has 21.4 percentage error in failure to predict actual reschedulings and only 2.6 percent error in falsely predicting reschedulings where none occur.

The choice of the threshold for classification as rescheduling versus nonrescheduling could be set lower to reduce type I error (a cutoff of 0.11 would eliminate one such error, improving the type I error rate to 14.3 percent). However, there appears to be a sufficient discontinuity between a group of three rescheduling cases with very low P_C^R, and all other rescheduling cases with considerably higher levels, that the most appropriate cutoff is at the level chosen (0.242).[34] Because there are considerable policy costs of misclassification in either direction, where a relatively clear separation exists in the distribution of P_C^R for rescheduling cases, such a zone would seem to be the appropriate place to establish the critical cutoff P_C^{R*}, as long as the resulting distribution of type I and type II errors is not seriously unbalanced.[35]

Some of the erroneous predictions in model L convey important information as well. Of the 10 type-II errors (prediction of rescheduling when none occurs), three are for Bolivia 1979, Brazil 1981, and Chile 1982. In all three of these cases the country did in fact reschedule in the year subsequent to the one when the false prediction occurred. Thus, the probability indicator soared from 0.03 in 1980 to 0.75 in 1981 for Brazil and from 0.0 in 1981 to 0.27 in 1982 for Chile—foreshadowing actual reschedulings in Brazil in 1982 and Chile in 1983. In short, the model appears to be relatively powerful in accurate prediction of rescheduling and pre-rescheduling situations.[36]

Creditworthiness Trends

The logit model estimated here may be used as a summary criterion for evaluating the trend of country creditworthiness over time. It provides a single composite indicator that is based in theory and empirical evidence, facilitating analysis in comparison with review of numerous individual indicators.

Table A-5 reports the level of the probability indicator for each of the largest

---

34. Thus, P_C^R is 0.015 for the Philippines, 1979; 0.054 for Romania, 1982; and 0.111 for Chile, 1972. There are no reschedulings at all for $.111 < P_C^R < .242$. There is then a cluster of 5 reschedulings for $.242 \leq P_C^R \leq .390$—a span of approximately the same width, followed by 6 reschedulings at still higher levels of P_C^R.

35. Methodologically the implication here is that the choice of the critical cutoff level, P_C^{R*}, should depend on three objectives: overall explanation, relative balance in percentage incidence of type I and type II errors, and apparent discontinuities in the distribution of P_C^R predictions for actual rescheduling cases. If these predictions had a constant frequency over a wide range (that is, no discontinuity between subgroups within the set of rescheduling cases), the first two objectives would suffice.

36. Most of the errors are of limited policy significance. Type I errors include early reschedulings (Philippines, 1970; Chile, 1972) and the special case of Romania, 1982, where credit contamination from Poland appears to have imposed problems disproportionate to underlying conditions. Of type II errors, 60 percent come from just two countries, Egypt and Zambia, and most of the others contain the policy information of pre-rescheduling situations, as noted in the text.

Table A-5 Logit indicators of debt-servicing difficulty[a]

Country	1971	1972	1973	1974	1975	1976	1977	1978	1979	1980	1981	1982
Algeria	.008	.000	.002	.000	.000	.000	.001	.001	.010	.003	.001	b
Argentina	.001	.101	.063	.000	.002	.339	c	.000	.000	.000	.002	.311
Bolivia	.003	.004	.008	.008	.000	.001	.004	.003	.265	.188	.388	c
Brazil	.000	.000	.000	.000	.0002	.006	.004	.001	.000	.026	.747	.810
Chile	.000	.111	c	.243	c	c	.009	.018	.002	.000	.000	.265
Colombia	.008	b	.006	.001	.004	.002	.000	.000	.000	.000	.000	.000
Ecuador	.002	.003	.000	.000	.000	.000	.000	.000	.001	.000	.000	.051
Egypt	.086	.259	.536	.027	.002	.131	.162	.021	.082	.049	.009	.197
Greece	.002	.000	.000	.004	.000	.001	.005	.001	.002	.003	.005	b
Indonesia	c	.005	.000	.001	.000	.003	.001	.000	.001	.000	.000	.001
Israel	.000	.001	.001	.001	.024	.118	.074	.006	.004	.003	.004	.033
Ivory Coast	.000	.002	.003	.003	.011	.000	.010	.019	b	b	b	b
Malaysia	.000	.000	.000	.000	.000	.000	.000	.000	.000	.000	.000	.001
Mexico	.004	.001	.001	.001	.004	.032	.250	.021	.090	.135	.021	.435
Morocco	.002	.007	.005	.000	.001	.002	.039	.157	.060	.144	b	b
Nigeria	.000	.001	.002	.003	.000	.000	.000	b	b	b	b	b
Peru	.000	.000	.000	.000	.000	.248	c	.525	c	c	.000	b
Philippines	c	.002	.000	.000	.000	.000	.000	.000	.001	.002	.001	.050
Portugal	b	b	b	.000	.002	.000	.001	.001	.002	.002	.016	.164
Romania	b	b	b	b	b	b	b	b	b	.018	.020	.054
South Korea	.000	.008	.001	.001	.006	.001	.001	.000	.001	.027	.004	.027
Spain	b	.000	.000	.000	.000	.000	.001	.000	.000	.000	.000	.001
Sudan	.006	.068	.201	.001	.021	.022	.210	.186	b	c	c	c
Syria	.001	.000	.009	.000	.000	.000	b	.003	.024	.002	.010	b
Thailand	.000	.000	.000	.000	.000	.000	.000	.000	.000	.001	.001	.024
Tunisia	.002	.000	.001	.000	.000	.000	.005	.002	.003	.001	.002	b
Turkey	.000	.000	.000	.000	.000	.011	.028	.738	c	c	c	.542
Venezuela	.001	.000	.000	.000	.000	.000	.000	.000	.000	.000	.000	.000
Yugoslavia	.006	.020	.002	.000	.001	.002	.000	.000	.000	.009	.007	b
Zaire	.001	.000	.010	.007	.006	.641	c	c	b	c	c	c
Zambia	.000	.000	.056	.002	.020	.058	.339	.137	.888	.036	.313	b

a. Critical level = 0.242.
b. Data not available.
c. Omitted because in year following rescheduling.

31 debtor nations, from 1971 through 1982. This indicator is from the large-debtor model "L" (table A-2). As the table shows, in the vast majority of cases the rescheduling indicator is far below the critical threshold (0.24). However, there is a general tendency for the indicator to rise in 1981–82. And the series for Mexico, Brazil, Argentina, and Chile in particular show the sharp deterioration that led to rescheduling in 1982 in the first three (and 1983 in Chile).

As a measure of the overall incidence of debt-servicing difficulty, it is useful to consider over time the debt held by countries shown to be above the critical value of the composite probability indicator (0.242). This measure is shown in table A-6. The table also reports the corresponding concept for countries that actually rescheduled (among the set of 31 large debtor countries). In both cases the total debt of the countries involved is expressed as a percentage of total debt of the 31 large-debtor countries shown in table A-5. Note that these countries, in turn, accounted for approximately 83 percent of the total external debt of nonoil developing countries, Eastern Europe, and four OPEC countries (Ecuador, Indonesia, Nigeria, and Venezuela) in 1982 (chapter 3).

The summary data in table A-6 show a strong recent acceleration of debt-servicing difficulties. Judged by actual reschedulings, the fraction of developing-country and East European debt (largest 31 countries) held by affected countries surged from an average of approximately 5 percent 1978–81 to 40 percent in 1982. Judged on the logit composite indicator, the acceleration was already in process in 1981, when 16 percent of developing-country debt was held by countries with the logit indicator above the critical level, rising to 41 percent in 1982.

A crucial implication of these results is that it was not merely market psychology but also underlying economic erosion that precipitated the debt problems of 1982. Otherwise, the measure of aggregate difficulty by actual rescheduling would not be matched by the measure based on the logit indicator (although the logit criterion does contain one element that incorporates market psychology: the behavior of aggregate lending). This diagnosis of underlying erosion implies that it will require more than psychological reversal to return to more normal debt servicing.

A second pattern evident in table A-3 is the relationship of debt-servicing difficulty to the global economic cycle. The incidence of difficulty is very low for most years, but rises in 1976–77 and again in 1981–82. These two periods were the troughs (or, troughs plus one-year lag) of the two most severe postwar recessions. This pattern is consistent with the view that global economic conditions have played a major role in precipitating debt difficulties.

Projections

A critical question for policy purposes is whether the debt problems of 1982–83 are temporary or permanent. Chapter 3 examines this question by carrying

Table A-6   Incidence of debt-servicing difficulty, 1972-82

| | | Actual reschedulings | | | Logit indicator above 0.242 | |
| | | Debt | | | | Debt | |
Year	Country	(billion dollars[a])	(percentage of total[b])	Country	(billion dollars[a])	(percentage of total[b])
1972	Chile	3.3	4.3	Egypt	2.2	2.9
1973	——	—	—	Egypt	2.5	2.6
1974	Chile	4.4	3.4	Chile	4.4	3.4
1975	Chile	4.7	3.0	c	c	c
1976	Argentina Peru Zaire	15.9	8.5	Argentina Peru Zaire	15.9	8.5
1977	Zaire	2.9	1.2	Mexico Zambia	28.7[c]	12.3[c]
1978	Peru Turkey	15.9	5.4	Peru Turkey	15.9	5.4
1979	Turkey Peru Sudan Zaire[d]	27.3	7.9	Zambia Bolivia	4.0[c]	1.1[d]
1980	Turkey Zaire	18.8	4.2	c	c	c
1981	Bolivia Sudan[d] Zaire	12.0	2.3	Bolivia Brazil Zambia	81.0[c]	15.7[c]
1982	Argentina Brazil Mexico Turkey Romania Sudan	242.3	40.4	Argentina Brazil Chile Mexico Turkey	245.1	40.9

a. Refers to total debt of country, not amount rescheduled.
b. Total is for 31 large-debt countries (table A-5).
c. Omits country with rescheduling because of additional rescheduling in previous year.
d. Case omitted from logit model because of missing data.

out projections of balance of payments and debt for the 19 largest debtor countries through 1986, under alternative global economic conditions. The composite logit indicator of debt-servicing difficulty provides a vehicle for a single summary evaluation of whether the degree of debt-servicing difficulty may be expected to intensify or accelerate in the next four years. Accordingly, the projections of underlying variables from chapter 3 may be applied to the logit model L (table A-4) for this purpose. The particular case projected is the base case scenario (see chapter 3).

The projections assume that global lending returns only gradually to its 1980–81 level after the severe 1982 contraction. Thus, the variable *EXBOR* is set at 13 percent (total borrowing as a fraction of imports) for 1983 (the same level as in 1982), 15 percent in 1984, 17 percent in 1985, and 19 percent in 1986 (the average level for 1980–81).

The results of applying the country projections of debt service, exports, reserves, economic growth, and other key variables to the logit model are shown in table 3.9, chapter 3. Two central findings stand out in the table. First, the degree of debt-servicing difficulty remains above the level associated with rescheduling through 1985 in Brazil and through 1984 in Mexico, Argentina, and Chile. But afterwards, all of the 19 countries examined return to "safe" levels of debt-servicing burden.[37] The two exceptions are Ecuador—where the logit indicator remains above the critical level throughout the period —and Algeria, highlighting the debt strain for oil exporters imposed by a declining real price of oil. The crucial implication of this pattern is that new lending may have to remain on an involuntary basis to Brazil through 1985 and to Mexico, Argentina, and Chile through 1984. Nonetheless, these countries should all return to creditworthiness within two to three years.

A second fundamental pattern in table 3.9 is that for most of the large debtor countries, the degree of debt-servicing difficulty should not reach levels associated with rescheduling, through 1986. Thus, for 9 of the 19 countries there is no year in 1983–86 when the logit indicator exceeds the critical level. The broad pattern of declining incidence of severe debt-servicing difficulty tends to confirm the conclusion of the simulation analysis in chapter 3, that the debt problem is one of illiquidity, not insolvency.

Other aspects of the projections warrant mention. The logit model predicts a rescheduling for Egypt, Portugal, and the Philippines in 1983–84. In the absence of in-depth country analysis, it can only be said that those predictions suggest special attention to creditworthiness of these countries. Indeed, events in the

---

37. It should be noted that these projections do not take into account the effect of reschedulings already conducted: rather, they refer to the debt servicing that would have occurred in the absence of these reschedulings. However, in all cases the reschedulings merely postpone principal, not interest. Principal postponement is relatively neutral in its effect on the debt-burden indicator, because while it reduces the debt-service ratio, it also reduces the amortization rate, with offsetting effects. More fundamentally, to the extent that the levels of debt service and amortization did show improvement in 1983–84 because of rescheduling, that improvement would be illusory as a guide to the ability of the country to return to voluntary lending capital markets, because it would understate the debt burden of the country.

Philippines in late 1983 bore out the rescheduling prediction here (completed in June 1983). The projections fail to capture the actual rescheduling difficulties of Venezuela and Peru in 1983. In the case of Venezuela, the high level of reserves yields an extremely low probability of rescheduling. The economic information contained in this estimate is broadly that the temporary problems of Venezuela in 1983 were more a manifestation of market confidence and mismanagement than a sign of underlying economic weakness. And for Peru the low level of the indicator suggests that, unlike the cases of Argentina, Brazil, Mexico, and Chile, the 1983 rescheduling was mainly a phenomenon caused by region-wide adverse psychology of the capital market rather than economic fundamentals.[38] A similar point applies to Yugoslavia, where East European credit contamination led to the need for a rescue package in 1983 even though on underlying fundamentals the debt problem was not severe. Moreover, the actual experience of Yugoslavia has been that there was only limited debt rescheduling and heavy emphasis on mobilization of new credits—a result consistent with the assessment given by the logit model of a relatively sound underlying economic situation.[39]

An important implication of table 3.9 in chapter 3 is that most of the Asian countries should be able to avoid debt rescheduling even in 1983–84. Thus, the logit indicator is low for Korea, Indonesia, and Thailand, although it does temporarily exceed the critical level (in 1983–84) for the Philippines.

Conclusion

Statistical analysis of debt reschedulings using the logit technique confirms the influence of key variables expected to play a role in capital-market breakdown for developing countries: debt service ratio (or, alternatively, ratio of net debt to exports), ratio of reserves to imports, amortization rate, current account deficit relative to exports, growth rate, and the level of international lending. A high degree of explanation of reschedulings may be achieved with this model, especially when applied separately to approximately 30 large debtor countries.

Application of the estimated model to trends over time confirms a severe erosion in 1981–82 and detects a smaller temporary erosion that occurred in 1976–77, suggesting the influence of the international business cycle. Projections of the logit indicator of debt-servicing difficulty confirm the general conclusion of the simulation model in chapter 3, that the debt situation should improve

---

38. This diagnosis is consistent with the fact that Peru long resisted rescheduling and rescheduled only when the large banks finally recommended that it do so in order that the new funds they contributed not merely leak away to small banks that were reducing their exposure. *Journal of Commerce,* 18 March 1983.

39. *Wall Street Journal,* 9 May 1983.

over the next few years and represents illiquidity rather than insolvency. The analysis here carries the evaluation one step further by not only measuring trends but also gauging the extent of improvement to determine whether it will be sufficient to permit a return to more normal creditworthiness and financing. In particular, the logit model projections indicate that by 1985–86 there should be sufficient improvement in the debt-servicing burden even for the major Latin American borrowers to permit reestablishment of levels of creditworthiness not associated with the need for debt rescheduling.

This analysis does contain the sobering finding that creditworthiness will not be restored in key Latin American debtor countries for one to two years. During that time it will be necessary to continue the process of involuntary bank lending orchestrated by pressure from the central bank, the International Monetary Fund, and the large banks. Moreover, the broadly sanguine implications of the analysis here are subject to the crucial assumption that economic growth in the industrial countries reaches a critical threshold of 3 percent in 1984–86. If this level of growth is not achieved, the prospects are for failure to improve creditworthiness of several major countries that have rescheduled, and the debt problem becomes transformed more and more into one of insolvency.

The broad policy implications suggest a social compact between the debtor and creditor countries. For their part the industrial creditor countries would undertake measures to ensure a strong and sustainable economic recovery.[40] In return, the debtor countries would remain committed to adjustment programs and normal implementation of the debt-rescheduling plans already in place. Under this strategy of mutual policy commitment, it should be possible to avoid the disruptions to the international financial system that could occur as the result of a breakdown in the debt-servicing and rescheduling process into extended moratoria (on interest and principal) or nonmarket reschedulings (at below-market interest), with or without either debtor collaboration in a debtors' cartel or implementation of sweeping debt reform proposals that involve write-downs of the debt.

---

40. A coordinated program for international recovery is outlined in Twenty-six Economists, *Promoting World Recovery: A Statement on Global Economic Strategy* (Washington: Institute for International Economics, December 1982). A US commitment to correct the over-valuation of the dollar would be a useful part of such a compact.

B A Projection Model for Balance of Payments and Debt

The analysis of chapter 3 examines the issue of illiquidity versus insolvency by projecting the prospective balance of payments and debt trends of the 19 largest debtor countries through 1986. This appendix sets forth the formal structure of the projection model and supplementary tables concerning its data base and results.

The Model

The model specification is as follows:

$$(1) \qquad X_t^o = X_1^o \left(\frac{P_t^o}{P_1^o} \right).$$

For oil-exporting countries, the value of oil exports in year t (X_t^o) *equals* their value in the base year 1 (1982) *multiplied* by the ratio of the international price of oil in year t (P_t^o) to the 1982 price, or \$34 per barrel. This approach makes no allowance for change in volume of oil exports. The continued efforts at conservation from current and lagged high prices will tend to offset increased volumes associated with world recovery. Moreover, it is anticipated that most of the increase in exports that might be associated with world recovery would be supplied by the swing producer, Saudi Arabia, a country excluded from the analysis.[1] Similarly, for oil-importing countries,

$$(2) \qquad M_t^o = M_1^o \left(\frac{P_t^o}{P_1^o} \right)$$

and the value of oil imports in the year in question (M_t^o) *equals* their value in the base year *times* the ratio of price in the year in question to price in the base year.

---

1. To the extent that oil trade volumes are expected to rise on a general basis, it is possible to capture this effect through specifying a correspondingly higher than expected oil price, so that the combined price-volume value captures the effect of higher volume.

The specification of nonoil exports is as follows:

$$X_t^{NO} = 0.97\, X_{t-1}^{NO}\, (1 + E_1\, g_t^{DC})\, (1 + E_2\Delta\, g_t^{DC})\, (1 + E_3\Delta\, g_{t-1}^{DC})$$

(3)
$$\cdot (1 + \dot{P}_t)\left(\frac{d_t}{d_{t-1}}\right)\left(1 + 0.5E_4\left[\left(\frac{R_t}{R_{t-1}}\right) - 1\right]\right)$$

$$+ X_{t-2}^{NO}\left(0.5E_4\left[\left(\frac{R_{t-1}}{R_{t-2}}\right) - 1\right]\right).$$

In this equation the initial elements, $0.97\, X_{t-1}^{NO}[1 + E_1\, g_t^{DC}]$, represent the influence of industrial country growth on export volume from the developing country.[2] As discussed in chapter 3, these exports decline by 3 percent in the absence of growth within the Organization for Economic Cooperation and Development (OECD), but rise by an additional 3 percentage points for each extra percentage point of OECD growth (the elasticity E_1 *equals* 3.0).

The next two elements in equation (3) capture the response of real export prices (terms of trade) to industrial country growth. The specification in equation (3) captures this phenomenon by stating an elasticity of "real" nonoil export prices for the country in question with respect to the change in industrial country growth. This formulation means that, once a stable growth rate plateau is reached, there is no further change in terms of trade. The formulation, based on empirical estimates discussed below, captures this effect for the current year (E_2 applied to Δg_t^{DC}) and for the lagged effect from the previous year (E_3 applied to Δg_{t-1}^{DC}; note that Δg_t^{DC} is defined as $g_t^{DC} - g_{t-1}^{DC}$).

The next element in equation (3) indicates that the value of exports increases along with the average rate of world inflation ($\dot{P}$) in the year in question. The following element is a similar inflator for the effect of dollar devaluation on the dollar price of goods in world trade. The term d_t is an index of the nominal exchange rate of the dollar per unit of foreign currencies. As (d_t/d_{t-1}) rises, the dollar depreciates relative to other major currencies.

The remaining elements in the export equation capture the effect of the country's own real exchange rate on its exports. With R_t defined as the amount of domestic currency (for example, pesos) per dollar, deflating both pesos and dollars by home country and US prices respectively (that is, the "real" exchange rate), the final multiplicative term states that a real devaluation in year t causes the country's exports to rise by one-half *times* the export elasticity (E_4) *times* the percentage change in the real exchange rate. In addition, exports in year t are augmented by a similar, lagged effect of devaluation in the previous year (the final, additive term in the equation). Thus, exchange rate stimulus to exports is spread evenly over two years. The export elasticity is a composite

---

2. That is, $0.97\, X_{t-1}\, (1 + E_1\, g_t^{DC})$ is approximately equal to $X_{t-1}\, [1 - .03 + E_1\, g_t^{DC}]$ so that the percentage change in exports is $-3 + E_1\, g_t^{DC}$ where g_t^{DC} is percentage growth in OECD real income.

elasticity reflecting both the elasticity of foreign demand and that of domestic export supply to a change in the real exchange rate. Broadly, the real exchange rate is a key element of domestic adjustment, whereas all of the other variables in the export equation are driven by the international economic environment.

Given equations (1) and (3), total exports are:

(4) $X_t = X_t^O + X_t^{NO}$.

Nonoil imports are influenced by domestic economic growth in the developing country, world inflation and dollar devaluation, and the real exchange rate. Thus:

$$M_t^{NO} = M_{t-1}^{NO} [(1 + E_5 g_t^i) + E_6(g_t^i - g_{t-1}^i)] (1 + \dot{P}) \left(\frac{d_t}{d_{t-1}} \right)$$

(5) $$\cdot [1 / (1 + [0.5E_7 \left(\left[\frac{R_t}{R_{t-1}} \right] - 1 \right)])]$$

$$- M_{t-2}^{NO}(0.5E_7[\left(\frac{R_{t-1}}{R_{t-2}} \right) - 1]).$$

In this formulation, nonoil imports in year t (M_t^{NO}) are based on the previous year's value. That value is increased, first, by a percentage reflecting the long-term growth relationship between real imports and real GDP: elasticity E_5 as applied to domestic growth $(g_t^i,$ with superscript i indicating the country in question). The shorter run cyclical response of imports to income is typically greater than the long-run trend response (because of factors such as inventory adjustments and temporary protection); that is, over the long run imports may grow in strict proportion to income (elasticity E_5 equals 1.0), but in the short run a cyclical decline of GDP by 1 percent may make possible a cutback of 3 percent or more in imports (as has been demonstrated dramatically in recent Latin American experience). Accordingly, there is an additional term to capture cyclical response of imports to income: E_6 $(g_t^i - g_{t-1}^i)$, where E_6 is the cyclical elasticity and $g_t^i - g_{t-1}^i$ is the change in growth rate from the previous year. The cyclical elasticity (E_6) equals 3, so that this parameter is symmetrical to the import function used for industrial countries; while the long-term import elasticity is set equal to 1.0 for proportionate import and income growth.

The next two terms in equation (5) are for world inflation $(1 + \dot{P})$ and dollar devaluation (d_t/d_{t-1}) their role is the same as that played in the export equation, (3).

The following term in the import equation measures the effect of changes in the country's real exchange rate. The multiplicative term places the percentage change in the real exchange rate *multiplied* by the (positively defined) import elasticity with respect to real exchange rate (E_7) in the denominator—so that larger devaluation causes a smaller volume of imports. As in the case of exports, half of the exchange rate effect is attributed to the current year; the other half is lagged one year the final, additive term in equation (5).

Given equations (2) and (5), total imports are:

(6) $M_t = M_t^O + M_t^{NO}$.

Exports and imports of nonfactor services (transportation, freight and insurance, tourism) are calculated, respectively, as constant proportions of nonoil exports and imports, determined from base-year levels:

(7) $X_t^s = X_t^{NO} \left(\dfrac{X_1^s}{X_1^{NO}} \right)$;

(8) $M_t^s = M_t^{NO} \left(\dfrac{M_1^s}{M_1^{NO}} \right)$.

Imports of services are defined to include net remittances of profits.

Interest payments are calculated as follows. The fraction of long-term debt that is at fixed interest rates is determined, as "f." The average interest rate paid on fixed interest debt in 1982 is determined, as "i_f." For all remaining external debt—short-term and long—it is assumed that the interest rate paid *equals* the international rate "r," London Interbank Offer Rate (LIBOR) *plus* a spread of 1½ percent (or, for Brazil, 2 percent). Interest earnings on nongold reserves (H) are assumed to be earned at a US Treasury bill rate (r'), assumed to *equal* 1½ percentage points below LIBOR. Net interest payments are thus:

(9) $I_t = i_f f D_{t-1}^{LT} + r_t [D_{t-1}^{ST} + (1-f) D_{t-1}^{LT}] - r'_t H_{t-1}$,

where I_t *equals* net interest payments, and D_t^{LT} and D_t^{ST} are long- and short-term debt at the end of year t, respectively. Note that interest flows result from interest rates in a given year applied to debt and reserve stocks at the end of the preceding year.

As final elements of the current account, transfers are estimated on the basis of simple 3 percent real growth as inflated by the path of dollar devaluation:

(10) $T_t = T_{t-1}(1.03)(1 + \dot{P}) \left(\dfrac{d_t}{d_{t-1}} \right)$.

The current account balance in year t is then the sum of the above elements:

(11) $C_t = X_t + X_t^s - M_t - M_t^s - I_t + T_t$.

Given the current account, the capital account is constructed as follows. The change in reserves is assumed to *equal* either zero, if imports decline, or one-fifth of the rise in imports if they rise—to maintain an acceptable reserve cushion relative to imports. Thus:

(12) $\Delta H_t = \text{Max} \begin{cases} 0.2[M_t - M_{t-1}] \\ 0 \end{cases}$.

Direct foreign investment is assumed to grow at a real rate of 3 percent annually, as inflated for dollar devaluation:

$$(13) \qquad DFI_t = DFI_{t-1}(1.03)(1 + \dot{P})\left(\frac{d_t}{d_{t-1}}\right).$$

Given the current account deficit, the needed increase in reserves, and the amount of direct foreign investment, the total amount of new net lending required to finance the balance of payments is:

$$(14) \qquad L_t = -C_t + \Delta H_t - DFI_t.$$

Total debt at the end of the year *equals* the previous year's debt *plus* net borrowing,

$$(15) \qquad D_t = D_{t-1} + L_t,$$

and the composition of debt between short- and long-term is assumed to remain the same as in the base period:

$$(16) \qquad D_t^{LT} = D_t\left[\frac{D_1^{LT}}{D_1}\right]; D_t^{ST} = D_t - D_t^{LT}.$$

Amortization on long-term debt equals the country's base period amortization rate, "a" (ratio of long-term debt amortization to end-of-year long-term debt in the previous year), applied to long-term debt at the end of the preceding year:

$$(17) \qquad A_t = aD_{t-1}.$$

Gross borrowing in year t *equals* net borrowing *plus* amortization:

$$(18) \qquad G_t = L_t + A_t.$$

To evaluate trends in debt-servicing burden and creditworthiness, four ratios are calculated: the ratio of net debt to exports of goods and services (NDX_t); the ratio of debt service to exports of goods and services (DSR_t); the ratio of the current account balance to exports of goods and services (CAX_t); and the ratio of reserves to imports of goods and services (excluding interest), RSM_t. Thus:

$$(19) \qquad NDX_t = \frac{(D_t - H_t)}{X_t^{GS}},$$

$$(20) \qquad DSR_t = \frac{(A_t + I_t)}{X_t^{GS}},$$

$$(21) \qquad CAX_t = \frac{C_t}{X_t^{GS}}$$

and

$$(22) \qquad RSM_t = \frac{H_t}{M_t^{GS}}$$

where X_t^{GS} and M_t^{GS} are exports of goods and services $(X_t + X_t^s)$ and imports of goods and services $(M_t + M_t^s)$, respectively.

The elasticities used in the analysis are as follows: E_1 *equals* elasticity of LDC export volume with respect to industrial country growth *equals* 3.0; E_4 *equals* elasticity of LDC export volume with respect to the country's real exchange rate *equals* 0.5; E_7 *equals* elasticity of import volume with respect to real exchange rate *equals* 0.6. The income elasticity of LDC imports E_5 is assumed equal to unity, while the cyclical elasticity of imports, E_6, is set at 3.0.

The terms of trade elasticities, E_2 and E_3, are based on simple regression estimates. Using data for 1961–81, the equations presented in table B-1 were estimated:

$$Z_t = a + E_2 \, \Delta g_t^{DC} + E_3 \, \Delta g_{t-1}^{DC},$$

where Z_t is the percentage change in the price index of the country's exports as deflated by the price index for industrial country exports and Δg^{DC} is the change in OECD country growth rate from year $t-1$ to year t. For countries with estimates of E_2, E_3 not significantly different from zero, the two elasticities are set at zero.[3] Table B-1 reports the cyclical terms of trade elasticities estimated.

Results

Chapter 3 presents the main results of the projection model. The discussion that follows concerns additional detail of the estimates. (Note, however, that subsequent, updated projections appear in the epilogue to this study, chapter 8.) The first set of results, in table B-2, indicates the projected trends for the 8 smaller debtor countries (projections for the 11 largest debtor countries appear in chapter 3, table 3.3).

As discussed in chapter 3, implausible trends in the initial estimates for some of the countries necessitated adjustments in the individual country assumptions on domestic growth and real exchange rate changes. These modifications are set forth in chapter 3. For purposes of more comprehensive reporting, however, tables B-3 and B-4 indicate the initial results obtained prior to introduction of the country adjustments.

---

3. In addition, for countries without data (Mexico, Argentina, Egypt, Ecuador) the average elasticities from the others are applied. For Chile, in the absence of an export price index, estimated cyclical elasticities for copper are applied with a weight of one-half, the approximate share of copper in exports. Also, the estimate for Hungary is applied as well to Romania.

In table B-3, the aggregate balance of payments projections are shown using the initial estimates without individual country modification. The projections refer to the base case (OECD growth of 3 percent in 1984–86, oil price of $29 per barrel, LIBOR trending down to 8 percent, and dollar depreciation by 15 percent; table 3.1). Comparison of table 3.2 to table B-3 indicates that the final estimates of this study are comparable to the initial estimates in the aggregate. However, in the final, adjusted estimates, projected trends for oil importers show somewhat milder improvement, while those for oil exporters show smaller deterioration.

For countries with special adjustments, the original, unadjusted projections appear in table B-4. Comparison with tables 3.3 and B-2 indicates the following modifications. For Brazil, a higher growth rate in 1984–86 moderates the favorable trend of the external account but still leaves sharp improvement over 1982. The modifications for Korea make a much larger reduction in its initially extremely favorable current account balances over the period. A comparably large adjustment for Venezuela occurs in the opposite direction, reducing its 1986 current account deficit from a highly implausible $18 billion to $11 billion, a figure that is almost certainly still overstated. A sharp reduction of projected deficits is also shown in the adjusted estimates for another oil-exporting country, Algeria. The remaining country adjustments are more moderate.

A central finding of this study is the strong influence of OECD growth on the debt problem. Table 3.4 reports this influence for the final year only (1986). To provide information on the profile of this influence over the earlier years, table B-5 reports comparable results (adjusted estimates) for each year through 1986. As the table shows, the differential growth impact (between case B and case D, for example) shows up strongly in 1984, with an even larger increment to current account balances in 1985 that is approximately repeated again in 1986.

The detailed balance of payments projections for Argentina, Brazil (adjusted), and Mexico appear in tables B-6 through B-8, under base-case assumptions about world economic conditions. From the vantage point of late 1983 it may be noted that Mexico's imports were far lower in 1983 than projected, leading to an actual account surplus of over $5 billion. In Brazil and Argentina, both imports and exports were moderately lower than projected, leaving trade and current account balances comparable to those projected but a lower export base for creditworthiness evaluation. In addition, actual direct foreign investment appeared to be significantly lower in 1983 than originally projected in Brazil and Mexico. (See chapter 8 for updated projections.) Finally, the corresponding detailed projections for the 19 largest debtor countries as a group appear in table B-9, with detail by oil importers and exporters.

Table B-1 Estimates of elasticity of real export price with respect to OECD growth[a] (t-statistics in parentheses)

Country	c	b_1	b_2	$\overline{R}^2$
Brazil	1.422	1.927	2.433	.306
	(.776)	(2.130)	(2.696)	
Chile (copper)[b]	3.554	4.946	5.033	.218
	(.719)	(2.026)	(2.068)	
Hungary	− 2.220	.755	—	.329
	(2.920)	(2.430)		
Israel	1.179	0.782	0.996	.101
	(1.003)	(1.346)	(1.720)	
Korea[c]	—	—	—	—
Peru	3.452	—	2.535	.088
	(1.097)		(1.655)	
Philippines	− .357	—	2.420	.105
	(.127)		(1.764)	
Thailand	.209	—	2.105	.119
	(.089)		(1.854)	
Turkey	− .096	—	1.403	.220
	(.058)		(2.025)	
Yugoslavia	1.365	—	0.606	.101
	(1.869)		(1.703)	

Source: IMF, *International Financial Statistics,* various issues; *OECD Outlook,* various issues.
a. From the 1961–81 regression $z = c + b_1 \Delta g_t + b_2 \Delta g_{t-1}$ where z = percentage change in country export unit value as deflated by industrial country export unit value index, g_t = OECD real growth in year t, and $\Delta g_t = g_t - g_{t-1}$.
b. For Chile, one-half the elasticity estimated here for copper is applied in the text analysis.
c. Results not significant.

Table B-2 Current account and debt projections, selected countries, 1982–86 (million dollars and ratios)

		1982	1983	1984	1985	1986
Egypt	CA	−2,500	−2,555	−3,033	−3,647	−3,806
	D	18,000	19,699	22,057	24,857	27,699
	NDX	2.398	2.595	2.416	2.457	2.424
Algeria[a]	CA	−2,935	−2,401	−4,824	−5,600	−5,481
	D	15,093	17,136	21,941	27,189	32,320
	NDX	1.283	1.668	2.072	2.561	2.667
Portugal	CA	−2,278	−1,736	−1,312	−1,236	−1,367
	D	12,900	14,538	15,939	17,166	18,530
	NDX	2.030	2.039	1.752	1.650	1.590
Peru	CA	−1,400	−2,260	−2,421	−2,578	−2,799
	D	11,100	13,187	15,427	17,748	20,245
	NDX	2.479	2.769	2.589	2.616	2.698
Thailand	CA	−1,100	−512	338	931	1,339
	D	10,500	10,688	10,207	9,016	7,366
	NDX	1.061	0.972	0.697	0.502	0.330
Romania[a]	CA	−600	407	1,522	2,217	2,501
	D	8,200	8,075	6,947	4,979	2,854
	NDX	0.595	0.497	0.317	0.171	0.038
Hungary	CA	−150	−961	−324	−241	−75
	D	7,500	8,632	9,303	9,797	10,126
	NDX	0.622	0.626	0.523	0.483	0.439
Ecuador	CA	−1,100	−1,243	−1,458	−1,687	−1,808
	D	6,300	7,535	9,017	10,694	12,476
	NDX	1.990	2.330	2.324	2.495	2.591

CA current account; D total debt; NDX net debt (deducting reserves) relative to exports of goods and services.
a. Adjusted estimates.

Table B-3 Unadjusted balance of payments projections, 1982–86 (base case, million dollars and ratios)

	1982	1983	1984	1985	1986
Oil importers[a]					
Exports	110,536	125,792	160,377	182,020	202,072
Imports	−125,552	−130,798	−152,112	−167,169	−185,638
Oil	−34,499	−29,426	−29,426	−29,426	−34,499
Interest	−29,464	−29,256	−29,458	−27,956	−27,332
Current account	−35,451	−24,724	−8,376	1,064	4,990
Debt	299,377	320,719	327,404	322,913	314,654
Net debt/exports[b]	1.94	1.83	1.45	1.25	1.08
Debt service ratio[c]	.39	.38	.31	.27	.23
Oil exporters[a]					
Exports	76,300	69,777	74,809	78,030	89,766
Oil	59,140	50,443	50,443	50,433	59,140
Imports	−64,756	−71,053	−87,836	−98,760	−108,364
Interest	−15,423	−16,520	−17,496	−19,437	−23,331
Current account	−20,989	−25,745	−40,114	−50,768	−53,268
Debt	184,778	208,188	247,393	295,732	345,932
Net debt/exports[b]	1.77	2.11	2.26	2.56	2.65
Debt service[c]	.34	.40	.39	.42	.44
Total, 19 debtors					
Exports	186,836	195,569	235,186	260,049	291,838
Imports	−190,308	−201,851	−239,948	−265,929	−294,002
Interest	−44,887	−45,775	−46,954	−47,392	−50,662
Current account	−56,440	−50,469	−48,490	−49,704	−48,277
Debt	484,155	528,906	574,797	618,646	660,586
Net debt/exports[b]	1.87	1.93	1.71	1.66	1.58
Debt service ratio[c]	.37	.38	.33	.31	.30

a. See table 3.6 for groupings.
b. Exports of goods and services.
c. Long-term amortization plus total net interest as a fraction of exports of goods and services.

Table B-4 Unadjusted current account and debt projections, by country, 1982–86ᵃ (base case, million dollars and ratio)

		1982	1983	1984	1985	1986
Algeria	CA	−2,935	−4,753	−7,237	−9,388	−10,278
	D	15,093	19,601	26,794	36,001	46,032
	NDX	1.283	1.936	2.599	3.485	3.907
Brazil	CA	−14,000	−7,131	−2,924	815	1,919
	D	88,200	93,060	93,833	90,379	85,870
	NDX	3.816	3.463	2.596	2.153	1.826
Chile	CA	−2,540	−4,548	−4,182	−4,285	−4,749
	D	18,000	22,436	26,280	30,151	34,449
	NDX	3.003	3.196	2.790	2.786	2.886
Korea	CA	−2,219	2,283	5,984	8,155	10,069
	D	35,800	33,380	27,907	20,072	10,430
	NDX	1.060	0.859	0.537	0.288	0.046
Romania	CA	−600	1,997	4,068	5,265	6,314
	D	8,200	6,232	2,477	−2,560	−8,571
	NDX	0.595	0.380	0.078	−0.193	−0.458
Turkey	CA	−1,100	−166	1,288	2,228	2,590
	D	19,000	19,035	17,780	15,522	12,988
	NDX	2.406	2.161	1.576	1.184	0.860
Venezuela	CA	−2,200	−8,044	−12,749	−16,727	−18,411
	D	31,285	39,702	52,914	69,932	88,575
	NDX	1.042	1.659	2.344	3.251	3.692

CA current account; D total debt; NDX net debt (deducting reserves) relative to exports of goods and services.
a. Includes only countries with adjustments in final estimates.

Table B-5 Influence of industrial country growth rates on balance of payments,[a] 19 major debtor countries, 1982–86 (million dollars)

	Current account				
	1982	1983	1984	1985	1986
Oil importers					
A	−35,451	−33,697	−34,360	−40,863	−55,730
B	−35,451	−30,890	−26,971	−29,292	−39,164
C	−35,451	−30,890	−23,598	−21,032	−26,141
D	−35,451	−30,890	−20,207	−12,564	−12,626
E	−35,451	−28,069	−12,455	139	6,210
Oil exporters					
A	−20,989	−20,375	−37,352	−47,723	−50,932
B	−20,989	−19,711	−35,573	−44,962	−47,008
C	−20,989	−19,711	−34,775	−42,973	−43,901
D	−20,989	−19,711	−33,973	−40,933	−40,674
E	−20,989	−19,044	−32,106	−37,895	−36,200
Total					
A	−56,440	−54,072	−71,713	−88,586	−106,662
B	−56,440	−50,602	−62,543	−74,254	−86,172
C	−56,440	−50,602	−58,373	−64,005	−70,042
D	−56,440	−50,602	−54,181	−53,498	−53,300
E	−56,440	−47,113	−44,561	−37,756	−29,990
Net debt/exports, total					
A	1.87	1.98	1.92	2.07	2.20
B	1.87	1.94	1.82	1.90	1.95
C	1.87	1.94	1.78	1.79	1.78
D	1.87	1.94	1.74	1.70	1.63
E	1.87	1.90	1.65	1.54	1.41

Growth rates: 1982 = 0 percent; 1983–86: case A, 1.0, 1.5, 1.5, 1.5; case B, 1.5, 2.0, 2.0, 2.0; case C, 1.5, 2.5, 2.5, 2.5; case D, 1.5, 3.0, 3.0, 3.0; case E, 2.0, 3.5, 3.5, 3.5.
a. Adjusted estimates.

Table B-6 Argentina: base-case projections[a] (million dollars and ratios)

	1982	1983	1984	1985	1986
Exports	7,700	8,815	11,466	13,136	14,584
Imports	−4,600	−6,182	−7,374	−8,278	−9,083
Services					
Exports	1,724	1,974	2,567	2,941	3,265
Interest	−4,619	−4,184	−4,028	−3,662	−3,512
Other imports	−2,153	−2,894	−3,451	−3,874	−4,251
Transfers	−4	−5	−5	−6	−6
Current account	−2,400	−2,476	−825	257	996
Direct investment	916	1,040	1,232	1,333	1,441
Amortization	−5,094	−6,750	−7,061	−7,031	−6,781
Net loans	1,157	1,752	−169	−1,409	−2,276
Gross loans	6,251	8,502	6,892	5,622	4,505
Reserves change	−327	316	238	181	161
Reserves	2,941	3,257	3,496	3,677	3,838
Total debt	38,000	39,752	39,583	38,175	35,898
Debt-service ratio	1.031	1.013	0.790	0.665	0.577
Net debt/exports	3.720	3.383	2.572	2.146	1.796
Current account/exports	−0.255	−0.230	−0.059	0.016	0.056
Reserves/imports	0.436	0.359	0.323	0.303	0.288

a. See chapter 8, table 8.3 for subsequent projections.

Table B-7 Brazil: adjusted base-case projections[a] (million dollars and ratios)

	1982	1983	1984	1985	1986
Exports	20,175	23,499	31,426	36,337	40,341
Imports	−19,394	−17,435	−21,160	−22,440	−25,521
Oil	−10,759	−9,177	−9,177	−9,177	−10,759
Services					
Exports	2,150	2,504	3,349	3,872	4,299
Interest	−10,700	−9,589	−9,421	−8,929	−8,758
Other imports	−6,613	−6,325	−9,177	−10,157	−11,305
Transfers	189	215	254	275	297
Current account	−14,000	−7,131	−4,729	−1,041	−647
Direct investment	2,000	2,271	2,690	2,909	3,147
Amortization	−8,605	−9,747	−10,284	−10,592	−10,413
Net loans	8,000	4,860	2,784	−1,612	−1,884
Gross loans	16,605	14,607	13,068	8,979	8,530
Reserves change	−4,000	0	745	256	616
Reserves	3,000	3,000	3,745	4,001	4,617
Total debt	88,200	93,060	95,843	94,231	92,347
Debt-service ratio	0.865	0.744	0.567	0.485	0.429
Net debt/exports	3.816	3.463	2.648	2.244	1.965
Current account/exports	−0.627	−0.274	−0.136	−0.026	−0.014
Reserves/imports	0.115	0.126	0.123	0.123	0.125

a. See chapter 8, table 8.3, for subsequent projections.

Table B-8 Mexico: base-case projections[a] (million dollars and ratios)

	1982	1983	1984	1985	1986
Exports	21,006	19,175	20,612	21,529	24,776
Oil	16,477	14,054	14,054	14,054	16,477
Imports	−14,422	−14,431	−19,794	−22,371	−24,546
Services					
Exports	8,463	9,570	12,255	13,969	15,508
Interest	−10,848	−8,798	−8,194	−7,909	−8,366
Other imports	−7,975	−7,980	−10,946	−12,370	−13,573
Transfers	125	142	168	182	197
Current account	−4,254	−2,321	−5,899	−6,970	−6,005
Direct investment	1,500	1,703	2,018	2,182	2,360
Amortization	−7,015	−7,867	−7,927	−8,402	−8,911
Net loans	−746	619	4,954	5,304	4,080
Gross loans	6,269	8,487	12,880	13,706	12,991
Reserves change	−3,500	2	1,073	515	435
Reserves	1,629	1,631	2,703	3,219	3,654
Total debt	82,000	82,619	87,573	92,877	96,957
Debt-service ratio	0.606	0.580	0.490	0.459	0.429
Net debt/exports	2.727	2.817	2.582	2.526	2.316
Current account/exports	−0.144	−0.081	−0.179	−0.196	−0.149
Reserves/imports	0.073	0.073	0.088	0.093	0.096

a. See chapter 8, table 8.3, for subsequent projections.

Table B-9   Base-case projections, 19 debtor countries, 1982–86 (million dollars and ratios)

	1982	1983	1984	1985	1986
Oil importers					
Exports	110,536	125,243	158,805	179,936	199,758
Imports	−125,552	−135,360	−159,308	−174,566	−194,848
Oil	−34,499	−29,426	−29,426	−29,426	−34,499
Services					
Exports	30,442	34,347	43,378	49,138	54,551
Interest	−29,464	−29,256	−30,058	−29,591	−30,187
Other imports	−35,076	−40,691	−50,587	−56,475	−62,444
Transfers	13,057	14,827	17,563	18,994	20,542
Current account	−35,451	−30,890	−20,207	−12,564	−12,626
Direct investment	4,426	5,026	5,953	6,439	6,963
Amortization	−25,612	−31,091	−33,571	−34,927	−35,159
Net loans	23,234	28,218	19,044	9,177	9,719
Gross loans	48,846	59,309	52,615	44,105	44,878
Reserves change	−7,791	2,353	4,790	3,052	4,056
Reserves	25,470	27,823	32,613	35,665	39,721
Total debt	299,377	327,595	346,638	355,816	365,535
Debt service/exports	0.391	0.378	0.315	0.282	0.257
Net debt/exports	1.943	1.878	1.553	1.398	1.281
Current account/exports	−0.251	−0.194	−0.100	−0.055	−0.050
Reserves/imports	0.159	0.158	0.155	0.154	0.154
Oil exporters					
Exports	76,300	69,783	74,836	78,072	89,813
Oil	59,140	50,443	50,443	50,443	59,140
Imports	−64,756	−66,835	−84,013	−92,747	−101,070
Services					
Exports	16,261	18,381	23,493	26,771	29,720
Interest	−15,423	−16,520	−16,886	−18,305	−21,284
Other imports	−26,434	−27,075	−34,429	−37,996	−41,391
Transfers	2,249	2,554	3,025	3,272	3,538
Current account	−20,989	−19,711	−33,973	−40,933	−40,674
Direct investment	3,171	3,601	4,265	4,613	4,989
Amortization	−15,925	−18,408	−20,136	−23,467	−27,248

Table B-9 Base-case projections, 19 debtor countries, 1982–86
million dollars and ratios *(Continued)*

	1982	1983	1984	1985	1986
Net loans	189	16,780	33,144	38,067	37,350
Gross loans	16,114	35,188	53,280	61,535	64,598
Reserves change	− 17,629	670	3,436	1,747	1,665
Reserves	20,930	21,600	25,035	26,782	28,447
Total debt	184,778	201,558	234,702	272,769	310,119
Oil importers					
Debt service/exports	0.339	0.396	0.377	0.398	0.406
Net debt/exports	1.770	2.041	2.132	2.346	2.356
Current account/exports	− 0.227	− 0.224	− 0.346	− 0.390	− 0.340
Reserves/imports	0.230	0.230	0.211	0.205	0.200
Nineteen debtors					
Exports	186,836	195,026	233,642	258,008	289,571
Oil	59,140	50,443	50,443	50,443	59,140
Imports	− 190,308	− 202,195	− 243,321	− 267,314	− 295,918
Oil	− 34,499	− 29,426	− 29,426	− 29,426	− 34,499
Services					
Exports	46,703	52,728	66,871	75,909	84,272
Interest	− 44,887	− 45,775	− 46,944	− 47,896	− 51,471
Other imports	− 61,510	− 67,766	− 85,016	− 94,471	− 103,835
Transfers	15,306	17,381	20,588	22,266	24,081
Current account	− 56,440	− 50,602	− 54,181	− 53,498	− 53,300
Direct investment	7,597	8,627	10,219	11,051	11,952
Amortization	− 41,537	− 49,500	− 53,707	− 58,395	− 62,407
Net loans	23,423	44,998	52,187	47,245	47,069
Gross loans	64,960	94,497	105,895	105,639	109,476
Reserves change	− 25,420	3,023	8,225	4,799	5,721
Reserves	46,400	49,423	57,648	62,447	68,168
Total debt	484,155	529,153	581,340	628,585	675,654
Debt service/exports	0.370	0.385	0.335	0.318	0.305
Net debt/exports	1.874	1.936	1.743	1.695	1.625
Current account/exports	− 0.242	− 0.204	− 0.180	− 0.160	− 0.143
Reserves/imports	0.184	0.183	0.176	0.173	0.171

C Managing the Debt Crisis: Mexico, Brazil, Argentina, Poland, and Yugoslavia

Despite the simultaneous impact of international economic shocks on many developing countries in recent years, ultimately debt crises occur at the level of the individual country. Successful debt management will depend on appropriate national policy as well as improved international conditions. This appendix reviews the recent debt experience of the three largest developing-country debtors and two East European countries that have faced debt difficulties.

Mexico

In August 1982 Mexico stunned the financial world by suspending payment temporarily on its external debt of approximately $80 billion.[1] This action marked the inauguration of the widespread crisis in international debt, whereas the previous episodes of near-default in Poland and payments suspension by Argentina because of the South Atlantic war had appeared to be isolated incidents. The Mexican suspension broke market confidence so severely that crises soon ensued in several other Latin American countries.

Mexico's economic problems stemmed from both external and internal factors. The external causes were a weakening of the world oil market since 1981 and higher world interest rates beginning in 1980. Oil constitutes three-fourths of

---

The sections on Poland and Yugoslavia were prepared by David D. Johnson.

1. The initial portion of this section also appears in William R. Cline, "Mexico's Crisis, the World's Peril," *Foreign Policy*, no. 49 (Winter 1982–83), pp. 107–9. The discussion of the cases of Mexico, Brazil, and Argentina draws on materials in the Latin American Economic Outlook, prepared by International Economic Analysis, Inc., Washington. See also John Williamson, ed., *Prospects for Adjustment in Argentina, Brazil, and Mexico: Responding to the Debt Crisis* (Washington: Institute for International Economics, June 1983). The discussion of the financial rescue packages for Mexico, Brazil, and Argentina draws upon "International Financial Rescue: Viability and Modalities" (Washington: 1984, mimeographed), prepared for the United Nations Development Program and United Nations Conference on Trade and Development. Portions of the discussion of interest capitalization and forgiveness in chapter 7 are also based on this study.

Table C-1   Mexico: economic indicators (billion dollars and percentages)

	1973	1974	1975	1976	1977
Exports	2.1	3.0	3.0	3.5	4.6
Imports	3.7	5.8	6.3	5.8	5.6
Current account	− 1.4	− 2.9	− 4.1	− 3.4	− 1.8
Reserves	1.2	1.2	1.4	1.2	1.6
Total debt	8.6	12.8	16.9	21.8	27.1
Short-term debt	2.1	3.3	3.6	3.3	3.2
Net debt/exports	154.6	182.0	243.8	286.5	309.7
Exchange rate index	104.6	101.7	100.1	105.1	116.1
GDP growth	7.6	5.9	4.1	2.1	3.3
Inflation	12.1	23.5	15.4	15.7	29.0

n.a. Not available.
Source: IMF, *International Financial Statistics,* various issues; Inter-American Development Bank, *Economic and Social Progress in Latin America,* various years; BIS, *Maturity Distribution of International Bank Lending,* various years; CEPAL, *Balance Preliminar* 1983; Banco de Mexico *Informe Anual 1983;* Solís and Zedillo, "A Few Considerations on the Foreign Debt of Mexico," 1984; and Institute for International Economics debt data base. Merchandise exports and imports. Nongold reserves. Net debt as percentage of exports of goods and services. Real trade-weighted exchange rate index, measured against five industrial country currencies. Consumer price inflation, year over year.

Mexico's merchandise exports. Yet in 1981 Mexico's oil exports amounted to only $14 billion instead of the $20 billion government planners had anticipated. In addition, higher international interest rates combined with rising debt drove Mexico's interest burden from $5.4 billion in 1980 to $8.2 billion in 1981. Together, these external forces helped cause an unusually high external deficit relative to exports. In 1981 the current account deficit was $12 billion compared with exports of approximately $20 billion (table C-1).

Internal policy made matters worse. An ambitious growth policy held real economic growth at an average of 8.2 percent in 1978–81, despite long-term capacity growth of about 6 percent. The result was an over-heated—and increasingly inflationary—economy out of step with slow growth internationally. Outsized budget deficits, reaching 17.6 percent of gross domestic product (GDP) in 1982, and an overvalued exchange rate aggravated the problem. Determined to maintain a fixed—or nearly fixed—exchange rate, authorities during 1977–80 held the peso at 23 to 25 per dollar in spite of 23 percent annual domestic inflation. The real, trade-weighted peso/dollar rate appreciated from an index of 116 in 1977 to only 89 in 1981 (table C-1). This overvaluation caused

1978	1979	1980	1981	1982	1983
6.2	9.3	16.2	19.8	21.2	21.4
8.0	12.1	18.6	23.1	14.4	7.7
−3.2	−5.5	−7.9	−11.7	−4.9	5.5
1.8	2.1	3.0	4.1	.8	3.9
33.6	40.8	53.8	74.1	84.1	87.6
4.6	7.6	15.5	24.0	25.2	n.a.
278.2	241.7	205.7	242.4	272.7	308.0
111.4	106.0	97.6	89.3	129.3	141.7
7.3	9.2	8.3	8.1	−0.5	−4.7
17.5	18.1	26.4	27.9	59.0	101.9

stagnation in nonoil exports. In combination with excess demand and import liberalization, the exchange rate prompted imports to rise from $6 billion in 1977 to $23 billion in 1981, outstripping even the once seemingly limitless bonanza of new oil exports. The overvalued exchange rate prompted capital flight of $8.4 billion in 1981. In February 1982 the government finally devalued the peso from 26 to 45 per dollar. During the final phase of a presidential election, however, the government was unwilling to make the politically painful adjustments—including budgetary cutbacks and wage restraint—that would have made devaluation more effective.

Ironically, the spark that ignited the August 1982 financial panic was an austerity measure. After a sound election victory for the official government party—Partido Revolucionario Institucional—in July, the government decreed increases of 100 percent in bread and tortilla prices and 50 percent in gasoline prices to reduce budget deficits caused by subsidies for these basic items. Anti-inflationary in the long run, these measures meant short-run corrective inflation. More significantly, they provoked the public—already shocked by a 60 percent annual inflation rate—frantically to convert pesos to dollars. Primarily in the first several months of 1982 capital flight amounted to nearly $9 billion. With sharply declining foreign exchange reserves, in August the government declared domestic dollar deposits in banks redeemable only in pesos, instituted a dual exchange rate, and temporarily closed the exchange market. When the market reopened, the peso soared from 70 to 120 per dollar. At the same time, on August 20, 1982, the government announced a 90-day suspension on payment of principal on foreign debt. Simultaneously, Western governments and international agencies extended support in a financial rescue package.

To meet Mexico's emergency financial needs, the international financial community rallied promptly and decisively in this rescue effort. The United States committed nearly $3 billion, with $1 billion in prepayment for purchases of oil for the strategic reserve, $1 billion in agricultural finance from the Commodity Credit Corporation (CCC), and $925 million in shorter term bridge lending from the Federal Reserve. European central banks matched this last amount in a bridge loan through the Bank for International Settlements (BIS). Official sources were also expected to provide $2 billion in export credits.

The Mexican government imposed exchange controls making it illegal for citizens to hold dollars domestically or abroad. It embarked on a comprehensive program of debt rescheduling, affecting $35 billion in principal payments ($19.5 billion public, $15 billion private) falling due through the end of 1984. The 90-day moratorium on principal was subsequently extended through August 15, 1983, as these arrangements were completed. For private debt the government established a special peso account (FICORCA) for debt servicing. In addition to agreeing to reschedule principal, by February 23, 1983, over five hundred foreign banks provided $5 billion in new lending for 1983, a 7 percent increase in their exposure.

The International Monetary Fund (IMF) provided the keystone for this financial architecture. It provided $3.7 billion financing over three years through the extended Fund facility, as well as $200 million through the first credit tranche. By making its support conditional on bank rescheduling and new lending, the IMF successfully orchestrated bank participation under conditions where banks acting individually would have had an incentive to withdraw rather than extend new funds (chapter 4). The IMF's policy conditions on its support included forceful fiscal measures, with the budget deficit scheduled to decline from 17.6 percent of GDP in 1982 to 8.5 percent in 1983, 5.5 percent in 1984, and 3.5 percent in 1985. After some anguish that the whole package would fall apart because of the nationalization of banks by the outgoing Lopez-Portillo administration, in November 1982 Mexico and the IMF reached agreement. By December the new De la Madrid administration began energetic implementation of the agreement. At the same time, it abolished the largely ineffective exchange controls and adopted a realistic flexible exchange rate policy as well as a tough wage policy.

Mexico's approach to the debt crisis after August 1982 was forceful and decisive. The balance of payments results for 1983 showed how strong the adjustment measures were. Correction of the external imbalance was far above target. Mexico achieved a current account surplus of $5.5 billion instead of the $3 billion deficit that had been planned under the IMF adjustment program. Although nonoil exports did achieve a brisk expansion of nearly 14 percent (while oil export revenue declined by 3 percent), this turnaround was primarily the result of a remarkable drop in imports by 46 percent (after a 40 percent decline in 1982). The sharp external sector adjustment came partially at the expense of severe domestic recession, as real GDP declined by 4.7 percent (after a decline of 0.5 percent in 1982). However, the reduction in imports was so extreme (from $23.1 billion in 1981 to $7.7 billion in 1983) that much of the decline was almost certainly associated with the real depreciation of the peso and the slimming down of an import bill that had been bloated by the oil bonanza, rather than being solely the consequence of domestic recession.[2]

Mexico also achieved its IMF targets in the area of domestic fiscal and monetary performance. Although its inflation was higher than anticipated (80.8 percent, December to December), the monthly rates showed deceleration. Because of its decisive progress in adjustment, by the September 1983 annual meetings of the IMF and World Bank, Mexico was the darling of the international financial community, after having been the proximate cause of widespread forebodings of international financial collapse at the same meetings just one year earlier. As discussed in chapter 8, Mexico further enhanced its prestige as a leader in recovery from the debt crisis by taking the initiative in a pathbreaking bridge loan from four Latin American nations (including Brazil, Colombia, and Venezuela) to Argentina, enabling that country to meet an important deadline in March 1984 on foreign bank loans.

Even though at first Mexico's suspension of payments may have appeared arbitrary to foreign creditors, analysts have favorably contrasted the country's decisive action with the more gradual approach of Brazil in dealing with the debt crisis.[3] There is considerable merit in this judgement, even though the adjustment process was probably more difficult for Brazil where import austerity and domestic recession had already begun considerably earlier. In the area of debt rescheduling, however, it is ambiguous whether Mexico's comprehensive approach (rescheduling $35 billion out of $82 billion in debt) was preferable to Brazil's more partial approach, considering the higher interest spreads paid on rescheduled debt and the implications for future bunching of maturities (chapters 4 and 5).

For the medium term, the projections of chapter 8 for Mexico suggest near balance in the current account after the surprising surplus performance of 1983. Mexico's reliance on oil exports, combined with probable stagnation of oil prices, implies medium-term pressure on external accounts. However, the sharp reduction in Mexico's imports suggests that, beyond a cyclical collapse, imports over the medium run may be significantly subject to domestic substitution. In any event, even the larger deficits projected in early estimates of this study (chapter 3) would appear to be manageable (see in particular the analysis of

---

2. Banco de Mexico, *Informe Anual 1983.*

3. M.S. Mendelsohn, *Commercial Banks and the Restructuring of Cross-border Debt* (New York: Group of Thirty, 1983), pp. 20–33.

Table C-2 Brazil: economic indicators (billion dollars and percentages)

	1973	1974	1975	1976	1977
Exports	6.1	7.8	8.5	10.0	11.9
Imports	6.2	12.6	12.0	12.3	12.0
Current account	−2.2	−7.6	−7.0	−6.6	−5.1
Reserves	6.4	5.2	4.0	6.5	7.2
Total debt	13.8	18.9	23.3	28.6	35.2
Short-term debt	2.2	4.5	4.3	4.4	4.3
Net debt/exports	106.1	145.9	194.3	195.8	207.6
Exchange rate index	96.2	98.4	100.0	94.0	94.8
GDP growth	11.4	9.6	5.7	9.0	4.7
Inflation	13.2	27.3	29.6	41.7	43.3

n.a. Not available.
Source: See table C-1, and Central Bank of Brazil.
a. For December to December, general price index: 211 percent.

chapter 5). In the absence of an unexpected political disruption, the prospects are for continued Mexican adjustment and return to creditworthiness, although the adjustment will presumably involve a return to considerably higher and more sustainable import levels than in 1983.

Brazil

In 1974 Brazil's external current account deficit soared to 90 percent of export earnings, as the consequence of the oil price shock as well as a sharp rise in nonoil imports and import prices. For the next few years Brazil consciously rejected the option of adjustment through reduction in the growth of domestic demand.[4] Instead, authorities chose a high-growth strategy relying on import substitution and the accumulation of foreign debt to deal with external imbalances. At the same time, they adopted a permissive attitude toward wage claims, creating the environment for reacceleration of inflation.

The policy of rapid growth meant rapid debt accumulation. The strategy of import substitution meant new distortions of high protection and partially

---

4. See William R. Cline and Associates, *World Inflation and the Developing Countries,* chapter 4, "Brazil's Aggressive Response to External Shocks" (Washington: Brookings Institution, 1981), pp. 102–35.

1978	1979	1980	1981	1982	1983
12.5	15.2	20.1	23.3	20.2	21.9
13.6	18.0	23.0	22.1	19.4	15.4
− 7.0	− 10.5	− 12.9	− 10.6	− 14.0	− 6.5
11.8	9.0	5.8	6.6	3.9	4.4
48.4	57.4	66.1	75.7	88.2	91.9
4.9	7.5	12.2	14.3	16.8	n.a.
252.2	269.3	259.1	256.6	365.3	336.6
99.9	107.9	116.0	99.1	97.4	122.1
6.0	6.8	7.9	− 1.9	1.1	− 3.3
38.8	52.8	82.8	105.6	98.0	142.0[a]

compensating export subsidies. Despite these distortions, the approach seemed to be working by 1979, as the ratio of imports to GDP had been squeezed from 9.8 percent in 1973–74 to only 7.2 percent in 1978–79 while Brazil's share in exports of nonoil developing countries had nonetheless been relatively well sustained (falling only from 6.6 percent to 6.3 percent),[5] although partly because of a windfall boost from high coffee prices in 1976–77.

The major risk was that rising debt meant increasing vulnerability to external shock and reversal of creditor confidence. The ratio of net debt (total debt *minus* reserves) to exports of goods and services rose from 106 percent in 1973 to 269 percent in 1979 (table C-2).

The second oil shock proved to be the undoing of the Brazilian strategy. From 1978 to 1980 oil imports rose by $5.7 billion, reaching $10 billion or nearly half of imports. In 1980 exports rose impressively mainly because of good harvests and continued growth of manufactured exports. Even so, the rising burden of oil imports and interest due on past debt overshadowed export gains. Moreover, despite important reforms at the end of 1979 devaluing the cruzeiro by 30 percent and reducing protection, the government quickly introduced a new and serious distortion of overvaluation by setting a limit of 50 percent on 1980 devaluation in the face of inflation that turned out to be 110 percent (general price index, December to December). An attempt to apply the Southern Cone strategy of prefixing decelerating devaluation as an anti-inflationary device failed, just as it did in Argentina and Chile. And a new policy of stabilization in early 1979 quickly yielded to renewed stimulus after

5. IMF, *International Financial Statistics Yearbook,* 1983, pp. 73–79, 144–47.

a change of planning ministers in mid-1979. By the final quarter of 1980, however, the resulting external imbalances as well as the level of inflation were so great that the government had no choice but to revise policy sharply, and adopt austerity policies. Accordingly, by 1981 the Brazilian recession had begun. Essentially, the inevitable adjustment to external shock, so long postponed through high borrowing, had begun in earnest. Economic growth, which had averaged 7 percent increase annually in 1974–79, fell to -1.9 percent in 1981 and only 1 percent in 1982.

The final blow came in 1982. Prolonged world recession, and severe cutbacks in Latin American and African markets, reduced the volume and prices of Brazil's exports by 13 percent, even as high interest rates raised debt-servicing costs. The current account deficit reached 63 percent of exports of goods and services and pushed debt to $88 billion, raising the ratio of net debt to exports of goods and services from 257 percent to an extraordinary 365 percent (table C-2). With this underlying erosion, it was not surprising that the Mexican shock to confidence in credit markets precipitated a drying up of new lending to Brazil. The result was the need for emergency international financial support in December and a rescheduling of debt payments due in 1983.

The package of international financial rescue for Brazil paralleled that for Mexico in size and commitment by foreign governments, agencies, and banks. The package was premised on a somewhat more gradualist approach, however, primarily in that it assumed that short-term foreign credits would remain at past levels and did not require formal rescheduling. The more limited rescheduling reflected an initial perception, eventually belied by actual external sector results for 1982 and subsequent developments, that Brazil's problems were caused primarily from psychological spillover in credit markets from the Mexican crisis and that on economic fundamentals and in terms of policy management the Brazilian case was less serious. Gradualism was also more feasible in Brazil because, having maintained exchange controls, Brazil did not experience the same massive loss of external reserves through capital flight that Mexico had faced, so that the Brazilian crisis was less abrupt. In contrast to Mexico, adjustment policy in Brazil during 1983 suffered a series of false starts. Only by the end of the year did the adjustment program seem to be firmly in place.

External financial pressure on Brazil had begun in mid-1982, primarily in the form of declining interbank deposits in foreign branches of Brazilian banks. From a level of approximately $10 billion, these deposits had declined to approximately $6 billion by the end of 1982. Pressure built up in September after the Mexican suspension of principal payments induced a cutback by approximately half in monthly capital inflows to Brazil. Although the government had resisted the politically unpopular step of seeking IMF assistance in view of forthcoming state and congressional elections in November 1982, it increasingly had no alternative. Before the election the government announced that it would seek the relatively automatic "compensatory finance" support from the IMF (for declines in export prices), and shortly after the election it announced its intention to seek a much broader support package from the IMF with policy conditions.[6]

At approximately the same time the US Treasury provided to Brazil a 90-day loan of $1.23 billion, which President Reagan announced at the turn of the month during his trip to Brazil. The Federal Reserve provided additional bridge lending of $400 million, and European central banks supplied $1.2 billion in bridge loans through the BIS. By the end of December 1982, Brazil had reached agreement with 125 large banks on a four-part financing package. Project 1 called for new medium-term loans amounting to $4.4 billion. Project 2 provided for the rescheduling over eight years of $4 billion in principal due on medium-term debt in 1983. Project 3 committed the banks to maintain short-term trade-related credit at its existing level of $8.8 billion. And in project 4 the banks pledged to restore interbank deposits in Brazilian foreign bank branches to the levels of mid-1982. To provide short-term bridging finance until the new funds were mobilized, six US banks committed $600 million and 34 foreign banks another $1.4 billion. An important motivating factor in the bank package, as in the case of Mexico, was the insistence by the IMF that bank support be forthcoming as a condition of its own support.

After a relatively brief period of negotiation, in January 1983 the IMF and Brazil reached agreement on a program of lending and adjustment. The letter of intent was the first of four that eventually emerged in the course of 1983 as successive difficulties in fulfillment arose. The program called for $4.6 billion in extended Fund facility lending over three years, in addition to $1.3 billion in compensatory finance. Brazil's policy commitments included the reduction of the operational budget deficit from 6 percent of GDP (including indexing costs on government debt the comprehensive figure was approximately 16 percent) to 3.6 percent, to be achieved by cuts in subsidies to agricultural credit, petroleum products, and wheat, and through higher prices for public services and lower budgets for state enterprises. Domestic credit expansion was limited to 63 percent for the year. As the key to external adjustment, the government set a target of $6 billion for the trade surplus.

As a whole the rescue package for Brazil was similar in format, magnitude, and principal actors to the arrangement for Mexico. The major difference was that in the Brazilian case the package relied heavily on the continuation of short-term credit lines on a voluntary basis (projects 3 and 4) instead of

---

6. For a discussion of the spillover from Mexico, see William R. Cline, "Mexico's Crisis," p. 111. Brazil's reluctance to seek IMF support is discussed in Edmar Bacha, "The IMF and Prospects for Adjustment in Brazil," in John Williamson, ed., *Prospects for Adjustment in Argentina, Brazil, and Mexico*, pp. 31–41.

including short-term debt in formal rescheduling. This strategy proved to be a weak link in the package. The banks failed to restore interbank deposits to the $10 billion level of mid-1982, or even to a subsequently reduced target of $7.5 billion, and these deposits stabilized at $6 billion. Primarily for this reason, Brazil began to build up arrears. Brazilian authorities concluded that more drastic action was necessary, and in February 1983 they carried out a maxidevaluation of 30 percent, leap-frogging the milder devaluation commitment under the IMF program (1 percent monthly in excess of domestic inflation).

By March inflation had accelerated to approximately 10 percent monthly (over 200 percent annually). The impact of maxidevaluation was one cause. For the year as a whole, however, a more important inflationary stimulus came from floods in the South and drought in the Northeast that caused food shortages and increases on the order of 300 percent to 400 percent for agricultural prices. By the end of 1983 inflation had reached a new threshold (211 percent) after having remained in the range of 100 percent yearly in 1980–82.

Higher inflation quickly outdated IMF financial targets stated in terms of cruzeiros, and by May 1983, Brazil was declared out of compliance with the IMF program. The agency suspended its disbursements. The government responded with additional measures on fuel and wheat prices and changes in the wage-indexing mechanism (purging of effects of natural disasters and elimination of overindexing for low wages), but the IMF judged the changes to be insufficient.

In an extraordinary episode in the history of international finance, on July 11 the BIS informed Brazil that it would not renew its loan due on the fifteenth, raising the specter of an officially declared default. President João Baptista de Figueiredo, about to leave the country for heart surgery, responded by decreeing a limit to wage indexation at 80 percent of inflation. Although the BIS then renewed its loan, the IMF welcomed the measure but refused to renew its own disbursements until after the Brazilian congress had approved the indexation decree within the 60-day review period provided by law. At this point the international financial system entered its most tense period since the Mexican payments suspension a year earlier. Brazil's arrears mounted to approximately $3 billion, and US banks came closer to the term of 90 days in interest arrears that determines classification of loans as nonperforming. (At that point they can no longer accrue interest into reported earnings, and overdue interest previously accrued must be removed from earnings. A more serious, but less automatic, deadline occurs after six months of interest arrears when loans may be reclassified as requiring loan-loss reserves.)

During this period Brazil went to the Paris Club of official creditors to reschedule its official debt. In addition, the US government adopted an innovative program of $1.5 billion in additional export credit guarantees available to banks that provided loans beyond the amounts agreed in the general bank lending package, and US authorities urged other industrial countries to provide an additional $1 billion in similar export credits.

The banks pursued their role by beginning the mobilization of $6.5 billion in new lending for 1984. However, approximately half of this amount merely represented funds the banks had failed to produce in 1983 because of the shortfalls in project 4. Furthermore, because the bank disbursements were tied to those of the IMF, by the third quarter of 1984 the banks had suspended drawdowns of their $4.4 billion in new lending (project 1) for 1983.

In mid-October, the Brazilian congress rejected the decree-law limiting wage indexation to 80 percent of inflation, casting into doubt the entire IMF–bank program. International perceptions of the Brazilian case deteriorated further, as did the stock prices of major US banks. By early November, however, the Brazilian congress approved a compromise measure guaranteeing full indexation for low-end wages and yielding an average indexation at 87 percent of inflation. The successful passage of this measure enabled the IMF and the banks to resume lending to Brazil. A major turning point seemed to have arrived as tensions in the international financial community eased.

The emerging data on Brazil's actual economic performance in 1983 further bolstered confidence, as the trade balance surplus exceeded (modestly) the $6 billion target, and the current account deficit ($6.5 billion) was somewhat below the government's forecast. By January 1984 over seven hundred banks had agreed to the package of $6.5 billion in new loans for 1984, in addition to rescheduling of principal due in 1984 and maintenance of short-term credit. And at the end of 1983 Brazil was in compliance with its revised IMF targets on monetary and fiscal performance as well.

For 1983 as a whole, however, the pattern was one of successive derailments in the Brazilian case in contrast to effective implementation of the adjustment program in Mexico. The difference was only partly attributable to program design (reliance on maintained short-term credit versus rescheduling). In addition, the burden of adjustment was probably more severe for Brazil than for Mexico. Brazil was in its third year of recession, whereas Mexico had enjoyed high growth through 1981. Brazil had pared imports to the bone beginning with the first oil shock, while Mexico's imports had ballooned as the oil bonanza made foreign exchange abundant. Moreover, Mexico had the political structure to be able to keep wage increases far below inflation, while in Brazil the attempt to deindex wages led temporarily to political impasse.

The medium-term prospects for debt management in Brazil depend importantly on political tolerance to adjustment, as discussed in chapter 5. The projections of this study suggest significant improvement in external performance, and the analyses of appendix A and chapter 5 indicate that this improvement should be sufficient by 1986 to permit renewed creditworthiness and a return to voluntary lending.

The Brazilian case is nonetheless subject to considerable uncertainty. Despite the renewal of the IMF stabilization program and the enactment of a compromise law limiting wage indexation in November 1983, the viability of the stabilization strategy for 1984 and beyond remained uncertain. There was a distinct possibility that a consequence of further cuts in the government budget deficit and additional monetary tightening would be substantial loss of production. If GDP fell sharply in 1984, and especially considering the timing of elections late in the year, pressures would be great to depart once again from the stabilization program.

The central prospect for Brazil is for continued external sector improvement, and for low growth in 1984 followed by substantially increased growth in subsequent years. As discussed in chapter 8, major increases in domestic oil production in 1984 should cut oil imports sharply. Moreover, by the first quarter of 1984 there were signs that industrial production was beginning to recover. Despite severe social strain the basic scenario of adjustment and recovery should be viable politically. If the strains prove unmanageable, however, the likely evolution of the Brazilian case would be toward some form of agreed interest capitalization to ease external pressure, coupled with a more gradual domestic adjustment program. There are difficulties with this option (chapter 7), especially in its consequences of increasing the level of total debt more rapidly (and reducing inflation more slowly). Moreover, it would be difficult for the Brazilian case to avoid becoming a model for treatment requested by other debtor countries. However, it would appear that even in this more adverse outcome the likelihood would be low of a still more serious rupture—such as outright unilateral moratorium on interest and principal over an extended period. Because Brazil has the largest external debt, it is perhaps the single country whose debt collapse would cause system-wide consequences (excluding Mexico, which appeared to be more firmly on the road toward adjustment in late 1983).

Argentina

The external sector performance of Argentina has experienced strong fluctuations. There have been recurrent crises despite Argentina's self-sufficiency in oil and food, which makes it much less subject to international shocks than many other developing countries. At the end of the Peronist regime in the mid-1970s the country was near bankruptcy. The military regime that took power in 1976 adopted orthodox, open economy policies, sharply cutting high protection, eliminating taxes on exports, and liberalizing interest and exchange rates. Exports nearly doubled over the next three years. However, after falling from even higher levels, inflation stuck at a threshold of over 150 percent per year.

At the end of 1978 Minister of Economy José Martinez de Hoz adopted a radical strategy. Beginning from a base of exceptional export strength, the government used the exchange rate and import competition as an anti-inflationary device. Exchange rate devaluation was prefixed at a scheduled, decelerating rate. The objective was to force domestic inflation to decelerate through the downward pressure of import competition on domestic prices. But because of inadequate monetary and fiscal measures, domestic inflation remained much higher than expected, and the exchange rate became seriously overvalued. Accordingly, the real, trade-weighted effective exchange rate appreciated from an index of 82 in 1977 to only 50 in 1980 (table C-3). As a result, exports decelerated while imports rose by 170 percent from 1978 to 1980. The corresponding external deficit was financed by massive capital inflow (thereby increasing debt) as foreign creditors took advantage of high domestic peso interest rates which, combined with lagging devaluation, meant rates of return on the order of 40 percent annually in dollars. By 1980, however, these inflows were insufficient to cover deficits, and foreign reserves declined. As market participants grew skeptical of the sustainability of the mechanism, capital flight reached a total of $11 billion in 1980–81.

Acute reserve loss in early 1981 led to a collapse of the preannounced exchange rate and a sequence of large devaluations that by 1982 raised the real peso/dollar rate by 74 percent over its 1979–80 level. Recessionary and inflationary pressure from such sharp devaluation, coming on top of a weakening of the industrial structure because of foreign competition, brought severe recession in 1981. Orthodox anti-inflationary measures in early 1982 were interrupted by a move toward controls at the time of the Falklands war. Thereafter in a brief policy interregnum the government applied controls on prices and interest rates, imposed high protection, raised wages, and adopted a domestic moratorium that wiped out nearly 40 percent of real domestic debt. The financial freeze and European trade embargo at the time of the war cut back exports and, even more sharply, imports.

Politics have dominated the vicissitudes of the Argentine rescue process even more than in the Brazilian case. Disruption to Argentina's debt servicing persisted for several months before the international financial community provided a rescue package, in contrast to the prompt action for Mexico and then Brazil. The smaller scale of Argentina's debt ($38 billion) may have played a role in this contrast, but so did the political complications resulting from the South Atlantic war. Because the military opposed an end to the freeze on British financial assets for several months after the war, Argentina did not enter into discussions with the International Monetary Fund until September, 1982. Agreement in principle was reached with the IMF by October, and formal agreement only in January 1983.

When it did materialize the financial rescue package for Argentina resembled those for Mexico and Brazil. The same principal actors were involved: the IMF, the BIS, and the private banks. The US Federal Reserve together with the BIS offered a loan of $500 million, although Argentina never drew on these funds because of their immediate callability and the requirement of collateral in gold.

Table C-3 Argentina: economic indicators (billion dollars and percentages)

	1973	1974	1975	1976	1977
Exports	3.3	3.9	3.0	3.9	5.7
Imports	2.0	3.2	3.5	2.8	3.8
Current account	.7	.1	−1.3	.7	1.3
Reserves	1.1	1.1	.2	1.4	3.2
Total debt	6.4	8.0	7.9	8.3	9.7
Short-term debt	1.5	2.4	2.6	2.1	2.8
Net debt/exports	140.8	145.2	211.5	145.7	96.8
Exchange rate index	65.1	66.4	100.0	64.4	82.0
GDP growth	6.1	6.5	−0.9	−0.2	6.0
Inflation	62.5	23.1	187.5	447.8	176.6

n.a. Not available.
Source: See table C-1.
a. December to December: 433.7 percent.

Because a new civilian government was scheduled to take power in early 1984, the IMF agreement was to cover only 15 months instead of the three-year program (with larger potential funding) available under the extended Fund facility, in order to leave policy flexibility for the new government. The IMF committed $1.65 billion in stand-by lending and $490 million in compensatory finance. The policy conditions of the agreement included reduction in the government deficit from 14 percent of GDP in 1982 to 8 percent by 1983 and 5 percent in early 1984; maintenance of realistic exchange and interest rates; limits on credit growth; and reduction of the balance of payments current account deficit to $1 billion in 1983. Inflation was to decline to 160 percent for 1983, although this objective was not a criterion for judging compliance.

The IMF made its support conditional on bank cooperation in rescheduling and new lending. The banks committed $1.5 billion in new five-year loans for 1983. They rescheduled over seven-year terms approximately $2 billion in arrears, $7 billion in public sector principal due in 1983 (both long- and short-term), $3.5 billion in long-term debt due in 1983, and private debt (postponing maturities for three to five years). The rescheduling structure was intermediate between those for Mexico and Brazil. As in the case of Mexico, the package rescheduled both long-term and short-term debt, public and private, amounting to nearly half of total debt (compared to only 5 percent in Brazil). As in the case of Brazil, however, the rescheduling covered only one year's maturities (1983), whereas the Mexican rescheduling covered principal through 1984.

1978	1979	1980	1981	1982	1983
6.4	7.8	8.0	9.1	7.6	7.8
3.5	6.0	9.4	8.4	4.9	3.9
1.9	− .5	− 4.7	− 3.8	− 2.4	− 2.6
5.0	9.4	6.7	3.3	2.5	1.2
12.5	19.0	27.2	35.7	38.0	44.0
2.6	6.0	9.3	10.0	11.0	n.a.
96.1	97.3	182.5	275.3	353.5	486.0
74.5	55.8	50.4	57.2	92.2	n.a.
− 3.9	7.1	1.5	− 6.1	− 5.0	2.0
175.3	159.6	100.8	104.5	164.8	343.8[a]

The rescheduling of Argentina's debt proved to be a more unsettled and protracted process than in the cases of Brazil and Mexico. Argentina took certain unilateral steps that disturbed creditors, including the postponement for five years of $5.5 billion in exchange guarantees (in November 1982) and unilateral rescheduling of $1.4 billion in swaps in March 1983. Disbursements of the $1.5 billion in new funds from banks in 1983 were seriously delayed, first because of issues concerning remittances to British firms (unresolved until August), then because of unwillingness of foreign banks to lend before changes in Argentine law giving preferential treatment to national creditors in bankruptcy cases, and finally because of suspension of IMF drawdowns as Argentina failed to comply with terms of the IMF agreement. As an indication of the political difficulties surrounding the rescheduling process, at one point the president of the central bank was imprisoned briefly when a local judge maintained that his signing of a rescheduling agreement violated Argentine law. Finally, once the new Alfonsín government took power it declared a debt moratorium on principal (and, as it turned out, on a considerable portion of interest) from December 15, 1983, through the end of June 1984 as a breathing space for renegotiation. During this period it sought better terms not only on new lending but also on rescheduling of payments due in 1982 and 1983, and foreign banks resisted reopening the terms of these reschedulings. Argentina's reschedulings had been packaged in a large number of individual agreements, and most of these had remained unsigned as the change in regime drew near.

Argentina's trade performance in 1983 was consistent with the objectives under the IMF agreement, as a sharp decline in imports (by 20 percent) permitted a sizable trade surplus (nearly $4 billion, or almost half the value of exports) despite limited growth in exports. In the first half of 1983 the IMF had found Argentina in compliance with the program despite accelerating inflation, but it found noncompliance by autumn, partly because of payments arrears that in turn were the consequence of delayed disbursements by the banks. Inflation then accelerated greatly as firms sought to defend themselves against price controls that might arise under a new government.

In early 1984 the new government of Raúl Alfonsín concentrated its efforts on domestic political issues, including labor union structure and processing of cases of human rights violations under the former military regimes. By the end of the first quarter Argentina had not yet reached a new agreement with the IMF, and correspondingly the foreign banks had still not disbursed the greater part of the $1.5 billion in new lending that had been committed for 1983. The government fell behind by more than 90 days in interest payments on a considerable portion of its external loans, and US banks were preparing to endure accounting losses on their first-quarter earnings as the loans went on nonperforming (and nonaccruing) status. At the last minute, however, an innovative financial package orchestrated by Mexico permitted Argentina to avoid nonperforming status. Mexico, Brazil, Colombia, and Venezuela jointly extended a bridging loan of $300 million to Argentina. The foreign banks lent $100 million and Argentina contributed $100 million from its reserves, permitting sufficient interest payments to be paid that no loans remained more than 90 days in arrears on interest. For its part the US Treasury provided a secondary bridge loan for $300 million, to come into effect once the letter of intent was signed between Argentina and the IMF, with the funds to be used to repay the Latin American participants in the package. The measure was deftly designed. Its significance was only partly that it permitted avoidance of the first major case of nonperforming status for US banks. Perhaps more importantly, it was a graphic demonstration that the major Latin American debtor nations were prepared to make major efforts to ensure that the lending process not break down. Far from forming a debtor's cartel to repudiate debt, they formed a debtor's club to support it. The reasons were relatively clear: these countries were concerned that nonperformance for Argentina would spill over into the credit markets more generally, making it more difficult for them to mobilize their own new lending. Indeed, Mexico was in the final phases of obtaining $3.8 billion in new borrowing for 1984 and wanted to avoid the unraveling of that effort.

The overall process of financial rescue in Argentina proved to be one with numerous mishaps and delays. The most favorable area of the process was Argentina's relatively successful performance in meeting its external sector goals. The most disappointing area of economic performance was in inflation, which reached 434 percent in 1983 (December to December).[7]

---

7. IMF, *International Financial Statistics,* May 1984, p. 83.

The prospects for Argentina's future debt management would appear to be more favorable. As discussed in chapters 3 and 8, the projections of this study indicate significantly improving external balances for Argentina as world recovery proceeds. As noted in chapter 5, the political change likely to follow the strong electoral victory of the Radical Party in October 1983 could facilitate forceful economic policy, aiding debt management. To be sure, the economic problems inherited by the new regime were extreme, especially inflation running at several hundred percentage points per year. However, with a commitment to a realistic exchange rate, external performance need not be seriously jeopardized even if success in reducing inflation is only gradual. Importantly, the early indications were that the general orientation of the new government will be to honor external debt commitments, although to bargain for the best terms possible with respect to interest rate spreads and maturities. (For a discussion of the threat to global debt management posed, nonetheless, by the temporary impasse between Argentina and the International Monetary Fund in mid-1984, see chapter 8.)

Poland

The Polish debt crisis emerged in a unique political context. Recent events are well known: in 1980–81, government austerity measures and economic mismanagement led to widespread labor unrest; the coalescence of political opposition under Solidarity brought Poland to the verge of major institutional reform. In December 1981 a military crackdown reestablished Communist party control. This provoked Western trade sanctions and the suspension of official talks on debt rescheduling. Although political events have made Poland's debt crisis a focal point for East-West confrontation, the crisis itself was long in the making.

Poland's debt accumulation began in the early 1970s as part of an ambitious strategy adopted by new political leadership. The Gierek regime came to power in 1971 in the wake of strikes and violence over food price increases. The regime regarded rapid growth and modernization of the Polish economy as prerequisites for political stability. Accordingly, the "new development strategy" called for major increases in investment and a general revitalization of Polish industry, combined with higher incomes as a reward for expected productivity gains.[8] Infusions of Western capital and technology were essential to the strategy, and external conditions were propitious: the atmosphere of detente gave Poland access to official Western credits, later augmented by private bank

---

8. Background on the "new development strategy" can be found in Zbigniew M. Fallenbuchl, "The Polish Economy at the Beginning of the 1980's," *East European Economic Assessment*, part 1, a Compendium of Papers Submitted to the US Congress, Joint Economic Committee, 97 Cong. 1 sess. (February 27, 1981), pp. 33–71.

Table C-4 Poland: economic indicators (billion dollars and percentages)

	1973	1974	1975	1976	1977
Exports	2.5	3.9	4.1	4.4	4.9
Imports	4.0	6.0	7.4	7.5	7.1
Current account	−1.3	−2.2	−3.1	−3.2	−2.4
Reserves	.6	.5	.6	.8	.4
Total debt	2.8	4.6	8.0	11.5	14.0
Short-term debt	1.5	2.2	2.7	2.8	2.6
Net debt/exports	88.5	105.6	180.0	242.7	276.2
Exchange rate index	n.a.	n.a.	n.a.	n.a.	n.a.
NMP growth	10.8	10.4	9.0	6.8	5.0
Inflation	2.6	6.7	3.0	4.4	4.9

n.a. Not available.

Note: Exports and imports with nonsocialist countries. Current account balance in convertible currencies; estimates for 1981–82 take account of unpaid interest. Net debt as percentage of merchandise exports to nonsocialist countries. Growth of net material product.

Source: Jan Vanous, *Centrally Planned Economies Current Analysis,* vol. 3, nos. 31–32, 38–39, 69–70; Richard Portes, *The Polish Crisis: Western Policy Options*; Zbigniew M. Fallenbuchl, "The Polish Economy at the Beginning of the 1980s"; David D. Driscoll, "Sovereign Debt: the Polish Example"; Central Intelligence Agency, *Handbook of Economic Statistics,* 1982.

lending. Planners were confident that viable export industries could be developed in the space of a few years to permit hard currency repayments.

The strategy implied a substantial reorientation of trade away from the member countries of the Council for Mutual Economic Assistance (Comecon) and toward the industrialized West. Accordingly, several industries were targeted for investment on the basis of expected demand growth in Western markets.[9] Certain of these industries (for example, automobiles, construction equipment, machinery, and electronics) were established through joint ventures or licensing agreements with European and US manufacturers.[10] Import-substituting industries also sought access to Western equipment and production techniques.

---

9. Gary Teske, "Poland: Performance and Prospects in Trade with the United States and the West," A Study Prepared for the Use of the US Congress, Joint Economic Committee, 97 Cong. 2 sess. (March 31, 1982), pp. 6–7, 28.

10. John Garland and Paul Marer, "US Multinationals in Poland: A Case Study of the International Harvester–BUMAR Cooperation in Construction Machinery," *East European Economic Assessment,* part 1, pp. 121–22.

1978	1979	1980	1981	1982
5.5	6.3	7.5	5.4	5.2
7.5	8.8	9.1	6.0	4.0
− 2.5	− 2.8	− 2.6	− 3.0	− 1.8
.9	1.2	.6	.8	1.1
17.8	22.7	25.0	26.4	26.6
2.8	4.1	3.1	2.8	2.7
308.6	341.3	324.9	469.2	491.0
n.a.	n.a.	n.a.	n.a.	n.a.
3.0	− 2.3	− 6.0	− 12.0	− 8.0
8.7	6.7	10.0	37.0	92.7

Technology transfers, in various forms, were expected to boost the efficiency of Polish industry and provide the basis for sustained economic growth.

The rapid growth rates achieved during 1971–75 (averaging nearly 10 percent) appeared to confirm this view.[11] However, the pattern of investment contained a number of weaknesses which only became apparent in the latter half of the decade. A large proportion of newly established industries were import-intensive. This presented special problems in the late 1970s when Polish import restrictions, imposed in response to widening trade deficits, reduced access to essential intermediate goods. Moreover, various industries developed in the early 1970s were not able to produce for export for several years. By the late 1970s many of these industries faced depressed foreign demand.[12]

Although trade deficits were a necessary feature of the new development strategy, the size of deficits in the mid-1970s far exceeded planners' expectations. Deficits in merchandise trade with nonsocialist countries grew sharply in three consecutive years, reaching $2.7 billion in 1975. Import growth was clearly excessive in 1971–75: average annual growth was 27 percent in constant prices, and 39 percent in current prices. These compare with export growth rates of 11 percent in constant prices, and 22 percent in current prices. Although import growth slowed markedly in 1976, export growth slowed even more, and the trade deficit with nonsocialist countries grew to $2.9 billion.[13]

11. Growth rates for "Domestic Net Material Product," a concept corresponding to net domestic product with most services excluded. See Fallenbuchl, "The Polish Economy at the Beginning of the 1980's," pp. 41–42, 67.

12. Teske, "Poland: Performance and Prospects," pp. 5–14.

13. Fallenbuchl, "The Polish Economy at the Beginning of the 1980's," p. 65.

The disappointing export performance was largely due to factors beyond Polish control. Some Polish exports, such as foodstuffs and basic manufactures, suffered from trade barriers imposed by the European Community in the mid-1970s. Higher prices for coal boosted export earnings for this sector, but recession caused foreign demand to stagnate after 1975.[14] Poor weather was partly to blame for declines in agricultural production in 1975. However, authorities devoted insufficient investment to agriculture in the early 1970s, and this contributed to poor sectoral performance. Poland became a net importer of foodstuffs in 1973, and subsequent domestic shortages had an important role in the erosion of political support for the Gierek regime.[15]

Excessive levels of investment were primarily responsible for rapid import growth and the deteriorating trade balance in the early 1970s. Investment grew at an average annual rate of nearly 19 percent in 1971–75—well above the targeted rate. The acceleration of investment spending exceeded absorptive capacity, as evidenced by long construction delays for some projects and the development of serious bottlenecks in transport and power generation.[16] The proliferation of investment projects and inadequate attention to infrastructural development caused many new industries to founder.

Wage increases were an important feature of the "new development strategy." Planners thought higher incomes would elicit large productivity gains, and indeed, plan targets for productivity were overfulfilled in 1971–75. However, average wage growth exceeded plan targets by a larger margin.[17] Wage growth was facilitated by new regulations introduced in 1973, which were intended to increase enterprise autonomy and reduce the scope for arbitrary and inefficient central controls. The new system made wage-bill growth dependent on output growth, as opposed to fulfillment of plan targets. Enterprises manipulated the new system in ways that permitted excessive wage increases, and by 1977 inflationary pressures prompted the reintroduction of some administrative controls.[18]

Personal incomes in 1971–75 grew more rapidly than wages, due to expanded social welfare payments and revised pensions. Nominal income growth averaged over 13 percent, while real income growth averaged 11 percent.[19] These rates were clearly unsustainable. Although increases in the cost of living were initially

14. Teske, "Poland: Performance and Prospects," pp. 11–12, 37.

15. William Newcomb, "Polish Agriculture: Policy and Performance," *East European Economic Assessment,* part 1, pp. 98–108.

16. Teske, "Poland: Performance and Prospects," p. 13, and Fallenbuchl, "The Polish Economy at the Beginning of the 1980's," p. 53.

17. Jan Adam, *Wage Control and Inflation in the Soviet Bloc Countries* (New York: Praeger, 1980), pp. 43, 47–48, 147.

18. *Ibid.,* pp. 141–45.

19. Fallenbuchl, "The Polish Economy at the Beginning of the 1980's," pp. 37–38, 65.

moderate, excess demand was reflected in product shortages and rising monetary balances. An unrealistic price structure, particularly for agricultural goods, exacerbated the problem of shortages. The government delayed necessary price adjustments, thereby ensuring strong consumer reaction when prices for meat and other basic foodstuffs were eventually increased.

Poland's net hard currency debt stood at roughly $11 billion in 1976; in the next three years it more than doubled, to $23 billion. Import restrictions led to some narrowing of hard currency trade deficits (from $2.9 billion in 1976 to $1.7 billion in 1979), but net interest payments rose simultaneously, causing the current account deficit to swell to $2.8 billion in 1979. The ratio of debt service to exports of goods and services increased from 34 percent in 1976 to 70 percent in 1979.[20] In order to relieve payments pressure (at least temporarily) Polish authorities began to seek trade credits with unusually long maturities. This was a signal of impending difficulty which Western banks apparently ignored.[21]

Poland did not encounter serious borrowing difficulties until early 1980. In late 1979 the French government refinanced official export credits coming due in 1980; Poland agreed to pay substantially higher interest in return for an eight-year stretchout, indicating severe liquidity pressures. The forseeable bunching of repayments in 1981 indicated to some Western bankers the need for a "sound restructuring" of commercial debt.[22] Yet Polish officials instead opened negotiations in early 1980 for a $550 million Eurodollar syndication. Banks were reluctant to extend more credit, largely because the government's economic plan for 1980 seemed unrealistic. The plan called for virtual elimination of the hard currency trade deficit (equal to $1.7 billion in 1979), through a 3 percent decline in imports and 19 percent increase in exports. National income and industrial production were expected to show moderate growth, despite declines in 1979, and productivity gains were expected to permit a rise in real incomes per capita.[23] The government raised its export growth target to 27 percent in the spring of 1980 on the basis of strong first quarter earnings, but this was completely implausible and only confirmed the desperation of Polish

---

20. Data on hard currency trade, debt, and debt service are from David D. Driscoll, "Sovereign Debt: the Polish Example," US Congress, Senate Committee on Banking, Housing, and Urban Affairs, *Polish Debt*, Hearing, 97 Cong., 2 sess., p. 72. Also see Fallenbuchl, "Poland's Economic Crisis," *Problems of Communism*, vol. 31 (March-April 1982), pp. 7–8, for estimates based on trade with nonsocialist countries.

21. Exposures of Western banks to Poland grew by 27 percent in 1979, to $15.8 billion. BIS, "Maturity Distribution of International Bank Lending" (Basle, June 1980; processed). See also Driscoll, "Sovereign Debt: The Polish Example," pp. 73–74, and Richard Portes, *The Polish Crisis: Western Economic Policy Options* (London: Royal Institute of International Affairs, 1981), p. 10.

22. Portes, *The Polish Crisis*, p. 10.

23. *Ibid.*, pp. 10–11, and Fallenbuchl, "Poland's Economic Crisis," pp. 6–8.

officials. The syndication eventually attracted only $325 million, including $45 million from East European banks.[24]

Economic deterioration led to a volatile political situation in 1980. Rapid expansion of money incomes in the 1970s had created unrealistic expectations. Real incomes had dropped precipitously, and government austerity measures promised no return to earlier growth rates. Industrial dislocations and idle capacity, due to import restrictions and a proliferation of new administrative controls, further undermined public confidence in government authorities. Given public dissatisfaction with economic policies generally, the explosive reaction to meat price increases in July 1981 could have been anticipated. A wave of strikes engulfed Poland in July and August, toppling the Gierek regime and establishing the Solidarity trade union movement as a major political force. After winning concessions from the government on work conditions and wages, Solidarity began to pressure for more far-reaching economic and political reforms. A political deadlock ensued, making even more remote any comprehensive program for reversing Poland's economic decline.

The hard currency trade balance showed some improvement in 1980 despite the labor turmoil. However, the current account deficit remained large ($2.7 billion) because of rising interest payments, and the ratio of debt service to exports reached 85 percent. The seriousness of Poland's financial situation in 1980 can be gauged from the fact that the government's hard currency reserves fell to $1 million in December; only an emergency loan from the Soviet Bloc allowed Poland to meet its debt-service obligations in the first quarter of 1981.[25]

In March 1981 Poland announced it could no longer guarantee repayments. Separate negotiations began with official and private bank creditors. By the end of April an agreement was reached between Poland and 16 Western governments on the rescheduling of official debt. The agreement called for rescheduling of 90 percent of the interest and principal due between May and December ($2.4 billion), with four years' grace period and four years' repayment.[26] The negotiations with private bank creditors were much more protracted. A 16-bank steering committee, representing 460 Western banks, finally reached agreement with the Polish government in October. The banks agreed to reschedule 95 percent of principal ($2.4 billion) but required that Poland pay all interest currently due. Other terms of the agreement were broadly comparable to those granted by official creditors. Formal signing was delayed until early 1982 because of Polish arrears on interest payments.[27]

---

24. Portes, *The Polish Crisis*, pp. 11–12.

25. Driscoll, "Sovereign Debt: The Polish Example," pp. 72, 80.

26. US Congress, Senate Committee on Appropriations, *Polish Debt Crisis*, Hearing, 97 Cong., 2 sess. (Washington, 1983), pp. 18–19.

27. Driscoll, "Sovereign Debt: The Polish Example," pp. 81–82.

In November 1981 Poland applied for membership in the IMF. This offered some encouragement to Western creditors, since IMF involvement would advance Polish adoption of necessary adjustment measures. It was nevertheless clear that 1982 debt repayments would have to be rescheduled. Polish exports to hard currency areas remained depressed, and worsening terms of trade suggested little chance of early improvement.[28]

The imposition of martial law in December led to a sharp reaction by Western governments. Talks on the rescheduling of official debts coming due in 1982 were indefinitely postponed, and trade sanctions were imposed as punishment for the repression against Solidarity.[29] The possibility of declaring Poland in default was actively considered—especially in the United States. This left private creditors in a quandary, since a formal declaration of default would eliminate all remaining prospects for repayment and leave banks with no choice but to write down the full value of their unguaranteed Polish assets (roughly $9 billion).[30] The threat of an official default declaration soon subsided, but trade sanctions and the suspension of official talks had an important bearing on the the banks' subsequent negotiations with Polish authorities.

Poland resumed negotiations with private creditors in July 1982. The cutoff of official Western credits, combined with trade sanctions, had further weakened Poland's financial position. Approximately $3.4 billion was due for payment to private banks in 1982, including $1.1 billion in interest charges. Poland sought a postponement of interest payments, and eventually the banks agreed to a formula which substantially eased the interest burden. Under the agreement reached in November, 95 percent of principal due in 1982 ($2.3 billion) would be rescheduled, with payments to begin after a four-year grace period. Poland agreed to pay all interest on condition that the banks provide new trade credits equal to half that amount.[31] This unusual arrangement represented a major concession by the banks. Nevertheless, the agreement implied a sizable net repayment, and the banks had no desire to force Poland into technical default by making unrealistic demands.

---

28. Terms of trade declined primarily because of depressed coal prices. For data on 1980–82 trade, see Jan Vanous, "Polish Foreign Trade Performance in 1982," *Centrally Planned Economies Current Analysis*, vol. 3, nos. 31–32 (29 April 1983), Wharton Econometric Forecasting Associates.

29. The economic sanctions imposed against Poland are discussed in Gary Clyde Hufbauer and Jeffrey J. Schott, *Economic Sanctions Reconsidered: History and Current Policy* (Washington: Institute for International Economics, forthcoming 1984). Also see Jerry F. Hough, *The Polish Crisis: American Policy Options* (Washington: Brookings Institution, 1982).

30. *Financial Times*, 9 July 1982. Estimate of unguaranteed bank assets is from US Congress, Senate Committee on Appropriations, *Polish Debt Crisis*, Hearing, p. 18.

31. *New York Times*, 15 September 1982, and Frederick Kempe, *Wall Street Journal*, 30 December 1982.

By early 1983 some banks were ready to give serious consideration to a multiyear rescheduling. When talks reconvened in the spring, Polish officials proposed rescheduling of debts coming due in 1983–85 over 20 years. The banks were anxious to avoid protracted negotiations with Poland; nevertheless, they were divided on the wisdom of a multiyear approach. American banks were generally less receptive, fearing the precedent that would be created for negotiations in Latin America; there was also concern about getting "too far ahead" of Western governments.[32] An agreement was finally reached in August on rescheduling 1983 principal due, with rescheduled maturities set at 10 years. As in the previous year the banks rescheduled 95 percent of principal ($1.4 billion), and agreed to recycle a large fraction of interest payments. Of the $1.1 billion in interest due in 1983, 65 percent would be returned to Poland in the form of new trade credits. In addition, the grace period on repayment was extended to 5 years.

Poland made no repayments to its official creditors in 1982. Western governments decided not to declare Poland in default in order to maintain economic and political leverage. The political situation began to ease in August 1983 when Poland lifted martial law. Subsequently Western governments announced their willingness to resume negotiations on the rescheduling of official debt. Talks were set to resume in November, with Poland expected to take a harder line than previously. Indeed, Polish authorities announced their intention to seek substantial financial compensation for US economic sanctions.[33]

Poland's hard currency trade balance has shown continued improvement because of extensive import cutbacks. Import volumes from nonsocialist countries declined by 50 percent between 1980 and 1982, while export volumes fell 23 percent. A modest trade surplus was recorded in 1982, and a larger surplus (of $1 billion) was predicted for 1983 on the basis of higher coal exports. The current account deficit in hard currencies fell from $2.9 billion in 1981 to $1.8 billion in 1982.[34] Substantial further improvement was expected in 1983, but there appeared to be little possibility of Poland's meeting its interest obligations to Western creditors in the near term without continued arrangements linking interest payments to new credits.

Industrial production, hard hit by work stoppages and import cutbacks in recent years, has begun to recover. Yet Polish industry faces major organizational problems (and material shortages) which will make growth difficult to sustain. In early 1982 the government announced a comprehensive set of economic reforms. The stated objectives were laudable—to promote efficiency through

---

32. *New York Times*, 19 August 1983.

33. *Washington Post*, 13 July 1983.

34. Vanous, "Polish Foreign Trade Performance in 1982," pp. 12–15. These estimates are larger than official current account estimates, owing to the inclusion of unpaid interest.

economic decentralization and enterprise self-management—but many of the announced reforms have not been implemented.[35] The introduction of worker self-management has been delayed, perhaps indefinitely, and little progress has been made toward self-financing of enterprises. The government had intended to dismantle the old system of detailed, quantitative planning, and place greater reliance on "economic parameters" (such as prices and interest rates) for guiding resource allocation. But after brief experimentation, direct administrative controls were reinstituted in many sectors, often to relieve specific shortages.

The economy still suffers from a massive monetary imbalance. Money incomes have grown faster than production of consumer goods in recent years, resulting in the accumulation of large private savings. The government has attempted to absorb some of this "inflationary overhang" through selected price increases, but the effort has been partially undercut by wage increases granted to keep labor peace.[36] Meanwhile, continuing shortages of consumer goods—and the prospect of further large price increases in early 1984—have accentuated public dissatisfaction with the government's economic program.

Yugoslavia

Yugoslavia has thus far avoided a formal rescheduling of its debt, thanks to a massive international rescue effort. In early 1983, Western governments, commercial banks, and international lending institutions agreed in principle to a rescue package totaling approximately $6 billion. The rescue package represented a major vote of confidence by Western creditors. However, it did not resolve Yugoslavia's financial difficulties. Although the package appeared more than sufficient for Yugoslavia to meet its 1983 debt-service obligations, continuing strain on external liquidity seemed likely in the medium term, given prospective 1984 payments and the uncertainty of future bank lending.

The need for a rescue package became apparent in early 1982, when Yugoslavia found itself shut out of commercial credit markets despite sharp improvement in its current account. Yugoslavia's current account deficit was reduced by roughly two-thirds between 1980 and 1981 (from $2.3 billion to $750 million) through a combination of deflationary policies, trade controls, and devaluation of the dinar.[37] Notwithstanding this improvement—and the approval of a $2.1 billion IMF stand-by credit in early 1981—bank lending to Yugoslavia came to

---

35. *The Economist,* 12 February 1983, pp. 71–73.

36. *The Economist,* 15 October 1983, p. 60.

37. For details of recent economic performance, see OECD, *Economic Surveys, Yugoslavia* (Paris, May 1983).

Table C-5 Yugoslavia: economic indicators (billion dollars and percentages)

	1973	1974	1975	1976	1977
Exports	2.9	3.8	4.1	4.9	5.2
Imports	4.1	6.9	7.1	6.8	9.0
Current account	.5	−1.2	−1.0	.2	−1.6
Reserves	1.3	1.1	.8	2.0	2.0
Total debt	4.6	5.4	6.3	7.7	9.6
Short-term debt	.3	.5	.5	.5	.6
Net debt/exports	76.0	75.6	88.8	81.8	100.1
Exchange rate index	113.3	102.1	99.9	100.0	99.9
GSP growth	3.9	7.5	2.5	2.8	7.0
Inflation	19.3	22.0	23.4	11.4	14.5

Note: Merchandise exports and imports. Nongold reserves. Net debt as percentage of exports of goods and services. Real trade-weighted exchange rate, measured against five industrial country currencies. Growth of gross social product. Trade and current account figures include transactions in nonconvertible currencies.

Source: IMF, *International Financial Statistics,* various issues; OECD, *Annual Economic Survey of Yugoslavia,* various years; BIS, *Maturity Distribution of International Bank Lending,* various years; Institute for International Economics debt data base.

a standstill. The exposure of Western banks to Yugoslavia actually declined 6.7 percent in the first half of 1982, after negligible growth in 1981.[38]

Several factors contributed to the contraction of credit in 1982. Among these was the Polish debt rescheduling, which radically changed the psychological atmosphere for lending to Eastern Europe. Although Yugoslavia was in a much stronger external position than Poland, its debt was larger in per capita terms. Moreover, only a third of Yugoslavia's debt was covered by explicit government guarantees. Political decentralization in Yugoslavia had permitted regional banks to accumulate substantial foreign debts with minimal government supervision. Uncoordinated borrowing by the regional banks had long been a source of concern for foreign creditors, and when a major Croatian bank fell behind in its foreign repayments in early 1982 the lending climate quickly deteriorated.[39]

---

38. BIS, "Maturity Distribution of International Bank Lending" (December 1982). Banks reporting to the BIS had combined exposure of $10.68 billion at the end of 1981, and $9.97 billion at mid-1982.

39. "Yugoslavia: Belt Tightening," *The Banker,* vol. 132, no. 682 (December 1982), p. 65, and *Financial Times,* 20 July 1982.

1978	1979	1980	1981	1982
5.8	6.8	9.0	10.2	10.2
9.6	12.9	13.8	13.3	12.2
−1.3	−3.7	−2.3	−.8	−.5
2.4	1.3	1.4	1.6	.7
11.8	14.9	17.6	18.5	17.9
.7	1.2	2.2	2.3	1.8
110.4	133.6	118.8	99.8	113.7
108.9	113.4	128.8	117.4	132.7
6.2	6.0	2.1	.7	−.5
13.6	21.3	29.9	39.7	32.9

Although there was some market overreaction to financial shocks in 1982, creditors had reason to be concerned about the Yugoslav economy. The stabilization program brought overall improvement in the current account, but a substantial trade deficit remained in convertible currencies. As a result of rising interest payments and stagnant export demand, debt service absorbed over a third of convertible currency earnings.[40] Yugoslavia's growth rate, formerly one of the highest in Europe, had fallen precipitously, and unemployment had risen to 9 percent of the labor force. Accelerating inflation (over 40 percent in 1981) undermined confidence in economic management, while regional unrest accentuated concerns about political stability in the post-Tito era.

An important component of the debt problem is Yugoslavia's trade pattern. During the 1970s, Yugoslav merchandise exports shifted away from industrial market economies and toward the Comecon countries. Exports declined to members of the Organization for Economic Cooperation and Development (OECD), as a percentage of total exports, from 56 percent in 1970 to 37 percent in 1980, while exports to Comecon countries increased from 32 percent to 46 percent of total exports.[41] The shift reflected recessionary conditions in Western Europe and a general loss of competitiveness for Yugoslav goods, largely due to overvaluation. On the import side, Yugoslavia continued to depend on industrial market economies for a major share of merchandise imports through-

40. Debt-service payments were roughly $4 billion in 1981. Exports of goods and services (excluding merchandise exports in nonconvertible currencies) were $11 billion, giving a debt-service ratio of 36 percent.

41. OECD, *Economic Surveys, Yugoslavia* (May 1983), p. 64.

out the 1970s. The OECD share of Yugoslavia's merchandise imports fell from 69 percent to 53 percent, while the Comecon share increased from 27 percent to 30 percent. Continued reliance on imports from the OECD area resulted in persistent bilateral trade deficits, which increased substantially during the decade.[42] Although workers' remittances and other invisibles helped to offset the imbalance in merchandise trade, Yugoslavia's current account remained in deficit in all but three years (1972, 1973, and 1976—years of low growth).

The commodity composition of Yugoslavia's trade complicates the process of external adjustment. Yugoslavia's merchandise imports consist primarily of capital goods, raw materials, and intermediate products; policies to compress imports therefore have a pronounced effect on potential growth rates. Merchandise exports (consisting largely of finished and semimanufactures, and chemicals) have a heavy import content, further reducing the scope for import controls.

Import substitution has been an important objective of Yugoslav trade policy, particularly since large trade deficits began to emerge in the mid-1970s. In 1976–78, the government expanded protection in light industry, raw materials, and agriculture in hopes of reducing import dependence.[43] Yugoslavia nevertheless remained in a vulnerable external position in 1977–78, with trade deficits in the range of $4.3 billion. The second oil shock resulted in substantial further deterioration: the trade deficit grew to $7.2 billion in 1979, and the current account deficit reached $3.7 billion (equivalent to 5½ percent of GDP)— a historic high.[44]

Debt accumulation was especially rapid in 1978–80. As in other developing countries, external finance permitted Yugoslavia to maintain high levels of investment and growth despite deterioration in the current account. Yugoslavia's rate of investment has historically been one of the highest in the world (roughly 28 percent of GDP during 1965–79).[45] Growth rates averaged 6 percent during 1965–79—high by comparison with most industrial economies, but lower than rates attained by other middle-income countries (notably Brazil and Korea).

Several factors have made investment relatively inefficient in Yugoslavia.

---

42. *Ibid.* Trade deficits with OECD countries during the 1970s accounted for over 80 percent of Yugoslavia's total trade deficit.

43. Diane Flaherty, "Economic Reform and Foreign Trade in Yugoslavia," *Cambridge Journal of Economics*, vol. 6, no. 2 (June 1982), p. 139.

44. Although oil price increases exacerbated Yugoslavia's trade and current account deficits, growth of domestic demand played a much larger role in the deterioration of external balances over the period 1973–80. See OECD, *Economic Surveys, Yugoslavia* (May 1981), pp. 24–26.

45. Rates of investment were especially high after 1973; investment in industry grew most rapidly (13 percent annually, compared to 7 percent in other sectors) during the period 1973–79. OECD, *Economic Surveys, Yugoslavia* (May 1981), pp. 22–23.

Prolonged periods of overvaluation, combined with import controls in various sectors, have penalized exports and discouraged product specialization. Yugoslavia produces a far wider variety of products than justified by its market size; moreover, the duplication of investment projects in different constituent republics has meant the loss of potential scale economies.[46] Because of the sectoral priorities of planners and low real interest rates, investment has been concentrated in capital-intensive industries, despite contrary indications for comparative advantage.[47]

Between 1973 and 1979, growth in aggregate demand was led by growth in fixed investment.[48] This pattern of demand growth produced some undesirable side-effects. Rapid growth of domestic demand diverted resources away from the export sector, thereby increasing pressure on the external accounts. Inflationary pressures also increased: the OECD has estimated a 3 percent excess of actual over potential domestic demand during the 1970s.[49] Yugoslavia's inflation rate, after stabilizing at around 13 percent (retail price growth) in 1977–78, increased sharply to 22 percent in 1979 and 30 percent in 1980. Higher import and energy prices explain much of the 1979–80 increase, but domestic inflation also accelerated, contributing 17 points to the 1980 rise in retail prices.[50]

High rates of domestic inflation and huge trade deficits prompted a major devaluation of the dinar in 1980. The dinar fell 53 percent against the dollar during 1980, reversing much of the previous decline in export competitiveness. However this provided only a temporary improvement in competitiveness; by early 1981 inflation had largely nullified the effects of devaluation.[51] Trade deficits nevertheless declined (from $6.1 billion in 1980 to $4.8 billion in 1981), due to lower imports from convertible currency areas and higher exports to nonconvertible areas.

Improved trade performance inspired some confidence in the economic plan

---

46. Examples include: "five plants producing five makes of cars, and five refineries operating at about one-half capacity." OECD, *Economic Surveys, Yugoslavia* (July 1982), p. 39. Decentralized decision making, and attempts to correct regional disparities are responsible for much duplication of investment. See Laura D'Andrea Tyson, *The Yugoslav Economic System and its Performance in the 1970's* (Berkeley: University of California Press, 1980), pp. 47–48.

47. Tyson, *The Yugoslav Economic System*, pp. 46, 67–69. Interest rates became highly negative in real terms during the late 1970s. See OECD, *Economic Surveys, Yugoslavia* (July 1982), pp. 32–33.

48. Before 1973 net exports contributed substantially more to GDP growth. OECD, *Economic Surveys, Yugoslavia* (May 1981), pp. 19–20.

49. *Ibid.*, p. 22.

50. Based on OECD estimates of the foreign and domestic contributions to inflation. *Ibid.*, pp. 17–18.

51. OECD, *Economic Surveys, Yugoslavia* (May 1983), pp. 20–21.

adopted for 1981–85. Principle objectives of the plan were the reduction of trade and current account imbalances, and lower inflation (running above 40 percent in 1981). Both objectives required highly restrictive policies of demand management, made especially difficult by institutional decentralization and the system of wage and price formation.[52] Led by major reductions in public spending (particularly on fixed investment), final domestic demand contracted by nearly 4 percent in 1981 and by an additional 2 percent in 1982. Depressed demand for imports led to further reduction in the trade deficit in 1982, to $3.1 billion. The current account deficit fell to $460 million despite high interest payments (nearly $2 billion) and lower remittances from workers abroad.[53]

Even as the current account improved, Yugoslavia's financial position became more precarious, as Western banks reduced their credit lines (especially short-term) and reserves fell to their lowest levels in a decade. In September the government applied to the Bank for International Settlements for a $500 million loan; in December, following high level consultations with US and European officials, an intergovernmental rescue package began to take shape. Fourteen Western governments announced $1.3 billion in official credits in January, shortly after Yugoslavia entered IMF-sponsored negotiations with its private bank creditors.

Yugoslavia had already fallen behind in repayment of its bank debt, and success of the rescue operations clearly depended on private refinancing.[54] Foreign banks wanted an assurance that federal authorities would assume responsibility for the borrowings of regional commercial banks. After protracted negotiations Yugoslavia acceded to this demand. The national bank agreed to supervise the foreign borrowings of regional banks and to act as joint guarantor on new foreign loans.[55] In turn, foreign banks agreed to refinance the debts coming due in 1983 and provide substantial new credits. Details of the agreement, formally signed in September, were as follows: banks would provide $1.2 billion in loans to permit repayment of principal due in 1983, and $600 million of additional medium- and long-term credits, with maturities of six to seven years and a three-year grace period. In addition, banks agreed to roll

---

52. Worker self-management and a multistage planning process have evolved into a system in which prices and wages are determined through extensive negotiations at industry, regional, and national levels. See OECD, *Economic Surveys, Yugoslavia* (July 1982), pp. 37–39.

53. Imports may also have been affected by moderate depreciation of the dinar after mid-1981. Final domestic demand data from OECD, *Economic Surveys, Yugoslavia* (May 1983), p. 12.

54. *Wall Street Journal,* 17 January 1983.

55. *Financial Times,* 7 September 1983, and F.B. Singleton, "Yugoslavia: Economic Grievances and Cultural Nationalism," *The World Today,* vol. 39, no. 7–8 (July-August 1983), pp. 289–90.

over $1.2 billion in short-term debts until January 1985.[56] Interest charges would be based on a spread of 1⅞ over LIBOR.[57]

Apart from the commitments of individual governments, various other forms of official credit were provided for Yugoslavia. The IMF continued its disbursements under the stand-by credit arranged in early 1981 (of which $600 million remained) and the World Bank committed over $500 million, to be divided between projects and a structural adjustment loan. The final piece of the package, the second installment of the $500 million BIS bridging loan, was disbursed in September.[58] Combined with bilateral loans from Western governments, credits from official sources totaled nearly $3 billion.[59]

This impressive level of official backing seems broadly due to three factors. First, Western governments were clearly motivated by the desire to preserve Yugoslavia's nonaligned status. Given the recent trends toward greater trade with the Soviet bloc, a rescheduling situation seemed fraught with political risks.[60] Second, there was a general recognition that Yugoslavia's debt-servicing difficulties stemmed from adverse credit market conditions. The stabilization policies adopted in 1980–82 produced considerable improvement in the external accounts, but the sudden contraction of credit in 1982 made further orderly adjustment impossible. By averting a formal rescheduling, the rescue package would permit an earlier return by Yugoslavia to normal commercial borrowing. Third, the show of support for Yugoslavia would help to shore up general confidence in the international financial system, badly shaken by the near-defaults of other major debtors. The IMF had a special interest in a successful outcome, since Yugoslavia was already in the third year of a stabilization program, and failure to arrange refinancing would tarnish the Fund's own credibility.

Yugoslavia has reasonably good prospects for continued improvement in its balance of payments. As of September 1983, hard currency exports were 15 percent above 1982 levels, while imports were virtually unchanged. A hard currency current account deficit of $500 million to $800 million was expected for 1983 (compared with $1.4 billion in 1982), and the government predicted a modest hard currency surplus in 1984.[61] However, this would not obviate the need for some additional debt refinancing or rescheduling.

---

56. *Wall Street Journal*, 9 May 1983, and communication with Manufacturers Hanover.

57. *Wall Street Journal*, 19 April 1983.

58. The second BIS installment was delayed because of a dispute over loan collateral. The BIS required gold collateral, and some commercial banks objected that this constituted favorable treatment. *Wall Street Journal*, 14 September 1983.

59. *Wall Street Journal*, 9 May 1983.

60. *Washington Post*, 24 January 1983.

61. *Financial Times*, 13 October 1983.

The government has pursued an active exchange rate policy. The dinar has been devalued substantially since October 1982, and authorities have announced their readiness to maintain exchange rates at low real levels.[62] Rules on the allocation of foreign exchange have been modified to facilitate debt servicing and meet the needs of exporters. Moreover, the federal government has begun to reassert primary authority over foreign transactions, formerly controlled by individual republics. Under revised foreign exchange laws, exporters are obliged to surrender 25 percent of export earnings to federal authorities, and lesser amounts to republican authorities, with the balance to be allocated among other producers according to nationally agreed criteria. This marks an improvement over the old system, which encouraged hoarding of foreign exchange by individual republics.[63]

Although important steps have been taken toward more effective exchange rate management, serious obstacles remain. One of these is the high proportion of households' deposits held in foreign currency. Foreign currency deposits have been encouraged by favorable interest rates and high domestic inflation; at the end of 1982, 60 percent of household deposits were in foreign currency accounts. The devaluations to date have produced sizable wealth effects, which may depress domestic savings. Another problem noted in a recent OECD survey is the system of foreign exchange rationing, which provides preferential access to established exporters. To avoid penalizing potential exporters, the criteria for foreign exchange rationing should be changed to take better account of relative opportunity costs.[64]

The OECD survey suggests that 1983 targets for devaluation may be too ambitious, given the limited short-term potential for diverting resources into export industries.[65] Recent devaluations have also contributed to an acceleration of inflation. After moderating somewhat in 1982, inflation accelerated to an annual rate of nearly 60 percent by the third quarter of 1983.[66] This may have an important bearing on the debt situation. Even with substantial progress expected in the current account, failure to control inflation will tend to undermine the confidence of foreign creditors, making it more difficult for Yugoslavia to refinance its 1984 maturities. (Of course, the expiration of the IMF stand-by program in early 1984 could also be unsettling.)

---

62. The "accounting exchange rate" used in trade with Comecon countries has been held constant, adding further incentive for exports to convertible currency areas. OECD, *Economic Surveys, Yugoslavia* (May 1983), pp. 20–22, 36.

63. The OECD has consistently recommended liberalization of foreign exchange transactions. For example, see OECD, *Economic Surveys, Yugoslavia* (July 1982), pp. 41, 50.

64. OECD, *Economic Surveys, Yugoslavia* (May 1983), pp. 46–47.

65. *Ibid.*, pp. 36, 41.

66. *Financial Times*, 13 October 1983.

The inflation problem has a number of difficult features. Market forces play a limited role in the system of price formation. Prices for certain goods are set directly by the government, while prices for a wide range of other goods are established through a process of negotiation involving producers and consumers, trade unions, and government officials. Consumer interests tend to be under-represented, and official pricing criteria are not rigorously defined, leaving ample scope for excessive price increases. Interregional barriers to trade and high levels of concentration within industries make inflationary pressures more difficult to resist.[67]

The system of wage determination has also imparted inflationary pressure. Under worker self-management, wages are based on sectoral agreements at the republican and local levels negotiated between trade unions, government officials, and chambers of commerce. The agreements conform in principle to federal guidelines, which until recently have emphasized real earnings, or the ratio of the wage bill to enterprise profits. Although real wages have been restrained, nominal wages have grown excessively, adding to the wage-price spiral. Recently steps have been taken to strengthen control over nominal wages. Stringent wage guidelines were contained in the 1983 Economics Resolution, and the government has sought to improve supervision by the Social Accounting Service—the official conduit for enterprise receipts and payments. Some proposed changes are bound to be controversial. It has been proposed, for example, that enterprises be forced to satisfy financial obligations before paying wages which formerly had first call on enterprise receipts. In the case of loss-making enterprises, nominal earnings would be adjusted downward, forcing workers to bear the costs of adjustment.[68] These measures would improve the financial discipline of self-managed enterprises, but it remains to be seen whether the government can implement them successfully.

Fiscal policies will remain highly restrictive in the near future. Republican and local governments account for roughly four-fifths of total public expenditures and are required by law to maintain balanced budgets; hence "fiscal tightening" in Yugoslavia has occurred through a declining government share in the economy. Public sector expenditure as a percentage of GDP has declined since 1978; this trend was expected to continue in 1983, with substantial real declines in most nondefense categories. The federal budget was expected to show a small surplus for the second consecutive year.[69]

Higher interest rates are the most conspicuous feature of recent monetary

---

67. See Tyson, *The Yugoslav Economic System*, pp. 74–86, concerning the system of price and wage determination and its inflationary impact. Also see OECD, *Economic Surveys, Yugoslavia* (May 1983), pp. 41–45.

68. OECD, *Economic Surveys, Yugoslavia* (May 1983), p. 42.

69. *Ibid.*, pp. 31–34, 37, 45.

policy. Since early 1982 there have been marked increases in the interest rates charged on business loans; together with new credit restrictions, these were expected to help reduce the volume of investment in 1983. Authorities also began more active monitoring of credit expansion, and prepared legislation to strengthen their control over the growth of interenterprise credit.[70] Such measures, combined with selective price freezes, are certain to increase financial pressures on Yugoslav enterprises.

Real incomes have declined in each year since 1979. While such adjustment was necessary for restoring external balance, depressed conditions have made for a more difficult political situation. At the time of Tito's death some observers were uncertain whether Yugoslavia would survive its own deep internal divisions. The system has proven remarkably resilient and adaptable, but stringent new economic policies may represent the severest political test to date.

---

70. *Ibid.*, pp. 28–30, 37–39.

D Notes on Data

In addition to the specific data sources cited for individual tables and estimates indicated in the main text of this study, the following data sources warrant mention. Total debt (for example, chapter 3 and table B-1) is estimated in a variety of ways. The World Bank's *World Debt Tables* provide data on long-term public debt for all of the countries examined, and for long-term private debt in some cases, although this source only covers information through 1981.[1] For 1982 debt, national sources, press reports, and other international official estimates are used.

Total debt is obtained by adding short-term debt to long-term debt. Short-term debt is estimated in the following way using data for 1977–82 from the Bank for International Settlements (BIS).[2] For a given year, these data report the amount of debt coming due within one year (D_t^1) and the amount coming due within the second year (D_t^2). It is possible to isolate short-term debt by subtracting from the total coming due within one year that portion that represents payment on previous long-term debt, as indicated by the principal due in the "second" year as reported in the previous year's data. Thus:

$$D_t^s = D_t^1 - D_{t-1}^2$$

where D_t^s is the estimate of outstanding short-term debt in year t. This approach ignores any short-term debt other than that owed to banks covered by the BIS reporting system.

Because the BIS data on bank debt maturities are unavailable for years before 1977, the estimates of short-term debt for earlier years are based on the ratio of short-term debt in 1978 to imports of goods and services (excluding interest) in that year, as applied to imports of goods and services for earlier years. This

---

1. World Bank, *World Debt Tables* 1982–83 ed.

2. BIS, *The Maturity Distribution of International Bank Lending*, various issues.

procedure assumes that, in 1978 and before, the principal use of short-term debt was as trade finance.

The debt-service ratio (table B-1) is defined as the ratio of total interest payments on all debt and amortization of medium- and long-term debt, *divided by* exports of goods and services. (Note that the interest payment concept is gross: interest receipts are not deducted.) The data sources are the International Monetary Fund's data tapes for *Balance of Payments Yearbook*, for interest and amortization, and *International Financial Statistics*, for exports of goods and services.

In table B-1, net debt *equals* the gross debt (including short-term) *minus* nongold reserves. Net debt relative to exports of goods and services is obtained using the data for these exports as just described.

Additional data required for the simulation model of chapter 3 include amortization rates, share of debt at fixed interest rates, and average interest rate on fixed-interest debt. These data are based on a variety of sources, including the Bank for International Settlements, the World Bank's *World Debt Tables*, financial press accounts, and the International Monetary Fund. *International Financial Statistics* provides data required for the model on merchandise trade, oil trade, direct foreign investment, transfers, and reserves, and for exports and imports of services the ratios to merchandise trade from the most recent data available in the IMF's *Balance of Payments Yearbook* are used. Country growth rates in the base year 1982 are from regional and official sources.[3]

The terms of trade elasticities in the model of chapter 3 are based on simple regression estimates, using data for 1961–81. The percentage change in the price index of the country's exports, as deflated by the price index for industrial country exports (*International Financial Statistics*), is related to the change in OECD country growth rate (OECD *Outlook*, various issues).

---

3. UN Economic Commission for Latin America, *Preliminary Balance of the Latin American Economy in 1982* (Santiago, January 1983); Asian Development Bank, *Annual Report 1982* (Manila, 1982); and IMF staff estimates.

E Statistical Appendix

Table E-1 Total debt[a] for 33 countries, 1973–82 (billion dollars)

Country	1973	1974	1975	1976	1977	1978	1979	1980	1981	1982
Algeria	3.1	3.7	5.0	6.3	9.0	13.5	15.7	15.8	15.1	n.a.
Argentina	6.4	8.0	7.9	8.3	9.7	12.5	19.0	27.2	35.7	38.0
Bolivia	0.7	0.9	1.0	1.3	1.6	2.0	2.4	2.4	2.7	n.a.
Brazil	13.8	18.9	23.3	28.6	35.2	48.4	57.4	66.1	75.7	88.2
Chile	3.6	4.4	4.7	4.5	4.9	6.4	8.2	10.7	15.0	17.9
Colombia	2.8	3.1	3.4	3.6	4.0	4.3	5.7	6.8	8.3	n.a.
Ecuador	0.6	1.0	1.1	1.3	2.1	2.7	3.2	4.1	5.3	6.3
Egypt	2.5	3.4	5.6	6.5	9.0	10.9	12.6	14.8	16.7	18.0
Greece	2.8	3.5	4.2	4.7	5.5	6.1	7.6	9.5	10.6	n.a.
India	10.5	11.6	12.4	13.4	14.7	15.6	15.9	17.7	18.5	n.a.
Indonesia	5.7	7.1	8.9	11.0	12.8	14.5	14.9	17.0	18.0	21.0
Israel	5.9	6.9	7.8	9.0	10.0	11.6	13.2	15.6	17.9	20.4
Ivory Coast	0.7	0.8	1.1	1.3	2.2	3.2	4.3	5.0	5.2	n.a.
Korea	4.6	6.0	7.3	8.9	11.2	14.8	20.5	26.4	31.2	35.8
Malaysia	0.9	1.2	1.7	2.0	2.4	3.1	3.6	4.0	5.8	n.a.
Mexico	8.6	12.8	16.9	21.8	27.1	33.6	40.8	53.8	67.0	82.0
Morocco	1.1	1.4	2.0	2.6	4.4	5.4	6.6	7.6	8.9	n.a.
Nigeria	1.3	1.5	1.5	1.4	1.6	3.0	4.6	5.2	6.4	n.a.
Pakistan	4.3	4.7	5.2	6.1	6.9	7.7	8.4	9.5	9.7	n.a.
Peru	2.4	3.8	4.9	5.3	6.4	6.7	7.4	9.0	9.8	11.1
Philippines	2.4	3.3	3.8	5.0	6.3	7.7	10.8	13.5	15.5	22.4
Portugal	1.5	2.0	2.1	2.4	3.3	5.1	6.0	7.6	9.0	12.9
Romania	1.6	2.7	2.9	2.9	3.6	5.2	7.0	9.5	10.7	9.8
Spain	5.7	8.6	10.7	13.5	16.3	18.4	22.2	27.4	33.2	n.a.
Sudan	0.7	1.3	1.7	2.2	2.5	2.5	3.0	4.2	5.3	n.a.
Syria	0.4	0.6	0.8	1.1	1.6	2.1	2.4	2.7	2.9	n.a.
Thailand	1.6	2.3	2.5	2.9	3.7	4.7	6.3	8.0	10.1	10.5
Tunisia	0.9	1.0	1.1	1.3	2.0	2.5	2.9	3.3	3.3	n.a.
Turkey	4.1	5.2	5.7	6.5	7.8	9.3	12.7	15.0	15.0	19.0
Venezuela	4.6	5.3	5.7	8.7	12.3	16.3	23.7	27.5	29.3	31.3
Yugoslavia	4.6	5.4	6.3	7.7	9.6	11.8	14.9	17.6	18.5	17.9
Zaire	0.9	1.3	1.7	2.3	2.9	3.6	4.3	3.8	4.0	n.a.
Zambia	0.8	1.0	1.4	1.5	1.6	1.6	1.8	2.7	2.6	n.a.

n.a. Not available.
a. Includes short-term.

Table E-2 Debt service[a] as percentage of exports,[b] 33 countries, 1973–82

Country	1973	1974	1975	1976	1977	1978	1979	1980	1981	1982
Algeria	10.9	12.9	13.2	16.2	18.3	24.9	27.9	27.9	n.a.	41.0
Argentina	19.9	21.3	31.9	26.2	19.1	41.6	21.3	32.2	37.5	102.9
Bolivia	22.7	16.0	22.6	21.8	27.4	58.2	34.9	39.9	42.6	n.a.
Brazil	36.7	36.0	40.8	45.3	48.7	59.3	65.6	60.8	66.9	87.1
Chile	35.1	37.4	42.7	41.7	45.9	49.7	44.4	41.3	61.0	60.4
Colombia	21.1	23.6	21.4	16.7	13.7	14.9	19.0	16.3	23.9	n.a.
Ecuador	8.2	8.9	6.3	8.6	10.9	23.2	52.7	37.5	47.7	62.6
Egypt	20.6	38.2	32.7	34.4	30.2	33.6	27.8	26.7	32.8	39.0
Greece	19.5	17.3	19.9	18.0	16.7	14.6	13.6	14.0	18.1	n.a.
India	23.6	63.7	14.0	11.5	12.3	11.4	11.2	n.a.	n.a.	n.a.
Indonesia	3.4	2.1	6.2	7.2	8.3	9.7	7.4	4.9	5.2	11.3
Israel	21.7	22.4	26.8	24.5	22.2	22.9	22.0	24.6	26.0	23.7
Ivory Coast	8.1	8.2	9.1	9.7	10.3	13.1	18.3	n.a.	n.a.	n.a.
Korea	11.5	11.8	12.5	9.8	10.2	12.0	13.9	17.3	18.8	21.1
Malaysia	2.8	2.9	3.1	2.6	3.7	4.4	3.7	3.8	5.0	n.a.
Mexico	28.7	21.9	30.3	40.7	53.6	64.9	67.7	36.4	48.5	58.5
Morocco	8.8	5.8	6.3	9.3	14.4	22.8	29.9	32.5	41.4	n.a.
Nigeria	0.9	0.6	0.6	0.4	0.6	0.6	2.9	1.3	5.4	n.a.
Pakistan	18.1	17.8	24.0	21.7	27.1	23.1	28.5	21.3	17.2	n.a.
Peru	35.8	30.1	45.7	47.2	45.1	64.4	44.6	50.9	n.a.	53.4
Philippines	17.3	19.0	18.3	19.5	21.1	29.6	25.5	18.1	27.9	36.1
Portugal	6.3	3.3	13.2	22.0	19.7	19.2	24.3	19.3	31.8	36.4
Romania	n.a.	n.a.	n.a.	n.a.	n.a.	n.a.	12.2	14.0	16.7	16.5
Spain	5.2	4.2	9.3	10.7	13.3	19.5	15.7	15.5	19.0	n.a.
Sudan	14.5	24.3	30.2	25.7	18.7	20.4	20.2	22.6	19.2	n.a.
Syria	14.9	11.7	10.2	n.a.	14.9	20.2	22.8	25.6	n.a.	n.a.
Thailand	14.3	11.2	14.4	12.6	12.5	18.6	20.7	24.3	25.4	21.9
Tunisia	15.7	8.7	11.6	11.9	13.4	15.8	13.8	16.1	17.1	n.a.
Turkey	28.7	14.6	16.5	31.9	22.3	28.7	68.1	71.2	48.0	32.4
Venezuela	3.8	3.3	3.5	8.4	10.0	15.6	16.4	15.6	19.0	20.7
Yugoslavia	21.7	21.7	21.1	18.3	19.4	21.0	20.8	20.0	n.a.	30.3
Zaire	10.6	15.2	24.1	28.5	45.6	n.a.	n.a.	n.a.	n.a.	n.a.
Zambia	9.3	8.9	11.0	12.7	19.5	38.0	21.3	17.9	20.9	n.a.

n.a. Not available.
a. Interest on long-term and short-term debt plus amortization on long-term.
b. Exports include services.

Table E-3 Net debt[a] as percentage of exports,[b] 33 countries, 1973–82

Country	1973	1974	1975	1976	1977	1978	1979	1980	1981	1982
Algeria	104.8	42.1	79.5	82.7	114.2	170.5	128.8	82.8	78.8	n.a.
Argentina	140.8	145.2	211.5	145.7	96.8	96.1	97.3	182.5	275.3	353.5
Bolivia	228.5	113.0	175.9	173.1	203.9	257.0	253.2	218.5	253.4	n.a.
Brazil	106.2	145.9	194.3	195.8	207.6	252.5	269.3	259.1	256.6	365.3
Chile	239.9	183.9	250.4	170.1	169.9	178.8	131.1	121.5	192.9	274.0
Colombia	141.7	136.8	131.8	88.2	63.3	46.1	38.6	35.5	72.9	n.a.
Ecuador	68.1	48.1	76.3	58.4	89.3	118.6	99.0	105.3	156.7	192.9
Egypt	173.5	149.3	238.1	222.8	236.4	285.5	275.9	210.3	231.0	236.2
Greece	79.9	84.9	94.6	93.8	96.8	86.2	81.1	97.8	104.5	n.a.
India	290.7	248.0	200.8	159.9	125.7	107.9	81.1	n.a.	n.a.	n.a.
Indonesia	146.9	75.2	118.0	108.9	94.6	104.7	69.8	52.2	54.9	86.2
Israel	145.5	154.8	173.3	168.9	150.3	131.6	121.8	120.7	132.6	180.9
Ivory Coast	60.1	52.3	65.6	64.1	71.3	88.7	124.7	181.1	221.0	n.a.
Korea	88.9	106.5	110.2	73.4	63.0	70.2	89.8	103.8	103.9	104.5
Malaysia	−10.3	−6.5	5.1	−7.3	−4.9	−2.1	−2.7	−2.6	13.3	n.a.
Mexico	154.6	182.0	243.8	286.5	309.7	278.2	241.7	205.7	242.4	272.7
Morocco	66.2	46.5	80.2	123.6	206.9	221.9	222.8	219.3	280.2	n.a.
Nigeria	21.0	−41.0	−44.2	−34.5	−19.5	9.2	−4.7	−18.5	13.6	n.a.
Pakistan	342.3	341.6	359.6	382.3	441.3	398.9	323.7	271.4	256.6	n.a.
Peru	138.5	151.7	258.2	286.3	280.6	260.7	141.6	143.8	204.6	259.9
Philippines	58.7	51.2	79.1	101.8	116.3	123.4	138.4	135.3	154.6	276.3
Portugal	−4.9	23.9	55.3	82.7	85.1	106.2	95.1	99.4	132.0	200.4
Romania	34.7	46.3	40.9	35.1	45.2	55.2	63.5	75.5	75.8	71.8
Spain	−4.1	21.0	37.7	60.3	60.3	37.4	30.0	46.0	66.2	n.a.
Sudan	135.1	259.8	323.3	306.1	310.2	330.2	403.6	404.5	416.0	n.a.
Syria	11.2	9.9	5.5	60.9	79.3	122.1	86.7	91.2	n.a.	n.a.
Thailand	20.7	16.4	28.0	30.8	45.5	53.9	69.3	79.0	94.8	102.9
Tunisia	77.7	47.9	57.0	70.1	121.8	125.2	89.7	87.8	83.9	n.a.
Turkey	114.9	162.5	238.3	193.0	280.3	274.7	366.8	352.2	220.3	234.6
Venezuela	51.2	−5.9	−37.3	−32.9	−8.7	35.6	41.5	33.2	29.3	104.2
Yugoslavia	76.0	75.6	88.8	81.8	100.1	110.4	133.6	118.8	99.8	113.7
Zaire	64.6	72.4	163.0	188.1	213.9	n.a.	n.a.	n.a.	n.a.	n.a.
Zambia	54.4	57.4	140.7	122.8	161.7	167.3	111.3	177.6	207.2	n.a.

n.a. Not available.
a. Debt *minus* external official assets, nongold.
b. Exports include services.

Table E-4 Ratio of total debt to gross domestic product, 33 countries, 1973–82 (percentage)

Country	1973	1974	1975	1976	1977	1978	1979	1980	1981	1982
Algeria	38.8	31.7	35.0	38.6	45.5	n.a.	n.a.	n.a.	n.a.	n.a.
Argentina	16.9	14.5	19.8	15.4	18.9	19.2	18.0	17.7	22.5	24.0
Bolivia	55.8	39.3	41.0	44.4	50.3	51.9	52.1	43.9	45.4	n.a.
Brazil	16.7	17.3	18.0	18.2	19.8	23.5	24.8	26.6	26.7	29.4
Chile	33.2	37.6	54.5	40.3	32.7	41.7	39.9	38.3	45.6	59.7
Colombia	26.9	24.5	25.5	23.6	20.3	18.2	20.4	20.3	22.5	n.a.
Ecuador	25.8	25.9	25.8	24.7	31.1	35.3	33.6	36.5	40.9	45.1
Egypt	27.4	31.7	45.3	40.8	42.8	43.7	70.7	62.1	59.3	57.3
Greece	17.3	18.8	20.3	20.9	21.2	19.3	19.6	23.8	28.9	n.a.
India	13.8	13.5	14.0	15.0	14.3	13.1	12.2	11.1	10.1	n.a.
Indonesia	34.8	27.5	29.1	29.6	28.0	28.2	29.0	23.4	21.1	23.3
Israel	63.9	57.2	64.0	72.5	73.0	85.6	75.2	76.4	83.2	90.4
Ivory Coast	27.0	26.8	27.8	28.9	34.3	41.0	n.a.	n.a.	n.a.	n.a.
Korea	34.5	32.4	35.3	32.3	31.7	31.1	33.8	45.3	48.4	50.1
Malaysia	12.3	13.0	18.1	17.9	18.6	19.6	17.4	16.8	23.5	n.a.
Mexico	15.6	17.8	19.2	24.6	33.1	32.8	30.3	28.9	28.0	32.7
Morocco	18.2	18.0	22.0	27.9	41.9	40.8	41.3	42.9	59.2	n.a.
Nigeria	9.9	5.5	4.7	3.5	3.7	6.6	n.a.	n.a.	n.a.	n.a.
Pakistan	64.0	53.9	45.9	45.8	45.8	44.1	42.4	39.6	34.2	n.a.
Peru	26.1	32.7	35.8	39.7	50.8	62.6	54.2	52.1	48.9	52.2
Philippines	22.9	22.2	24.2	28.0	30.4	32.0	36.1	38.1	39.9	53.5
Portugal	13.4	15.3	14.0	15.2	20.4	28.5	29.5	31.6	45.8	60.9
Romania	n.a.	n.a.	n.a.	n.a.	14.1	17.4	21.1	27.6	25.0	21.1
Spain	8.1	9.7	10.2	12.5	13.5	12.5	11.3	13.0	17.9	n.a.
Sudan	27.7	36.0	38.7	40.6	36.6	32.4	n.a.	n.a.	n.a.	n.a.
Syria	17.3	13.6	13.8	17.5	23.6	25.4	24.1	20.8	18.2	n.a.
Thailand	15.7	17.1	17.1	17.6	19.2	20.4	23.2	24.0	27.3	26.0
Tunisia	31.4	28.9	26.4	29.2	39.0	42.5	40.3	38.3	40.7	n.a.
Turkey	19.7	17.7	15.9	15.8	16.4	17.7	18.1	26.3	26.2	30.3
Venezuela	27.2	20.1	20.6	27.5	33.9	41.0	48.3	45.8	43.3	43.9
Yugoslavia	24.2	21.0	21.7	23.5	23.9	24.5	24.3	28.2	26.3	n.a.
Zaire	30.6	37.3	44.8	64.0	62.3	54.7	66.1	64.0	59.7	n.a.
Zambia	34.3	34.5	56.1	56.7	66.4	59.8	54.6	70.7	n.a.	n.a.

n.a. Not available.

Table E-5 Argentina: conversion to voluntary lending (million dollars)

Year	Current account (A)	Change in reserves (B)	Direct investment (C)	Borrowing requirements (D = − A + B − C)	Net borrowing from banks (E = .67 D)
1983	−2,426	316	1,040	1,752	1,500[d]
1984	−825	238	1,232	0[e]	0
1985	257	181	1,333	0	0
1986	996	161	1,441	0	0
1987	500	200	1,400	0	0
1988	500	222	1,400	0	0
1989	500	241	1,400	0	0
1990	500	273	1,400	0	0

a. *Equals* 0.666 *times* total amortization, based on bank share in total debt.
b. Beginning in year of conversion, *equals* 30 percent of total bank amortization.
c. Prior to conversion, *equals* 70 percent of E. Thereafter, *equals* E + G.
d. Actual lending commitment.
e. Minimum borrowing *equals* zero.

Table E-6 Brazil: conversion to voluntary lending (million dollars)

Year	Current account (A)	Change in reserves (B)	Direct investment (C)	Borrowing requirements (D = − A + B − C)	Net borrowing from banks (E = .67 D)
1983	−7,131	0	2,271	4,860	5,450[d]
1984	−4,729	745	2,690	2,784	5,450[d]
1985	−1,041	256	2,909	0[e]	0
1986	−647	616	3,147	0	0
1987	−1,000	561	3,200	0	0
1988	−1,000	623	3,200	0	0
1989	−1,000	692	3,200	0	0
1990	−1,000	768	3,200	0	0

a. *Equals* 0.627 *times* total amortization, based on bank share in total debt.
b. Beginning in year of conversion, *equals* 30 percent of total bank amortization.
c. Prior to conversion, *equals* 70 percent of E, thereafter, *equals* E + H.
d. Actual lending commitments.
e. Minimum borrowing *equals* zero.
f. Includes $1,072 million short-term.

Amortization to banks[a] (F)	Repayment to small banks[b] (G)	Borrowing from large banks[c] (H)	Large bank exposure (I)	Percentage increase, large bank exposure (J)
0	0	1,050	18,760	5.9
4,020	0	0	18,760	0.0
4,266	1,280	1,280	20,040	6.8
9,278	2,783	2,783	22,823	13.4
8,092	2,248	2,428	25,251	10.6
6,260	1,878	1,878	27,129	7.4
6,260	1,878	1,878	29,007	6.9
4,262	1,279	1,279	30,286	4.4

Amortization to banks[a]		Repayment to small banks[b] (H)	Borrowing from large banks[c] (I)	Large bank exposure (J)	Percentage increase, large bank exposure (K)
Long-term (F)	Short-term (G)				
3,603	10,032	0	3,815	42,525	9.9
1,746	10,584	0	3,815	46,340	9.0
7,059	10,901	0	0	46,340	0.0
6,947	10,718	3,156[f]	3,156	49,496	6.8
7,026	10,504	3,180[f]	3,180	52,676	6.4
7,026	10,504	3,180[f]	3,180	55,856	6.0
7,026	10,504	2,108	2,108	57,964	3.8
7,888	10,504	2,366	2,366	60,333	4.1

Table E-7 Mexico: conversion to voluntary lending (million dollars)

Year	Current account (A)	Change in reserves (B)	Direct investment (C)	Borrowing requirements (D = A + B − C)	Net borrowing from banks (E = .67 D)
1983	−2,321	2	1,703	619	5,000[d]
1984	−5,899	1,073	2,018	4,954	3,319
1985	−6,970	515	2,182	5,304	3,554
1986	−6,005	435	2,360	4,080	2,734
1987	−6,000	477	2,552	3,925	2,630
1988	−6,000	524	2,760	3,764	2,522
1989	−6,000	575	2,985	3,590	2,405
1990	−6,000	631	3,228	3,403	2,280

a. *Equals* 0.785 *times* total amortization, based on bank share in total debt.
b. Beginning in year of conversion, *equals* 30 percent of total bank amortization.
c. Prior to conversion, *equals* 70 percent of E. Thereafter, *equals* E + G.
d. Actual lending commitments.

Amortization to banks[a] (F)	Repayment to small banks[b] (G)	Borrowing from large banks[c] (H)	Large bank exposure (I)	Percentage increase, large bank exposure (J)
0	0	3,500	48,580	7.8
1,453	0	2,323	50,903	4.8
7,419	2,226	5,780	56,683	11.4
11,597	3,479	6,213	62,896	11.0
16,699	5,010	7,640	70,536	12.1
18,332	5,500	8,022	78,558	11.4
16,352	4,906	7,311	85,869	9.3
17,509	5,253	7,533	93,402	8.8

Select Bibliography*

Alexander, Sidney S. April 1952. "Effects of a Devaluation on the Trade Balance." *IMF Staff Papers,* vol. 2.

Aliber, Robert Z. October 1980. "A Conceptual Approach to the Analysis of External Debt of the Developing Countries." World Bank Staff Working Paper, no. 421. Washington.

Asian Development Bank. *Annual Report 1982.* Manila.

Avramovíc, Dragoslav, et al. 1964. *Economic Growth and External Debt.* Baltimore: Johns Hopkins Press.

Bacha, Edmar L., and Carlos F. Diaz-Alejandro. May 1982. "International Financial Intermediation: A Long and Tropical View." *Essays in International Finance,* no. 147. Princeton, NJ: International Finance Section, Department of Economics, Princeton University.

Bailey, Norman A. 10 January 1983. "A Safety Net for Foreign Lending." *Business Week.*

Banco de Mexico. 1982, 1983. *Informe Anual.* Mexico City.

Bergsten, C. Fred, and William R. Cline. November 1982. *Trade Policy in the 1980s.* POLICY ANALYSES IN INTERNATIONAL ECONOMICS 3. Washington: Institute for International Economics.

————. December 1983. "Trade Policy in the 1980s: An Overview." In *Trade Policy in the 1980s,* William R. Cline, ed. Washington: Institute for International Economics.

Bergsten, C. Fred, and Lawrence R. Klein. 23 April 1983. "Assuring World Recovery: The Need for a Global Strategy." *The Economist.*

BIS (Bank for International Settlements). 1978. *Annual Report.* Basle.

————. June 1981, June 1982, July 1983, and various other issues. *The Maturity Distribution of International Bank Lending.* Basle.

Black, Stanley W. 1981. "The Impact of Changes in the World Economy on

---

* For additional country references, see notes to appendix C.

Stabilization Policies in the 1970s." In *Economic Stabilization in Developing Countries*, William R. Cline and Sidney Weintraub, eds. Washington: Brookings Institution.

Bolin, William H., and Jorge Del Canto. Summer 1983. "LDC Debt: Beyond Crisis Management." *Foreign Affairs*, vol. 61, no. 5.

Bronfenbrenner, Martin. April 1955. "The Appeal of Confiscation in Economic Development." *Economic Development and Cultural Change*, vol. 3.

Chenery, Hollis B., and Alan M. Strout. September 1966. "Foreign Assistance and Economic Development." *American Economic Review*, vol. 56, no. 4.

Chicago, University of, and the Johnson Foundation. May 27, 1983. "Solvency, Stability and the External Debt of Developing Countries." Conference sponsored by the University of Chicago and the Johnson Foundation. Racine, Wisconsin.

Cline, William R. 1981. "Brazil's Aggressive Response to External Shock." In William R. Cline and Associates, *World Inflation and the Developing Countries*. Washington: Brookings Institution.

———. Spring 1982. "External Debt: System Vulnerability and Development." *Columbia Journal of World Business*, vol. 17, no. l.

———. Winter 1982–83. "Mexico's Crisis, the World's Peril." *Foreign Policy*, no. 49.

———. (Forthcoming). *Exports of Manufactures from Developing Countries: Performance and Prospects for Market Access*. Washington: Brookings Institution.

Cline, William R., and Sidney Weintraub, eds. 1981. *Economic Stabilization in Developing Countries*. Washington: Brookings Institution.

Cooke, W.P. June 1981. "Developments in Cooperation Among Banking Supervisory Authorities." *Bank of England Quarterly Bulletin*, vol. 21, no. 2.

Dale, Richard S. April 20, 1983. Statement before the US Congress, House Committee on Banking, Finance, and Urban Affairs. 98 Cong., 1 sess.

De Saint Phalle, T., ed. 1983. *The International Financial Crisis: An Opportunity for Constructive Action*. Washington: Georgetown University Center for Strategic and International Studies.

Dhar, Sanjay. Autumn 1983. "US Trade with Latin America: Consequences of Financing Constraints." *Federal Reserve Bank of New York Quarterly Review*, vol. 8, no. 3.

Dhonte, Pierre. March 1975. "Describing External Debt Situations: A Rollover Approach." *IMF Staff Papers*, vol. 22, no. 1.

Diaz-Alejandro, Carlos F. 1983. "Some Aspects of the 1982–83 Brazilian Payments Crisis." *Brookings Papers on Economic Activity*, no. 2.

Dornbusch, Rudiger. February 1983. "Real Interest Rates, Home Goods and Optimal External Borrowing." *Journal of Political Economy*, vol. 91, no. 1.

———. October 24, 1983. Presentation at a seminar held by Corporación de Investigaciones Económicas para America Latina. Santiago, Chile.

Eaton, Jonathan, and Mark Gersowitz. 1981. "Debt with Potential Repudiation: Theoretical and Empirical Analysis." *Review of Economic Studies,* vol. 48.

Economist. 30 April 1983 and 9 July 1983.

Enders, Thomas O., and Richard P. Mattione. 1984. "Latin America: The Crisis of Debt and Growth." *Studies in International Economics,* Washington: Brookings Institution.

Feder, Gershon, and Richard Just. March 1977. "A Study of Debt-Servicing Capacity Applying Logit Analysis." *Journal of Development Economics,* vol. 4, no. 1.

Federal Financial Institutions Examination Council. *Country Exposure Lending Survey.* Washington; processed. Various issues.

Federal Reserve Board of Governors, Federal Deposit Insurance Corporation, and Comptroller of the Currency. April 7, 1983. "Joint Memorandum: Program for Improved Supervision and Regulation of International Lending." Washington; processed.

Frank, Charles R., and William R. Cline. August 1971. "Measurement of Debt Servicing Capacity: An Application of Discriminant Analysis." *Journal of International Economics,* vol. 1, no. 3.

Fundaçao Centro de Estudos do Comercio Exterior. September 1983. *Balança Comercial e Outros Indicadores Conjunturais.* Rio de Janeiro.

Furtado, Celso. 1983. *Não à Recessão e ao Desemprego.* Rio de Janeiro: Paz e Terra.

Group of Thirty. 1981. *Balance of Payments Problems of Developing Countries.* New York.

————. 1983. *The IMF and the Private Markets.* New York.

Gutentag, Jack, and Richard Herring. April 26, 1983. "Overexposure of International Banks to Country Risk: Diagnosis and Remedies." Testimony before the US Congress, House Committee on Banking, Finance, and Urban Affairs, Subcommittee on International Trade, Investment, and Monetary Policy. 98 Cong., 1 sess. Washington.

————. May 1983. "The Lender-of-Last-Resort Function in an International Context." *Essays in International Finance,* no. 151. Princeton, NJ: International Finance Section, Department of Economics, Princeton University.

Hardy, Chandra. February 1982. "Rescheduling Developing-Country Debts, 1956–80: Lessons and Recommendations." Overseas Development Council Working Paper No. 1. Washington.

Holsen, John A., and Jean L. Waelbroeck. May 1976. "The Less Developed Countries and the International Monetary Mechanism." *American Economic Review,* vol. 66, no. 2.

House of Commons. March 15, 1983. Fourth Report from the Treasury and Civil Service Committee. *International Monetary Arrangements: International Lending by Banks,* vol. 1, sess. 1982–83.

IMF (International Monetary Fund). 1976. *Annual Report*. Washington.

———. September 1980 and July 1982. *International Capital Markets, Recent Developments and Short-Term Prospects*. Washington.

———. 1983. *International Financial Statistics*, various issues. Washington.

———. 1981 and 1982. *International Financial Statistics Yearbook*. Washington.

———. 1982–1984. *World Economic Outlook*. Washington.

———. July 11, 1983. *IMF Survey*. Washington.

Inter-American Development Bank. 1983. *Economic and Social Progress in Latin America: 1983 Report*. Washington.

——— 1984. *External Debt and Economic Development in Latin America*. Washington.

Internal Revenue Code. 1980. New York: The Research Institute of America, Inc.

Kissinger, Henry A. 24 January 1983. "Saving the World Economy." *Newsweek*.

Kravis, Irving B., Alan W. Heston, and Robert Summers. June 1978. "Real GDP Per Capita for More than One Hundred Countries." *The Economic Journal*, vol. 88, no. 351.

———. 1982. *World Product and Income: International Comparisons of Real Gross Product*. Baltimore: Johns Hopkins University Press for the World Bank.

Krueger, Anne O. 1981. "Interactions between Inflation and Trade Regime Objectives in Stabilization Programs." In *Economic Stabilization in Developing Countries*, William R. Cline and Sidney Weintraub, eds. Washington: Brookings Institution.

Kuczynski, Pedro-Pablo. Fall 1983. "Latin American Debt: Act Two." *Foreign Affairs*, vol. 62, no. 1.

Leven, Ronald, and David L. Roberts. Autumn 1983. "Latin American Prospects for Recovery." *Federal Reserve Bank of New York Quarterly Review*, vol. 8, no. 3.

Lomax, David. January 1983. "Sovereign Risk Analysis Now." *The Banker*.

Mendelsohn, M.S. 1983. *Commercial Banks and the Restructuring of Cross-Border Debt*. New York: Group of Thirty.

Morgan Guaranty Trust Company. October 1982 and February and June 1983. *World Financial Markets*.

Naciones Unidas, Comisión Económica para América Latina (CEPAL). December 16, 1983. Balance Preliminar de la Economía Latinoamericana durante 1983, cuadro 2. Santiago.

OECD (Organization for Economic Cooperation and Development). 1982. *Development Cooperation*. Paris.

———. 31 July 1982. *OECD Economic Outlook*.

———. September and June 1983. *Monthly Statistics of Foreign Trade*.

Paine, Webber, Mitchell, Hutchins, Inc. June 14, 1983. "Earnings Models for Large US Banks." *Status Report*.

Roett, Riordan. 1984. "Democracy and Debt in South America." *Foreign Affairs*, vol. 62, no. 3, pp. 695–720.

Rohatyn, Felix. January 17, 1983. Testimony before the US Congress, Senate Committee on Foreign Relations. 98 Cong., 1 sess. Washington.

Sachs, Jeffrey D. 1981. "The Current Account and Macroeconomic Adjustment in the 1970s." *Brookings Papers on Economic Activity,* no. 1. Washington: Brookings Institution.

Saini, Krishnan, and Philip Bates. September 1978. "Statistical Techniques for Determining Debt-Servicing Capacity for Developing Countries: Analytical Review of the Literature and Further Empirical Results." Federal Reserve Board of New York, Research Paper 7818.

Sargen, Nicholas. Fall 1977. "Economic Indicators and Country Risk Appraisal." Federal Reserve Bank of San Francisco, *Economic Review.*

Simonsen, Mario Henrique. 1983. "The Financial Crisis in Latin America." Rio de Janeiro: Getúlio Vargas Foundation; processed.

Smith, Gordon W. 1979. "The External Debt Prospects of the Non-Oil-Exporting Countries." In *Policy Alternatives for a New International Economic Order,* William R. Cline, ed. New York: Praeger Publishers for the Overseas Development Council.

Solomon, Robert. 1977. "A Perspective on the Debt of Developing Countries." *Brookings Papers on Economic Activity,* no. 2. Washington: Brookings Institution.

Stiglitz, Joseph, and Andrew Weiss. June 1981. "Credit Rationing in Markets with Imperfect Information." *American Economic Review,* vol. 71, no. 3.

Twenty-six Economists. December 1982. *Promoting World Recovery: A Statement on Global Economic Strategy.* Washington: Institute for International Economics.

US Congress. 1984. *Supplemental Appropriations Act.* PL 98–181, sec. 805 and 905.

UN Economic Commission for Latin America. January 1983. *Preliminary Balance of the Latin American Economy in 1982.* Santiago.

US Congress, Congressional Budget Office. March 1983. "Economic and Budgetary Consequences of an Oil Price Decline—A Preliminary Analysis." Washington; processed.

———, House Committee on Banking, Finance, and Urban Affairs. 1983. *International Recovery and Financial Stability Act.* H.R. 2957. 98 Cong., 1 sess.

———, House of Representatives. March 11, 1983. *Reckless Risk Recovery Act of 1983.* H.R. 2069. 98 Cong., 1 sess.

Weinert, Leslie. Spring 1983. "Bank and Bankruptcy." *Foreign Policy,* no. 50.

Williamson, John. August 1982. *The Lending Policies of the International Monetary Fund.* POLICY ANALYSES IN INTERNATIONAL ECONOMICS 1. Washington: Institute for International Economics.

———, ed. June 1983. *Prospects for Adjustment in Argentina, Brazil, and Mexico: Responding to the Debt Crisis.* Washington: Institute for International Economics.

———. September 1983. *The Exchange Rate System.* POLICY ANALYSES IN INTERNATIONAL ECONOMICS 5. Washington: Institute for International Economics.

World Bank. *Annual Report 1980.* Washington.

———. *Annual Report 1982.* Washington.

———. 1983. *World Debt Tables, 1982–83 Edition.* Washington.

———. *World Development Report 1982.* Washington.

———. *World Development Report 1983.* Washington.

Index

Economic growth
  Critical threshold for, 67
  Demand for rescheduling and, 213–14
  Importance of imports to, 178–80
  Inflation constraint on, 180–81
  Oil price impact on, 58–59
  Projection model, 45–48
  Recovery in, *1983–84*, 151, 152, 159
  See also Organization for Economic
    Cooperation and Development
Economist, The, 281n
Ecuador
  Current account and debt projections,
    51, 52
  External debt, 1, 11, 68
Egypt
  Current account and debt projections,
    51
  Potential debt problem, 68
Enders, Thomas O., 42n, 171, 172n
Ercilla (Chile), 86n
Exchange rate
  Export and import response to, 43,
    241–43
  External debt and policies relating to,
    14–15
Export Development Fund, proposed,
  133n
Exports, developing countries
  Actual versus projected, 156–57, 159
  Calculation of value, 41–43
  Debt service as percent of, 3, 295
  Factors influencing, 41–43, 241, 247
  GDP growth versus, 2
  Interest rates compared with, 6–8, 9
  Net debt as percentage of, 296
  Response to exchange rate changes,
    43
  Stagnation in, 5
External debt
  Challenge to policymaking, 201
  Crisis in illiquidity and, 144, 145;
    information gap hypothesis on,
    114; international financial system
    vulnerability to, 21; rescue
    operations for, 29–34; stages of,
    26–29
  Factors contributing to: capital
    outflow, 15–16; dollar value, 61–63; exchange rate policies, 14–15;
    interest rates, 11–12, 59–61; oil
    prices, 8–11, 58–59; psychological,
    17–18; terms of trade deterioration,
    13–14
  Financing availability and, 155

Growth, 1, 2–3
  Illiquidity versus insolvency in, 34,
    39–40
  Impact on banks, 26–29
  Interest payments on, 43, 60n
  Involuntary lending implications, 78–79
  Long-term viability, 95, 100
  Medium-term viability, 39–40, 123;
    maturity bunching and, 95–100;
    political feasibility of, 104–09;
    reconversion to voluntary lending
    and, 100–03
  Policy recommendations for, 147–49
  Private, 2, 85–86
  Relief from, 189
  Sovereign, 1–2; default on, 21;
    involuntary lending and, 71;
    proposed regulatory reforms for,
    115–16
  Trends in, 5, 6, 294–97
  See also Projection model for balance
    of payments and debt; Reform
    proposals, for external debt

Fallenbuchi, Zbigniew M., 273n, 275n,
  276n, 277n
FDIC. *See* Federal Deposit Insurance
  Corporation
Feder, Barnaby J., 132n
Feder, Gershon, 205n, 219, 225n
Federal Deposit Insurance Corporation
  (FDIC), 29, 80n, 116, 119, 144
Federal Financial Institutions
  Examination Council, 18n, 113n,
    115–16n
Federal Reserve, 80n, 119
  Actions on free-riders, 76
  Interest rate on rescheduled debt, 82
  Measures to offset foreign loan losses,
    28–29, 32
  Proposed foreign lending reforms,
    116, 144
Federal Reserve Bank of New York,
  balance of payments and debt
  projections, 64, 170, 171
Feinberg, Richard E., 174n
Financial Times, 33n, 85n, 286n, 287n,
  288n
Fishlow, Albert, 173n, 174, 182n
Flaherty, Diane, 284n
Forced lending. *See* Lending,
  international
Foxley, Alejandro, 193n
Frank, Charles R., Jr., 205n, 225n

Free-riders
  Methods to overcome, 76–78, 137, 144, 148
  Small banks as, 30, 75
Furtado, Celso, 105n

GAB. *See* General Arrangements to Borrow
Garland, John, 274n
Gazeta Mercantil, 33n
GDP. *See* Gross domestic product
General Arrangements to Borrow (GAB), 124, 125, 144
Gersowitz, Mark, 87n, 206n, 214n
GNP. *See* Gross national product
Gross domestic product (GDP)
  Gross domestic savings as percent of, 16
  Per capita, 195–96
  Projection model simulations for, 44
  Real growth, 2, 104, 105, 107, 108
  Resource transfers as share of, 177–78
  Total debt ratio to, 297
Gross national product (GNP), 16, 67, 152
Group of Thirty, 120n, 124n, 126n
Gutentag, Jack, 119n
  Reform measures for external debt, 132–33, 135

Hardy, Chandra, 118n
Herring, Richard, 119n
  Reform measures for external debt, 132–33, 135
Heston, Alan W., 223n
Holsen, John A., 112n
Hough, Jerry F., 279n
Hufbauer, Gary Clyde, 279n
Hungary, 52

IFS. *See International Financial Statistics*
IIF. *See* Institute for International Finance
Illiquidity
  Debt problem and, 34, 144, 145
  Insolvency versus, 39–40, 67
IMF. *See* International Monetary Fund
Imports
  Developing countries, actual versus projected, 155–58; cutbacks in, 52; and economic growth, 178–80; increase in value of, 13; response to exchange rate changes, 43; for services, 43, 44

Ratio of foreign reserves to, 213
  Restrictions on industrial country, 147
Income distribution, international, 195
Indonesia, 1, 11, 50, 51
Industrial countries
  Borrowers from IMF, 124
  Economic growth, 12, 152, 159, 246, 251
  Lower oil price impact on, 58–59
  Projection model implications for policies of, 68–69
  Protectionism of, 147, 197–99
Inflation
  Debt rescheduling and, 220
  Debt repayment and, 3
  Constraint on economic growth, 180–81
  Oil price effect on, 59
  Projection model assumptions for, 44–45
  Projections, 160–61
Institute for International Finance (IIF), 114–15
Inter-American Development Bank, 104n, 162n, 192
  Balance of payments and debt projections, 172–74
Interest
  Capitalization of, 78, 136; loss of bank influence from, 138–39; operational problems with, 137–38; unilateral country action from 139–40, 143
  Forgiveness of, 140–42
  Payments, 60n, 66; calculations of, 43, 243; deferred, 68; ratio to net new borrowing, 87–89
  Rates: debt repayment and, 3; debt sensitivity to, 11–12, 59–61, 181–83; effect on resource transfers, 176–77; excess, 12; export growth compared with, 6–8, 9; projection model assumptions for, 46; proposed ceiling on, 183–87; on rescheduled debt, 80–83
Internal Revenue Code, 27n
Internal Revenue Service, 119
International Debt Discount Corporation, proposed, 130–31, 134
International Financial Statistics (IFS), 222–23
International financial system
  External debt risk to, 143
  Rescue operations for debt crisis, 29–32; bridging loans, 34–35, 146;

progress under, 143–44; results of, 32–34; tactical changes in, 34–37
International financial system
External debt risk to, 143
Vulnerability, 21, 26
International Monetary Fund (IMF), 2n, 10n, 11n, 12n, 13, 14n, 15n, 18, 41n, 49n, 52, 62n, 112n, 113, 152, 157n, 161n, 292
Adjustment program, 106, 107–08, 126–27, 191
Argentina and, 152, 189, 192, 193, 194
Balance of payments and debt projections, 127–28, 170–71
General Arrangements to Borrow, 124, 125, 144
Proposed interest stabilization facility, 186–87
Proposed role in external debt reform, 113–14, 131–32, 133n
Quotas for bank lending, 111, 123–26, 144, 145, 147
Role in rescue operations, 30, 32, 33, 260, 266–68, 269–71; considered tactical changes in, 35–37; debt reschedulings, 32, 80; for debt problems with new involuntary lending, 71–72, 75, 79
Stabilization program, 207
Supervision over interest capitalization by, 139–40
International Trade Commission, 198
Investment, direct foreign, 44, 128, 129, 244
Involuntary lending. See Lending, international
Israel, 51, 68

Jacobs, Andrew, Jr., 132n
Johnson, David D., 257n
Journal do Brasil, 105n
Journal of Commerce, 131n, 238n
Just, Richard, 205n, 219, 225n

Kallab, Valeriana, 174n
Kempe, Frederick, 279n
Kenen, Peter B., Reform proposal for external debt, 130–31, 134, 135
Kennecott Copper Corporation, 90
Kissinger, Henry A., 146
Klein, Lawrence R., 69n, 152n, 159n
Korea, 6, 50, 52
Kravis, Irving B., 223n

Krueger, Anne O., 109n
Kuczynski, Pedro-Pablo, 80n

Latin America
Economic growth forecasts, 171–72
Projected debt and balance of payments, 158–59, 171–72
Restricted capital flows, 17, 18
US bank exposure in, 23, 24
Latin American Economic Conference, 189
Lender of last resort (LLR), 119–21, 148
Lending, international
Bridge, 34–35, 146
Central bank coverage of, 111, 119–21
Concessional, 128
Cutbacks in, 127
Global versus country-specific, 219
IMF quotas for, 111, 123–26, 144, 145, 147
Incentive for continued, 144
Involuntary, 66; defined, 71; incentive for, 72–74; model of, 75–76; overcoming free-riders with, 76–77; policy implications of, 78–79
Large versus small bank, 101–02
Market disequilibrium, 208–11
Needed changes in, 113–15, 116–19
OPEC surplus deposits for, 111–12, 113
Regulations, 144, 148
Voluntary, 100–03, 139
Leven, Ronald, 42n, 64n, 170n, 173n, 182n
Lever, Harold, 133n
LIBOR. See London Interbank Offer Rate
LINK model, 68, 152n, 159, 160
LLR. See Lender of last resort
Loan subordination, 77–78
Logit model of debt rescheduling, 65, 205–06
Alternative versions of, 227, 229
Countries in, 226
Data for, 222–25
Debt-service difficulties and, 207–08
Indicators of performance of, 229–30
International lending and, 208–10
Policy implications, 239
Projections, 65, 235, 237–38
Reduced form of, 220–22
Results, 225–31
Lomax, David, 111n, 206n

London Interbank Offer Rate (LIBOR),
    11–12, 43, 113, 142
  Developing country debt and, 3, 61n
  OECD growth and, 182–83
  Projections, 160
  On rescheduled debt, 80–81, 82

Marer, Paul, 274n
Mattione, Richard P., 42n, 171, 172n
Mendelsohn, M.S., 261n
Mexico
  Bank lending to, 22, 23, 113
  Current account and debt projections,
    49, 50, 52, 54, 164–67, 246, 254
  Current account surplus, 152, 155
  Debt crisis: domestic policies
    contributing to, 14, 15–16, 257–59;
    management of, 259–62; political
    response to, 104–05; rescue
    package for, 30–33, 35, 91, 260
  Debt rescheduling, 32, 36, 66;
    duration, 84–85; interest rate on,
    80–81, 82; treatment of private
    debt in, 85
  Economic indicators, 258–59
  External debt: amortization profile
    for, 96–100; default, 195; oil price
    rise and, 10; ratio to exports, 6
  FICORCA special peso account, 260
  Involuntary lending to, 66, 71, 73,
    75, 76
  Nonoil exports, 154, 164
  Real GDP growth, 104, 105
  Trade balance, 33–34
  Voluntary lending to, 103, 298–99
Moral hazard problems, 121, 135
Moral suasion, debt rescheduling
    versus, 84, 148
Moratorium, loan, 26, 73–74
  Debt reschedulings compared with,
    207–08
Morgan Guaranty Bank, balance of
    payments and debt projections, 64,
    128, 170, 171
Multi-Fiber Arrangement, 197
Multilateral lending organizations, 128,
    129, 144, 146, 147
Municipal Assistance Corporation, 131

Nación, La, 107n
Napier, Ron, 159n
Net foreign resource transfer, 66–67
Netto, Antônio Delfim, 190, 191n
Newcomb, William, 276n
New York Times, 124n, 130n, 131n,
    279n, 280n

Nicaragua, 68
Nigeria, 1, 11
Nonoil developing countries
  Current account balance, 127–28,
    153
  External debt, 1, 2–3, 181–82;
    burden of, 5; deteriorating terms of
    trade and, 13–14; high interest
    rates and, 12; oil price rise and, 8–
    10; projected, 128, 129
  GDP real growth, 2
  Interest payments, 87
  Recycling of OPEC surpluses to, 111–
    12
  US bank exposure in, 22–23
North Korea, 90, 92

OECD. *See* Organization for Economic
    Cooperation and Development
O Globo, 33n
Oil
  Prices: balance of payments and, 55–
    56, 59; debt burden and, 8–11, 58;
    projected, 46
  Recycling of surplus, 206
Oil-exporting developing countries
  External debt, 10–11, 58–59
  Oil trade, *1982,* 57
  Projections of balance of payments
    and debt, 46–48, 52–56
  Value of oil exports, 41
Oil-importing developing countries
  External debt, 58–59
  Oil trade, *1982,* 57–58
  Projections of balance of payments
    and debt, 46–49, 52–56
  Value of oil imports, 41
OPEC. *See* Organization of Petroleum
    Exporting Countries
Organization for Economic Cooperation
    and Development (OECD), 128n
  Economic growth, 41–42, 146, 151;
    developing country exports and,
    241, 247; effect on debt problem,
    52–55; interest rate and, 60–61,
    182–83; LIBOR and, 182–83; oil
    price impact on, 58–59; projection
    model, 45; terms of trade response
    to, 42
  Inflation, 42n, 49n
  Survey of Yugoslavia economic
    performance, 281n, 283n, 284n,
    285n, 286n, 288, 289n
Organization of Petroleum Exporting
    Countries (OPEC)

Rout, Lawrence, 151n
Rowe, James L., Jr., 80n

Sachs, Jeffrey, D., 16n
Saini, Krishnan, 205n, 220n
Sargen, Nicholas, 205n, 220n
Savings, 16, 66–67
Schott, Jeffrey J., 279n
Schumer, Charles E., Reform proposal
    for external debt, 130, 131–32,
    134, 135
SDRs. *See* Special drawing rights
Simonson, Mario Henrique, 7
Singleton, F.B., 286n
Smith, Gordon W., 206n
Solomon, Anthony M., 183n
Solomon, Robert, 205n
Special drawing rights (SDRs), 42n,
    124, 125, 192, 222n
Stiglitz, Joseph, 208n
Stretchouts, loan, 39, 130, 131
Strout, Alan M., 179, 209n
Summers, Robert, 223n

Teske, Gary, 274n, 275n, 276n
Thailand, 51, 52
Trade, international
    Elasticities in, 43, 292
    Protectionism in, 147–48, 197–99
    Response to economic growth, 41
Transfers, debt, 44
    Interest forgiveness and, 142
    Level of financing through, 128, 129
Treasury, US, 32
Turkey, 51
Twenty-six Economists, 68n, 239n
Two-gap model, 179
Tyson, Laura D'Andrea, 285n

United Nations Economic Commission
    for Latin America, 15n, 18n, 153n,
    223n, 292n
United States
    Banks, 21–24, 26–29, 113, 115, 143
    Budget deficit, 46
    Prime rate, 80–81, 181, 187
    Role in rescue operations, 30
    Tight money policy, 12

Vanous, Jan, 279n, 280n
Venezuela
    Current account and debt projections,
      50, 51–52, 54, 164–67
    Current account surplus, 152, 155
    Debt-servicing interruptions, 23, 26
    External debt, 1, 6, 11, 15
    Potential debt problem, 68

Waelbroeck, Jean L., 112n
Wallich, Henry C., 112
Wall Street Journal, 41n, 76n, 82n, 83n,
    108n, 111n, 238n, 286n, 287n
Washington Post, 27n, 30n, 76n, 77n,
    82n, 86n, 106n, 124n, 145n, 280n,
    287n
Weinert, Leslie, 130n
Weintraub, Sidney, 17n, 109n, 113n,
    193n, 216n
Weiss, Andrew, 208n
Wharton Econometric Forecasting
    Associates, 1n
Williamson, John, 32n, 61n, 179n,
    257n, 265n
Wolf, Martin, 197n
World Bank, 1, 2n, 16n, 49n, 67n, 97n,
    192, 291
    Multilateral net disbursements, 128n,
      129–30
Write-offs, loan, 28, 29, 39, 131, 133

Yugoslavia
    Debt crisis: factors contributing to,
      281–86; rescue package for, 30, 32,
      287
    Debt rollover, 84n
    Economic plan, 285–86
    Exchange rate policy, 288
    Inflation, 289
    Involuntary lending to, 72
    Political response to debt problem,
      107–08

Zero coupon bonds, as instrument for
    lending, 136–37
Zombanakis, Minos, 133n

Other Publications from the Institute

POLICY ANALYSES IN INTERNATIONAL ECONOMICS

BOOKS

SPECIAL REPORTS